POST-REVOLUTIONARY
POLITICS IN IRAN

For my father, of blessed memory.

POST-REVOLUTIONARY POLITICS IN IRAN

Religion, Society and Power

DAVID MENASHRI

Tel Aviv University

FRANK CASS
LONDON • PORTLAND, OR

First published in 2001 in Great Britain by
FRANK CASS PUBLISHERS
Crown House, 47 Chase Side
Southgate, London N14 5BP

and in the United States by
FRANK CASS PUBLISHERS
c/o ISBS, 5824 N. E. Hassalo Street
Portland, Oregon, 97213–3644

Website: www.frankcass.com

Copyright © 2001 D. Menashri

British Library Cataloguing in Publication Data

Menashri, David
Post-revolutionary politics in Iran: religion, society and
power
1. Religion and politics – Iran   2. Iran – Politics and
government – 1979–1997   3. Iran – Politics and government –
1997–   4. Iran – Foreign relations – 1979–1997   5. Iran
Foreign relations – 1997–
I. Title
320.9'55'09045

ISBN 0-7146-5074-9 (cloth)
ISBN 0-7146-8121-0 (paper)

Library of Congress Cataloging-in-Publication Data

Menashri, David.
    Post-revolutionary politics in Iran: religion, society and
power / David Menashri.
    p. cm.
    Includes bibliographical references and index.
    ISBN 0-7146-5074-9 (cloth) – ISBN 0-7146-8121-0 (paper)
1. Iran – Politics and government – 1979–1997.   2. Iran – Politics and
government – 1997–   3. Iran – Foreign relations – 1979–1997.   4.
        Iran – Foreign relations – 1997–   I. Title.
            DS318.825 .M476 2001
    955.05'4 – dc21   00-050862

Typeset by Regent Typesetting, London
Printed in Great Britain by
MPG Books Ltd, Bodmin, Cornwall

Contents

PART TWO: IRAN, THE WEST AND THE MIDDLE EAST PEACE PROCESS

Preface

The Islamic Revolution in Iran has undoubtedly been one of the most momentous developments in the modern history of the Middle East. It has led to a dramatic change in the domestic landscape and had a far-reaching influence in the region and far beyond Iran's borders.

Since its outbreak, the revolution has attracted a great deal of public opinion, as well as the interest of scholars, the media and policy-makers worldwide. Some of its unique features, such as mass participation, Ayatollah Ruhollah Khomeini's charismatic leadership, the revolutionary movement's ideology and the politics of the new regime, turned Iran into a focus of public attention from the outset. Thereafter, the process of Islamization, the *modus operandi* of the clerical regime, the Iran–Iraq war, and the revolution's influence in the Muslim world continued to fascinate observers. More recently, the emergence of President Mohammad Khatami and the wave of reformism have further fired the imagination of observers. Iran's relatively free press, the open domestic debate and deep soul-searching process, the colorful election campaigns (notably to the presidency in 1997 and to the Majlis [parliament] in 2000), and the subsequent countermeasures by the conservative elite, have turned the reformers into the main focus of attention.

More than two decades after the revolution, the Islamic Republic remains in many respects an enigma. The power structure, decision-making process and exact politics of the Islamic regime are far from clear, and the struggle over the revolutionary path is not yet decided. Moreover, at the time of writing, the main developments under discussion seem to have reached a new, more complex and convoluted peak. The principles of the revolutionary philosophy and politics are now being examined in a fierce and open debate about religion and state, Islam and politics, Islam and democracy, state interest versus revolutionary ideology, and Iran's relations with the outside world. This book does not pretend to resolve all such complexities. It strives, however, to shed some additional light on the main processes in post-revolutionary Iran and to try clarify Iran's political landscape.

This book analyzes the developments in the 'second republic' (that is, since the death of Ayatollah Khomeini in 1989) until the end of 1999. The Epilogue, which should be read as an integral part of the discussion, updates the discussion to cover the Majlis elections in early 2000 and the politics of the aftermath of the elections, thus extending the study until the summer of 2000 – three years after Khatami's election, and less than a year before the next presidential elections are scheduled.

This study is the result of an ongoing attempt to follow contemporary Iranian politics. Since 1978, I have written all the 22 annual essays on Iran in the Moshe Dayan Center's yearbook, *Middle East Contemporary Survey*. The opportunity to study such developments in continuum since the revolutionary change in Iran erupted has resulted, I hope, in an intimate familiarity with the Iranian scene, its nuances and vicissitudes over the years. The chapters of the first decade of the revolution have been collected into one volume, *Iran: A Decade of War and Revolution* (New York, Holmes & Meier Publishers, 1990). This book seeks to provide a comprehensive and updated analysis of the momentous developments in revolutionary Iran in the 'second republic'.

Still, some issues have been deliberately excluded from this study, such as a discussion of the opposition movements, the army and the Revolutionary Guards, and Iran's security concerns and politics. In other cases, only some aspects of more general questions are discussed. Thus, while analyzing the social and political ramifications of the economic situation, this book does not provide a detailed study of the economy. In the field of foreign relations, again, the discussion is limited to certain key questions, while other areas of foreign policy are discussed only briefly.

The convulsions in Iranian domestic landscape make it difficult accurately to identify the competing tendencies. In the early 1990s, domestic differences seemed to revolve essentially among groups usually referred to as pragmatists, radicals and conservatives. Over time, the main actors changed their outlook significantly and the relative power of individual leaders and groups varied considerably. Against a background of such shifting complexities, mapping the domestic forces (in terms of doctrine and association) is not an easy matter. Some of the radicals of the early 1990s turned into the flag-bearers of the reform movement at the end of the decade, and some powerful figures of the early 1990s appeared much weaker only a few years later. Therefore, the portrayal of groups or individuals in terms of policy and influence can relate only to the specific context and period being discussed; and their place in the hierarchy of power should be construed in conjunction with the timeframe and policy areas being examined.

I have used 'Islamism' to denote a phenomenon often referred to as 'political Islam', 'radicalism' or 'fundamentalism'. Yet 'Islamism', too, is a problematic term, since it may imply that its dogma represents Islam, or that there is only one interpretation of Islam. However, for convenience, I have preferred to use 'Islamism'. For the sake of consistency, the term 'Iran' is used throughout the book, even for periods in which 'Persia' would have been more appropriate. I have used a simplified system of Persian transliteration, making allowances for pronunciation. I have omitted diacritical marks, yet have retained the *ayn* and *hamza* (such as in *'ulama'*). Some Persian and Arabic consonants and vowels have been transliterated differently, when pronunciation so required (for example, Reza, Mohammad, *velayat-e faqih*, *marja'-e taqlid* in Persian; but Rida, Muhammad, *wilayat al-faqih*, *marja' al-taqlid* in Arabic). Names of individuals are rendered in the way they are most commonly known. Thus, appellations and titles often serve as family names (such as Rafsanjani). In cases of well-known proper names, or Islamic terms for which a different orthography has become established in English usage, I have consciously departed from the system of transliteration. In references to the Foreign Broadcast Information Service (FBIS), Daily Report (DR), until August 1996 (when a hard copy was published) I quoted the original source as well as the date of the DR publication. Since then (when it has appeared on line), I have only added in brackets (DR), indicating that the source used was from the DR.

I am indebted to the Dayan Center for making available to me the research material essential for my ongoing research on Iran. Some parts of the book were further facilitated by research grants from the Washington Institute for Near Eastern Politics (Washington, DC) and the Tami Steinmetz Center for Peace Studies (Tel Aviv University). The above studies were then published, respectively, in my papers: 'Revolution at Crossroads: Iran's Domestic Politics and Regional Ambitions' and 'Iran after Khomeini: Revolutionary Ideology versus National Interests'. The main findings of the above studies are incorporated in different parts of the present book. I am indebted to The Washington Institute and the Tami Steinmetz Center for their permission to do so.

I am grateful to Itamar Rabinovitch (President of Tel Aviv University), for his friendship, generosity and support all along. Special thanks should also go to Martin Kramer (Director of the Dayan Center), Ami Ayalon and Bruce Maddy-Weitzman (the editors of *Middle East Contemporary Survey*). Many other colleagues and friends have offered important insights into the subject matter of this book, and helped me obtain resources and data. Wholehearted thanks should also go to Ali

Banuazizi, Farhad Kazemi, Joseph Kostiner, Meir Litvak, Orly Ram, Soli Shahvar, Asher Susser, David Wasserstein and David Yerushalmi. Several research assistants provided significant help and they deserve much gratitude: Haggai Etkes, Alexis Pavlich, Shiri Rotem, Ayelet Savyon, Anat Shekhori and Sanaz Yashar. Special thanks to Rami Regavim. His devotion and talent were of special value throughout the research and in the preparation of the manuscript for press. Thanks should also go to the Dayan Center's documentation unit, mainly to Haim Gal, Marion Gliksberg, Dorit Paret; to Elena Lesnick, and especially to Amira Margalit, the Assistant Director of the Center, for all her hard work, devotion and care, which allowed me and my colleagues to pursue our research. I would likewise wish to thank the Gulf2000 project, especially its director Gary Sick, for making available for those interested in the Gulf region valuable information on line. I wish to extend my deepest gratitude to Frank Cass, my publisher, for his encouragement and support. Thanks should also be given to my editor, Andrew Humphrys, and the copy-editor, Farzana Shaikh. It gives me special pleasure to thank Jack Mahfar, for his friendship and support. Finally, I would like to express my deepest gratitude to my wife, Gila, for her patience and encouragement and for being such a faithful companion in my long journey to study Iran and its people.

Special thanks to the Maccabee Foundation in New York, for their support in conducting this research. Finally, I wish to thank the Parviz and Pouran Nazarian Chair for Modern Iranian History at Tel Aviv University for the valuable support that made the publication of this book possible. Long-time supporters of education and scholarship, Pouran and Parviz Nazarian have contributed significantly to the expansion of Iranian Studies at Tel Aviv University. Their support has been instrumental in facilitating this research.

List of Abbreviations

AFP	Agence France Presse
AIPAC	American–Israel Public Affairs Committee
CIA	Central Intelligence Agency (USA)
DR	Daily Report (Middle East), Foreign Broadcast Information Service (FBIS)
EIU	Economist Intelligence Unit
EU	European Union
Hamas	*Harakat al-Muqawama al-Islammiyya* (Islamic Resistance Movement; Palestinian)
ICO	Islamic Conference Organization
IMF	International Monetary Fund
IRNA	Islamic Republic News Agency (Tehran)
ISNA	Iranian Students News Agency
JRM	*Jame'eh-ye Ruhaniyyat-e Mobarez* (Society of Combatant Clergy)
JPRS	Joint Publication Research Services
KDP	Kurdistan Democratic Party
MRM	*Majma'-e Ruhaniyyun-e Mobarez* (Association of Combatant Clerics)
MECS	Middle East Contemporary Survey
MEED	Middle East Economic Digest
NATO	North Atlantic Treaty Organization
OECD	Organization for Economic Cooperation and Development
OPEC	Organization of Petroleum Exporting Countries
PLO	Palestine Liberation Organization
SAVAK	*Sazeman-e Amniyyat va Ettela'at-e Keshvar* (State Intelligence and Security Organization), prior to the revolution
SNSC	Supreme National Security Council
SWB	Summary of World Broadcasting (British Broadcasting Corporation)
UAE	United Arab Emirates

UNESCO   United Nations Educational, Scientific and Cultural
           Organization
WB   World Bank

Introduction:
Revolutionary Politics in Iran

For the past two centuries, Iran has oscillated between extremes as the country searched for a viable response to the multiple challenges of Western-style modernity. Having been generally insulated from the outside world until the late eighteenth century, Iran gradually underwent a transformation that became increasingly apparent in the period immediately preceding the collapse of the monarchy and the establishment of the Islamic Republic in 1979.

Iranian views of the West have changed. After prolonged geographical and political isolation from the West – far more so than the predominantly Sunni Muslim communities of the Middle East – Iran under the Qajars and the Pahlavis gradually moved towards emulation, and later to enthusiastic imitation, of everything Western, until the Islamic Revolution reversed the trend with its disdain for, and indeed total rejection of, the Shah's 'Westoxication'. The dichotomy that has characterized Iran's recent history and politics is, therefore, best exemplified in the contrasting visions of the country's two leading figures of recent times: the last Shah, Mohammad Reza Pahlavi, and Ayatollah Ruhollah Khomeini.

While the Shah sought to promote an essentially new collective identity rooted in the country's pre-Islamic heritage, and in loyalty to the monarchy and to Iranian territorial nationalism, the leaders of the Islamic Republic have attempted to ground collective identity in strict adherence to Islamic religion and cultural values. The attachment to the legacy of Cyrus the Great that typified the Shah's projected vision of history was superseded under Ayatollah Khomeini by the return to the Shi'i Islamic heritage of Imam 'Ali, the first Shi'i Imam.

Thus, the overthrow of the monarchy in Iran was not merely a revolution in name, achieving no more than a change of government. It was designed from the outset to achieve a complete revolution in all spheres of life – *Islamic* both in name and in character. For its leaders, the 'Islamic Revolution' was a vision of an ideal Islamic order, not only in Iran itself but as a model for other Islamic communities to imitate.

Above all, however, the revolution was intended to provide a fundamental cure, based on Islamic doctrine and revolutionary politics, for the ideological, social and economic malaise that has plagued Iranian society in modern times.

The revolution in Iran therefore represented a new prototype of political philosophy, but one couched in terminology with which the populace was intimately familiar, generating a new pattern of power seizure in the modern history of the Muslim Middle East. Generally, the countless *coups d'états* in this region from the mid-twentieth century onwards were executed by small groups of men, usually led by army officers, who mobilized popular support for themselves and their new ideology *after* seizing power. The Islamic Revolution was a striking exception: it was led primarily by clerics; it enjoyed massive popular support of men and woman not as a consequence of, but as a prerequisite for the seizure of power; and its 'new' vision was essentially based on the glorious heritage most familiar to Iranians – that of Islam.

Though markedly divergent from the pattern of Middle Eastern coups, the Islamic Revolution was generally consistent with earlier opposition movements in the modern history of Iran. Three earlier outbursts over the last century are especially noteworthy in this regard. First, the Tobacco Movement (1891–92), which rallied support against the tobacco concession (and the system of capitulations in general), forcing the Shah to revoke the concession to a foreign company. Second, the Constitutional Revolution (1905–11), which coerced the Shah to approve a constitution limiting his own power. Finally, the national movement headed by Mohammad Mosaddeq (the prime minister in the years 1951–53), which drove Mohammad Reza Shah into temporary exile.

The Islamic Revolution shared certain characteristics with all these earlier movements. First, each began in reaction to the reigning Shah's policies, which were injurious to various socioeconomic groups and motivated diverse forces to unite around a common cause. Second, in all but the national movement under Mosaddeq, the clerics were the driving force and proved their ability successfully to mobilize popular support. Third, mass support played a decisive role in each of the movements. Fourth, mounting social and economic tensions, intensified autocratic rule, growing secularization and extensive foreign (Western) influence in the country were instrumental in garnering opposition to the regime. Finally, notwithstanding their internal differences, the various groups within each movement rallied around a powerful, unifying symbol: tobacco (and the system of capitulations) in the late nineteenth century;

constitutionalism (symbolizing the struggle for freedom) in the early twentieth century; oil, or the nationalization of the oil industry (and, more generally, nationalism and national independence) in the early 1950s; and Islam in the late 1970s. All four movements were successful in achieving their initial goals, but, whereas the earlier popular uprisings had limited objectives (i.e. to change one major item on the government's agenda), the Islamic Revolution sought and managed to change the regime itself, replacing the monarchy with an Islamic Republic.

The first two decades of clerical rule following the Islamic Revolution were characterized by the attempt to attain two main goals. First, the new regime sought to consolidate, institutionalize and perpetuate its own control. Second, and more importantly, it sought to implement Ayatollah Khomeini's revolutionary ideology, which offered to alleviate the general feeling of disillusionment in the country and to transform Iran into a prosperous country, thereby entrenching and legitimizing the rule of the clerics.

Although generally successful in maintaining political stability throughout the first two decades of revolutionary rule, the Islamic regime proved to be far less successful in translating its dogma into an effective instrument to resolve the mounting political, social and economic problems that had been the root cause of the revolution.[1] Indeed, the urge to provide practical solutions to the pressing problems facing the people was to pose the most severe challenges to the regime in the 1990s.

To appreciate fully the degree of profound change that has taken place in Iran since the revolution, four issues seem particularly pertinent.

(1) *The extent to which the Iranian Revolution was religious in its roots and goals.* The Islamic imperative is both individual and collective. Islamic religion and jurisprudence encompass all aspects of the believer's life, making no distinction between the religious, the political, the scientific or other spheres of human endeavor. Thus, from a purely Islamic perspective, solutions to the prevailing economic distress, social disparities, political repression, foreign exploitation and the unsettling consequences of rapid Westernization and modernization, which had combined to serve as the catalysts for the revolution, could not be found in isolation from religion. Indeed, Iranians rose against the Shah for a variety of reasons, but viewed Islam as the panacea to end the social and economic crisis, to provide their children with a better life and to lead their country to a brighter future. The revolutionary credo 'Islam is the solution' (*al-Islam huwa al-hal*) best embodied this deep-rooted and multi-dimensional vision. Islam gave the movement its basic ideology

and leadership, and helped recruit popular support. The Islamic Revolution, much like other Islamist movements in the region, was religious in this more comprehensive sense, even though the motives which led people to join the movement exceeded what in Western terms might narrowly be defined as strictly 'religious' grievances and goals. Ultimately, however, the demise of the monarchy led to the creation of an Islamic regime, which continues to be led by clerics, and in that sense it was, undeniably, an Islamic Revolution.

(2) *The extent to which Khomeini's doctrine represented traditional Islam or a departure from conservative Islamic thought.* Following the Iranian Revolution, Western analyses generally associated its basic precepts with the principles of Islam – specifically Shi'i Islam. Yet Islam (like Judaism and Christianity) is an infinite body of knowledge and belief, whose interpretation and meanings change over time. This last point has recently been re-emphasized by leading Iranian intellectuals, who note that there is no single interpretation of Islam, that no single interpretation enjoys supremacy over any other, that there is no final or ultimate interpretation and, finally, that there can be no official interpretation of Islam.[2] Throughout history, there have been varied interpretations of the tenets of Islam, and this was as evident on the eve of the Islamic Revolution as it is today. When judged against the beliefs and practices of early Islam, Khomeini's vision appears conservative in many respects. However, if 'tradition' refers to more recent trends in Islamic thought and politics, Khomeini's ideas were comparatively innovative and revolutionary.[3] Upon close examination of Khomeini's political thought one can also detect significant changes in his own world-view over time.[4] In many ways, Khomeini's doctrine represents a revolution in recent Islamic political thought, and it was the Islamic Revolution that enabled such interpretations to prevail by making them integral to the ideology of Iran's clerical system.

(3) *The degree to which the Islamic regime remained loyal to its dogma after assuming power.* Like other ideological movements in history, the new regime upon assuming power faced complex demands of governance, forcing it to adapt to new realities. In opposition, the revolutionary clerics could advance a theoretical model of the ideal Islamic state. Once in power, however, the new leaders of Iran were unable to govern by revolutionary slogans only. Obliged to manage rather than theorize about affairs of the state, they often had to make compromises, not from a new-found moderation, but in pragmatic response to the exigencies of their situation (see mainly Chapters 1 and 4). Yet, in terms of specific areas of policy and with respect to appro-

priate degrees and rates of change, the various domestic factions differed widely among themselves. Iranian revolutionary policies thus remained fluid, divergent and often contradictory – in constant search of an appropriate balance between idealistic convictions and the realities of life. (See Chapter 2.)

(4) *Why Islam became the symbol of the revolution.* Despite the process of modernization, Islam remained the most profound symbol of Iranian identity and the most cohesive element to unite the Iranian society. The enormous difficulties facing large segments of Iranian society, now led people to Islam in search of salvation. Apparently, the magnitude of the malaise necessitated reverting to a solid philosophy that had proved itself effective in the past. In addition, the failure of the new 'imported' philosophies (such as Westernization, constitutionalism, nationalism or socialism) to resolve the basic problems facing the modern Middle East, coupled with the failure of the quietist (traditional) clergy to meet popular expectations, encouraged people to view Islam as a source of hope and direction. The profound challenges – cultural, political, economic and military – presented by the West also led to a growing reliance on Islam as a panacea for existing social problems.

Against this background, Ayatollah Khomeini suggested the most authentic, familiar and simple solution: a return to the basic tenets of Islam as the cure for the current malaise in Muslim society. He offered the people hope and championed his cause in terms that every Muslim could comprehend and could identify with. He offered a solution to the country's problems arising from rapid modernization and mass economic and social dislocation. The disillusionment and despair experienced by many Iranians in the decades preceding the Islamic Revolution, and their deep identification with Islam, made them especially receptive to such a philosophy. The charismatic personality of Ayatollah Khomeini, combined with his long and courageous struggle against the Shah, his religious credentials and unique leadership qualifications, made him an attractive and respected leader who could lead the revolution to success. His dogma, thus, became in the eyes of many revolutionaries, the hope for salvation and for a brighter future.

The revolution did not end, however, with the downfall of the Shah and the establishment of the Islamic Republic. In many ways the takeover of government was just the first phase – the revolution then had to prove that its dogma could cure society's ills. In fact, this task has become the main challenge for the revolutionary regime, particularly since the end of the Iran–Iraq war in 1988, and the death of Ayatollah Khomeini, the founding father of the revolution, in 1989.

It became abundantly clear soon after the change of regime in 1979 that there were significant differences within the revolutionary camp over the formulation of concrete policy programs and the response to the challenge of governance. One reason for these differences lay in the existence of opposing factions within the heterogeneous coalition that had led the new regime to power. With the consolidation of the clerical regime, these differences became more visible among the hard core of Khomeini's own disciples. Since Khomeini's death opinions have polarized as respective leaders and political camps vie for ultimate authority in dealing with social problems. The formulation of policy has often led to serious disputes within revolutionary ranks and has often generated inconsistent and contradictory policies.

Another reason for these apparent differences was the varied response to simultaneous and momentous domestic and regional changes in the period following the revolutionary takeover. In the initial stages of the revolution these included the translation of the general philosophy of the revolution into a concrete program of action. The most serious difficulties included the political struggle for power between the different groups in the revolutionary movement; the social and economic challenges following the revolutionary takeover (and the drop in oil income); the Iran–Iraq war; tension with the United States (and other Western powers); and tense relations with most of Iran's immediate neighbors. This book focuses on developments in Iran since the late 1980s. The following outline, therefore, considers only the major domestic challenges and the main changes affecting Iran and the Middle East since that time.

On the domestic front, three main challenges evolved.

(1) *The death of Ayatollah Khomeini* in 1989 ended his all-powerful, charismatic style of leadership and called into question the essence of the religio-political guardianship of the revolution and the very nature of clerical rule itself. (See Chapters 1 and 5.)

(2) *The resulting struggle for power between Ayatollah 'Ali Khamene'i and Hojjat ul-Islam 'Ali Akbar Hashemi Rafsanjani (1989–97) and the election of President Mohammad Khatami in 1997,* widened the gap hitherto contained by Khomeini's authoritative and charismatic rule. None of these leaders had Khomeini's religious authority, political power, mass appeal or personal charisma. Khomeini's most important decisions went unchallenged (such as his declaration of the cease-fire with Iraq in 1988), those of his successors did not. Generally speaking, the power struggle within the revolutionary camp was played out on two levels: an open conflict between ideological purists and their more

pragmatic and reformist rivals, and a more latent and personal struggle between the leaders of such trends (over and above their common struggle against the opposition movements). The election of Hojjat ul-Islam Mohammad Khatami as president did not change the system of government although domestic alliances shifted and rivalries deepened further; public opinion gained greater significance in domestic politics and the demand for social improvement became more pressing. (See Chapters 2 and 3.)

(3) *Growing social and economic difficulties and the quest for greater personal freedoms* have given rise to intense popular dissatisfaction and marked disillusionment. This has resulted in greater political realism and a growing emphasis on 'reasons of state' over the 'ideological crusade'.[5] Yet even this pragmatic attitude has not helped ease the difficulties facing the *mostaz'afin* (disadvantaged classes), or solve their problems. (See Chapter 4.) Moreover, the popular struggle to secure more liberty of expression which assumed greater intensity at the end of the 1990s led to open confrontation within the regime. (See Chapter 5.)

Furthermore, developments on the domestic front were coupled with unprecedented regional developments that had a direct influence on Iran and its revolutionary policy.

• *The disintegration of the Soviet Union* removed Iran's traditional threat from the north and provided her with new opportunities as well as significant challenges. The fall of the 'Islamic iron curtain'[6] made it possible for Iran (at least in its own view) to open a new chapter in its relations with Russia on more equal terms. In addition, Iran recognized the potential for Islamic and other developing countries to fill the vacuum created by the demise of the Soviet Union. Iran itself wished to be the leading force in such an effort to secure regional dominance. The collapse of the Soviet Union also led to the emergence of six Islamic republics close to Iran's borders that created new opportunities to advance Iran's regional ambitions. But this also posed significant challenges for Tehran. They included the need to preserve regional stability; to limit the influence of unfriendly countries competing for influence in the Islamic regions of the former Soviet Union; and to prevent the possible penetration of competing ideological influences into Iran from newly independent republics, like Azerbaijan. More importantly, the disintegration of the Soviet Union notwithstanding, Russia remained an important neighbor whose interests and influences Iran could not ignore. Finally, the collapse of the Soviet Union further strengthened the position of the United States on the international scene and in the Middle East – much to Iran's dismay.

- *The 1991 Gulf War* (and the renewed attack on Iraq in 1998), considerably weakened (at least temporarily), Iran's major rival: Iraq. The war also led to tensions between Iraq and its Arab neighbors (Saudi Arabia and Kuwait, for example), which further stimulated the Iranian drive to secure regional hegemony in the Persian Gulf and beyond. Not surprisingly, Iran's attempts were challenged by local Arab states and by US policy in the Gulf. (See Chapters 6 and 7.)

- *The Arab–Israeli peace process* – and the participation therein of Iran's main Arab ally, Syria – further isolated Iran as the leader of the anti-peace axis. Having made Palestine a major issue on its foreign policy agenda, Iran was now willing (or felt obliged) to offer its leadership to this camp. Although support for Islamist movements became a means for Iran to champion Iranian and Islamic dominance, the precarious situation has also presented Tehran with dilemmas that often posed serious challenges to the regime. (See Chapter 8.)

- *The growth of Islamism* was inspired largely by Iran and enjoys its committed loyalty. This required Iran to provide patronage, support, and guardianship in order to substantiate its claim to leadership of Muslim communities outside Iran's borders. Iran's self-perception as a regional patron has presented the government with new opportunities to strengthen and expand its regional and ideological influence. At the same time Iran also faced challenges that included increasingly precarious relations with regional states and expectations of Iranian support by Islamist movements worldwide.

In the context of these changes and the aftermath of the death of Ayatollah Khomeini, Iran appears to have entered a new revolutionary phase. Some scholars viewed Khomeini's death as the beginning of the 'second republic'.[7] Others maintained that the direction of the Islamic Republic had changed course even prior to Khomeini's death, like following the cease-fire with Iraq: 'The people saw the cease-fire as a humiliating defeat.' After making enormous sacrifices for the war effort in the belief that they were fighting a holy war, 'Iranians were suddenly faced with the grim reality that God has not triumphed over Satan (Saddam Husayn). The people were traumatized and that led to a marked change in their perception of the state and the clergy.'[8] Still others viewed the fall of the Soviet Union as having ushered in 'the second phase' of Iranian foreign policy.[9] Clearly, a decade after taking power, both domestic and regional realities have changed significantly. The *Iran Times* went so far as to suggest that, with such enormous changes, the 'world [has] turned upside down'.[10]

Although the revolutionary nature of these changes is beyond argument, their combined impact did not necessarily generate a clear-cut policy. At times they led to ambiguity, dualism, and even contradictions as the Islamic Revolution struggled to consolidate itself and respond to the growing needs and expectations of the people. The 1997 election of President Khatami may be considered yet another turning point, signaling at least greater support for reform among large segments of Iranian society, including officials.[11]

The objective of this book therefore is to analyze Iran's domestic and foreign policies in the era of this 'second republic', that is, since the death of Ayatollah Khomeini in June 1989. It sets out to examine the forces, both domestic and regional, that influence Iran's policy-making, with special emphasis on the nature of politics in Iran in the three years or so following the election of President Khatami.

The first part of the study focuses on internal developments and their impact on the regime's domestic policies. The second part explores the evolution of Iran's regional ambitions and policies since the death of Ayatollah Khomeini until after Khatami's election to the presidency. In studying developments in this fashion, the book will similarly attempt to examine some of the complex inter-relationship between Iran's domestic dynamics and its foreign policies. The Epilogue will provide a tentative appraisal of the developments from late 1999 until after the Majlis election in the spring of 2000.

NOTES

1. For a discussion of their initial success in consolidating their rule, see David Menashri, 'The Islamic Revolution in Iran: The Consolidation Phase', *Orient*, 25/4 (April 1984), pp. 499–515; and *Iran: A Decade of War and Revolution* (New York, NY: Holmes & Meier, 1990), pp. 4–11.
2. For a detailed discussion of such arguments by leading intellectuals, and for some basic differences between leading theologians in the early stages of the revolution, as well as in the 1990s, see Chapter 1.
3. Nikki Keddie, 'Iran: Change in Islam, Islam and Change', *International Journal of Middle East Studies*, 2 (1980), p. 532. See also Hava Lazarus-Yaffe, 'Ha-Shi'a be-torato ha-politit shel Khomeini' [Shi'ism in Khomeini's Political Thought], *Ha-Mizrah Ha-Hadash*, 30 (1982), pp. 99–106.
4. Compare his views expressed in his book *Kashf al-Asrar* [Unveiling the Secrets] (written in the early 1940s) and *Velayat-e Faqih* [The Rule of the Jurisconsult] (representing his thought since the late 1960s).
5. R. K. Ramazani, 'Iran's Foreign Policy: Both North and South', *Middle East Journal*, 46/3 (Summer 1992), p. 395.
6. Shireen Hunter, 'The Emergence of Soviet Muslims: Impact on the Middle East', *Middle East Insight*, 8/5 (May–June 1992), p. 32.
7. See Anoushirvan Ehteshami, *After Khomeini: The Iranian Second Republic*

(London: Routledge, 1995); Udo Steinbach, 'The "Second Islamic Republic": A Theocracy on the Road to Normality', *Aussenpolitik*, 1 (1990), pp. 73–90.

8. Eric Rouleau, 'The Islamic Republic of Iran: Paradoxes and Contradictions in a Changing Society', *Middle East Insight*, 11/5 (July–August 1995), p. 56. Rouleau was quoting the views of Naser Hadiyan and Hadi Semmati (professors of political science from Tehran University).

9. See editorial in *Hamshahri*, 9 February 1993 – DR, 23 February 1993.

10. *Iran Times*, 1 October 1993.

11. See article by Bahman Baktiari and Scott Harrop in *Christian Science Monitor*, 16 April 1996.

Part One:
The Domestic Scene

1

The Guardianship of the Jurisconsult:
The Ideological Dilemma

KHOMEINI'S SUCCESSION AND RETREAT FROM DOGMA

Perhaps the most profound achievement of the 1979 revolution was the unification of religion and state, and the transfer of all power – theological and political – to the highest religious authority, the *marja'-e taqlid* (source of imitation), or, as the concept became known in revolutionary parlance, the *velayat-e faqih* (guardianship or vicegerency of the jurisconsult).[1] Yet, it was in this very realm that Khomeini's disciples faced their most crucial ideological challenge, both in defining the authority of the Islamic government and in settling the identity and powers of the new Supreme Leader in succession to Ayatollah Khomeini.

The problem consisted of two inter-related elements. First, there was the conflict between the philosophy of the revolution (which held, among other things, that leadership should be entrusted to a prominent cleric and defined the authority of the government under Islamic rule), and the particular interests of the Iranian state. Second, there were conceptual, factional and personal conflicts among the revolutionaries themselves regarding questions of succession, the power structure and actual policies to be followed. In a clear deviation from the creed of the revolution, the regime was forced over time to give greater weight to national interests and practical considerations than to dogmatic principles. At the same time, power moved gradually from prominent theologians to religio-politicians, who were charged with the task of running the state.[2] The dogmatic and political controversies that had begun to emerge in the initial stage of the Islamic Republic thus gained further significance after the death of Ayatollah Khomeini.

Faced with the challenge of governance and mindful of the practical needs of the state, Khomeini himself often intervened to sanction the authority of religio-politicians at the expense of prominent clerics. Under the constitution, the 12-man Council of Guardians (*shura-ye negahban*), comprising of six clerics appointed by the Supreme Leader and six jurists chosen by the Majlis with his approval, is charged with reviewing laws passed by the Majlis to determine whether they are in conformity with Islamic law and compatible with the Iranian constitution. Because of its conservative approach, already well established at the outset of the revolution, the Council of Guardians vetoed many laws that the government deemed essential for the effective running of the government (e.g. land redistribution, the nationalization of foreign trade, taxation, and labor practices), to the point of obstructing government functions.[3] Khomeini was then forced to intervene personally to pressure the Council to reverse its decision and approve laws it had previously vetoed.

In a series of notes exchanged with President Khamene'i and with the Council of Guardians (in December 1987 and January 1988), Khomeini further elaborated on one of the principal questions in Shi'i theology: the limits of government power.[4] His ruling was an important step in stripping the Council of its exclusive constitutional authority. At the same time, he sanctioned the authority of the state even 'to destroy a mosque' or suspend the exercise of the basic religious duties, if state interest (*selah-e keshvar*) so required.[5]

In February 1988 he went one step further. In response to an appeal by a group of prominent officials, who sought to bypass the Council of Guardians in a case of a disagreement with the Majlis, Khomeini decreed that such an impasse should be resolved by a council consisting of six theologians from the Council of Guardians and six state officials (the president, the prime minister, the speaker of the Majlis, the president of the supreme court, the prosecutor general and representative of Imam Khomeini), and the minister concerned with the proposed legislation. The Council's decision, he then decreed, 'must be accepted'.[6] This represented another blatant retreat from his own revolutionary doctrine. The authority to determine the state's interest (a phrase worked into the name of the new body, *shura-ye tashkhis-e maslahat*; roughly translated as the Expediency Council), was thus entrusted to a mixed assembly (i.e. one composed of theologians, religio-politicians and government officials with no Islamic training), a decision which deprived the Council of Guardians of its exclusive right to approve legislation. In August 1988, prompted by the urge to adopt new policies to resolve post-war difficulties, Khomeini ordered the formation of a four-man council (*shura-ye ta'yin-e siyasatha-ye bazsazi*), made up of the heads of the three branches of government (Rafsanjani, Khamene'i and Ayatollah 'Abdul-Karim Ardabili), and the prime minister (Mir-Hosein Musavi), to resolve disagreements over post-war reconstruction policy and ministerial appointments.[7]

In so doing, Khomeini in fact sanctioned the supremacy of the state over the philosophy of the revolution, which was whittled down in the face of harsh realities. Such a decision 'in favor of state paramountcy in society's affairs' gave 'dramatic new power to the state', sanctioned its dominance over society,[8] and even 'permitted the state to violate citizens' rights for the common good'.[9] The Speaker of the Majlis, Rafsanjani, then interpreted Khomeini's guidelines in a most revealing way: the 'law should follow Islamic doctrine. However, if necessary, priority will be given to government decision over doctrine.'[10] This was inevitable for the actual running of the state, although it constituted a serious blow to one of the most basic doctrines of the revolution. The question of the succession presented the regime with yet another challenge.

In a sense, Khomeini's doctrine constituted a revolution in recent Shi'i Islamic political thought. He introduced new interpretations and gained support mainly from low-ranking (and relatively young) clerics, or religio-politicians, over the heads of senior theologians (see below). The succession issue thus presented the regime with both a theological challenge and severe political obstacles. According to Shi'i tradition (now embodied in the Islamic regime and the 1979 Iranian constitution), the Supreme Leader was supposed to be the most learned and righteous *faqih* (*a'lam va asdaq*). Yet the most prominent theologians were not politically suited for the succession, and the religio-politicians lacked the proper religious credentials. In fact, the leading theologians of the rank of *Ayatollah 'uzma* (grand Ayatollah) did not fully identify with Khomeini's revolutionary doctrine, and none of Khomeini's loyal followers had the prominent religious standing (not to mention the charisma and political authority) of Khomeini himself to qualify for the succession.

Most of the leading theologians of 1979 were either resentful of the *velayat-e faqih* concept as practiced by the ruling clerics (thus, Kazem Shari'atmadari, 'Abdollah Shirazi, and Abul-Qasem Kho'i), or distanced themselves from daily politics (such as Seyyed Shihab al-Din Najafi-Mar'ashi, Mohammad Reza Golpaygani and apparently Mohammad 'Ali Araki). Some of the leading *'ulama'* (clerics) vehemently opposed Khomeini's doctrine and were forcibly silenced; others were less vocal, or, acknowledging the commanding power of the Islamic regime, gave their blessing to the facts established by Khomeini or his disciples. It soon became evident that the very concept and the criteria for the selection of the *velayat-e faqih* mentioned above were (as Khomeini's first prime minister Mehdi Bazargan once said), 'a garment fit only for Mr Khomeini'.[11]

Nevertheless, given the prominence of the *vali-ye faqih* as the Supreme Leader in the Islamic regime, it was crucial to guarantee a smooth transfer of power. Since there was no theologian endowed with both religious and revolutionary credentials who appeared fit for the succession, the regime could either opt for a collective leadership or rally behind a less prominent though fully loyal cleric. Khomeini's disciples opted for the second option, prompting yet another sharp deviation from the revolutionary concept of *velayat-e faqih*.

It is true that there were numerous instances in Shi'i history in which no single *faqih* was accepted as the sole source of authority, and the result was often a kind of collective spiritual leadership in which, as Khomeini pointed out, there was a continuing debate over theological issues among senior clerics.[12] Major Shi'i thinkers have even argued that having a single guide (*marja'*) 'ran counter to the principles of Shi'ism'. All the more, since the current guide's (Khamene'i) career has been in politics, not religion.[13] Yet, in the past, their ideological differences, as Khamene'i once said, had 'existed [only] in books'.[14] Now, on the other hand, given the civil power clerics had assumed, their disputes could, as they often did, disrupt the effective administration of the government. The fact that the clerics now wielded complete power made the selection of a (single) successor essential for the effective running of government.[15]

With this in mind, and keen to avoid a succession crisis, Khomeini and his disciples first 'recognized' Ayatollah Hosein 'Ali Montazeri as an *Ayatollah 'uzma* (Grand Ayatollah) at the outset of the revolution, and then officially selected him (by means of the Council of Experts) as Khomeini's heir apparent in 1985.[16] In 1987, Khomeini also revised his will, apparently to avoid a struggle for succession after his death. Although Montazeri's religious credentials were significant, his selection which defied traditional practice and Khomeini's own creed (since there were greater religious authorities still alive), had more to do with his role in the revolutionary movement than with pure scholarship or piety. Yet, despite the fact that loyalty was an essential element in his selection, Montazeri's subsequent criticisms of the government and its revolutionary politics led to his disqualification in March 1989, an event which provided another example of the supremacy of political considerations over doctrinal ones.[17]

Given Khomeini's failing health, changes to the 1979 constitution were necessary to adapt the revolutionary doctrine to the then prevailing realities and to guarantee a smooth succession.[18] A series of constitutional amendments in 1989 gave official blessing to the separation of the positions of *marja'iyya* and *velayat*, thus allowing any *faqih* (jurist) with 'scholastic qualifications for issuing religious decrees' to assume the position of Supreme Leader (Articles 5 and 109). The 1979 stipulation (Article 5) that the Supreme Leader be 'recognized and accepted' by 'the majority of the people' (a requirement for the *marja'iyya*), was also dropped. At the same time, the new constitution stressed that preference must be given to those better versed in 'political and social issues' (Article 107). Thus, while the level of religious scholarship required for leadership was lowered, political experience was given greater weight – another step in the retreat from dogma.[19]

The selection of Khamene'i (until then only a hojjat ul-Islam, a lower ranking than ayatollah) as Supreme Leader, and the subsequent smooth transfer of authority, were undeniable signs of political stability.[20] Yet, they also constituted additional evidence of the ideological impasse facing the regime. Although clerics (albeit of lesser rank) were still in charge, ultimate authority was no longer exercised by the supreme religious sources or by prominent theologians. Khamene'i had neither emerged by popular consensus nor received the endorsement of the leading authorities for his pre-eminent religious credentials, but was in fact 'promoted' to the position of Supreme Leader by the religio-politicians then wielding power.

Having entrusted the leadership to Khamene'i, the regime rallied behind Ayatollah Araki (who was very old and in failing health), as the ideal choice for the *marja'*. Araki possessed adequate religious credentials, was inclined to support the government but unlikely to usurp power, and would probably not live long. This gave the regime a free hand to pursue its preferred policies with Araki's assured blessing, while paving the way for Khamene'i to claim the *marja'iyya* in the not too distant future – again a move of evident political maneuvering rather than theological sincerity. The revolutionary leadership managed to pursue its preferred policy, but proved less successful in securing significant endorsement from prominent religious authorities.

The selection of Khamene'i to succeed Khomeini and the eventual separation of *marja'iyya* from *velayat* constituted another severe blow to the revolution's most fundamental ideological creed, and represented a blatant retreat from its most significant and revolutionary achievement. If the Islamic government had its origins in the spiritual leadership of the *marja'*, the appointment of Khamene'i demonstrated that 'not only individuals but also ideas had played musical chairs'. After all, Khamene'i had never been considered a 'doctor of law' (*mujtahid*) qualified to give an independent opinion.[21] No *mulla* (cleric), religious student, or even ordinary Iranian, another observer maintained, 'would seek a *fatwa* [religious judgment]' from him.[22]

Official attempts to justify the selection of Khamene'i as the new Supreme Leader made the enduring gap between ideology and reality even more strikingly evident. Rafsanjani and other officials claimed that Khomeini had expressed the initial idea of separating the *marja'iyya* and *vilaya* 'in private discussions' before his death. Quoting from Khomeini's letter of April 1989 to Ayatollah 'Ali Meshkini, the head of the Council of Experts, Rafsanjani then added: 'Since the very beginning', Khomeini had 'insisted' that *marja'iyya* was not a necessary condition for leadership and that any *faqih* (even if he was not a *mujtahid*), could be the *vali*.[23]

Moreover, the religio-politicians then claimed that Khomeini had sanctioned the selection of Khamene'i in advance, as the preferred candidate for the position. Making the point, Rafsanjani said that in a meeting with Khomeini, the heads of the three branches of government had expressed their concern that the (old) constitution's stipulations regarding his successor might lead to a political vacuum. Khomeini said this was unlikely, 'since we have the appropriate people for the position'. When Khomeini was asked about the identity of such a person, Rafsanjani disclosed, 'he pointed to Khamene'i'.[24] Ayatollah 'Abdul-Qasem Khaz'ali (a member of the Council of Guardians), added similarly that, shortly before his death, Khomeini had indicated three times that he viewed Khamene'i as the most appropriate successor.[25] It was very clear that the attribution of such ideas and intentions to Khomeini ran counter to his last will and testament and thus carried no legal weight.[26] They clearly stood in marked contrast to his writings and statements since the late 1960s.

Eager to stress Khamene'i's qualifications to serve as Khomeini's successor, Iranian officials then raised further arguments that wildly contradicted Khomeini's own creed. Although Khomeini had endorsed rule by a prominent cleric, they now placed greater emphasis on political and administrative qualifications than on scholarship and piety for leadership. 'Familiarity with national issues', Rafsanjani tellingly maintained, is 'far more important' than knowledge and piety. Khamene'i had eight years' experience as president, he noted. 'If we selected a Supreme Leader from a seminary, by the time he became familiar with national issues', Iran might 'suffer irreparable harm'.[27] Ayatollah Ahmad Jannati then opined that political shrewdness was one of the most important qualities for the *marja'*.[28] Ayatollah Meshkini observed that prominent clerics were not automatically qualified for leadership, since they lacked sufficient knowledge of world conditions 'and the political, social, and cultural issues facing Muslims'.[29] These were 'obvious reference to Khamene'i' but 'a complete reversal of 150 years of Shi'a tradition', Mottahedeh observed.[30] In fact, taken only one step further, such arguments would countenance rule by most of the leaders of Muslim states (whom Khomeini did not regard as qualified to govern), since each could claim significant political credentials. Clearly, then, the interpretations of those holding power were made to appear as if they were Khomeini's views, and their preferred candidate ultimately assumed the position of the Supreme Leader.

Since then, the religio-politicians have pursued their own agenda but have sought to achieve a *modus vivendi* with the leading theologians, who more often than not have given government policy their perfunctory blessing (for some significant exceptions, however, see below).

The deaths of three prominent authorities (*maraje'*) in the early 1990s – Kho'i (in August 1992), Golpaygani (in December 1993), and Araki (in December 1994) – forced a further reckoning with reality and distancing from doctrine. The same dilemma of succession remained. If senior clerics were chosen for *marja'iyya* from outside the political structure they could challenge it; if they were chosen by those in power, religion would be subordinated to the state and belief made subject to the 'vicissitudes of politics', thus constituting 'a threat to historical Shi'ism'.[31]

Signs of clerical opposition to a government-imposed *marja'* became especially evident after Golpaygani's death.[32] Khamene'i and his supporters realized that he was unlikely to obtain recognition as the supreme *marja'* in the short term. Aware that he lacked the full religious credentials, his associates again emphasized his political qualifications. Khamene'i was already a senior *marja'*, argued Ayatollah Mohammad Yazdi (the president of the supreme court and one of Khamene'i's most ardent supporters), and therefore his instructions in matters of jurisprudence were binding. Moreover, Yazdi questioned whether a pious person who lacked the rudiments of political and social experience was at all qualified to serve as the supreme *marja'* as that distinction implied a separation between religion and politics.[33] According to Yazdi,

Khamene'i was 'the most qualified compared to all his peers and equals with regard to his awareness of the requirements of time, management ability, administrative skills', and also had the necessary religious credentials. If a pious candidate for supreme *marja'* 'fails to understand the most basic social and political issues of the Islamic community', he asked, 'should he be the source of emulation?'[34] Khamene'i failed to muster popular support as the *marja'*, however, and the regime – while preparing for the next opportunity – rallied once again around Ayatollah Araki.[35] The Association of Seminary Theologians of Qom (*Jame'eh-ye Modarresin-e Howzeh-ye 'Elmiyyeh-ye Qom*) stated that the 'source of imitation' was henceforth to be embodied in Araki,[36] while Ayatollah Mohammad Javadi-Amoli said that the *marja'iyya* of the world's Shi'is 'rests today' with him.[37]

But Araki's death came sooner than expected, and well before Khamene'i could significantly enhance his chances to qualify for the position (on the basis of pure scholarship). A new round of 'electioneering' began, with establishment figures promoting Khamene'i's candidacy for the position of the *marja'* once again. However, since he had but recently failed to gain such recognition, they had to be content with his recognition as one of those possessing *marja'iyya* qualifications. The deceased Araki was quoted as having given Khamene'i 'generous, decisive, unequivocal and all-embracing support' as the custodian of the affairs of the world's Muslims.[38] The Speaker of the Majlis, 'Ali Akbar Nateq-Nuri,[39] and Ayatollah Yazdi[40] presented Khamene'i as the future *marja'*. Yazdi referred to him as 'the esteemed leader and fully qualified theologian' in charge of 'leading the Muslims on behalf of the lord of the era'.[41] His name also appeared on numerous lists of those fully qualified (*jame' ul-sharayet*) to serve as *marja'* issued by various organizations, including the Association of Seminary Theologians of Qom,[42] the *Jame'eh-ye Ruhaniyyat-e Mobarez* (Society of Combatant Clergy),[43] and the *Majma'-e Ruhaniyyun-e Mobarez* (the Association of Combatant Clerics).[44] More prominent clerics were once again by-passed. (Among the personalities usually regarded as *maraje'* were: Montazeri, Hasan Tabataba'i Qomi, Mohammad Ruhani, Seyyed 'Ali Hoseini Sistani [who lived in Iraq], Naser Makarem Shirazi, Shaykh Mohammad Hoseini Shirazi, Yusef Sane'i, Mohammad Taqi Behjat, Fazel Lankarani, Vahid Khorasani, and Lotfollah Safi Golpaygani.)

In addition to decrying Khamene'i's lack of religious qualifications and the fact that greater authorities had been passed over, dissident clerics also protested at the government's interference in the selection of the *marja'* and its politically motivated departure from Islamic doctrine.

Mehdi Ha'iri, living in exile in Germany, argued that the regime had made its intentions clear after Golpaygani's death by arresting Ayatollah Sadeq Ruhani, a prominent scholar who advocated the separation of religion and state, and raiding his residence.[45] In what purported to be an open letter to the Iranian authorities, Ruhani then asked for an exit visa, complaining that life in Iran had become 'unbearable for those who abide by the true principles' of Islam. He was quoted as claiming that 'armed criminals' had attacked his home in Qom and threatened to kill him unless he declared allegiance to Khamene'i. He added that he could not 'remain a spectator while Islam is violated daily' and 'true religious leaders' are silenced in a country which is 'claiming to be an Islamic Republic'.[46] In July 1995, a group of armed men reportedly attacked Ruhani's residence. A statement by a close associate of the Ayatollah reportedly called the attackers messengers of the *'taghut* [idol-worshipping] regime', a term normally used to refer to the Shah's government. Ruhani's followers called for the release of his son, Javad, and other supporters, whose sole crime was to follow a legitimate *marja'*. Several other clerics joined the protest in Iran, as did Ruhani's brother, Mehdi Ruhani, who lived in exile in Paris.[47]

Government officials denied that the recognition of the new *marja'* represented any challenge to the Islamic establishment following Araki's death. Khamene'i said that the West had found a handful of 'illiterate . . . pseudo-clerics' and supplied them with money and microphones in order to use them as tools in a propaganda campaign against the Islamic Republic. They were aiming, he said, to 'undermine the lofty and divine status' of the *marja'iyya* and to insinuate that the public had turned their backs on the clergy.[48] Nateq-Nuri referred to them as the 'sultans' preachers' (*vo'az ul-salatin*), and 'court clerics' (*akhundha-ye darbari*), who had fled Iran because of their black record.[49] Rafsanjani dismissed the whole issue as simply Zionist-imperialist propaganda and the 'most basic form of [Western] cultural onslaught'.[50] Yet, evidently, the question of the *marja'iyya* continued to present the Islamic regime with a serious ideological and political challenge.

More recently, some leading intellectuals went on the offensive, criticizing the government for its actual failures and decrying Khamene'i's inadequate religious credentials for the *velayat-e faqih*, as well as the interpretation given to this dogma under the Islamic Republic.

THE CHALLENGE FROM THE CLERGY

As in the past, developments relating to the *marja'iyya* were often linked to the 1989 disqualification of Ayatollah Montazeri as Khomeini's heir apparent. Yet, Montazeri was not the first Ayatollah whose status was affected by political considerations, just as Sadeq Ruhani was not the first to be forcibly silenced. Similarly, they were not the only prominent clerics who challenged the extensive authorities and the application of the concept of *velayat-e faqih* in Islamic Iran. The challenge to such basic revolutionary creed by some of the prominent clergy continued throughout the first two decades of the revolution, and reached a new peak following Khatami's election, when Montazeri intensified his criticism and was joined by Ayatollah Ahmad Azari-Qomi (d. 1999).

In the early days of the revolution, Ayatollah Kazem Shari'atmadari (d. 1986) was intimidated into silence by recurrent verbal and physical assaults on his home and followers.[51] The most outstanding differences between Shari'atmadari and Khomeini were over ways in which the divine law should be interpreted and how it should be applied in Islamic Iran. Shari'atmadari advocated the application of Islamic laws in a correct (*sahih*) and progressive (*moteraqqi*) mode.[52] According to him, the main goal of the revolution was to end dictatorial rule and to establish a democracy based on the will of the people in the light of Islamic law.[53] While for Khomeini the accent was on social justice, for Shari'atmadari, the term *'edalat* (justice) implied, above all, the safeguarding of political democracy. In his view, an Islamic regime 'is a democratic regime based on the people's will'. It is 'the government of the people, for the people and against dictatorship and despotism'.[54] Shari'atmadari also advocated that clerical involvement in day-to-day politics be limited to guidance, instruction, and supervision,[55] and was therefore strongly opposed to Khomeini's regular interference in day-to-day politics as well as to the activities of extra-governmental bodies operating under his auspices and in the name of religion. Khomeini and Shari'atmadari also differed in their approach to the question of Iran's national identity and their attitude towards ethnic minorities (see Part Two). After the formation of the new regime in 1979, Shari'atmadari continued to voice his independent positions, presenting Khomeini with a serious challenge from the highest echelons of the religious leadership. Late in 1979, tension between supporters of these two leading authorities reached a peak. In 1982, Shari'atmadari was accused of having supported a plot against the regime. The *Jame'eh-ye Ruhaniyyat-e Mobarez* then announced that he was not qualified to be a *marja'*[56] or even be recognized as a grand ayatollah.[57] Demonstrators demanded that he be stripped of his religious title; some even called for his execution.[58]

From the late 1980s, however, it was Montazeri who was perceived as the main challenge. Indeed, with the passage of time, his criticism became more open and fierce, finding a receptive audience within sections of the clergy, lay intellectuals, some political factions and within society at large.

Although Montazeri's nomination as Khomeini's heir apparent in 1985 was not entirely in line with Khomeini's doctrine, nor his religious qualifications of such merit as to succeed to the 'leadership', he was the most distinguished cleric among Khomeini's loyal disciples and had significant religious credentials. He also had sufficient revolutionary credentials, as he had long been active in opposition to the Shah. However, he gradually expressed independent positions and was associated with people that were not highly regarded in Khomeini's inner circles. Finally, it became evident that Montazeri, because of his public criticism of the politics of the Islamic regime, could no longer be considered sufficiently loyal to the philosophy of the revolution, let alone to the policies of Khomeini's disciples wielding power. (Montazeri's association with Mehdi Hashemi, a supporter and relative of Montazeri who was executed as an enemy of the revolution by the Islamic regime in 1987, was another reason often cited to cast doubt on his credentials and loyalty to the revolution.)

Montazeri repeatedly criticized Khomeini's disciples in government and supported its critics. In a strongly worded letter to Prime Minister Mir-Hosein Musavi on 1 October 1988, for example, Montazeri criticized the government for shortages, inflation, continuing unemployment and mismanagement, as well as for maintaining costly parallel organizations and agencies. He deplored the intervention by the Revolutionary Guards and the Foundation of the Martyrs (*Bonyad-e Shahid*) in commerce, and condemned the brutal behavior of judicial and security organizations and the lack of coherence among government agencies in domestic and foreign policy.[59] In February 1989, Montazeri declared that the tenth anniversary celebrations of the Islamic Revolution should be used for reviewing 'past mistakes' since 'we had slogans in the past that turned out to be mistakes'. Young Iranian revolutionaries resentful of the realities of their life under the Islamic regime, he claimed, 'are justified', since there was 'a big gap between what they have gained and what they were promised'. He went on to point to some prevalent problems under clerical rule: 'unprofessionalism, extremism, selfishness, group inclinations, injustices and ignoring the people and the genuine values of the revolution'. All these, he said, caused 'damage for the revolution'. Hinting that his own views had been censored, while that of many other Iranians suppressed, he warned that radio and television should not be a monopoly in the hands of the few. There are, he said, people in Iran 'who are so afraid of persecution they cannot [even] breathe in peace'.[60] He continued to criticize the government from time to time, challenging its politics and even its legitimacy.

On 26 March 1989, Khomeini asked Montazeri to resign. Montazeri replied in writing the next day, declaring himself unqualified for the position of the next leader. Khomeini wrote again a day later, noting that the task of a leader was a 'heavy and august responsibility which requires more strength' than Montazeri had manifested. He continued: 'Everyone knows that you have been the product of my life and that I am very fond of you', but he then criticized Montazeri harshly for associating himself with improper elements, including people whom Khomeini considered enemies of the regime (such as Mehdi Hashemi). He advised him that 'in order that former mistakes' are not repeated, '[you should] cleanse your household of unsuitable individuals and seriously prevent the coming and going [to your house] of the opponents of the [Islamic] system'.[61]

Although Montazeri had in the past criticized the functioning of the executive, his remarks on the eve of the tenth anniversary of the Islamic Republic were much harsher than anything he had publicly stated before. *Ettela'at* went as far as to claim that Montazeri's latest views were not a critique but an echo of the propaganda of groups who were anti-state and anti-revolutionary.[62] In a letter to Montazeri, Ayatollah Khomeini's son, Ahmad Khomeini, produced a long list of accusations to demonstrate that Montazeri's succession would be harmful to the revolution. He charged Montazeri with ignoring Khomeini's warnings not to allow 'misguided people' to infiltrate his house and 'create catastrophe'. Ahmad further challenged Montazeri: 'Was it not because of your affection for Mehdi Hashemi that you created so many problems for Islam and the revolution?' He went on to wonder: 'What hand was at work which separated you so far from the Imam that you [said that you] consider the Intelligence [officers] and the officials' of the Islamic regime to be 'worse than the Shah's SAVAK'.[63]

After his disqualification, Montazeri was often accused of opposing government policy and his activities were closely monitored. He still posed a challenge to the regime, mainly at the ideological level, but with political implications as well. He had many supporters, and his lectures – in which he occasionally criticized the government – incurred the authorities' anger. In February 1993, for example, he decried the amount of money spent to celebrate the anniversary of the revolution. He portrayed himself as the 'midwife' of the revolution and as one of its 'wet nurses', and criticized ruling clerics for usurping his right of succession.[64] In response, government supporters marched to his house chanting pro-regime and anti-Montazeri slogans. The demonstration soon developed into a violent clash.[65] *Jomhuri-ye Islami*, like other newspapers, then described Montazeri as simple-minded and influenced by satanic forces, and threatened to publish a letter written by Khomeini in 1989 which, it claimed, was critical of Montazeri and would lead people to 'realize their duty'.[66] (The letter was ultimately published in 1997, see below.) Opposition sources then claimed that some of Montazeri's associates had been detained and that five had been executed.[67] In March 1993, anti-Montazeri figures distributed a copy of a letter he had written to Ayatollah Golpaygani protesting against low-ranking clerics taking control of the revolution. In 1994, Montazeri condemned the monopolization of the revolution by 'a certain group'. He blamed the authorities for deviating from the path of the revolution, and criticized injustice and the absence of security for the public.[68] Nine clerics close to him were reportedly arrested on charges of instigating sedition by distributing his statements.[69] Anti-Montazeri demonstrations continued, his freedoms were restricted, but he continued to express displeasure and criticize the government occasionally.

Montazeri resented the realities established by Khomeini's disciples in power and his charges touched upon highly sensitive issues. He stressed the religious qualifications required for leadership (implying criticism of Khamene'i's lack of such credentials), and pointed to the mishandling of the affairs of the state (implying criticism of President Rafsanjani). That Montazeri 'stood apart' from the regime and was believed to entertain political ambitions concerned the regime. The government's response to his charges also indicated 'extreme sensitivity to any challenge' to Khamene'i's authority.[70] It was therefore not surprising that a visit by a group of Majlis deputies to Montazeri in Qom in November 1991 turned into a major political incident.[71] *Resalat*, suggesting that 'the radical' faction (see Chapter 2), may have been behind the release of another critical letter by Montazeri in March 1993, criticized them and called upon the newspaper *Salam* to clarify its attitude concerning Montazeri.[72] *Salam* replied tersely that, given the atmosphere, it had decided to remain silent on the issue so as not to participate in creating unrest.[73] In this way, the identity and status of the Supreme Leader became enmeshed in factional rivalries.

Montazeri continued to express his views on occasion, challenging the very legitimacy of the regime and criticizing its conduct in practice. His criticism intensified and assumed a more threatening dimension following Khatami's election.

In a Friday sermon to his followers in Qom on 14 November 1997 Montazeri vigorously reiterated his charges, criticizing even more pointedly the ruling elite and the application of the principles of the *velayat-e faqih* under the Islamic Republic. He argued that the guardianship was conditional upon having proper qualifications (which in his view Khamene'i lacked). Moreover, he maintained, the *vali-ye faqih* is not 'in charge of everything'; his principal responsibility is merely 'supervision' (*nezarat*) over the affairs of society to make sure they do not deviate from Islamic rules and Islamic justice. In this regard, he maintained, the *vali-ye faqih* must be 'like the Prophet', who (only) 'supervised affairs of the state', thus underlining the point that Khamene'i 'should not interfere in these affairs'. Touching upon the current Supreme Leader's lack of sufficient religious credentials for the position, he added that the essence of *velayat-e faqih* was to be a fair, learned and competent jurisprudent. Khamene'i, however, did not even have the authority 'to issue a *fatwa*', he charged. By appointing him, the regime had trivialized the *marja'iyya* and ridiculed it, Montazeri added. Whenever he raised such issues, he reported: 'I am warned not to trespass beyond the red line.' However, the only red line that should not be crossed, he said, was the sanctity of God, the Prophet and the Imams.

Touching on more mundane issues, Montazeri went on to deplore the actions of the then government, stating that the leader ought not to build up a separate governmental apparatus with royal pomp and indulge in ceremonial travel that cost fortunes. Such practices were not compatible with the guardianship of the religious jurist, he noted. The term Hezbollah (members of God's party, often used to denote the supporters of the government), should not be applied to 'individuals who are incited to chant slogans and create a climate [of fear]', for the world would no longer accept the rule of such wielders of clubs. Moreover, decisions ought not to be taken by a few individuals 'who sit at the top and issue orders'. The concept of a 'republic', he added tellingly, 'meant the people's rule' and the people's freedom to express their views. Montazeri reminded the ruling clerics that governments, after all, 'are brought to power [and dismissed] by the people', adding that the people have the right and the duty to be active in politics and to prevent the misuse of the rulers' power.

In what could be interpreted as encouraging active opposition to the government, Montazeri further noted that by simply 'sitting and praying no prayer is ever granted'. More significantly, Montazeri also disclosed that he had sent a message to President Khatami 'to warn him that with the style he is pursuing, he will not achieve anything'. He urged Khatami, therefore, to be more assertive in pursuing his reform program and in demanding authority. Montazeri suggested that Khatami go to the Supreme Leader and point out to him that over 22 million people had voted for him, knowing full well that his views were different from those of Khamene'i and that Khamene'i had endorsed the rival candidate, Nateq-Nuri, who was defeated in the presidential elections. The people, he concluded, had not endorsed Khamene'i's policies: rather, they had voted for the alternative path, that advocated by Khatami. If the president's conditions were not accepted, Montazeri advised him, he should resign.[74]

Montazeri's harsh criticism coincided with similarly grave charges made by another prominent Ayatollah, Ahmad Azari-Qomi (who had served variously as managing director of the conservative paper *Resalat*, a judge of the Revolutionary Court and member of the Majlis and the Council of Experts). Having occasionally criticized the *modus operandi* of the Islamic regime Azari-Qomi issued a strong statement on 19 November 1997 opening with the theme: 'God is the avenger'. Azari-Qomi then tellingly cited another tradition: anyone who witnesses an unjust ruler and keeps silent becomes a partner in his crimes. Leaving no room for error, he went on to assert that 'Khamene'i kills the pious and tortures them, reviles the good and [sends them] to slaughter, and continues usurping the Office of the Guardian'. People may not remain idle while witnessing 'such crimes', but must move on to 'perform the [religious] duty of preventing evil'. He concluded: 'I am weary of the injustice and oppression of Khamene'i. If he had guardianship, he is stripped of it, and related institutions, from Friday Imam to other positions, are all null and void.'[75]

Following the subsequent forceful attack on Montazeri and Azari-Qomi and their supporters by the conservatives, Montazeri issued another, harsher statement. The point of his statement, Montazeri declared, was to express disdain for the damage done to Islam by the regime's attack on clerics and religious seminaries following his statement of 14 November. Montazeri then enumerated acts of vandalism, including physical attacks on students and the damage to books in his own *madrasa* (seminary). He accused the authorities of detaining several of his associates and making statements as though they represented a victory for the *velayat-e faqih*. By doing so, they were reinterpreting the remit of the *velayat-e faqih* and degrading religious seminaries and attacking clerics.[76]

Clearly, the charges levelled by the two leading ayatollahs not only touch upon the politics of the Islamic regime but also challenged some of the major principles of the ruling system. The government could not be indifferent to such a criticism. There have since been occasional rallies against Montazeri (as well as numerous rallies by his supporters), in different cities. Official sources have confirmed that the police used tear gas to disperse demonstrators chanting 'death to the opponents of *velayat-e faqih*', 'death to dissident rejectionists', and 'death to Montazeri'.[77]

The official response to Montazeri's vociferous criticism was similarly harsh. Once again Mohammad Yazdi rushed to support the ruling system and to defend Khamene'i personally. On 21 November he announced, echoing typical charges by Khamene'i, that outside agents had been responsible for the recent 'conspiracy' and that anyone who claimed that governance (*hokumat*) was not part of Islam or that the Prophet Muhammad had restricted himself to consultation (*moshavereh*), as Montazeri had suggested, did not know what Islam really was. Some critics, he went on, claimed that they accepted the Islamic revolutionary system (*nezam*) but disapproved of the governor (*nazem*), while others depicted the *velayat* as 'rule over people who are insane (*majanin*) and imbecilic (*sofaha*)', or maintained that its only function was supervision (*nezarat*). Yazdi went on to say that Montazeri had questioned Khamene'i's *marja'iyya* qualifications even though Khamene'i 'is both the leader of the state and the *marja'* of Muslims worldwide'. By continuing to behave in this way, the president of the supreme court warned Montazeri, he would provoke 'a stronger response'.[78]

In a similar vein, the Chairman of the Council of Experts, Ayatollah 'Ali Meshkini, accused Montazeri of inciting (*tahrik*) President Khatami against the Supreme Leader Khamene'i and of encouraging Khatami to demand greater authority for himself under threat of resignation. Montazeri's 'ugly' and 'corrupting' speech, Meshkini added, went against his own interests and the interests of the revolution. 'Our leadership is correct; our leadership is complete; our leader is fully eligible and his leadership is faultless', Meshkini stressed.[79] Those who claimed that *velayat-e faqih* had no practical functions did not understand that the principle of *velayat-e faqih* superseded the stipulations of the constitution, he declared, going so far as to equate the role of the *vali-ye faqih* under the Islamic Republic with that of the Prophet Muhammad.[80] Another angry reaction came from the head of the *Majma'-e Hezbollah-ye Majlis* (the Association of the Majlis Hezbollah), Hojjat ul-Islam Majid Ansari, who also challenged the claim that the *faqih* was a mere supervisor (*nazer*), devoid of actual authority (*faqed-e ekhtiyar*) or the right to interfere in politics.[81] Mohammad Reyshahri (a former minister of intelligence), announced that Montazeri's statements were tantamount to promoting sedition (*fitna*).[82] Similarly, *Kayhan* (a major organ of the conservatives), dismissed the view that Khamene'i should not interfere in politics, and rejected claims that he was behaving like a dictator or a king, or the leader of witless people who required a shepherd.[83] Doubts (*shabahat*) regarding the *velayat-e faqih* have always existed, added Ayatollah Mohammad Javadi-Amoli, branding those raising such arguments as 'a kind of virus' that keeps recurring.[84]

On 26 November 1997, Khamene'i himself censured Montazeri and Azari-Qomi, although not by name. The people, he warned, must 'understand the depth of the conspiracy'. The enemy hides 'behind the curtain', he said, using its [domestic] agents to employ deviationist arguments. Having tried all sorts of methods to fight the revolution, the Supreme Leader added, the enemy has now turned to directly 'targeting the leadership'. Those who incite by creating discord, he said, have 'committed acts of treason (*khiyanat*) against the people, the revolution, and the country'. He concluded very tellingly that if 'those actions are illegal, which they are, if they are acts of treason, which they are', then the legal authorities must put those carrying them out on trial for implementing the foreigners' conspiracies.[85]

Finally the conservatives published the hitherto undisclosed letter that Ayatollah Khomeini had written to Montazeri on 26 March 1989, setting out the reasons why he was not qualified to be his successor. In this letter, which the authorities had long threatened to publish (see above), Khomeini charged Montazeri with serving as a mouthpiece for hypocrites, and with inflicting heavy blows on Islam and the revolution. Should he become the successor, Khomeini then warned, Montazeri would 'hand over' Iran to the liberals, and through them to the *monafeqin* (hypocrites, a term generally used to refer to the opposition movement, *Mojahedin-e Khalq*). This made him ineligible for the succession. Khomeini also blamed Montazeri for supporting Mehdi Hashemi. 'It breaks my heart and my chest is full of agonizing pain', Khomeini wrote, seeing you, 'the fruit of my life's labor', being 'so ungrateful'. Calling him 'simple-minded' (*sadeh luh*) and a man 'easily provoked', Khomeini forbade Montazeri to engage in politics at all. Montazeri's deeds were tantamount to treason, and he was advised by Khomeini to confess to all his sins and mistakes. 'Maybe then God will help you', he wrote to him.[86]

Jomhuri-ye Islami (one of the conservatives' main organs) then wondered: Is there still room for hesitation? Any person who claims to follow Ayatollah Khomeini must prove his sincerity today, the newspaper suggested. Otherwise, the way will remain open 'for the enemies of Khomeini's aspirations'.[87] Deputy Speaker of the Majlis, Hojjat ul-Islam Mohammad 'Ali Movahedi-Kermani, declared that 'violators and transgressors' must be chastised, and that if Montazeri did not admit to his errors and apologize to the nation, the divine decrees would be 'implemented against him and his cohorts'.[88] Hojjat ul-Islam 'Ali Razini, head of the Special Court for the Clergy, announced that the court would investigate 'a certain simple-minded element' that had violated the conditions laid down by Ayatollah Khomeini. Montazeri had hurt Khomeini immensely in his lifetime, and had reiterated his allegations now, Razini charged. Montazeri should know that the followers of the Imam would not allow his valuable legacy to be tarnished.[89] (For rejection of the letter as reflecting Khomeini's actual views, see below.)

Action against Ayatollah Azari-Qomi took the form of his dismissal from the Association of Seminary Theologians of Qom, a step taken, according to *Iran News*, in the light of a protest by some thousand clerics against the 'irresponsible remarks' he had made against the *velayat-e faqih* and the basic tenets of the revolution. The Association warned those proposing aberrant (*enherafi*) philosophies in deceitful forms not to fall into the arms of 'American Islam' and not to separate themselves from the true Islam and the genuine revolutionary path.[90] Responding to Khamene'i's demand for his trial, Azari-Qomi denied committing any offense but announced that he was ready for martyrdom and welcomed any sort of trial in a true court of Islamic justice, even if it ended in his execution. However, he claimed, the judicial system in Iran was corrupt, deviant, and removed from any judicial foundations of Islam.[91] (Ayatollah Azari-Qomi, who had reportedly been under house arrest ever since, passed away on 11 February 1999.)

Harsh steps continued to be employed against dissident clerics. In a highly critical letter to the UN Secretary-General Kofi Annan, on 10 September 1998, Mehdi Ha'iri detailed the 'deplorable situation' in which the theologians (even most prominent *maraje'*) were under the control of the authorities and could not leave their residencies. They were, he said, 'deprived of the most basic civil rights'. This includes

Montazeri, who has been under house arrest since November 1997, and Sadeq Ruhani, who, Ha'iri wrote, was under house arrest for many years. Ha'iri portrayed a gloomy situation in the special courts for the clergy (see Chapter 5), including death sentences, depriving clerics from performing religious duties and arrests. The authorities take harsh steps against the clerics who advocated separation of religion and state, Ha'iri added. The attitude of the Islamic regime is even worse than that of the previous regime, it was claimed. A similarly gloomy situation was reported by Akbar Ganji (a critical journalist, who is well known for using extremely harsh language to denounce the politics of the Islamic Republic). Having visited Qom recently, he witnessed the pressure on the theologians, which is stronger than ever in history, he wrote. This is a *dowlat-e dini* (religious government) that wants to impose *din-e dowlati* (governmental religion) on the *maraje'*. The theologians do not have the right even to criticize the violence exercised or the attribution of despotic (*estebdadi*) qualities to religion, nor to secure their own independence.[92]

Although the harsh criticism of Montazeri and Azari-Qomi was almost unanimous, there were also few more moderate responses. Initially they were hesitant and indirect, but gradually they turned more unequivocal. Two years later, 'Abdollah Nuri supported Montazeri's right to express his views loudly and clearly. Nuri then combined the debate over Montazeri with more basic questions of the right to interpret dogma in light of the changing circumstances, and criticism of the restrictions of liberties in Iran. Such harsh actions taken against Montazeri, he said, had rarely been taken against clerics in the past. The authorities' reference to the letter attributed (*mansub*) to the Imam, from 26 March 1989, ignored Khomeini's genuine thoughts as well as his own letter two days later, on 28 March 1989. In the latter, Khomeini acknowledged his deep appreciation for Montazeri's scholarship, urged him to continue and guide the regime and the people, and stressed his own strong affection (*'alaqeh-ye shadid*) for him. Unfortunately, ten years later, Nuri added, the clerics in power pulled out Khomeini's doubtful (*tardid-amiz*) letter from 26 March, even though it was nullified by the subsequent letter. Obviously, one can doubt (*tardid*) this letter. How could the Imam possibly accuse Montazeri of being under the influence of the *Monafeqin*, and two days later express 'great affection' for him? Could Khomeini possibly allow a person with such qualities (as described in the first letter) to pass on religious edicts (as he outlined in the subsequent letter)? Is it possible that Khomeini, who had repeatedly stressed the political aspects of the clerics' duties, would forbid a cleric from engaging in politics? Therefore, the very publication of the second letter, Nuri argued, constituted a 'grave injustice' (*zolm-e faheshi*) not only to Montazeri, but also to the Imam. Why should they tarnish Khomeini's reputation in such a way, he wondered. Akbar Ganji seconded him, and in his customary way, even more bluntly. Montazeri, he said, was the theoretician of the idea of *velayat-e faqih*, who tried to reconcile the ideal of clerical rule with the spirit of democracy. Khomeini supported Montazeri and (in his letter from 28 March 1989) called upon him to guide people. How can one put Nuri on trial for support-ing Montazeri's views, Ganji asked, while Khomeini himself acknow-ledged his scholarship and called the people to follow his advice? How could Khomeini forbid clerics from engaging in politics, while this was one of the main pillars of his own thought? Yet those who demand absolute authority, Ganji concluded, denied Montazeri's right to guide people. In his view, thus, the 'hand of the absolutist' (*tamami-khwah*) faction stretches from the sleeves of the radical (fascist) right.[93]

On the whole, public discussion of the *velayat-e faqih*, which had generally remained taboo, has changed significantly in recent times. In addition to the statements by prominent clerics already noted, lay intel-lectuals and student leaders also expressed views on the issue which were not dissimilar to those held by dissident clerics. Even in 1997, some observers in Iran hinted at a 'great deal of coordination' between Montazeri and 'Abdul-Karim Soroush, or, at least, some affinity in their views.[94] This became even more evident in 1999.

Generally speaking, both groups – dissident clerics and lay intel-lectuals as well as many students, were closer in their views to Khatami than to Khamene'i. In any case, since Khatami's election the debate over the issue of the guardianship of the religious jurist has carried on almost openly, gathering momentum in 1999. The discussion over *velayat-e faqih* has also become enmeshed with domestic factional rivalries and with the heated struggle for individual freedom. (See also Chapter 5.)

RELIGION AND THE STATE: AN ALTERNATIVE CONCEPT

In recent years Iran has experienced a flowering of an 'alternative thought' (*andisheh-ye digar*), i.e. 'the expression of viewpoints that are different from and often in opposition to official policy positions'.[95] Professor 'Abdul-Karim Soroush, Hojjat ul-Islam (and Professor) Mohsen Kadivar and Hojjat ul-Islam Mohammad Mojtahed Shabestari have become the most eloquent spokesmen of such viewpoints. Some students' associations and segments of the press have also supported such new thinking. They have raised penetrating questions on various aspects of the domestic debate, and although they seem to have distinctive views, there are also some major points they share in common. The views most relevant to the discussion in this chapter are those on the inter-relationship of religion and state, Islam and democracy and their stress on the need for greater freedom (*azadi*), openness and respect for civil rights. In one way or another, each of the above arguments has had a bearing on the role and function of the *velayat-e faqih*, its application in revolutionary Iran and on its implication for Islamic rule in modern times.

Soroush's idea, founded on relativism, stressed that although the sacred texts are immutable, human perception of them depends on many variables, including time and location. Imposing a single, specific interpretation upon religion gives it a superficial and official mold and makes it dogmatic (*qeshri*) and one-dimensional (*yek bo'di*).[96] As stated above some intellectuals maintained that there was no single, correct interpretation of Islam, nor an interpretation that had precedence over another; there was no final interpretation and, most significantly, no official and abiding interpretation of Islam. This, in itself, was perceived as a serious challenge to the revolutionary doctrine and to the *modus operandi* of Khomeini's disciples in power.

Soroush, who has been a devout supporter of the Islamic Revolution, delved further into the difference between religion and ideology.[97] According to his view, the 'ideologization of religion' is the beginning of its vulgarization and leads to its deterioration.[98] With the transformation of faith from *nehzat* (the awakening movement) to *nehad* (ruling institution), he said, the blood which had initially kept the Islamic movement alive had been converted into opium.[99] Faith, Soroush argued, is not a mold with a fixed cast (*qalebi jehat-dar*), and Khomeini's movement 'will not bear the appropriate fruits' unless his followers nurture 'a new understanding of religion'.[100] Religion is more substantial (*farbehtar*), more comprehensive (*kameltar*), and more humane (*ensanitar*) than ideology. It generates weapons, tools, ideals, but is not itself the tool. Religion is like air (*hava*), essential for every human being but lacking a fixed mold in itself. As one of the essentials of its eternity, he said, religion does not strive for a specific historical society. Ideology, by contrast, is like a garment or mantle (*jameh va qaba*) designed to fit a particular individual, or a medicine prescribed for a specific patient. In sum, religion is like a scale (*tarazu*), lamp (*cheragh*), rope (*risman*), and ladder (*nardeban*) – none of them has a defined destination of its own.[101] Such articulation could not be perceived as mere abstraction and

Iranians – accustomed to reading between the lines – found them relevant to their situation and identified accordingly.

Moreover, Soroush argued that the rule of the clergy is 'based on the logic of power, not the logic of liberty'. Using religion as an ideology 'makes it intolerant and authoritarian', he added. Government and economics, for example, are the province of intellect and reason, not the domain of faith. Clerics should be 'freed' from state or public financial support so that they are not forced to propagate official views. Religion, he said in 1995, is for 'the lovers of faith', not for 'the dealers of the faith'.[102] In 1999, he went so far as to state that the Shi'i jurisprudence (*fiqh*) 'lacked any virtue' for the proper administration of the community and for the guidance of the citizens. In fact, in two decades of Islamic rule, he claimed, except for censoring some pornographic scenes from movies and forcing dress codes on women, the clerics in power did not seem to have 'anything of worth to say', and had not engaged in 'any useful action' at all. In his view, they even failed to comprehend the proper meaning of a 'modern revolution', which they confined to the creation of a society based exclusively on religious laws as they understood them. In his words: 'The religious intellectuals [equipped with modern education] have brought about a reconciliation (*ashti*) between religion and revolution, and are now endeavoring to reconcile religion with democracy.' But the clerics now wielding power in Iran 'have never reconciled religion and revolution in the modern sense of the term, but only made use of religion as a platform for their struggle against dictatorship'.[103]

The relevance of Soroush's ideas and their implicit and explicit criticism of life in Islamic Iran is clear and painful for the regime. His views and his open criticism have led both supporters and critics to compare his role in reforming Islam with that of Martin Luther in reforming Christianity.[104] His views also included an 'implicit attack on the institution of the *velayat-e faqih*'. Paradoxically, his challenge was well received by some (primarily younger *mullas*), who believed that by becoming too closely identified with the state Islam was in danger of 'losing its soul'.[105] Gradually, an increasing number of Iranians seem to be endorsing this new thinking to agree that the clerics' political involvement is 'compromising their historic spiritual role' and that it would be better for both Iran and Islam if the clergy 'returned to the mosques and left the task of government to professional politicians'.[106]

In many ways, Mohsen Kadivar raised similar arguments in an equally harsh tone. His arguments proved extremely sensitive for the Islamic regime. The authorities were aroused by his views on religion and state as discussed, for example, in his recent book *Views on Government in Shi'i Jurisprudence*.[107] Above and beyond any specific argument, the point was made that throughout history there were different, often conflicting views on Islamic rulings, and that in any case there could be no exclusive interpretation of Islam. Early in 1999, Kadivar went as far as to claim, explicitly and in public, that in order for a society to advance and for freedom to prosper, the community needs to free itself from the shackles of past traditions and adopt new (social, political and democratic) systems, in line with the spirit of the time. In his view, had the Prophet Muhammad set out on his mission today, he would probably have 'observe[d] some of the fundamentals' of religion, but followed a different path to the one he himself had adopted 1,400 years ago. There was no reason to believe that, if the leaders of early Islam were to rule Muslim states today, they would follow the same path as their ancestors. The meaning and essence of religion in the twentieth century, he believed, are bound to be different due to the passage of time, and perception today may – and even should – differ from that of early Islam. He called for the formation of a social pact (*qarardad-e ejtema'i*), based on collective logic and on public interest (although not in violation of the fundamentals of faith). In short, it follows that past rulings and their interpretation cannot be viewed as permanent, but rather as open to re-examination in the light of changing circumstances. In a direct challenge to the Islamic government, he stated that 'no government' should ever think that it possesses 'a special mission from God', or that it carries the exclusive responsibility, or that others lack credible authority. This, he believed, could lead to 'tremendous problems in society', giving rise to misconceptions that are bound to suppress freedoms in society (see note 108 below).

According to Kadivar, autocratic regimes, by their nature, prevent freedom. A society that does not respect social and political rights, and international principles of human rights, is by definition undemocratic. In his view, the people should supervise (*nezarat*) the government and have the right to question it and experience freedom – there is nothing in Islam to prevent such a sacred right. In his view, 'religion has left most of the questions in the realms of politics and faith to human intellect ('*aql-e bashari*), outlining only the basic principles'. Basing his arguments on the statements of Ayatollah Mohammad Hosein Na'ini (a leading cleric in the constitutional revolution), Kadivar stated that if not properly followed, religion can turn into the worst kind of dictatorship. Kadivar went as far as to challenge the basic revolutionary concept of *velayat-e faqih*, stating that not all prominent authorities supported the

concept of '*velayat-e motlaqeh-ye faqih*' (absolute rule of the jurisconsult), as practiced in revolutionary Iran. In any case, he noted, no
ruling can exceed the boundaries of the law. 'Human rights' are sacred,
just like the right 'to life, security, freedom and the right to resist injustice'.[108]

A recent article by Kadivar in which he argued that 'The Basic
Problem of Iran is *Velayat-e Faqih*' (*moshkel-e asli-ye Iran, velayat-e
faqih ast*), demonstrates his critical stance. Invoking the principles of
Islam, he attempts to prove that the concept of *velayat-e faqih* is baseless, and that the way it was implemented has led to the severe problems
with which Iran is currently faced. According to Kadivar Islam regards
every person as grown-up and mature (*rashid* and *balegh*), unless otherwise proven, whereas the principle of *velayat-e faqih* is based on the
notion that people are irresponsible and incapacitated (*mahjur*).[109] Not
only did Kadivar personally support greater separation of religion
and state; he stated that the vast majority of clerics in Iran suffer from
the growing unpopularity of the clergy, which is held collectively responsible for the mistakes and violations of the few who wield power.[110] His
criticism has become more equivocal, with some similarity to the criticisms voiced by other intellectuals and clerics, notably Shari'atmadari,
Montazeri and Azari-Qomi while gaining popularity among students.
Kadivar was also charged with having distinguished between eliminating the 'form (*surat*) of the Shahanshahi [monarchical] system' and
changing the foundations (*bonyadha*) and the attributes (*monasebat*) of
the former ruling system. The revolution, he was said to have argued,
only terminated the appearance of the old system, 'but the same old
attributes' are now reappearing 'in new forms'. Although Kadivar denied
having said this, he admitted saying that 'the same attributes and modes
of operation (*hanjarha*)' are still dominant (*hakem*), 'as if it were an
Islamic monarchical system' (*kanah nezam-e saltanati-ye Islami*). In both
regimes, he said, the head of state possessed absolute power and merely
changing the name of the ruling system and of a few other attributes did
not represent a basic change.[111] (For the government campaign against
Soroush and the arrest of Kadivar, see Chapter 5.)

Mohammad Mojtahed Shabestari combined the questions of freedom, traditionalism and the need for change, and similarly advocated
greater efforts to adapt dogma to the evolving realities. He argued that
while Islam subscribes to the notion of freedom and basic human rights,
in practice Muslim communities have often neglected to follow such
principles or to respect basic rights. 'Our past political, social and
cultural structure (*sakhtar*) was by no means democratic.' There have

been changes in our systems over time, he claimed, but all these had one thing in common: 'obedience (*eta'at*) to superiors and to the different sources of power'. Moreover, in our heritage 'there was nothing reminiscent' of popular 'participation in power' and in 'decision-making'. In fact, 'the people' did not even figure as an entity capable of making decisions. Therefore, in practice, there seems to be a conflict between traditional principles that continue to prevail in current Muslim communities and the spirit of the new era, which is based on democratic principles.

The perpetuation of old practices, Shabestari added, is the main reason for the absence of freedom, and the prevailing violence in Muslim society stems from a lack of sufficient respect for human rights. In his view, the principles of religion and human rights are not necessarily identical. The latter, he noted, derive from a philosophical concept of equality, based on the idea that 'the humanity of an individual has priority over his belief', unlike religious principles in which equality is based on the faith of people. Proceeding from this premise, Shabestari stressed the need for dialogue between faiths, which in his view was essential (see also Chapter 6). According to Shabestari, a major obstacle to freedom in Muslim societies has been the fear of innovation. Shabestari thus came close to advocating deviating from the prevailing structure (*sakhtar*), or paradigm. The previous structures, he said, failed to meet the requirement of a democratic society, and maintaining the old social and political system would lead to violence. Only in a democratic political system would it be possible to elevate the people to the highest levels of their capabilities (*tavan*) and potential (*este'dad*). They must, he said, therefore change the old structure, which was 'painted with religious colors', and adopt 'a new political-social structure and [a new] political culture'. This is 'both possible and essential'.[112]

Shabestari argued that it was impossible to ignore that today, 'whether we like it or not, numerous new human forces have been released in Muslim communities, and especially in our society, which no one can control any more'. Persistence in preserving the past structure only exacerbates the problem. We are now 1,400 years from the days of the Prophet Muhammad, he declared, and this fundamental fact cannot be ignored while formulating today's principles and politics. Our understanding now of the message of the Prophet differs essentially from that of previous generations. But this should not mean that we 'exceed the boundaries of Islam', nor that the previous generations had failed to follow the appropriate path. Neither they, nor we, should be considered erroneous in our different interpretations. Each possesses his own understanding, and all of them are legitimate.¹¹³

Such notions, which challenged the views held by the conservative elite in power in Islamic Iran, found fertile ground particularly among students, who supported them and propagated them further. This became particularly evident after Khatami's election, and even more so during 1999. Heshmatollah Tabarzadi, the Secretary General of the Islamic Union of University Students and Graduates, gave voice to similar views in numerous statements. Other student leaders, such as Manuchehr Mohammadi, one of the leaders of the Union, also expressed similar views. They were asserted much more forcefully during the student riots in July 1999. The slogans chanted by student demonstrators at that time attest to the severity and the depth of the domestic dichotomy. Some challenged the authority of the Supreme Leader, the conservative elite, the lack of freedoms under the Islamic Republic and even the very concept of *velayat-e faqih*. (For more on student protests and Montazeri's support for them, see Chapter 5.) Others were particularly revealing: 'Khamene'i be ashamed (*haya kon*), abandon the leadership (*raha kon*)'. Yet others expressed anger at the abuse of the concept of Islamic Republic which, they argued, had become synonymous with a *velayat-e motlaqeh-ye faqih* (an absolute *velayat-e faqih*) ruled by one person, and transformed the Islamic regime into despotism (*estebdad*). These charges were aimed, in one way or another, at the very nature of the revolutionary system and the functioning of the *vali-ye faqih*.

A link has been thus formed, that included leading clerics of the early revolutionary period, senior contemporary religious authorities, leading intellectuals and students and some liberal and national movements (such as the Freedom Movement). All of whom, in one way or another expressed resentment concerning the consequences of the revolutionary doctrine espoused by the government in power. They certainly confronted the regime with a major ideological challenge.

Since the early days of the revolution, many people have criticized the extensive powers bestowed on the Supreme Leader and the subsequent lack of freedom under clerical rule, claiming that the divine law should be reinterpreted in light of emerging realities and by means of logic (*manteq*). Shari'atmadari was the most adamant critic at the outset of the revolutionary regime. Even before the revolutionary takeover, he said that 'the ideal state' of early Islam, while still 'worthy of imitation' in many respects, 'does not mean that we ignore all [other] innovations' made during the 1,400 years since the advent of Islam.¹¹⁴ He spelled out the contradiction between the constitutional assertion of popular sovereignty (Articles 6, 56 of the 1979 constitution) and the expropriation of this very right as a result of unlimited power enjoyed by the Supreme Leader (articles 5, 110).[115] His main criticisms were shared by many liberals at the time and seemed to have gained even greater support since. The Iranian Association of Jurists similarly asserted in 1979 that the constitution of the Islamic Republic 'openly violates' the principles of 'government by the people', adding that the power of the Supreme Leader might give rise to 'a new dictatorship'. They claimed that 'it would have been more logical and more honest if, instead of all the articles, only one [Article 4] had been submitted to the plebiscite since it gives absolute authority to the Council of Guardians [to approve legislation]'.[116] Mehdi Bazargan then expressed the fear that such a concentration of power would lead to a 'class rule or monopoly'.[117]

More recently, Nuri took such arguments even further. Religious knowledge (*ma'refat-e dini*), he said, is relative and may have varied interpretations. No red lines exist via which to express opinions, besides those stipulated in the constitution. One-mindedness is not possible, nor is it desired. Moreover, no individual or group can claim exclusiveness and the sole right to interpret dogma. Indeed, dogma should be reconsidered in light of changing realities. Thus, for example, Ayatollah Khomeini had repeatedly stressed, that even if Iran developed relations with Saddam Husayn, it would not forgive the crimes committed by Saudi Arabia (for its anti-Iranian policies in the 1980s). Yet, Iran now has relations with both of them. Similarly, Khomeini was opposed to Britain and the USSR, not only to the United States. If Khomeini's (past) stances are the criteria for actual policy, 'they should be followed on all issues', not only in matters that those wielding power now find acceptable. Moreover, Nuri went on to exhort, Khomeini's past views on the various questions should not be used to settle factional rifts or to advance the aims of a particular group.[118] Ganji argued, similarly, that scholars should use the tools they possess to reach new interpretations. In his view, a royalist and fascist interpretation of religion may lead to the destruction of faith, the state and the regime, while a divine-logical-human (*rahmani-'aqlani-ensani*) interpretation would strengthen all three. For 14 centuries, Ganji went on arguing, scholars had studied Islam. The analysis offered by Ayatollah Khomeini is another in a long series of interpretations, but it should by no means be viewed as the last and the only abiding one. He therefore called upon reformists (*eslah-talab*), to strive for reform in the interpretation of religion.[119]

The arguments raised by Montazeri and Azari-Qomi on the one hand,

and Soroush, Shabestari and Kadivar on the other, represent the two
main trends challenging – each in its own way – the same fundamental
revolutionary creed. Their basic contention seems to have gathered
further support among many Iranians, particularly among liberals
and students. The regime could not altogether silence such emerging
voices, although it kept a strict watch on the activities of their proponents.

Clearly, the issue of the *marja'iyya* posed the most serious ideological
threat to the clerical government with significant political implications.
As Hashim has observed, the 'severe crisis of political legitimacy' was
'eroding the foundations of the system'. To begin with, the separation of
marja'iyya and *rahbariyya*, which occurred after the death of Ayatollah
Khomeini, was 'a major blow to the regime's conception of itself as an
Islamic state'.[120] Clearly, after Khomeini, the country was not led by the
most prominent *marja'*. By seeking *marja'iyya* status, Khamene'i wished
eventually to acquire the sweeping powers and the supreme authority
enjoyed by Khomeini. His succession, as Mottahedeh has observed,
inspired him 'to be a genuine holy man'.[121] He takes 'seriously his role
as heir to Khomeini's mantle', added Bakhash. Though he has hitherto
failed to gain full theological endorsement, his recognition as one of the
maraje' (in addition to his political power), reinforces his authority and
serves as an important asset. Nevertheless, it would be difficult to regard
his rulings 'as authoritative, binding, [or] superior to those of other
eminent jurists' and 'as the guidelines by which state, society and individuals should conduct themselves'. Clearly, his religious rulings lack
jurisprudential authority.[122] This constitutes a severe ideological retreat
from the concept of *velayat-e faqih* and the ideological creed of the
revolution.

The harsh social, economic and political realities that persist after two
decades of Islamic rule, and the restrictions on freedom have led some
Iranians to attribute the government's failures to Islam. (See the
Conclusion to Part I). This indictment in turn led some clerics 'increasingly, though still indirectly, to criticize the religious office of the
Guide'.[123] Seyyed Mahmud Qomi (son of Ayatollah Seyyed Hasan
Tabataba'i Qomi), gave rise to such concerns. He claimed in 1995 that,
by nature, state and religion 'are incompatible' and 'must [thus] be
separated'. In any case, he argued, *marja'iyya* was not an issue for
governments to deal with.[124] The realities of two decades of Islamic
government have also raised questions about the basic concepts of the
new regime and the way dogma has been implemented.

Clearly, leading theologians have challenged basic revolutionary

principles. This has become an 'urgent national issue' as well as a theological question.[125] Yet in the immediate aftermath of Khomeini's death,
as Bakhash wrote, it seemed 'impractical, if not impossible', to combine
spiritual and temporal leadership in one person, and 'equally impractical' to separate the two roles.[126] The result, added Olivier Roy, was a
'divorce' of the supreme religious function from the highest political
function: for him, the concept of *velayat-e faqih* 'is defunct'.[127] Moreover, 'the crisis of religious legitimacy' in revolutionary Iran has led to a
supremacy of political consideration. Ultimately, Roy observed, there is
a 'growing tendency, not only among democrats and liberals, but also
traditional clerics, to separate religion and politics, this time to save
Islam from politics'.[128]

In sum, the *marja'iyya* saga reflects a significant retreat from the most
important principle of the revolutionary philosophy, with state interests
gaining supremacy over dogma and religio-politicians over theologians.
This constitutes a severe blow to the ideology; it leads to domestic strife
and it has, in fact, already damaged the functioning of the revolutionary
institutions of the Islamic Republic. The idea of a supreme religious
authority, which Khomeini wished to retain – and to a great extent
succeeded in keeping – beyond argument and above political factions
has gradually become an issue in public debate. Moreover, unlike the
situation under Khomeini's leadership, the person of the Supreme
Leader is now identified with one of the rival factions and has become
an issue in the political struggle for power. (See Chapters 2 and 3.) In
the absence of an all-powerful and generally accepted authority, the
domestic political divisions have become even more pressing, as the next
chapter will attempt to show.

NOTES

1. The 1979 Iranian constitution (Articles 5, 107, and 112) vested paramount
   religious and political authority in the Supreme Leader (*rahbar*) – a position
   unparalleled in Iran's earlier constitutional history but consistent with
   Khomeini's concept of *velayat-e faqih*. The Supreme Leader (among others) is
   responsible for 'delineating the general policies' of the state and 'supervising the
   execution of those policies' (Article 110). For the amendments to the constitution after Khomeini's death in 1989, see below. For a discussion of the 1979
   constitution, see Menashri, *Decade of War and Revolution*, pp. 116–26.
2. The distinction between theologians and 'religio-politicians' is complex.
   Leading politicians such as Rafsanjani and Khatami have religious credentials,
   and eminent clerics often engage in politics. In the context of this discussion,
   persons who gain prominence on the basis of their religious scholarship and

authority are deemed theologians, whereas those clerics who exercise authority primarily as a result of their political power are referred to as religio-politicians.

3. On the constitutional authority of the Council, see Menashri, *Decade of War and Revolution*, pp. 117, 192–3. On the use of such power to block radical legislation, see ibid., pp. 173, 183, 224, 246, 327–8 and 356–8. For criticism of the wide constitutional authority and the even greater *de facto* powers exercised by the Council, see below.

4. *Ettela'at*, 7 and 12 January 1988.

5. *Kayhan* (Tehran), 7 January 1988.

6. *Ettela'at*, 7 February 1988.

7. *Ettela'at*, 31 August 1988.

8. Farhad Kazemi, 'Civil Society and Iranian Politics', in Augustus Norton (ed.), *Civil Society in the Middle East* (Leiden: Brill, 1996), Vol. II, pp. 123–4.

9. Ervand Abrahamian, *Khomeinism: Essays on the Islamic Republic* (Berkeley, CA: University of California Press, 1993), p. 57.

10. NHK Television (Tokyo), 1 February 1988, in British Broadcasting Corporation (BBC), Summary of World Broadcasts (*SWB*), The Middle East, 3 February 1988.

11. *Middle East Policy*, 3/4 (1995), p. 26.

12. *Jomhuri-ye Islami*, 7 November 1988; *Kayhan* (Tehran), 26 November 1988.

13. Laurent Lamote [pseudonym], 'Iran's Foreign Policy and Internal Crisis', in Patrick Clawson (ed.), *Iran's Strategic Intentions and Capabilities* (Washington, DC: National Defense University, 1994), pp. 10–12.

14. Radio Tehran, 11 November 1988 – SWB, 14 November 1988.

15. See Menashri, 'Iran', in *Middle East Contemporary Survey [MECS] 1989* (Tel Aviv: Dayan Center, Annual), pp. 347–50.

16. In September 1979 Montazeri was appointed Imam Jum'ah of Tehran. On 22 May 1980 he was appointed Imam Jum'ah of Qom in recognition of his 'high religious credentials' (*Ettela'at*, 22 May 1980). He was then promoted to succeed Khomeini. See Menashri, *Decade of War and Revolution*, pp. 128, 266–8, 339, 380–7.

17. For his disqualification, see *MECS 1989*, pp. 341–4. For Khomeini's letter dismissing him, see below.

18. Khomeini died before the constitutional amendment body had made its final decisions.

19. See details on the amendments in Menashri, 'Iran', pp. 347–50.

20. A detailed discussion of Khamene'i's nomination, and the reasoning given for his selection, see Menashri, 'Iran', pp. 350–3. Khamene'i was thereafter referred to as an ayatollah.

21. Roy P. Mottahedeh, 'The Islamic Movement: The Case of Democratic Inclusion', *Contention*, 4/3 (Spring 1995), p. 112.

22. Edward G. Shirley [pseudonym], 'Fundamentalism in Power: Is Iran's Present Algeria's Future?', *Foreign Affairs*, 74/3 (May–June 1995), p. 38.

23. Radio Tehran, 9 June 1989 – SWB, 12 June 1989; *Kayhan* (Tehran), 11 June 1989.

24. Radio Tehran, 9 June 1989 – SWB, 12 June 1989.

25. *Resalat* as brought in Foreign Broadcast Information Service, Daily Report, Middle East and North Africa (DR) 5 June 1989.

26. Arguments based on what Khomeini may have said in private bear no legal weight, because his last will explicitly warned that no views attributed to him should be given credence 'unless I said it in my own voice [i.e. on tape] or it has my signature [on it, verified by] the affirmation of the experts, or what I said on the television of the Islamic Republic'. *Imam Khomeini's Last Will and Testament* (Washington, DC: Interest Section of the Islamic Republic of Iran, Algerian Embassy, 1989), p. 62.

27. *Kayhan* (Tehran), 10 June 1989; Radio Tehran, 9 June 1989 – SWB, 12 June 1989.

28. Mottahedeh, 'Islamic Movement', pp. 114–15.

29. Islamic Republic News Agency (IRNA), 16 June – SWB, 19 June 1989.

30. Mottahedeh, 'Islamic Movement', pp. 114–5.

31. *Iran Times*, 24 December 1993.

32. *Al-Sharq al-Awsat* as quoted by the *Iran Times*, 31 December 1993. Clerics then reportedly signed a letter protesting against the regime's efforts to control the selection of the *marja'*. See *Iran Times*, 24 December 1993 and 7 January 1994.

33. IRNA, 10 December 1993 – DR, 12 December 1993; *Iran Times*, 7 December 1993.

34. Radio Tehran, 17 December 1993 – DR, 20 December 1993; *Salam*, 18 December 1993; *Iran Times*, 17 and 24 December 1993.

35. *Iran Times*, 28 January 1994.

36. *Ettela'at*, 12 December 1993; *Iran Times*, 17 December 1993.

37. Tehran TV, 25 December 1993 – DR, 27 December 1993.

38. Tehran TV, 1 December 1994 – DR, 2 December 1994.

39. Tehran TV, 3 December 1994 – DR, 5 December 1994.

40. Radio Tehran, 9 December 1994 – DR, 12 December 1994.

41. Tehran TV, 30 November 1994 – DR, 30 November 1994.

42. Tehran TV, 2 December 1994 – DR, 5 December 1994.

43. IRNA, 2 December 1994 – DR, 5 December 1994.

44. Radio Tehran, 9 December 1994 – DR, 12 December 1994.

45. *Iran Times*, 7 January, 1994. IRNA, 5 January 1994, quoted Ruhani's son's denial of this report; see DR, 5 January 1994.

46. *Al-Sharq al-Awsat*, 25 January 1995.

47. In September 1995, Javad Ruhani was sentenced to three years in prison; broadcast over Israel Radio (Persian Service), 5–12 August and 16 September 1995; and quoted in *Kayhan* (London), 27 July 1995 – DR, 13 September 1995. More details are given in Mehdi Ha'iri's letter to the UN Secretary-General on 10 September 1998 (see below).

48. Radio Tehran, 14 December 1994 – DR, 15 December 1994.

49. Radio Tehran, 3 December 1994 – DR, 5 December 1994.

50. Radio Tehran, 30 December 1994 – DR, 30 December 1994. See similar statement in this context by Khamene'i, Radio Tehran, 14 December 1994 – DR, 15 December 1994.

51. For the rivalries between Shari'atmadari and Khomeini, see David Menashri, 'Shi'ite Leadership: In the Shadow of Conflicting Ideologies', *Iranian Studies*, 3/1–4 (1980), pp. 119–45; and Menashri, *Decade of War and Revolution*, pp. 82–90, 129–30, 224–5, 239–40.

52. *Ettela'at*, 19 and 31 May 1979.

53. *Kayhan* (Tehran), 24 February 1979; Agence France Presse (AFP), 28 January 1979; DR, 30 January 1979.
54. *Kayhan (Tehran)*, 24 January 1979. See similarly, *Ettela'at*, 31 August 1978, 28 January, and 31 May 1979.
55. *Le Monde*, 17 July 1979.
56. Radio Tehran, 21 April 1982 – DR, 22 April 1982. Among the signatories were Rafsanjani, Khamene'i, Musavi, Nateq-Nuri, Ardabili, and Mahdavi-Kani.
57. *Ettela'at*, 22, 24, 26 April 1982; *Jomhuri-ye Islami*, 22 April 1982; *Tehran Times*, 1 May 1982.
58. *The Guardian*, 22 April 1982.
59. *Iran Focus*, December 1988, pp. 2–3.
60. *Abrar*, 6 February 1989 – SWB, 8 February 1989.
61. *Ettela'at*, 29 March; Radio Tehran, 28 March 1989 – SWB, 30 March 1989; see also below.
62. *Ettela'at*, 5 April 1989.
63. *Resalat*, 15, 16, 17 May 1989 – DR, 16 July 1989. SAVAK is the State Intelligence and Security Organization, so called after the initials of its name *Sazeman-e Ettela'at va Amniyat-e Keshvar*.
64. *Jomhuri-ye Islami*, 15 February 1993.
65. *Kayhan* (London), 14 and 18 February 1993, in *Echo of Iran*, no. 61 (February 1993), p. 14; DR, 19 February 1993.
66. *Jomhuri-ye Islami*, 15 February 1993.
67. IRNA, 16 February 1993 – DR, 17 February 1993; *Al-Sharq al-Awsat*, 16 February 1993.
68. *Kayhan* (London), 20 October 1994 – DR, 1 December 1994.
69. *Al-Sharq al-Awsat*, 2 November 1994.
70. Shaul Bakhash, 'Iran: The Crisis of Legitimacy', in *Middle Eastern Lectures* (Tel Aviv: Moshe Dayan Center, 1995), Vol. I, p. 99.
71. *MECS* 1991, pp. 389–90.
72. *Resalat*, 30 March 1993.
73. *Salam*, 21 December 1994.
74. *Resalat*, 23 November 1997.
75. *Kayhan* (London), 4 December 1997.
76. Voice of Israel, in Persian, 1 December 1997 – SWB, 3 December 1997. See also Ha'iri's letter, cited below.
77. IRNA, 19 November 1997 [DR]; Tehran TV, 21 November 1997 [DR].
78. *Jomhuri-ye Islami*, 22 November 1997.
79. *Jomhuri-ye Islami*, 22 November 1997; *Kayhan* (Tehran), 23 November; Tehran TV, 22 November 1997 [DR].
80. *Kayhan* (Tehran), 27 November 1997.
81. *Kayhan* (Tehran), 23 November 1997.
82. *Jomhuri-ye Islami*, 22 November 1997.
83. *Kayhan* (Tehran), 15 and 16 November 1997.
84. *Kayhan* (Tehran), 15 November 1997.
85. *Jomhuri-ye Islami*, 27 November 1997; Tehran TV, 26 November 1997 [DR].
86. *Jomhuri-ye Islami*, 20 November 1997; *Abrar*, 22 November 1997.
87. *Jomhuri-ye Islami*, 20 November 1997.
88. *Hamshahri*, 24 November 1997.

89. *Resalat*, 20 November 1997.
90. *Iran News*, 11 November 1997 [DR]; *Jomhuri-ye Islami*, 9 and 11 November; *Resalat*, 9 November 1997.
91. *Kayhan* (London), 4 December 1997.
92. The author has a copy of Ha'iri's letter. For Ganji statements, see Akbar Ganji, *Naqdi Bara-ye Tamam-e Fosul: Goftogu-ye Akbar Ganji ba 'Abdollah Nuri* [Critique for all Seasons: Akbar Ganji's Conversation with 'Abdollah Nuri] (Tehran: Tarh-e Now, 1999–2000), pp. 77–80.
93. 'Abdollah Nuri, *Showkaran-e Eslah* [Hemlock for Advocate of Reform: The Complete Text of Nuri's Defense at the Special Clerical Tribunal] (Tehran: Tarh-e Now, 1999), pp. 186–98; Ganji, *Naqdi bara-ye Tamam-e Fosul*, pp. 77–80; Akbar Ganji, *Talaqqi-ye Fashisti az Din va Hokumat* [Fascist Interpretation of Religion and Government] (Tehran: Tarh-e Now, 2000), pp. 136–43.
94. *Resalat*, 1 December; *Akhbar*, 7 December 1997 [DR].
95. Eric Hooglund, 'The Pulse of Iran Today', *Middle East Insight*, 11/5 (July–August 1995), p. 41.
96. 'Abdul-Karim Soroush, *Farbehtar az Ideolozhi* [More Substantial than Ideology] (Tehran: Sarat, 1993), pp. 122–3.
97. Soroush, *Farbehtar az Ideolozhi*. For an insightful discussion of Soroush's thinking see Valla Vakili, *Debating Religion and Politics in Iran: The Political Thought of Abdolkarim Soroush* (New York: Council for Foreign Relations, 1996) and Judith Miller, *God Has Ninety-Nine Names: Reporting from a Militant Middle East* (New York, NY: Simon & Schuster, 1996), pp. 429–64. For a criticism of Soroush's views, see Jahangir Salehpur, 'Naqdi bar Nazariyeh-ye "Farbehtar az Ideolozhi"', *Jahan-e Islam*, 5 (June–July, 1994), pp. 23–7.
98. Rouleau, 'Islamic Republic of Iran', pp. 55–6.
99. Soroush, *Farbehtar az Ideolozhi*, pp. 114–17.
100. 'Abdul-Karim Soroush, 'Dark-e 'Azizaneh-ye Din' [Precious Understanding of Religion], *Kiyan*, 4/19 (May–June 1994), pp. 2–9.
101. Soroush, *Farbehtar az Ideolozhi*, pp. 122–30.
102. *Los Angeles Times*, 30 December 1995; *Kiyan*, 4/23 (February–March 1995), pp. 2–36.
103. *Neshat*, 22 June 1999.
104. *Los Angeles Times*, 27 January and 30 December 1995.
105. Rouleau, 'Islamic Republic of Iran', pp. 55–6.
106. Hooglund, 'Pulse of Iran', pp. 41–2.
107. Mohsen Kadivar, *Nazariyeha-ye Dowlat dar Feqh-e Shi'eh* (Tehran: Nashr-e Ney, 1376 [1997/98]).
108. Debate with Shabestari on 'Din, Modara va Khoshunat' [Religion, Tolerance and Violence], *Kiyan*, 8/45 (January–March 1999), pp. 6–19.
109. *Ruzegar-e Now*, 205 (February–March 1999), pp. 31–3.
110. Rouleau, 'Islamic Republic of Iran', p. 56.
111. Such charges were raised in Nuri's trial, against Kadivar as well as Nuri, who published them in *Khordad* in February 1999, Nuri, *Showkaran-e Eslah*, pp. 107, 110–11.
112. Shabestari on 'Din, Modara va Khoshunat', pp. 6–19; Mohammad Mojtahed Shabestari, 'Islam va Masihiyat-e Orupa'i' [Islam and European Christianity] *Siyasat-e Khareji*, 4/3 (Sept.–Nov. 1989), pp. 409–15.

113. Shabestari on 'Din, Modara va Khoshunat', pp. 6–19.
114. *Der Spiegel*, 27 August 1978.
115. For this and other points made then by Ayatollah Shari'atmadari, see *Bamdad*, 28 and 30 November 1979; *Guardian*, 30 November and 3 December; Radio Tehran, 23 December 1979 – DR, 25 December 1979; *Cambio 16*, 23 December 1979 – DR, 28 December 1979.
116. *Bamdad*, 28 November 1979.
117. *Bamdad*, 27 and 28 November; *Kayhan* (Tehran), 28 November; *al-Dustur* (London), 24 December 1979.
118. Nuri, *Showkaran-e Eslah*, pp. 176–9, 252–3.
119. Ganji, *Talaqqi-ye Fashisti az Din va Hokumat*, pp. 116–24, 143–51; Ganji, *Naqdi Bara-ye Tamam-e Fosul*, pp. 58–9.
120. Ahmed Hashim, *The Crisis of the Iranian State* (Adelphi Paper 296; London: International Institute for Strategic Studies, 1995), pp. 5, 23.
121. Mottahedeh, 'Islamic Movement', p. 112.
122. Bakhash, 'Crisis of Legitimacy', pp. 104, 109, 113–4.
123. Lamote, 'Iran's Foreign Policy', pp. 10–12.
124. *Kayhan* (London), 15 December 1994 – DR, 20 January 1995.
125. Abdulaziz Sachedina, 'Who Will Lead the Shi'a? Is the Crisis of Religious Leadership in Shi'ism Imagined or Real?', *Middle East Insight*, 11/3 (March–April 1995), p. 25.
126. Bakhash, *Crisis of Legitimacy*, p. 99.
127. Olivier Roy, *The Failure of Political Islam* (Cambridge, MA: Harvard University Press, 1994), p. 179.
128. Olivier Roy, 'The Crisis of Religious Legitimacy in Iran', *Middle East Journal*, 53/2 (Spring 1999), p. 202.

2

The Political Scene: Rival Factions and Conflicting Tendencies

CONFLICTING TENDENCIES WITHIN 'THE LINE OF THE IMAM'

By their very nature, revolutionary movements often deviate from their professed doctrine once they have made the transition from opposition to power. Iran's Islamic Revolution was no exception. As the leader of a movement in opposition, Ayatollah Khomeini had depicted a 'new Iran' modeled on his idealistic design. Once in power, however, he (and even more so his disciples after him), realized that they could not rule by means of slogans alone. Governing required the management of, and attention to, evolving practical difficulties, which often necessitated deviation from pure dogma. Therefore, a measure of pragmatism and realism was inevitable for the effective running of the state. Yet, the various political trends seemed to differ, often drastically, on the actual policy to be followed, the degree of flexibility required, and the particular areas and pace of change.

It should be stressed at the outset of this discussion, however, that the grave rivalries and the fundamental differences discussed here were still primarily among groups which were generally loyal to the basic revolutionary dogma and to the Islamic revolutionary system.[1] In fact, given all the challenges facing the clerical regime and the vicissitudes of its rule, there was an impressive measure of continuity with the regime generally remaining stable throughout its two decades in power. As demonstrated throughout Iran's constitutional history, the duration in office of individual governments provides a valid yardstick of such stability. In the four years that followed the autumn 1977 revolutionary crisis, which led eventually to the overthrow of the Shah, ten prime ministers served in office – five of them between the revolutionary takeover in February 1979 and October 1981. Between January 1980 and October 1981, there were three presidential elections. By contrast, between October 1981 and the summer of 1989, Iran had the same president (Khamene'i), Majlis speaker (Rafsanjani), prime minister (Mir-Hosein Musavi), president of the supreme court (Ayatollah 'Abdul-Karim Ardabili), and the same Supreme Leader (*rahbar*), Ayatollah Khomeini. Stability and continuity also marked the passing away of the founding father of the revolution, Ayatollah Khomeini, in June 1989. Khamene'i then became the *rahbar* and Rafsanjani replaced him as newly elected president. (Since then Mehdi Karubi and Nateq-Nuri have served as Speakers of the Majlis; and Ayatollah Yazdi as the president of the supreme court.) After two terms in office, Rafsanjani was replaced in 1997 by Khatami. Majlis elections have been similarly held on schedule every four years since 1980. Ayatollah Yazdi served ten years as the president of the supreme court and was replaced, in August 1999, by Ayatollah Mahmud Hashemi Shahrudi. Elections to the Council of Experts were held on schedule. In February 1999, 20 years after the change of regime, municipal elections were held – for the first time since the revolution – throughout the country. The fierce rivalries and struggle for power throughout the 1990s, and the growing signs of popular discontent, had not overshadowed this overall picture of stability, at least at the time of writing.

With the consolidation of the regime, the opposition also weakened. The expatriate opposition was initially vocal, but divided and sterile, and seemingly lacking in organization and determination. Numerically speaking, its ranks expanded somewhat as some who had initially supported the revolution grew disillusioned. Yet, the different opposition factions have offered neither a viable alternative ideology to unite them in a common struggle to challenge the Islamic regime, nor proved successful in recruiting significant members of important power groups (i.e., the armed forces or clergy). Rather than forming a single 'opposition in exile', there were many 'oppositions', each as hostile to one another as they were to the Islamic regime. Ideological divisions and personal conflicts divided them, with rifts so deep that no single expatriate movement, leader or creed, proved capable of unifying the groups in the direction of concrete action. In their attitude, also, a resignation to their fate as exiles became gradually prevalent. Only the National Resistance Council – with the *Mojahedin-e Khalq* at its core – seemed still to have preserved a significant clandestine network within Iran (mainly among the ethnic minorities). However, with its leadership in exile, their capability for action was limited. Those movements within Iran with a different vision (such as the Freedom Movement), were under strict control and their activities restricted, as were those of dissident clerics and intellectuals. (See Chapter 1.) While those opposing the ruling system from abroad did not seem to give the Islamic government much cause for real concern in the 1990s, growing popular disillusionment at home did. Nevertheless, the government managed to control signs of disloyalty – such as riots in different cities in the early 1990s and the student demonstrations at universities in 1999 – to prevent them from assuming threatening proportions. (See Chapters 4 and 5.)

Yet, while the revolutionary leadership seemed firmly in command, a fierce struggle for power became evident within its ranks. The differences between the various groups emerged for a variety of reasons. These ranged from different interpretations of Islamic law to divergent doctrinal convictions arising from the inherent tension between the doctrine of the revolution and Iran's national interests. Different political considerations and tendencies and factional and personal rivalries also played a part.

In the early 1990s, Western opinion viewed these differences, by and large, as existing essentially among three distinct factions, which were commonly termed: pragmatists, radicals and conservatives. In fact, even within these vaguely defined parameters, the situation was much more complex; mapping the domestic forces allied to these groups (in terms of doctrine and association), and identifying individuals as members of a specific group was no easy matter. The various trends never actually organized into clear-cut factions – let alone into competing parties with coherent, collective ideologies. In addition, there were significant subgroups within each trend, all of them proclaiming loyalty to Imam Khomeini's 'line' (*khatt-e Imam*). Moreover, it was impossible to distinguish between genuine ideological differences and political rivalries. Similarly, participants frequently changed their positions, sometimes drastically, speaking in pragmatic terms on one occasion (or on one particular topic), and adopting more hard-line views on other occasions (or on a different issue). As one newspaper noted caustically in the early 1990s, Iranian officials often speak 'sweet words in English to foreigners, but it's strictly Satan-as-usual when they speak Farsi on the home front'.[2] Other observers regretted that when officials moved away from public forums (or visited distant countries), they expressed less categorical views, than when at home.[3] More importantly, there were significant changes, over time, in the political outlook of many groups, which often changed their stance in response to momentous developments in Iran and abroad. Consequently, political alignments also changed occasionally.

Yet after carefully considering the position of different groups, their cumulative statements and policy priorities over the last two decades, it seems possible broadly to identify three main political trends in the early 1990s. These were: (a) radicals (sometimes called 'hard-liners'); (b) pragmatists, realists, or reformists; and (c) conservatives, or ideological purists (often also termed 'hard-liners' and 'extremists'). Towards the late 1990s, even such categorization no longer seemed valid. However, two general 'trends' were then visible. One, a pragmatic or reformist faction (led by Khatami and supported by some of the groups formerly known as radicals). The other, a faction of conservatives and ideological purists (identified with the Supreme Leader), which was usually described as the hard-line camp.

Although these generalizations are rife with inaccuracy and error, it may be said that those who held executive power and shared the burden of running the state were generally more pragmatic. Conversely, those outside the administration usually comprised hard-liners and ideological purists. But even this has not always been the case. Thus, for example, Hojjat ul-Islam 'Ali Akbar Mohtashami remained extremely radical even while serving as minister in Musavi's government, while many of those who did not share administrative responsibilities (including Khatami, before his election to the presidency, and 'Abdollah Nuri, before his return to government in 1997), were among leading pragmatists. Even more significantly, 'Abdollah Nuri was generally viewed as a radical while serving as the minister of the interior in the 1980s, but a pragmatic supporter of government reforms when out of office and since his return to the same ministry in 1997 (and his impeachment in 1998). However, it should be remembered that, generally, the pragmatists were also devoted revolutionaries, aligned with Khomeini's doctrines. It was mainly the practical difficulties of running the government and perpetuating Islamic rule, as well as the experience of the years of Islamic rule, that gave their thinking a belated pragmatic tinge. As the problems facing the regime multiplied (and politicians became more experienced and mature over time), the tendency toward pragmatism became more marked and the pressure for reform more noticeable. Many more elements within the regime gradually became more aware that perpetuating revolutionary rule required a greater measure of realism, however, others continued to uphold pure dogma.

In the second half of the 1990s, another categorization seemed even more appropriate to identify domestic tendencies – the popular trends in society (mainly the youth and women), and growing elements within civil society (and segments of the press, students' associations, women's organizations), which generally supported more practical solutions and reform, and the revolutionary institutions and organization (such as the

Revolutionary Guards, Council of Guardians, Council of Experts), that remained strictly more loyal to the conservative line. Khatami offered another distinction, between those who supported the law and those who did not. It may be possible to make yet another distinction, between those who preach to obey the laws, and those who strive to change them altogether. (See Chapter 5.) Even such vague definitions, do not capture the diversity of the political scene in the 1990s, and the alignments were still far from clear. Interestingly, however, many of those known as radicals in the early 1990s came to support greater pragmatism and reform in the late 1990s. Therefore, the definitions in this chapter – which covers the period up to 1997 – may be somewhat different from those used in the next chapter – covering the late 1990s. It is with these reservations and for the sake of convenience only that such terms as radicals, pragmatists, conservatives and other similar categories, are used in this study in the context of the given revolutionary phase.

Be that as it may, the categorization and the identity of various groups, and the differences between domestic trends, were deep, touching upon significant policy preferences. These diverse approached colored the political scene from the initial stages of the revolution. Significant differences within the ruling Islamic Republican Party developed following the 1979 revolution;[4] these intensified and became more public following Khomeini's death. Such differences came to the fore more forcefully during the parliamentary elections of 1996, reaching a peak in the 1997 presidential elections and intensifying in the three years since Khatami entered office. (See the following chapter and Epilogue.)

The fact that Khamene'i – as Khomeini before him – periodically exhorted the different 'camps', 'trends', or 'wings' (as they were variously described), to maintain their unity demonstrated the intensity of the domestic rivalries in the early 1990s. Rafsanjani, who was often viewed as the head of the pragmatists at the time, said in 1991, that there were 'two currents' in Iran: 'a radical one and a more moderate one'.[5] Mohtashami, commonly regarded at the time as a leading radical, alluded to the depth of such divisions. Khomeini's death, he said, had plunged Iranian society into a period of deep despondency, in which the true revolutionaries (i.e., the radicals) no longer had 'a voice' in formulating policy and had been 'eliminated from the scene'. He accused 'some members of a particular faction [i.e., the pragmatists] of spreading venom and distorting facts to prevent us [radicals] from continuing our rightful course'.[6] The fluctuating power of rival camps inescapably left its imprints on the government policy.

Consequently, actual policy often seemed fluid and at times conflicting. Broadly, however, the first 21 years of the Islamic regime indicate
an increasing trend toward pragmatism, interspersed with occasional
outbursts of radicalism – a pattern that has persisted despite changes in
personalities, alignments and issues under discussion.

In 1979, a confrontation between Prime Minister Mehdi Bazargan
(who wished to pursue pragmatic policies), and his hard-line rivals
(radicals and conservatives), led to the seizure of the US embassy and a
subsequent interval of greater extremism. In 1981, in response to President Abul-Hasan Bani Sadr's attempts to introduce somewhat greater
openness, his opponents forced his expulsion and introduced another
period of greater revolutionary zeal. In 1983–84, the religio-politicians
– then in charge of the executive – introduced an interlude of relative
pragmatism that culminated with the arms deals with the United States
in 1985–86. This was followed by a new interval of hard-line policy, as
demonstrated by the clash with the US Navy in the Gulf in 1987, riots
during the 1987 *hajj* (pilgrimage) in Saudi Arabia, and the election of a
more radical Majlis in 1988. A new pragmatic trend introduced in the
summer of 1988 was most clearly reflected in the approval of a cease-fire
with Iraq in July 1988, the subsequent discussion of plans for economic
rehabilitation, and a measure of liberalism on the eve of celebrations
marking the first decade of the revolution in February 1989. This
triggered another phase of extremism which was manifested in the disqualification of Montazeri as Khomeini's heir apparent and the latter's
fatwa against the author Salman Rushdie in February 1989. After that,
the pragmatists reinforced their power, and the tendency toward pragmatism became even more evident, although their attempts to pursue
such policies were often blocked (or delayed) by the more ideological
and conservative factions in the establishment. The election of President
Khatami in 1997 further accelerated this tendency, as he sought to
introduce more comprehensive reforms which were harshly opposed by
revolutionary purists. (See Chapter 4.)

At the outset of each wave of extremism, its leaders would seize
upon an issue with which all the revolutionaries could easily identify to
challenge their pragmatic rivals and their preferred politics. Thus, the
1979 seizure of US hostages targeted Bazargan; the 1981 expulsion of
Westernized liberals from power was aimed against Bani Sadr; the Iran–
Contra affair threatened Rafsanjani, and the 1989 *fatwa* against Salman
Rushdie pointed at Ayatollah Montazeri (and probably Rafsanjani). In
one way or another, all were manifestations of the ongoing ideological,
political, and personal struggles for power.

The growing influence of ideological hard-liners, which typified the political *milieu* on the eve of Khomeini's death, was modified following Rafsanjani's election to the presidency in 1989. His first act in power was to exclude the then radical ministers Mohtashami (in charge of the interior portfolio) and Mohammad Reyshahri (in charge of the intelligence portfolio) from his government. In October 1990, on the eve of the elections to the Council of Experts (which is empowered to select a new Supreme Leader), the struggle between hard-liners and pragmatists reached another peak. This was provoked by the decision of the Council of Guardians to hold examinations for candidates to determine their proficiency in jurisprudence in order to serve in the Council. The issue was plagued by acrimonious accusations, primarily in the Majlis, where a scuffle was reported to have occurred between members of opposing camps. Although the Council of Guardians claimed that decisions on candidates' eligibility were based on purely legal and religious foundations, the examinations were ultimately used to obstruct the radicals. Among those rejected were some leading radicals at that time, including Majlis Speaker Mehdi Karubi, former head of the Revolutionary Courts Ayatollah Sadeq Khalkhali, and Mohtashami. That they were found to lack sufficient religious credentials to sit on the Council of Experts was a humiliating indictment for these hojjat ul-Islams, to say nothing of the speaker of the Islamic Majlis. Khalkhali then accused 'some elements' of attempting to monopolize the revolution.[7]

Having eliminated the 'ideologue-purists' (to use Mohtashami's word) first from the executive, in 1989, and then from the Council of Experts, in 1990, Rafsanjani and his men then went on to curtail the influence of the radicals in their main power base, the Majlis.

The 1992 Majlis campaign pitted the two main camps against each other vigorously. They were then usually portrayed as pragmatists and radicals. Both factions, viewing the contest as a struggle to determine the path of the revolution, fought resolutely, in what was depicted as the 'mother of all election campaigns' (*umm al-ma'arek al-intikhabiyya*).[8] At the head of each camp stood the two major clerical associations, the *Jame'eh-ye Ruhaniyyat-e Mobarez*, and the *Majma'-e Ruhaniyyun-e Mobarez*. Although these clerical associations were formally restricted to the capital only – in line with Khomeini's 1984 ban on clerics from one constituency interfering in the electoral affairs of others[9] – the effect of their contest was felt across the entire country. As Ahmad Khomeini has put it, each of them had its supporters on every street and in each *bazaar* around the country.[10] The election thus typified the larger pragmatist–radical contest in the early 1990s.

The *Jame'eh-ye Ruhaniyyat-e Mobarez* included most figures then considered pragmatic as well as many conservative leaders, who at that time were generally allied to President Rafsanjani (this was known as 'the right' or the 'traditional right'). This association was headed by former interior minister Ayatollah Mohammad Reza Mahdavi-Kani. Its prominent figures included close associates of President Rafsanjani and those identified with the more pragmatic trend, such as First Vice-President Hasan Habibi, Vice-President 'Ata'ollah Mohajerani, and the minister of finance, Mohsen Nurbakhsh. They drew their support from the middle classes, including government employees, technocrats, professionals and elements of the business community.[11]

The prominent figures of the *Majma'-e Ruhaniyyun-e Mobarez* and those identified with it, were commonly known as radicals (often defined as 'the left'). At its head were some prominent figures from the previous government, including former interior minister Mohtashami, Majlis Speaker Karubi, former Prosecutor-General Mohammad Musavi Kho'iniha, the former head of the Revolutionary Courts Khalkhali and Deputy Majlis Speaker Asadollah Bayat. Their support came mainly from student associations (whose active members were at that time mostly radicals), and younger, more militant clerics.

The support they had in the Majlis, and the key positions their members enjoyed within it (such as Speaker Karubi, Deputy Speaker Bayat, defense committee chairman Mohtashami) increased their influence. Although unable to block the government's major policies in the Majlis, e.g., the approval of the Economic Plan, acceptance of foreign loans, the release of Western hostages in Lebanon, the radicals nevertheless continued to challenge Rafsanjani and his relatively pragmatic policies. They became a significant, well-organized power group, basing their arguments on Khomeini's initial doctrine. They were much weaker, however, in the executive branch of government in the early 1990s.

The pragmatists (supported by the conservatives) used their power in the executive branch to propagate their policy in the campaign and curtail their rivals' campaign. Acting on their behalf, the Council of Guardians used its constitutional power to 'supervise' the elections to disqualify many leading radicals from contesting the 1992 legislative elections. In fact, some 40 members out of a total of 270 of the outgoing Majlis, were found to be unqualified to participate in the 1992 election.[12] Among them were leading radicals including Bayat, Khalkhali, Hojjat ul-Islam Hosein Musavi Tabrizi, Ebrahim Asgharzadeh, Hadi Ghaffari, 'Ateqeh Sadiqi Raja'i, and former minister Behzad Nabavi.[13]

The interpretation of Article 99 of the constitution although the subject of much debate during earlier elections, evolved into a major issue in the 1992 contest (and continued to remain so until 2000). 'Supervision', the radicals charged, does not include the right to approve, or disqualify candidacies.[14] They argued that since disqualification violates the candidates' basic constitutional rights, it should be applied in extreme cases only, i.e. against counter-revolutionaries or criminals. They maintained that concrete supervision should be the prerogative of the interior ministry, with the Council of Guardians only dealing with appeals of disqualified candidates. In fact, in all election campaigns, the Council exercised its right to disqualify candidates and, by so doing, acted primarily against the conservatives' rivals. Council members made clear that they did not intend to allow those whom they considered unfit to be elected. Ayatollah Abul-Qasem Khaz'ali sparked a row when he said on 8 February 1992 that he and his colleagues would block 'bad elements' [i.e., radicals] from the Majlis, adding 'we will spray [them] with DDT'.[15] Not surprisingly, this comment angered the radicals, prompting Khalkhali to reply that it was an insult to compare Majlis deputies to insects. 'DDT is an insecticide. Now are Majlis deputies cockroaches or centipedes or something of this sort?'[16]

Khalkhali, whose candidacy had been rejected by the Council of Guardians, said that he and his colleagues were being targeted only because of their bravery, honesty and unequivocal opposition to US interests. Like many of the candidates who were found unfit to run, he asked the Council to disclose the reasons for his disqualification.[17] Other rejected candidates also protested against their disqualification.[18] In its defense, the election committee of the Council claimed that the reasons for their disqualification were not made public in order to avoid infringing their privacy.[19] Yet, many rejected candidates considered their formal disqualification even more damaging to their reputation than any possible allegation that might have been leveled against them.

The radicals had hoped that Khamene'i would support them in the general interests of the revolution much as Khomeini had supported the rights of minority groups so long as they worked within the Islamic consensus. They therefore proposed that the Supreme Leader should decide,[20] but Khamene'i chose not to pass judgment, thus serving the interests of the pragmatists, the conservatives and of Rafsanjani. Instead, he stressed the last-mentioned's main propaganda line, by advising voters to elect representatives who would enact laws that would 'enable the duly-elected government . . . to carry out its work'.[21]

As is the case in all elections everywhere, the incumbent (more pragmatic) government had a considerable advantage over its radical rivals out of government. In December 1991, the government replaced many of the provincial governors. (Those acting previously had been appointed by the former interior minister Mohtashami.) The pragmatists, supported by the conservatives, used the government-controlled radio and television (which at the time were run by Rafsanjani's brother, Mohammad Hashemi), to further promote their propaganda. They also benefited from their close ties with provincial Jum'ah imams (leaders of Friday prayers) for indoctrination throughout the country,[22] and used their influence in the judiciary to launch investigations of prominent radicals, and spread rumors concerning their alleged offenses. According to the *Echo of Iran*, the pragmatist faction 'shrewdly succeeded in compiling evidence of embezzlement' against individuals including Ardabili, Ghaffari, Hasan Karubi, Asadollah Bayat and Khalkhali, and presenting this as 'evidence' to the public in order to 'to destroy their image'. Charges of mishandling funds belonging to the Foundation of the Martyrs', headed by Mehdi Karubi, were also made public.[23] Mohtashami and Morteza Alviri were among many who were summoned to the special court for the clergy to respond to charges against them.[24]

In fact, the atmosphere soon became 'poisoned with rumors' which blemished the radicals' reputation.[25] Khalkhali claimed that the actions undertaken by the government would only 'breed dictatorship'.[26] Members of the *Jame'eh-ye Ruhaniyyat-e Mobarez* were accused of being 'monopolists' (*enhesar-talab*) who wished to eliminate (*hazf*) the loyal revolutionary elements[27] in order to 'create a one-track Majlis'.[28] The radicals also complained that they were not given a fair chance to compete for popular vote.[29] They accused the Council of Guardians of rejecting their candidates and criticized the pragmatists for their 'organized and directed' (*sazeman yafteh va hedayat shodeh*) campaign to eliminate their camp.[30] Mohtashami claimed that had there been no 'infringement [*takhallof*], fraud [*taqallob*], intimidation [*er'ab*] and fear [*vahshat*]', the 'true representatives' of the people could have been elected.[31] As events developed, the radicals began to lose support; their morale was weakened, their actions became less effective and they lost credibility amongst the people.

Consequently, they also failed to nominate a candidate to run against Rafsanjani in 1993. Following the presidential elections, however, the *Majma'-e Ruhaniyyun-e Mobarez* resumed its activities. This move was probably prompted by the large vote against Rafsanjani and the belief that the deteriorating economic situation (see Chapter 4), could be its 'ticket to success'.[32] However, while the *Majma'-e Ruhaniyyun-e*

Mobarez continued to admonish the government's deviation from the revolutionary path, the collective activities of the group declined significantly. Its members did not 'consider the conditions favorable' for such activities.[33] They acknowledged that their movement was 'not involved in political activities in the true sense of the word',[34] but pledged nevertheless to continue to follow Khomeini's true path. Consequently, the pragmatists tightened their control over the government, but did not succeed either in solving the numerous problems that faced the people, or in overcoming the strong conservative opposition to many of their policy preferences. (See below.)

The radicals and the pragmatists held contrasting attitudes to almost every issue, notably, how strictly one should adhere to the revolutionary dogma, and how the government should formulate its policies and define its priorities. Some experts have viewed the differences between the two camps as primarily differences of domestic policy,[35] arguing that Iran's foreign policy is generally seen through 'the prism of domestic issues'[36] and that 'foreign policy is now dependent' on 'internal crises'.[37] Others claim that 'perhaps in no other realm . . . is the impact of factionalism and ideology as apparent' as in foreign policy.[38] Yet, in Iran, as elsewhere, the two realms can hardly be separated[39]; in fact, the differences between the two factions encompass all spheres of life.

The pragmatists demanded that revolutionary slogans be toned down in favor of a policy of expediency. They considered economic rehabilitation to be the government's primary task, and advocated improved relations with other countries, including Western and even 'reactionary' Muslim states, as a means to boost the country's economy. On the whole their policies reflected Rafsanjani's orientation at the time.

Rafsanjani seemed fully aware of the difficulties that hindered the pursuit of 'pure' revolutionary dogma. He declared repeatedly, especially after the cease-fire with Iraq, that the days of early Islam had long passed and that 'today . . . we live under new conditions'.[40] In March 1991, he reiterated the need to adjust ideology to reality[41], stating that it was no longer necessary for Iran 'to speak fanatically' or 'chant impractical slogans'. Instead, the country required 'a prudent policy' that could be employed without being blamed for prompting 'terrorism [and] without anyone being able to call us fanatics'.[42] In his view, Iran could well safeguard the principles of the revolution, but 'only under the aegis of a rational (*ma'qul*) and logical (*manteqi*) policy'.[43] He added that he and his colleagues did not consider the revolution 'beyond the framework of reasonable methods'. We 'must not be radical' nor abandon principles and values, he warned in 1993. 'We are not dogmatic. We do not support absolutism.'[44]

The pragmatists did not abandon revolutionary goals, but once aware of existing constraints they sought more pragmatic means to achieve their basic aims. Their pragmatism in policy prevailed only to a certain degree and only in specific areas. Moreover, this pragmatism may be regarded as such only if judged by Iranian standards. In fact, their pragmatism occasionally followed the same ideological lines as the radicals, for example, their approach to the 1992 dispute over the Gulf islands. (See Chapter 7.) Furthermore, when radical and/or anti-US sentiments ran high, Rafsanjani himself adopted the more extreme rhetoric characteristic of the hard-liners (both conservatives and radicals). In May 1989, for example, after Khomeini issued his *fatwa* against Salman Rushdie, he called upon the Palestinians to retaliate against Israel by attacking Westerners and Western interests, thus demonstrating that pragmatism was not necessarily synonymous with moderation. (See Chapter 6.) Nevertheless, despite the occasional harsh statement, Rafsanjani was then more pragmatic than both the radical and the conservative factions, and demonstrated greater dogmatic flexibility and political maturity.

The more radical faction, for its part, believed then that Iran could solve its problems by strict adherence to dogma, regardless of changing realities. It criticized the government for its political impotence[45] and its failure to recognize the strength of the revolution. For example, Mohtashami admonished the government because it had abandoned the 'pure stances of the revolution' and failed to 'gauge the extent of the honor and prestige of the Iranian system'.[46] The radicals objected to improved ties with the West, especially the United States (see Chapter 6), but advocated an expansion of the revolution beyond Iran's borders. They emphasized that, unlike the government, they remained fully committed to the revolution[47] and that the weakening of their camp, and, in turn, the revolution, would serve US interests, claiming that it was only their strength that prevented the United States from reasserting its hegemony over Iran.[48]

The radicals' main criticism of the government revolved around its social and economic policy. The two camps differed in opinion regarding policy and priority. Just how vital was economic rehabilitation and how should one achieve social and economic goals? In the aftermath of the Iran–Iraq war, Rafsanjani, with the general support of Khamene'i, stressed the centrality of economic reconstruction and made it a key issue of his presidential campaign. It remained so during his term in office. In contrast, the radicals viewed the emphasis on economic reconstruction as a pretext to engage in pragmatic reforms and strengthen Iran's ties with the West. In 1989, Mohtashami listed Iran's main challenges 'in order of priority' as 'political, cultural, social and, finally, economic problems'. He added that only Iran's enemies stressed the primacy of economy, in order to divert attention away from the crucial issues of 'political and cultural independence'.[49] A year later, he stated that the 'proposition that we should first address ourselves to economic issues . . . is a mere fallacy. That is simply a pretext . . . to remove the core of the revolution'.[50] In 1993, he reiterated: 'If you set the economy as the principle and sacrifice everything at its altar, there would remain nothing by which you could be powerful, free, and independent.'[51]

The radicals therefore opposed many of the government's initiatives to boost the economy and used their influence to curtail government-proposed reconstruction programs. When they did stress economic goals, their emphasis was on the need to improve the lives of the underprivileged and advance Iran's economic independence. Towards that end, they called on the government to take control of foreign trade, limit land holdings, impose higher taxes on the rich, and reform Iran's economic structure and resource management. They also criticized the government's efforts to facilitate the return of expatriate professionals and to encourage investment by exiled capitalists, and railed against private enterprise, negotiating foreign loans and debt rescheduling. In their view the economic programs recommended by the World Bank and International Monetary Fund (IMF) were only designed to achieve their own 'evil imperialist' goals.[52] They often argued that these 'international economic institutions . . . operate within the framework of the West's hegemonic policies'. 'We will not be able to satisfy our hunger with the loaf of bread that the West will loan us.'[53] On this point then the domestic politics of the radicals was consistent with their foreign outlook. (See Part Two.)

The radicals considered ideology, economics and foreign relations to be inter-related, and therein lay their criticism. They criticized Rafsanjani's government for its indifference to the people's suffering and claimed that his ministers, mainly technocrats rather than ideologues, had never suffered 'poverty and hunger'.[54] The radicals accused the government of serving the interests of the arrogant (*mostakbarin*), both domestically (the wealthy) and abroad (the superpowers). Such accusations were meant not only to censure the government's failures, but also to stress its betrayal of a primary pledge of the revolution: to improve the situation of the *mostaz'afin*.

For their part, the pragmatists dismissed the radicals as only superficially (*zaheran*) concerned about the weak and accused them of raising such arguments as a means to gain popular support. They claimed that whereas the government persistently endeavored to solve problems, its adversaries only 'poke sticks through its spokes' and raised 'hollow slogans'. Thus, on the eve of the 1992 Majlis elections Rafsanjani reportedly called on the radicals to substitute reason (*sho'ur*) for empty slogans (*sho'ar*).[55] The radicals were accused of providing ammunition to Iran's enemies with their repeated criticism and accusations against the government.[56] Vice-President Habibi dismissed them as 'professional revolutionaries', expert only in raising untimely slogans. Vice-President Mohajerani called them 'dubious elements' who gamble with popular despair 'with pure opportunism, to present themselves [as] . . . an alternative to the present leadership'.[57]

The third faction, the conservatives, was much more influential than it appeared in the early 1990s, but less vocal in the domestic debate. Its members appeared pragmatic on some issues, such as the economy, but ideologically hard-line on others, such as cultural Islamization and ties with Islamist movements outside Iran. They advocated the strict application of Islamic law and social and cultural norms. They derived their strength from the clergy, *bazaar* circles, and the traditional middle class. They were very influential in revolutionary institutions, such as the Council of Guardians, the Council of Experts, the Foundation of the Dispossessed and Self-Sacrificers (*Bonyad-e Mostaz'afin va Janbazan*) and the Foundation of the Martyrs, and emerged as the dominant faction in the fourth Majlis (1992–96). Despite the pragmatists' electoral victory, the fourth Majlis was no more supportive of Rafsanjani's reforms than the third Majlis (1988–92). In many ways the conservatives blocked reform initiatives even more vigorously than the radical-dominated third Majlis. They also vehemently supported the campaign to counter the Western 'cultural onslaught'.[58]

In the early 1990s, members of this group strengthened their hold over some key positions. Nateq-Nuri replaced the then radical Karubi as Majlis Speaker, Mohammad Yazdi replaced Ardabili as head of the judiciary, 'Ali Mohammd Besharati became interior minister and 'Ali Larijani replaced Rafsanjani's brother as director of state radio and television. These changes occurred over and above the continued services of conservative officials who had previously held major posts, such as *Bonyad-e Mostaz'afin* director Mohsen Rafiqdust.[59] Thus, while many radicals were driven out from office, 'they were replaced by social conservatives who had little use for [pragmatist] reforms'.[60] In many ways, therefore, hard-liners set the terms of the debate. 'They take a "show me" attitude toward change, shifting the burden of proof to any party proposing change.' With decisions defaulting to the extremist line, this created a bias in favor of continued conservatism: pragmatism had to be defended, while generalized revolution-inspired activity did not. The government was thus 'tied to a hard line' from which any departure 'must be justified'.[61] One other factor that ensured strict adherence to revolutionary ideals was the support of the Supreme Leader. (See more on the dogma and strength of conservatives in Chapter 5 and about their weakness on the eve of the 2000 Majlis elections, see the Epilogue.)

The division between different ideological camps then cut much deeper into the political climate than the authorities admitted, but less than often depicted in the West. Yet, there was a genuine contest between factions over the fate of the revolution. The differences were great and the struggle for power forceful. President Rafsanjani managed to control the domestic rivalry and maintain a measure of pragmatism, but he failed to use his power to ease the burden on the people or even fully to advance his own professed policies. In due course, it became clear that the main struggle for power was between the pragmatists and the conservatives. In a sense, it was also a contest between revolutionary institutions and growing popular pressure for change. (See Chapters 4 and 5.) This became increasingly evident during Rafsanjani's second term as president (1993–97).

RAFSANJANI AND THE CHALLENGE OF THE PRESIDENCY

While the main challenge facing Khamene'i centered on the question of his religious credentials to serve as the *marja'*, that confronting President Rafsanjani was the heavy burden of governance. This involved two major problems. First, to assert Rafsanjani's primacy at the head of the revolutionary executive and policy-making. Secondly, to resolve Iran's mounting problems and meet popular expectations. However, it soon became clear that Rafsanjani did not have adequate authority to implement many of his preferred programs, nor sufficient means to meet growing expectations.

It should be recalled that in Iran, the head of state is the Supreme Leader, currently Khamene'i, and not the president, as Rafsanjani was at the time. The two men appeared to differ in opinion on many issues – at least as long as Rafsanjani was president – and often seemed to challenge one another for power. (See also Chapter 3.) Yet, at other times, they supported each other and united against their common opponents.

Over the years, relations between the two leaders fluctuated between cooperation and competition. They have long been close associates, publicly supporting each other and cooperating with one another: first in the struggle for revolution and later in their drive to consolidate the new regime.[62] However, the gap between the two men, discernible from the early days of the Islamic regime, became more apparent after Khomeini's death. In many cases each man identified with a different ideological trend in the mid-1990s. Rafsanjani identified with the more pragmatic faction whereas the conservatives were supported by Khamene'i. In the absence of Khomeini's omnipotent command, factional rivalries and the struggle between Rafsanjani and Khamene'i hindered decision-making although both men worked together to preserve the government's stability.

In the public sphere, Rafsanjani and Khamene'i supported one another. Khamene'i often mentioned their common struggle against the Shah in the late 1950's and recounted tales of their shared experiences in the opposition in the mid-1960s.[63] In 1984, Khamene'i described Rafsanjani as the most 'talented, wise, and brave' man he had ever known. 'I pray to Allah that he will take [days] off of my life and add them to the life of Rafsanjani', he said.[64] On the eve of the 1992 Majlis elections, Khamene'i praised him again and lent him important support in the Majlis elections. 'Which [previous] head of government was comparable to him?' he asked. 'Which of them was as trusted [by Khomeini . . . and] served the revolution as much as him?'[65] He described Rafsanjani as 'one of the Imam's most dedicated associates and a celebrated pillar of the revolution'.[66] Following Rafsanjani's 1993 re-election to presidency, Khamene'i described him once again as 'cherished [*mahbub*] by all' and 'worthy of the job',[67] and later added that the president has a 'shining personality' and is a 'strong arm and eloquent tongue of the revolution'.[68] For his part, Rafsanjani portrayed his relations with Khamene'i as the most fulfilling two people could possibly have. They had struggled together for some 40 years, stood alongside each other since the revolution, and were always in full agreement. 'I view him as the most appropriate individual to be leader of the state', he said. 'The rumors about rivalry and competition reflect only the jealousy of others.' Reviewing their long struggle, he said: 'Now as then, when I have no access to him, I feel weak. My faith in him increases as time goes by.'[69] Rafsanjani continued to express support for

Khamene'i following Khomeini's death and, again, following Khatami's election. (See Chapter 3.)

Their praise for one another notwithstanding, a measure of competition between Rafsanjani and Khamene'i has also been evident. This began when Khamene'i served as president (and secretary-general of the Islamic Republican Party in the early 1980s), and Rafsanjani as Speaker of the Majlis (1980–89), continuing until Khamene'i became Supreme Leader, in June 1989, and Rafsanjani President in August 1989. Their respective roles in government, i.e. Khamene'i in the capacity of Supreme Leader and Rafsanjani as President, often created an atmosphere of competition, in which Khamene'i had several advantages. Unlike Rafsanjani, he had no direct administrative responsibilities and was thus not identified personally with the failures of the executive branch of government (at least so long as he was not identified with a particular faction). Moreover, whereas Khamene'i's position was to be held during his lifetime (his removal being possible only in extreme circumstances), Rafsanjani's second (and last) term as president was due to end in 1997.

President Rafsanjani's policies were at the time often convoluted and inconsistent, but, nevertheless, generally pragmatic. Khamene'i's line was no less confusing and, although initially much less pragmatic, gradually grew more strictly conservative. Whether from sincere belief, sense of responsibility to the fate of the revolution, or the need to highlight his religious credentials, Khamene'i frequently voiced conservative views on topics such as culture and Islamism and, of course, the concept of *velayat-e faqih*. At other times, mindful of the need to solve the country's mounting problems, Khamene'i supported Rafsanjani's more pragmatic policy, mainly in the realm of the economic rehabilitation.

Despite their differences, both men were aware of their shared responsibility to serve the country and the revolution, and to overcome the challenges posed by existing realities and their common adversaries. Some observers have used the metaphor of the drivers of a tandem bicycle to characterize their rule in the early 1990s: they labored jointly to move Iran forward, but had to cooperate, coordinate, consult, or at least inform each other before any 'sharp turns' (i.e., critical decisions) were made.[70] Nevertheless, the question of which of them occupied the driver's seat remained open. Generally speaking, there appeared to be an informal division of labor between them, with Rafsanjani taking the lead on economic and foreign policy, and Khamene'i directing cultural issues and ties with Islamist movements. But such divisions are not always totally clear. Khamene'i had a role in formulating foreign relations, just as Rafsanjani had a say in Iran's attitude toward Islamist movements and culture. Moreover, foreign relations were not totally devoid of religious aspects in Islamic Iran as demonstrated by the *fatwa* against Rushdie and its impact on Iran's relations with European countries, mainly Britain, where Rushdie lives under government protection, or the issue of pilgrimage to Mecca and ties with Saudi Arabia. It appears that these two leading revolutionary figures often discussed critical, and perhaps less critical, issues before making decisions.

After Khomeini's death, Khamene'i still consulted Rafsanjani on many issues although he became 'far more assertive' in formulating policy and controlling key positions. Rafsanjani and his associates apparently dismissed Khamene'i's potential for becoming 'a magnet for the vested interests' threatened by government reforms. All in all, Khamene'i is often identified with the conservatives and occasionally supported their cause. After the 1993 presidential elections, Khamene'i began to exercise his political convictions even more forcefully, and to secure important posts for his proteges.[71] (See below.)

Rafsanjani, on the other hand, appeared to have lost support since first elected president in 1989. Although the 63 per cent share of the vote received in 1993 would have been considered a comfortable margin of victory in most Western countries, it was small by Iranian standards. In 1989, by comparison, Rafsanjani received 94.5 per cent of the vote, while Khamene'i won 95 per cent in 1981 and 88 per cent in 1985. In fact, Rafsanjani became president in 1993 with less support than Bani Sadr in 1980 (who gained 76 per cent) – thus securing the lowest percentage of votes ever for an Iranian president up until then. The results of the 1993 presidential election were thus considered 'a warning' indicating popular disenchantment with the domestic (mainly economic) situation and disappointment with the president himself.[72]

Economic rehabilitation was Rafsanjani's central theme in the 1989 elections. He promised a 'decade of reconstruction' that would extricate Iran from its economic difficulties after eight years of war with Iraq and improve the lives of the *mostaz'afin*. He described his first term (coinciding with the First Economic Plan) as 'successful' and 'satisfactory', and promised that the Second Economic Plan would further stabilize the economy.[73] He said that the distribution of wealth had been unfair under the rule of the Shah and during the Iran–Iraq war, but since the implementation of his five-year plan 'the wealth of the higher strata is gradually decreasing and the wealth of the lower strata [is] increasing'.[74] In making such statements, Rafsanjani also raised public expectations. On the fourteenth anniversary of the revolution in February 1993, just prior to the elections, he expressed the hope, that 'all the problems facing the country' would be solved by the twentieth anniversary of the revolution in February 1999 (see Chapter 4). Following his re-election, he reiterated his hopes and declared that at the end of the Second Economic Plan, Iran would be a developed (*abad*), independent (*mostaqel*), and advanced (*pishrafteh*) country, and would enjoy much greater social welfare (*moraffah*).[75] The public's expectations rose following the conclusion of the war with Iraq and were further encouraged by promises made by prominent officials, including Rafsanjani.

However, while people expected to see tangible results, many of the economic and foreign policy goals outlined at the beginning of Rafsanjani's presidency were either overlooked or unsuccessfully targeted. By his second term in office, 'Ali Akbar Rafsanjani, 'once nicknamed "Akbar Shah", an allusion to his king-like powers', was viewed by many as 'a lame duck with an uncertain future'.[76] Early in 1996, Majlis member Hojjat ul-Islam 'Ali Movahedi-Savoji declared Rafsanjani 'incompetent' and ill-suited for the presidency and called for the dismissal of his government.[77] Although Rafsanjani was not entirely to blame for the bleak economic situation in Iran, as head of the executive and with significant influence over other branches of government, he could not evade responsibility altogether.

Another area in which Rafsanjani (and, after him, Khatami) was at a disadvantage *vis-à-vis* Khamene'i was the latter's control over the armed forces and the security apparatus. Iran's military force is divided into two main organizations: the regular army, a professional organization with a national as well as revolutionary affinity; and the *Pasdaran-e Enqelab-e Islami* (Revolutionary Guards; or The Guardians of the Islamic Revolution), a paramilitary organization with a strong ideological affinity to the conservative leadership. Both are subordinate to the Supreme Leader. While the president is a prominent member of the Supreme National Security Council (SNSC) and serves as its chairman, the Supreme Leader wields actual control over the SNSC. Its decisions generally 'rise above internal divisions', yet, as a rule, it 'tends to adopt lowest common denominator positions that associate all groups with policy decisions',[78] which was an additional advantage for the ideological purists in the first two decades of revolutionary rule.

Khamene'i also strengthened his hold over the numerous extra-governmental bodies and revolutionary organizations including the *Bonyad-e Mostaz'afin* (a charitable foundation that had become a sizeable industrial conglomerate) and *Bonyad-e Shahid*. Added to this are the strong (and conservative) supreme court, the revolutionary courts, the network of Friday Imams, and a large segment of the media. These entities remain channels by which Khamene'i can exert his influence and control, and further weaken the president. (On the emergence of a pro-reform press, see Chapter 5 and the Epilogue.)

An immediate problem facing Rafsanjani was the constitutional limit on two consecutive presidential terms. Some of Rafsanjani's close associates sought to ease this constraint, whether because they thought his continued service was essential or out of concern that Majlis Speaker Nateq-Nuri would ultimately replace him. The vice-president for parliamentary affairs, Mohajerani, hinted at the outset of Rafsanjani's second term that 'there may be an amendment' to this constitutional provision.[79] He said that if this were the case, Rafsanjani would be the most qualified person for the office. However, the idea did not gain much support either because of the commitment of many Iranians to their constitution, or due to factional rivalries. Many political figures, conservatives and radicals, also resented the idea of amending the constitution to suit the interests of an individual or a particular faction. *Jomhuri-ye Islami* wrote that such an amendment would be tantamount to instituting 'permanent sovereignty', contrary to the interest of the revolution.[80] *Gozaresh-e Hafteh* described 'the spirit' of the proposed change as 'disagreeable and reproachable, for it lays the foundations for an authoritarian and autocratic government'. Unlike North Korea, Syria, and Libya, it wrote, Iran does not have 'a lifetime president'.[81] Nateq-Nuri rejected the amendment as wrong in principle, because it aimed to favor a particular person. Such an amendment, he feared, would signal that the revolution depended on a few individuals while in fact there were a number of qualified candidates[82] – including himself. Ultimately, the idea did not gain much support. Some viewed this as a sign of Rafsanjani's dwindling popularity at the time.

Since the revolution, Rafsanjani has proved to be a shrewd, sophisticated, and powerful politician. Despite declining support for the government, Rafsanjani remained personally popular. After eight years as Speaker of the Majlis and two terms as president, he survived the vicissitudes of political change and remained in the upper echelon of Iranian politics. (For his nomination as the head of the *shura-ye tashkhis-e maslahat* [the Expediency Council], with extended authorities, see Chapter 3). Then a pragmatist by Iranian standards, Rafsanjani seemed to have correctly diagnosed Iran's troubles and identified the proper remedy for them. Many Iranians believed that his approach was the correct way to extricate Iran from its economic difficulties. Yet these unfulfilled economic expectations also angered the Iranian public. Although he was undeniably faced with major factional challenges,

Rafsanjani did not demonstrate the necessary determination, or persistence to pursue his own preferred policies.

Thus, when Mohajerani and Sa'id Raja'i Khorasani called for dialogue with the United States in the early 1990s, Rafsanjani retreated. (See Chapter 6.) Similarly in August 1995, when the free market experiment came under attack, he bowed to criticism and replaced Vice-President and Director of the Planning and Budget Organization Mas'ud Rowghani-Zanjani – one of the architects of his economic program.[83] On other occasions, he often joined lines with the ideological purists and allowed himself to be carried away by waves of extremism. (See Chapter 6.) Referring to these occasional hard-line policies as attempts to appease domestic audiences, the *Echo of Iran* observed that Rafsanjani's 'kinder, gentler foreign policy' is not simply 'a hoax'. Rather, he and his aides know their preferred policies 'rile the radicals' and 'feel they must feed some "red meat" to keep them at bay'.[84] Whatever the cause, Rafsanjani proved more successful in convincing Khomeini to take bold steps when acting as speaker than in exercising sufficient authority to advance his reform programs while president.

After being first elected in 1989, Rafsanjani wasted a great deal of time and political effort in his first years in the presidency. Although the cease-fire with Iraq and the death of Khomeini created the kind of 'breaks in historic continuity' which often facilitate the acceptance of new ideas, he failed to produce significant policy changes when the time seemed ripe. Despite these missed opportunities, he still possessed one significant advantage – there seemed to be no better alternatives to the policies he advocated for economic rehabilitation. (This remained true until Khatami emerged and became the new symbol of hope.)

Aware that time was slipping by, Rafsanjani became more assertive in his attempt to secure power and to advance his preferred policies on the eve of the 1996 Majlis elections. This signaled a recognition that an immediate and decisive step was essential to promote his preferred policies and preserve his own standing, as well as to secure positions of influence and power for his close associates. This was also an important juncture at which to stress the centrality of economic reconstruction and bring new forces to the fore. Thus, eventually, the Majlis elections served as the prelude to the 1997 presidential elections both in terms of the major issues in public debate and existing political alignments.

The significance of the 1996 parliamentary elections lay in part in the important place given to the Majlis throughout Iran's parliamentary history (since the 1905–11 Constitutional Revolution), and the significance attached to the Majlis since the Islamic Revolution.

The Constitutional Revolution, which first introduced the concept of free elections, is still perceived by many Iranians as the greatest achievement in Iranian modern history (at least until the Islamic Revolution), and the main guarantor of civic rights and freedom. Revitalizing the parliamentary tradition was a major goal for many revolutionaries at the end of the Shah's rule. Khomeini, too, repeatedly stressed the importance of the Majlis, which he often described as the most significant institution in Iran (i.e., after that of the Supreme Leadership). With Khomeini's support, the Majlis consolidated itself as a prestigious and powerful institution. In addition to playing a vital role in shaping policy, Khomeini transferred to the Majlis the power to make decisions (or to give its seal to the decisions he had made; see above) on important issues, such as the impeachment of Bani Sadr and the release of the US hostages in 1981. Similarly, the Majlis held serious deliberations regarding law and general policy, and its members' speeches, often broadcast live on radio and television, were occasionally used to raise controversial issues and criticize the government. Majlis members also used their prerogatives to approve, or disqualify, ministerial nominees and to impeach ministers. The Majlis has thus established itself as a vital body that debates important issues and influences policy. The personal prestige that Rafsanjani lent to the Majlis (he served as its Speaker for the first two terms), added to its prominence.

Beyond the importance of the elections as a vehicle for political struggle, rival camps viewed the 1996 elections as a critical precursor to the forthcoming presidential election. Rafsanjani and his supporters sought to control the Majlis to advance more pragmatic policies (mainly in the realm of economics) and establish their supremacy; their conservative rivals wished to preserve their strength, uphold the true principles of the revolution and promote their candidate (Nateq-Nuri) for the presidency.

In the early stages of the campaign, the contest appeared similar to the previous rounds, at least as far as the domestic debate and the alliances were concerned. Months before the elections, *Salam*, the mouthpiece of the radicals, still maintained allegiance to this line and targeted Rafsanjani and the pragmatist policy. It dismissed Rafsanjani's earlier promise to allow elections free of government interference as a 'drug for a dead patient'.[85] His instructions, the newspaper contended, were either too late or merely 'smoke in the eyes'. The ministry of interior had already appointed key provincial officials (e.g., mayors, district governors, governor-generals) to secure their victory – a measure taken, according to *Salam*, under pressure from the 'right wing' (i.e., the conservatives) to eliminate the 'left' (i.e., the radicals). Kho'iniha, a prominent member of the group, censured as late as January 1996, the 'ruling masters' of Tehran as vociferous politicians who strive to expand their power through fraud and mischief.[86] Mohtashami was again confident that in 'a free competition, the radical revolutionaries will win'.[87] As events developed, however, the contest emerged not between the groups that had competed in 1992 (*Jame'eh-ye Ruhaniyyat-e Mobarez* and *Majma'-e Ruhaniyyun-e Mobarez*), but essentially between ideological purists (conservatives) on the one hand, and pragmatist and technocrats on the other. By then, the leading figures of the *Majma'-e Ruhaniyyun-e Mobarez* had gradually moved to support the more pragmatic camp.

Beyond this, the most important political development was the January 1996 decision, made by 16 of the president's close aides, to compile a list of candidates to compete in the elections. They called for support for the hero of reconstruction, Rafsanjani, as the best way to advance the revolutionary goals and to secure Iran's progress. Among the signatories were vice-presidents Mohajerani and Reza Amirollahi, ministers Isma'il Shushtari (Justice), Mohammad 'Ali Najafi (Education), Morteza Mohammad Khan (Economy), Gholamreza Foruzesh (Construction), 'Isa Kalantari (Agriculture), Akbar Turkan (Transportation), Mohammad Gharazi (Communication), Gholamreza Shafe'i (Cooperatives) and Rafsanjani's brother Mohammad Hashemi.[88] The group became known as the *Kargozaran-e Sazandegi-ye Iran,* or the Executives of Iran's Construction. Following Khamene'i's instructions, to acting ministers not to run for seats in the legislature, the group was led by four vice-presidents, Central Bank Governor Nurbakhsh, and the popular Mayor of Tehran, Gholamhosein Karbaschi. The *Kargozaran,* often referred to as the G-6 or the 'modern right', placed economic reconstruction at the top of its political agenda and stressed the importance of administrative expertise for members of the Majlis and government ministers. Their slogans combined *'ezzat-e Islami* (Islamic glory), *tadavom-e sazandegi* (enduring reconstruction) and *Iran-e abad* (developed Iran).[89] The newspapers *Hamshahri, Bahman* and *Iran* were the main organs that supported this group, among others.

Both camps, pragmatists and conservatives, perceived the contest as a struggle for the fate of the revolution, the destiny of the state, and their own role therein, and they competed fiercely for support.

The leading figure in the *Jame'eh-ye Ruhaniyyat-e Mobarez*, the group which held the majority of seats in the outgoing Majlis, was Majlis Speaker Nateq-Nuri. Other prominent figures included Mohammad

Javad Larijani, Ayatollah Mohammad Reza Mahdavi-Kani, Ahmad Tavakkoli, Mohammad Yazdi, Mohammad Reza Bahonar, Mohammad 'Ali Movahedi-Kermani and Hasan Ruhani, who also enjoyed the support of the main revolutionary organizations. They adopted the old social justice jargon and focused their attention on preserving Islamic conduct and preventing the Western 'cultural onslaught' (*tahajom-e farhangi*). They were often referred to as the 'traditional right'. *Resalat* was their primary mouthpiece with *Jomhuri-ye Islami* and *Kayhan* also lending them support. Khamene'i backed this group.

The conservatives, alarmed by the new initiative, criticized the formation of the *Kargozaran* list as an illegal intrusion by the executive branch into the legislature's affairs.[90] Majlis member Maryam Behruzi, one of the leaders of the socio-religious organization *Jame'eh-ye Zaynab*, described the move as divisive and accused the *Kargozaran* of seeking only to safeguard its own position in the next government.[91] Raja'i Khorasani, by contrast, welcomed the move as a means of creating a healthy atmosphere of competition.[92] *Salam* now accused the *Jame'eh-ye Ruhaniyyat-e Mobarez* of rejecting any alternative line.[93] Although Khamene'i did not yield to pressure to denounce the *Kargozaran* he advised against moves that would lead to tension and divisions.[94] He approved the formation of the new list, but prohibited ministers from subscribing to it. Rafsanjani vowed to observe neutrality and refrain from supporting any candidate or group,[95] but given the platform maintained by the *Kargozaran,* as well as the personalities involved in it, it was clear that they generally supported the line taken by Rafsanjani and that he, too, sanctioned their group. The *Majma'-e Ruhaniyyun-e Mobarez* did not run as an electoral list, but generally supported the candidates of the *Kargozaran*.

Ironically, *Jame'eh-ye Ruhaniyyat-e Mobarez* attacked the *Kargozaran* with the same rhetoric that the *Majma'-e Ruhaniyyun-e Mobarez* had used against the *Jame'eh-ye Ruhaniyyat-e Mobarez* themselves in 1992 – a major change of approach and alignments, from one election to another.

The conservatives' campaign focused on calls that favored values over reconstruction and revolution-inspired zeal over expertise. Thus, Nateq-Nuri reminded Rafsanjani that building bridges and paving highways had nothing to do with 'preserving revolutionary values'. If that were the yardstick by which Islamic governments were measured, he said, Malaysia would be a better model for an Islamic State.[96] The conservatives' election slogans pledged to 'follow the line of the Imam [Khomeini], obey the leadership [Khamene'i], and support Hashemi

[Rafsanjani]'.[97] They called on the public to vote only for those 'who do not weaken the pillars of Islamic thought under the pretext of liberalism and freedom'. They portrayed the *Kargozaran* as liberals, seeking Western-style development and soft Islamic principles. 'Not only do the new liberals not resist the hegemony of America', they charged, 'they even think about negotiations and relations with the Great Satan'.[98]

Another list of rival candidates was the *E'telaf-e Goruhha-ye Khatt-e Imam* (Coalition of Groups Aligned with the Imam's Line) which supported candidates who are 'brave, faithful, and follow the line of the Imam'.[99] This included some of the more hard-line groups such as *Jam'iyyat-e Defa' az Arzeshha-ye Enqelab* (Association for the Defense of Revolutionary Values), led by Reyshahri, which emphasized cultural values and social justice.[100] There was also the *Ansar-e Hezbollah* (Champions of the Hezbollah), an extremist revolutionary faction close to the Revolutionary Guard and the *Basij*, whose most prominent spokesmen included Hosein Allahkaram, Ayatollah Jannati, and Mehdi Nasiri. Their views were reflected in the newspapers *Kayhan* and *Sobh*. Other groups included the *Mojahedin-e Enqelab-e Islami* (Mojahedin of the Islamic Revolution), led by Behzad Nabavi, whose views were expressed primarily by *'Asr-e Ma*; the *Anjoman-e Mohandesin-e Enqelab-e Islami* (Association of the Engineers of the Islamic Revolution), and several other associations comprising university professors, students, and teachers.[101]

No fewer than 2,946 candidates competed in the first round of elections held on 8 March 1996, for 270 Majlis seats (including 566 candidates in Tehran who vied for 30 seats). Figures for previous elections show that 2,200 candidates ran in 1992, 1,600 in 1988, 1,584 in 1984, and approximately 2,000 in 1980. In the 1996 elections 139 candidates across the country secured enough votes in the first round to win seats (compared with 135 in 1992, 179 in 1988, 123 in 1984, and 97 in 1980). In Tehran only two people secured seats in the first round – Nateq-Nuri and Rafsanjani's daughter, Fa'ezeh Hashemi (compared with two in 1992 and half of the seats in each of the earlier campaigns). Although neither of the main trends seemed to have secured an absolute majority in the new Majlis, and while the pragmatists (and the *Kargozaram*) managed to gain significant support (see below), the conservatives emerged as the more dominant faction.[102]

The elections were held on schedule and the identity of candidates from their respective lists attests to the degree to which clerics had consolidated their rule since the first elections in 1980. The campaign was restricted to groups which, despite their differences, all claimed to be 'followers of the Imam's line'. As in 1992, the Council of Guardians exercised its right to 'supervise' the elections by disqualifying some 40 per cent of the roughly 5,000 candidates – including about 40 members of the outgoing Majlis.[103] This mass disqualification effectively precluded genuine change. Thus, rather than national elections, some observers noted, they were elections only within one group.[104] Given these realities, some even wondered whether there was any need for elections at all as the seats had already been designated.[105]

Given the legacy of revolutionary politics and previous elections, it was not easy to draw definite conclusions about the results. From the inception of the *Jame'eh-ye Ruhaniyyat-e Mobarez* in 1981, its members (or those allied with it) controlled the Majlis. Prior to the 1988 elections, its more radical members broke away to form the *Majma'-e Ruhaniyyun-e Mobarez* and gained substantial influence in the Majlis. In 1992, the *Jame'eh-ye Ruhaniyyat-e Mobarez,* which at the time ran under a slogan of 'defense of Hashemi' (*hemayat az Hashemi*), won a decisive victory. Over time, however, the Majlis has taken a more conservative course. Many of those aligned with Rafsanjani in 1996 were essentially the same as those who competed against 'his' list in 1992. Moreover, many candidates appeared on several electoral lists and were supported by various (even competing) groups. For example, on the Tehran lists in the first round in 1996, ten candidates appeared on both the *Jame'eh-ye Ruhaniyyat-e Mobarez* and *Kargozaran* lists, eight of them also appeared on the *Jam'iyyat-e Defa' az Arzeshha-ye Enqelab* list formed by Reyshahri. (Altogether the latter shared 11 candidates with the *Jame'eh-ye Ruhaniyyat-e Mobarez* and ten with the *Kargozaran.*) Moreover, many of the winners were notable figures who ran in their own constituencies and who eventually received support regardless of the list with which they were affiliated. There were, in fact, many new faces in the fifth Majlis (some 156 out of the total 270).[106] Many of those elected in the provinces were unknown, 'unopened melons' as some observers put it, and it was not clear what line they would ultimately take.

Similarly it was difficult to weigh the success of the *Kargozaran*. Given that it had joined the race at a very late stage in the election campaign, its achievements may be considered a great success. Indeed, Rafsanjani had been hesitant to throw his full weight behind the new group, while Khamene'i preserved some equilibrium by allowing it to contest the election at the same time as preventing ministers from officially aligning themselves with it.

Although Khomeini delegated to the Majlis the authority for major decisions, it was not the most important authority in shaping policy. In the past its role in decision-making was usually subordinate to that of Supreme Leader Khomeini who often called on the Majlis to give his actions its seal. This does not mean, however, that the Majlis is an insignificant institution in Iran. In fact, compared with other parliaments in the region, it shows strength and vitality and a greater degree of independence. Nevertheless major policy decisions are still made outside the Majlis, and the main obstacles to change (e.g., in attitudes toward cultural Islamization or relations with the West) resolved within a range of revolutionary institutions, of which the Majlis is only one. These factors ultimately set the stage for a continued struggle to establish control over issues of public debate and, more generally, to determine the shape of politics of revolutionary Iran.

Generally speaking, however, the elections were a 'microcosm of pending changes in relations between the clergy and the state, between elected and non-elected organs within the state, and between moderation and extremism'. It is clear that the elections changed Iran's internal 'political landscape' and suggested 'hints [of] a potential change' in its policy'.[107] The results of the campaign also reflected the popular mood at the time: disillusionment with empty slogans and hopes for genuine improvement in the conditions of life. The Majlis elections confirmed, once again, the urge to address central issues such as social and economic problems and the lack of personal freedoms that enraged growing segments of the population. (See Chapters 4 and 5.) The importance assumed by these problems, the significant shift in domestic alignments and the emergence of forces upholding the need for change, were significant facets of the election campaign. Thus, in many ways, the 1996 Majlis elections signaled the prelude to the presidential contest that brought Khatami to power.

Notes

1. This chapter discusses the differences among the revolutionaries themselves. Views of those opposing the Islamic system altogether, including those who had initially supported the Islamic Revolution, are not discussed here.
2. *Echo of Iran*, no. 41 (June 1991), p. 17.
3. See, for example, *Salam*, 26 September and, similarly, ibid., 3 October – DR, 7 October 1993; *Jomhuri-ye Islami*, 27 September 1993 – DR, 6 October 1993.
4. For some earlier examples of differences within the ruling system and the Islamic Republican Party, see Menashri, *Decade of War and Revolution*, pp. 115–16, 147–50, 174–5, 219–25, 268–71, 345–7, 378–84.

5. *Der Spiegel*, 25 March 1991. The Rafsanjani interview is also quoted in *Ettela'at*, 27 March 1991.

6. *Salam*, 17 March 1991 – DR, 8 April 1991.

7. *Resalat*, 1 October 1990 – DR, 18 October 1990. Majlis member Eliyas Hazrati characterized the decision as a conspiracy 'by one specific faction' to extermi-nate the others; see IRNA, 2 October 1990 – DR, 3 October 1990.

8. *Al-Majallah*, 18 March 1992.

9. *Kayhan* (Tehran), 9 April 1984; see also *MECS* 1983–84, pp. 433–4. For more on their competition in 1988, see *MECS* 1988, pp. 491–2.

10. As quoted in *Abrar*, 26 April, and *Salam*, 27 April 1992.

11. Ali Banuazizi, 'Iran's Revolutionary Impasse: Political Factionalism and Societal Resistance', *Middle East Report*, 24/191 (November–December 1994), p. 4. See also Ali Banuazizi, 'Faltering Legitimacy: The Ruling Clerics and Civil Society in Contemporary Iran', *International Journal of Politics, Culture, and Society*, 4/4 (1995), pp. 563–78.

12. *Salam* (31 March 1992) wrote that, in general, those disqualified all belonged to the same political trend.

13. *Salam*, 3 April 1992.

14. See, for example, Mohtashami's arguments quoted in *Jahan-e Islam – Echo of Iran*, October 1991, p. 12.

15. *Salam*, 16 February 1992; *New York Times*, 23 March 1992.

16. *New York Times*, 23 March 1992. See also *Salam*, 16 February 1992.

17. *Salam*, 5 April 1992.

18. *Salam*, 7 and 20 April 1992.

19. IRNA, 7 April 1992 – DR, 9 April 1992.

20. See, for example, words of Asadollah Bayat quoted in *Abrar*, 5 December 1991.

21. Radio Tehran, 27 March – DR, 30 March 1992; *Ettala'at*, 28 March 1992.

22. According to *Salam* (14 January 1992), the *Jame'eh-ye Ruhaniyyat-e Mobarez* sent 'secret bulletins' to the Jum'ah imams which included accusations 'against individuals and social and political groups'.

23. *Echo of Iran*, 40 (May 1991), pp. 12, 14, 19.

24. For such practices see *Salam*, 21 September 1991.

25. *Salam*, 21April 1992.

26. Tehran TV, 2 June 1991 – *Echo of Iran*, 41 (June 1991), p. 12.

27. *Salam*, 30 April 1992.

28. See their complaint to Khamene'i in *Salam*, 29 March 1992.

29. *Salam*, 15 April 1992.

30. See, for example, articles in *Salam*, 21 April 1992.

31. *Salam*, 3 May 1992.

32. *Iran Times*, 5 November 1993.

33. *Salam*, 21 October – DR, 1 November 1993.

34. Mohtashami, explaining their failure to put forward a candidate in the 1993 presidential elections, in *Salam*, 16 and 17 May 1993; see also DR, 28 May 1993.

35. Patrick Clawson, *Business as Usual? Western Policy Options Toward Iran* (Washington, DC: American Jewish Congress, 1995), pp. 10, 15. But Clawson is aware that 'the positions that each side takes on domestic issues also have foreign policy implications', see pp. 10–11.

36. Patrick Clawson, 'Alternative Foreign Policy Views among the Iranian Policy Elite', in Clawson (ed.), *Iran's Strategic Intentions*, pp. 29, 31.
37. Lamote, 'Iran's Foreign Policy', pp. 5, 17.
38. Banuazizi, 'Iran's Revolutionary Impasse', pp. 4–5.
39. Farhad Kazemi, 'All Politics is Local', in Clawson (ed.), *Iran's Strategic Intentions*, pp. 49–54.
40. Radio Tehran, 25 September – SWB, 27 September 1988.
41. Interview in *Der Spiegel,* 25 March 1991. Also quoted in *Ettela'at,* 27 March 1991, and *DR,* 26 March 1991.
42. Radio Tehran, 20 December – DR, 23 December 1991. It should be noted that these phrases were deleted from the otherwise lengthy reports of his Friday sermon in *Kayhan, Ettela'at,* and *Abrar.* See also *MECS* 1991, p. 385.
43. Radio Tehran, 23 August 1992 – DR, 24 August 1992.
44. Interview with Beirut TV, 28 November 1993 – DR, 3 December 1993.
45. *Jahan-e Islam*, 24 May 1993 – DR, 4 June 1993; *Iran News*, 9 February 1995 – DR, 17 February 1995.
46. *Jahan-e Islam*, 24 May 1993 – DR, 4 June 1993. See also Introduction to Part II.
47. For a typical argument of this type see *Salam*, 14 March 1992.
48. *Al-Sharq al-Awsat*, 23 March 1992.
49. *Ettela'at*, 12 December 1989. Similarly, see his interview in *Kayhan* (Tehran), 21 December 1989.
50. IRNA, 13 November 1990 – *SWB*, 15 November 1990.
51. Clawson, *Business as Usual?*, p. 12.
52. *Salam*, 5 January 1993; *Echo of Iran*, no. 60 (January 1993), p. 4.
53. *Salam*, 13 October 1993 – DR, 25 October 1993.
54. *Bayan*, January–February 1992 – DR, 27 February 1992. For Rafsanjani's governments as formed in 1989 and 1993, see, respectively, Menashri, 'Iran' in *MECS* 1989, pp. 356–9 and *MECS* 1993, p. 325.
55. *Kayhan* (London), 16 April 1992.
56. See, for example, Rafsanjani's Friday sermon in *Jomhuri-ye Islami,* 18 April 1992.
57. *Al-Majallah*, 13 November 1991.
58. Banuazizi, 'Iran's Revolutionary Impasse', p. 5.
59. Ibid.
60. *Los Angeles Times,* 7 February 1994.
61. Shahram Chubin, *Iran's National Security Policy: Capabilities, Intentions, and Impact* (Washington, DC: Carnegie Endowment, 1994), pp. 68, 71.
62. For their relations in the 1980s, see Menashri, *A Decade of War and Revolution*, pp. 264, 307–9, 350–2.
63. *Jomhuri-ye Islami,* 26 September 1984. See also his statements quoted in Menashri, *Decade of War and Revolution*, pp. 264, 307, 350–2.
64. *Jomhuri-ye Islami,* 24 November 1984.
65. *Ettela'at*, 28 March 1992; Radio Tehran, 27 March 1992 – DR, 30 March 1992. Earlier he denounced some of Rafsanjani's rivals as financially, morally, or ideologically corrupt, and accused them of weakening the system by 'poking sticks through the government's spokes'. See *Ettela'at*, 23 February 1992; *Echo of Iran*, no. 49 (February 1992), p. 13.

66. *Salam, Abrar,* and *Jomhuri-ye Islami,* 30 May 1992.
67. *Abrar, Jomhuri-ye Islami,* and *Ettela'at,* 17 June 1993.
68. IRNA, 3 August 1993 ; Radio Tehran, 3 August 1993 – DR, 3 August 1993; *Ettela'at,* 4 August 1993; *Iran Times,* 13 August 1993.
69. *Jomhuri-ye Islami,* 29 December 1994.
70. See, for example, Ramazani, 'Iran's Foreign Policy', p. 394.
71. Hashim, *Crisis of the Iranian State,* p. 18; Bakhash, *Iran: Crisis of Legitimacy,* pp. 113–14; and Mottahedeh, Islamic Movement, p. 112.
72. Tehran TV, 26 May 1993 – DR, 28 May 1993; *Tehran Times,* 14 June 1993; and *Jomhuri-ye Islami,* 14 June 1993 – DR, 29 June 1993.
73. See, for example, his broadcast on Radio Tehran, 3 June 1993 – DR, 4 June 1993.
74. Radio Tehran, 5 February 1993 – DR, 8 February 1993. See also his 1993 New Year's speech on Tehran TV, 20 March 1993 – DR, 22 March 1993.
75. *Salam,* 15 June 1993. See also *Kayhan* (Tehran), 17 June 1993.
76. *Los Angeles Times,* 13 December 1994.
77. *Salam,* 24 January 1996.
78. Chubin, *Iran's National Security Policy,* pp. 68, 70. See also, Beaver Paul and Rathmell Andrew (eds), *Jane's Sentinal – Security Assessment – The Gulf States* (London, Jane's Information Group, 1996).
79. *Iran News,* 30 October 1994 – DR, 4 November 1994. Alternatively, Mohajerani said, Rafsanjani could return to his previous post as speaker; see *Al-Majallah,* 6 November 1994; *Resalat,* 28 November 1995.
80. *Jomhuri-ye Islami,* 15 November 1994.
81. *Los Angeles Times,* 13 December 1994.
82. *Salam,* 28 January 1995. *Jahan-e Islam,* 24 November 1994 – DR, 7 December 1994, warned that such an amendment could lead to further deviation in the future from the spirit and principles of the constitution.
83. Agence France Presse, 12 August 1995 – DR, 15 August 1995.
84. *Echo of Iran,* 41 (June 1991), p. 17.
85. *Salam,* 28 September 1995.
86. *Salam,* 21 January 1996.
87. *Famiglia Cristiana* (Milan), 15 October 1995 – DR, 16 October 1995.
88. *Ettela'at* and *Salam,* 18 January 1996; *Resalat,* 20 January 1996.
89. *Abrar,* 19 February 1996.
90. *Resalat,* 22–24 and 29 January 1996.
91. *Resalat,* 22 January 1996.
92. *Kayhan* (Tehran), 24 January 1996.
93. *Salam,* 24 January 1996.
94. *Resalat,* 29 January 1996.
95. *Abrar,* 22 January 1996.
96. *Jomhuri-ye Islami* and *Kayhan* (Tehran), 1 May 1996.
97. *Sobh,* 19 February; *Resalat,* 29 February 1996.
98. *Iran,* 10 April. See also SWB, 15 April 1996.
99. *Salam,* 15 April 1996.
100. Reyshahri defended its creation by saying that political organizations were essential for the revolution and the regime, and did not represent division or the pursuit of power. He accused those stressing reconstruction over social

justice of imitating the West; see *Kayhan* (Tehran), 19 February and 6 March 1996.

101. *Resalat*, 29 February 1996.
102. The number of clerics in the Majlis has been gradually declining. There were roughly 50 in the fifth Majlis, compared with 128 in the first, 127 in the second, 81 in the third, and 36 in the fourth. Over the same period, the number of members with modern higher education has risen significantly; see *Jomhuri-ye Islami*, 27 May 1992, and 21 April 1996. For an examination of the Majlis since 1980, see: Bahman Baktiari, *Parliamentary Politics in Revolutionary Iran: The Institutionalization of Factional Politics* (Miami, FL: University of Florida Press, 1996).
103. Such a massive disqualification begs the question of whether the screening committee had failed to detect their lack of qualifications when they were first nominated, or whether candidates had behaved unbecomingly, or in a 'politically incorrect' fashion while acting as members of the Majlis. Such questions were raised by some observers during the Majlis elections in 1992 and 1996.
104. *Salam*, 21 December 1995.
105. *Salam*, 11 October 1995.
106. *Akhbar*, 14 March 1996 – DR, 19 March 1996; IRNA, 11 March 1996; *Abrar*, 22 April 1996. Only 12 members served in the Majlis from 1980 until 1992, less than ten until 1996.
107. *Christian Science Monitor*, 16 April 1996.

3

Khatami's Emergence

The landslide victory won by Hojjat ul-Islam Mohammad Khatami in the presidential elections of 23 May 1997 was an impressive show of strength for the newly elected president and a signal of popular demand for reform. At the same time, however, major obstacles continued to hinder significant transformation. Three years after the elections, with domestic rifts widening, Iranian policy continues to be subject to contradictory pressures.

The facts that the elections were held on schedule and that contending candidates remained loyal to basic revolutionary tenets attested to a measure of continuity. While the elections marked a widespread desire for change, they were still conducted essentially within the framework of the post-1979 Islamic system. Yet, Khatami's victory signaled growing disillusionment and disenchantment and a pressing urge to resolve the numerous difficulties, mainly those facing the underprivileged class, whose expectations still remained largely unfulfilled. It was, therefore, also a sign of protest – against societal conditions, the ruling conservative elite and rigid official dogma – as well as a yearning for greater pragmatism and liberalization and a more decisive role for Iran's emerging civil society, of which Khatami had become the symbol. Yet, in the three years since his election there have been no dramatic policy shifts or tangible improvements in living conditions. Although some subtle statements have been made and much greater political openness has become visible, the actual results were far short of meeting the fast-growing expectations.

The domestic contest over the direction of Iran's revolutionary course continued – even intensified – so that policy directions remained far from clear. At this stage, the contest was primarily between two main trends – one generally depicted as 'pragmatic', 'reformist' (*eslah-talab*) or 'traditional left' (*chap-e sonnati*), which was supported by groups hitherto described as 'modern right'; and the other 'conservative', 'ideological purists', or 'the traditional right' (*rast-e sonnati*), which were also supported by the groups known as the 'radical right' (*raste-e efrai*). Curiously, many of those usually depicted as radicals in the early 1990s now supported reformism and openness and the ideas of civil society. Beneath the surface, however, more basic divisions sharpened – between those fully committed to the basic doctrine of the ruling system and those challenging it, either for reasons of principle or due to its perceived impracticality. There were also growing signs of a deeper divide between the ruling establishment and the various tendencies within it, and emerging civil society, particularly the youth, women, segments of the press and intellectuals. Domestic rivalries entered a new phase, in which the urge for pragmatism and dogmatic flexibility conflicted with devotion to the original ideals of the Islamic Revolution.

The short time that has elapsed since Khatami's election and the fierce domestic rifts do not allow us to determine with any certainty the exact course that the revolution is taking, the pace and areas of transformation or the relative power of competing groups. Moreover, the extent of the new president's power to lead Iran in an entirely new direction also remains largely unclear. With these caveats in mind, this chapter will seek to analyze the developments in Khatami's initial steps in the presidency, weighing the achievements and the difficulties he faced and exploring, as far as possible, Iran's general policy directions and the factors influencing the balance of power after two decades of the Islamic rule. (See also Chapter 5 and the Epilogue.)

KHATAMI: THE PEOPLE'S CHOICE

Until shortly before polling day, the presidential contest did not appear to be so different from the previous elections under the Islamic Republic. Majlis Speaker Hojjat ul-Islam 'Ali Akbar Nateq-Nuri appeared confident of his victory – having long been groomed for the post by the ruling conservative establishment, and enjoyed the implicit backing of Supreme Leader Khamene'i. He had also secured the support of some of the main revolutionary institutions and significant organizations, including the Council of Guardians, the Council of Experts, and the revolutionary *bonyads*, as well as many Friday prayer leaders and the religio-political group, the *Jame'eh-ye Ruhaniyyat-e Mobarez*. As polling day approached, however, popular support for Khatami gathered momentum, with the two main candidates being regarded as representative of two entirely different trends. Khatami became the symbol of an establishment outsider, who would promote reform and lead Iran to greater openness. He represented the hope for a brighter future with the

capacity to 'shake things up'. Nateq-Nuri, on the other hand, turned
into a symbol of the status quo and conservatism. He thus represented
the ruling establishment, which in the eyes of many, had failed to fulfill
the initial pledges of the revolution.[1] Although far from meeting the
Western definition of free elections, the latest presidential elections
seemed to be a genuine contest, offering a real choice.

Khatami's past record, his election program and his pragmatic
statements heightened expectations, at home as well as abroad, of a
dramatic policy change. Khatami was not an 'average mullah', a
Western observer typically noted, but a president 'with one foot in
Western civilization'.[2] He was not 'the best representative of the ruling
religious institution', one newspaper wrote, but 'a completely different
prototype' of leader, who diverged 'to a large extent' from the world-
view governing the ruling system. Others observed that, above all
Khatami 'is an intellectual'; this is his main trait, it was often noted.[3]
Some referred to him as 'Ayatollah Gorbachev'.[4] Others, more soberly,
viewed him as a 'peaceful evolutionist', aiming to lead the way to an
'Iranian-style perestroika'.[5]

Khatami (b. 1943), combined traditional education (at the Islamic
centers in Qom and Isfahan), and modern schooling (at the universities
of Isfahan and Tehran). He had been active in the Islamic opposition to
the Shah's regime, and in 1978 was assigned to head the Islamic Center
in Hamburg. He served as a member of the first Islamic Majlis, was
named Khomeini's representative and head of the *Kayhan* group of
newspapers, and in 1982 was appointed minister of culture and Islamic
guidance, a post he held until 1992, when he was forced to resign in
light of fierce conservative opposition. Speaking a number of foreign
languages, he is also familiar with Western literature and political
thought, and enjoys a reputation for personal probity. His decade-long
tenure as minister of Islamic guidance was widely viewed as a relatively
'golden age' for Iranian culture and intellectual pursuits.[6] At the same
time he 'encouraged Iranian filmmakers to flourish, eased constraints on
the content of books and magazines, and expanded the list of foreign
publications to enter the country'.[7] Following his forced resignation
from the government he headed Iran's National Library, a period of
'exile' during which he maintained close contact with intellectuals and
artists and gave them his support. This also helped to cultivate his image
as a symbol of change and hope for reform.

By Iranian standards Khatami is a liberal. He signaled relative
openness, advocating greater political and social freedom, political flexibility, a broader education for young people, women's rights, greater

emphasis on social welfare, the relaxation of cultural Islamization and economic rehabilitation. He 'is not someone who considers democracy alien to Islam'. In fact, he 'thinks it's right there, but the Muslims have missed it', a foreign commentator observed.[8] This also implied a more pragmatic attitude towards the outside world, as he regarded foreign influences as unavoidable, even advantageous, provided Iran preserved its identity and independence. Resigning from his ministerial post in 1992, he warned that if the revolutionary path were not modified, Iran would see 'the beginning of a dangerous trend'.[9] He feared that the regime's repressive tendencies would fan out from Iran's borders, discouraging Islamists elsewhere and even endangering Islam.[10] His aim was not to abandon the revolutionary path but to return it to its 'appropriate track', by honoring dogma and simultaneously improving people's living conditions, thereby serving, and possibly saving the revolution.

Much of his world view was reflected in his writings and speeches prior to the election.[11] In his view, the 'gravest problems' facing the world of Islam were that 'our culture' (*thaqafatuna*) belonged 'to a civilization that has long passed away', while Muslims live today under the dominant impact of Western civilization, with which they have to comply.[12] For centuries Islam had not been engaged in the actual running of the state;[13] it therefore lacked the essential experience for the challenge, he believed. While recommending selective borrowing from the West, the birthplace of a new and powerful civilization,[14] he was aware that this necessitated a reappraisal of Muslims' own sources, including the Qur'an and the Sunna – taking present needs into account when interpreting them.[15] Such an approach paralleled Islamic reformist thought elsewhere in the world of Islam in modern times, as in Egypt at the end of the nineteenth century. They were also reminiscent of views held by the late Ayatollah Shari'atmadari (see Chapter 1), and Khomeini's first prime minister, Mehdi Bazargan – all of whom were vigorously rejected by the conservative establishment.

Khatami reiterated such views during his campaign, though somewhat less explicitly – stressing in equal measure his revolutionary credentials and dogmatic devotion to the principles of the republic.

Basing his campaign on edicts issued by Ayatollah Khomeini, Khatami highlighted the centrality of state interests (*maslahat*) in shaping politics. According to Khomeini, he declared, proper governance is one of the 'primary commands' of religion. This 'system and this order have one important requisite', he said – *maslahat*, 'the best interests', of Islam, of Iran and of the people.[16] The accent on 'interest' and 'proper governance' justified some dogmatic deviation. This, in a nutshell, was Khatami's basic conception, though conceivably with much greater doctrinal flexibility than envisioned by Khomeini. Khatami's stricture that 'chanting slogans' could not secure Iran's revolutionary goals was also reminiscent of President Rafsanjani's challenge in 1992 to his rivals (some of whom now supported Khatami), to substitute reason for slogans. (See Chapter 2.) Khatami reiterated the need to abandon empty rhetoric and replace it with practical solutions. In his view, demonstrating economic and political viability, for example, would advance Iran's revolutionary values far more than impractical slogans.[17] He also pleaded for dialogue with Western civilization and greater dogmatic flexibility while dealing with the outside world. (See Part Two.)

Khatami came out most vigorously against the restriction on individual freedoms under the Islamic government. Iran, he said during the campaign, is 'a society in which the government belongs to the people and is the servant of the people, not its master'.[18] He advocated social liberalization, political tolerance, greater rights for women, and the rule of law. Moreover, he often stressed that the *harim* (privacy) 'deserves respect' and that all people should enjoy 'security and freedom within their private life'. Emphasising the need for social justice, he pleaded for equal opportunities for 'all groups in every region' of the country.[19]

Khatami has shown special sensitivity to the widespread alienation and discontent of Iranian youth, and made the improvement of their situation a major issue of his platform. He therefore advocated investment in 'job-generating projects', called for 'change in the educational system', and stressed the need to solve the country's urgent housing problem.[20] Speaking frequently at universities, he promised a 'better tomorrow' for frustrated, jobless youth, maintaining that a 'fresh approach to youth issues' was one of the government's main duties.[21] In fact, these 'children of the revolution', the 'most volatile segment of the population',[22] now considered the system 'as their own'.[23] Many of them welcomed Khatami's proposals with enthusiasm and embraced him. 'Fed up with a regime that meddles in their social lives without providing them with education or jobs', Baktiari writes,[24] they sought what he represented.

Another major issue in Khatami's election campaign was the elevation of the status of women. Aware that the problem was deeply rooted in the 'male-chauvinist attitude' in Iran,[25] Khatami called 'to do away with male supremacy'.[26] Men 'are not in charge of the women', he admonished. The obstacles to women's progress should be eliminated,[27] he said, and women should be present on all political, social and religious forums.[28] Asked whether, if elected, he would appoint women as ministers, he said: 'In this regard, I make no distinction between men and women.'[29] (A promise he failed to fulfil – see below.) For women too, therefore, Khatami symbolized hope for change.

Khatami's program combined religion with state, with a clear emphasis on Iran's national interest. (See also Chapter 7.) His campaign platform stipulated: 'The great Iranian nation has a great Islamic and national heritage.' His stress on the country's national interests also molded his foreign outlook. 'Foreign policy does not mean guns and rifles', he stated, but the utilization of all legitimate 'international means' to persuade others.[30] Iran wanted good relations with all the nations which respect its independence, dignity, and interests. In a mixture of pragmatism and revolutionary devotion, he added that Iran 'will not interfere in the affairs of others', nor would it allow any power to interfere in its domestic affairs. However, defending 'the deprived and oppressed' and the 'freedom-seeking countries' worldwide, especially the Palestinians, was Iran's 'Islamic and revolutionary obligation'.[31] He stressed the need for dialogue between civilizations and faiths and appealed for an end to religious fanaticism.[32] Later, addressing the UN General Assembly on 21 September 1998, Khatami appealed for the year 2001 to be designated the 'Year of Dialogue among Civilizations', in the hope that such a dialogue would promote universal justice and liberty.[33] (For more on his foreign outlook, see Part Two.)

Nateq-Nuri, by contrast, epitomized the conservative approach. Unlike Khatami, he came from a rural family in the province of Mazandaran, had little knowledge of the outside world, and traveled out of Iran only on brief official visits (e.g., to Russia, North Korea and Sudan). He continued to adhere ardently to the original dogma of the revolution, regardless of the passage of the time and changing realities.

His campaign regarding the West focused on the 'cultural onslaught' emanating from it. According to him, this was the West's vehicle for attacking the Iranian nation's ideology, religious thinking, national identity and revolutionary values.[34] Elaborating on the 'Western cultural onslaught', Nateq-Nuri was extremely radical. He blamed the West for 'spreading corruption and obscenity; ridiculing sacred Islamic terminology, sanctities, and divine traditions; propagating debauchery, raunchiness, and homosexuality; consuming alcohol; insulting clerics; instilling the impression that girls who are outwardly chaste and noble are in reality extremely profligate; and mocking religious chanting'.[35] In his view, the Islamic regime should not be measured by economic growth or construction programs, but by morals and values. (See also Chapter 2.) The gulf between the United States and Islamic Iran, he maintained, was, and remains unbridgeable, because 'our struggle against America has its origin in our ideology'. Inasmuch as the United States by 'its nature' was domineering, Iran's struggle against it would continue.[36] Thus, whoever was elected for the presidency, he believed, must maintain Iran's revolutionary foreign policy guidelines, which are 'based on safeguarding our principles, national interests, and mutual respect'. Neighboring states and Islamic countries, however, should realize that 'we are no threat to them'. A strong Iran would be their 'powerful brother'. After all, he said, echoing the old revolutionary jargon, 'we are all members of the same family. We should safeguard this family's security.'[37] Another central tenet was the defense of Palestine, as a religious duty (*taklif*) for Islamic Iran.[38] (See Chapter 8.)

Preserving Islamic values and the struggle against the Western 'cultural onslaught' was, thus, a major theme in Nateq-Nuri's campaign. In his view, among the main weapons of the Western cultural onslaught were communications satellites and the media in general. This 'foreign culture is launching an onslaught against the cultural foundations of our nation in order to dominate this nation', he warned. While in the past foreign powers used to dispatch their armies to capture new territories and to enslave nations, now they sought to dominate other people 'by attacking their thoughts and ideologies' and promoting 'the culture of corruption, decadence, and idleness'. He proposed creating 'immunity', i.e., strengthening national culture and values, as a response.[39] He also focused on the plight of the youth in Iran, listing job opportunities, economic security, and the reform of the administrative and tax systems as among 'the most important priorities for the next government'.[40] Basing his discussion on Khomeini's philosophy, he declared that 'women in our society are active in every arena, as are men, and they [women] have the right to be active in society'. Responsibilities should 'be given based on talents', and Iranian women 'have shown their value, they have proved that they have talents'.[41]

Within the parameters of political dialogue in Iran, therefore, Khatami and Nateq-Nuri represented two conflicting approaches. Nateq-Nuri was perceived as the symbol of establishment conservatism, while Khatami was perceived as a symbol of reformism, openness and change. This obliged Khatami to stress his revolutionary credentials and devotion to Khomeini's creed during the campaign, and encouraged Nateq-Nuri to try and shake off his reputation as an uncompromising ideologue. In view of the constraints of the language of Iranian political discourse, voters had to read between the lines. Eventually, the public seemed far more influenced by what the candidates represented than by what they actually said during their campaign. In the public mind, Nateq-Nuri epitomized the conservative establishment, regardless of the milder language he adopted as polling day approached. Conversely, Khatami turned into symbol of the reformist approach, regardless of his attempt to stress his revolutionary credentials and his loyalty to basic revolutionary tenets. In fact, the public 'saw a choice it had not been offered previously and decided to make a choice'.[42]

Ever since the Constitutional Revolution, civil liberty has been a major goal for Iranians. (See Chapter 5.) That may not yet have been achieved, owing to the limited scope for change under the existing political system. Yet, the Iranian people once again demonstrated their massive political will to determine their country's destiny. As on several earlier occasions in the last century (the Constitutional Revolution, Mosaddeq's National Movement, and Khomeini's Islamic Revolution), the people's voice was heard loud and clear, notwithstanding prevailing constraints. In fact, the measure of freedom of expression during the campaign was exceptional by Iranian and regional standards.

The vitality of the political process, the lively election campaign and the surprising results attracted world attention. By regional standards, the defeat of the establishment candidate and the massive vote in favour of Khatami were astonishing, as was Iran's adherence to its constitution. The results might not have been 'one of the most stunning electoral upsets in world history' as some observers viewed them,[43] nor was Khatami a total outsider as others seemed to argue. Yet, the candidate supported by the ruling establishment had been defeated – in itself a refreshing development by regional standards. The parameters of change, however, were still significantly confined.

Given the precedent of the large-scale disqualification of candidates in previous elections, and the establishment's undisguised wish to secure massive support for Nateq-Nuri, there was no doubt that presidential candidates would be subject to a process of vetting. Indeed, the Council of Guardians fulfilled its responsibility 'to supervise' the elections and to thin out the list of candidates drastically. Of the 238 presidential aspirants (many others eventually failed to register, believing that they would be ultimately rejected), only four were found qualified to run.[44] By narrowing the list so sharply, the screening committee not only limited freedom of choice, but practically confined the framework of possible change. In a way, it effectively made the selection, allowing voters only to grade the four candidates who were deemed acceptable.

(For such charges by Ayatollah Montazeri, in 1999, on the eve of the Majlis elections, see Chapter 5.)

While the massive rejection of candidates was customary, and the candidacy of women unprecedented in a presidential election (unlike Majlis elections), the disqualification of all nine women aspirants became a focus of resentment this time, in the light of heightened consciousness among women of their right to stand for high office. In particular, the disqualification of A'zam Taleqani, the daughter of the popular Ayatollah Mahmud Taleqani, became a rallying point for protest. Her candidacy took on the symbol of a struggle for women's rights. Formally, she was rejected because she lacked 'the necessary religious political prerequisite', based on the screening committee's interpretation of the constitutional clause (Article 115), which stipulated that the president must be elected from the country's political and religious *rejal*. The term *rejal* (borrowed from the Arabic) means men, but it can also be construed in a gender-neutral sense meaning people or person, an interpretation regarded as valid by women's organizations.[45] The disqualification of Taleqani encouraged women to vote for Khatami, who persuaded them that he was more attentive to their cause.

The massive popular participation in the elections was reminiscent of the early days of the revolution. There was a sense that the people could make a difference and that their vote might determine the course of the revolution. Of the estimated 32m eligible voters, over 29m (roughly 91 per cent), cast their ballots – significantly higher than the 57 per cent turnout in 1993.

Khatami won over 20m votes (69 per cent), more than out-going President Rafsanjani had gained four years earlier (63 per cent) when he ran as the main establishment candidate.[46] Khatami's greatest support came from the provinces of Yazd, his home province (nearly 85 per cent), Bushehr (84 per cent), Ilam (81 per cent) and Fars (80 per cent). His lowest support was registered in Mazandaran (Nateq-Nuri's home province, 44 per cent) and Lorestan (45 per cent). In the Central Province (which includes Tehran) both Khatami and Nateq-Nuri won slightly less than their total average (some 68 per cent and 22 per cent, respectively). Nateq-Nuri's total in percentage terms was nearly 25 per cent (highest support in Lorestan, 53 per cent, and in Mazandaran, 52 per cent; and the lowest, close to 13 per cent in each of the provinces of Yazd, Bushehr and Kermanshah). The two other candidates, deputy head of the judiciary Seyyed Reza Zavare'i and former minister of intelligence Mohammad Mohammadi Reyshahri, received only 2.6 per cent and 2.7 per cent of the votes, respectively.[47] The vote thus marked a landslide victory for Khatami. He 'won in Tehran and in the provinces; he won in the villages as well as cities; he won the votes of the poor as well as the rich', trumpeted the *Iran Times*.[48] This was a devastating result for the establishment candidate, Nateq-Nuri, who was viewed shortly before the elections as unbeatable, and for the conservative elite that had endorsed him.

The results signaled popular displeasure with prevailing realities, illustrating a marked preference for practical solutions instead of dogmatic purity. The vote for Khatami 'was definitely the anti-establishment vote', commented one of his aides.[49] That such a large proportion 'chose to reject the establishment candidate', the *Iran Times* noted, also testified to growing popular dissatisfaction.[50] If the elections were to be viewed as a referendum, the conservative approach would be deemed to have suffered a significant setback. The result was thus perceived as a mandate for change, even if only within the framework of the Islamic system. If Khatami had once feared that the realities in revolutionary Iran would discourage Islamists elsewhere and even endanger Islam, he was now set to prevent such a scenario by providing tangible improvement.

Khatami's most immediate challenge was to form a government that would be a vehicle for translating his campaign pledges into substantive programs. Taking his oath in the Majlis on 4 August 1997, he reiterated his main campaign pledges, vowing to serve the people, uphold justice, guard against authoritarianism, and promote civic freedoms. The government 'is the servant of the nation, not its master', he declared. To attain its objectives, he promised to provide 'a safe atmosphere for the clash of ideas' in the framework of Islam and the constitution. His government, he added, 'will attach great importance' to maintaining Iran's prestige and defending the rights of Muslims worldwide, the oppressed generally, and the Palestinians in particular.[51]

Khatami mounted an intensive campaign to have all 22 of his ministerial nominees approved, as a means of entrenching his authority and promoting his goals. Presenting his nominees for the approval of the Majlis on 12 August 1997, he described his team as a cohesive, harmonious, competent and capable collective that combined 'experience, innovation, and new thinking (*now-andishi*)', which would enable Iran to fulfill its 'religious, revolutionary, and national obligations'. Khatami stressed that in selecting his ministers, he had ensured that they did not hold views opposed to those of Supreme Leader Khamene'i.

Promising to uphold campaign pledges, Khatami pointed out that his nominees' platforms were open to debate. The Majlis, he said, should exercise its right to assess the qualifications of each of his nominees and their proposed program, although he urged it to approve the entire list.[52] *Salam*, supporting Khatami, also urged members of the Majlis to help him 'with any tool he finds expedient'. Otherwise, it wrote, 'wittingly or unwittingly, they would be committing a violation of their duty'. Members had been selected 'to reflect the nation and the legitimate wishes of the people', *Salam* wrote, advising the Majlis to hold 'a magnifying glass' in its hands, not 'a sledge hammer'.[53] It added that the nominees met the requirements for the 'necessary spring cleaning' in the ministries, and urged the Majlis to give them its 'unequivocal support'.[54] In the same vein, one paper wrote: Today's vote will have an impact on the tomorrow of the Iranian people, the ones who created the Epic (*hamaseh*) of the Second of Khordad (the election day, 23 May 1997) by casting their 30m votes.[55]

Conservative Majlis members, however, censured Khatami for failing to carry out his pledge to form a supra-factional (*fara-jenahi*) government that included representatives of all trends. The conservative *Jomhuri-ye Islami* regretted that Khatami's campaign rivals 'have no share' in the new government.[56] Ahmad Nejabat then cynically wondered if 'the word cross-faction has changed in the dictionary', since contrary to promises, the cabinet 'does not include ministers from other factions at all'.[57] The *Majma'-e Ruhaniyyun-e Mobarez*, which supports the president, accused the conservatives of preventing Khatami from appointing leading politicians close to their own movement. 'Those who lost the last elections are putting pressure' on Khatami's 'choice of ministers', charged veteran member of the group, Mohtashami.[58]

In fact, Khatami retained only a few of the out-going ministers. He dropped 'Ali Akbar Velayati, Iran's foreign minister for 16 years, who had been influential in shaping Iran's hard-line stance toward the West, appointing instead Iran's former ambassador to the United Nations, Kamal Kharrazi. The hard-line Intelligence Minister 'Ali Fallahiyan, was replaced by Qorban 'Ali Dori Najafabadi.[59] Contrary to expectations, however, Khatami did not include any women on his list, though he appointed Ma'sumeh Ebtekar as vice-president, a nomination that did not require Majlis approval – an initial signal of recognition of the limits of his power.

Khatami's cabinet included 17 newcomers, mostly young, highly educated technocrats who, much like the out-going government, constituted a professional team with strong revolutionary credentials but generally pragmatic inclinations. Nearly half the nominees had served in previous governments ('Abdollah Nuri, Hosein Namazi, Bijan Namdar Zanganeh, Mostafa Mo'in, Mohammad Sa'idi-Kiya, Gholamreza Shafe'i, 'Isa Kalantari, Hosein Kamali, Mohammad Farhadi and Admiral 'Ali Shamkhani). Five were governors-general (Mahmud Hojjati, Habibollah Bitaraf, 'Ali 'Abdul'alizadeh, Ishaq Jahangiri and Morteza Hajji), one was a former ambassador (Kamal Kharrazi) and eight had previously served as Majlis members (Hosein Kamali, 'Ata'ollah Mohajerani, 'Abdul'alizadeh, Isma'il Shushtari, Jahangiri, Qorban 'Ali Dori Najafabadi, Nuri and Mo'in). Many of the new ministers were signatories of the *kargozaran-e sazandegi* 1996 manifesto (Mohajerani, Shushtari, Kalantari, Shafe'i and Zanganeh), or associated with the movement.[60] Immediately upon taking oath, Khatami reappointed Hasan Habibi as first vice-president. Later he appointed several other vice-presidents, the most conspicuous being Ma'sumeh Ebtekar, 37, a US-educated lecturer at Tehran University, who was named head of the Organization for the Protection of the Environment – the first woman to serve in such a prominent position since the revolution.

Three of Khatami's ministerial nominees were targeted for particular criticism in the Majlis (as well as by the conservative press).

(1) Mohajerani (Islamic Guidance) had antagonized the conservatives by openly criticizing the restriction of freedom in Iran. He had also supported the amendment of the constitution, allowing Rafsanjani to run for a third term, at a time when Nateq-Nuri's election seemed assured. This was viewed as a step against Nateq-Nuri and the conservatives. (See Chapter 2.) Worst of all, he had written a highly publicized article in *Ettela'at* in 1990 pointing to the advantages of a dialogue with the United States. (See Chapter 6.) During the Majlis debate Mohajerani denied having advocated the resumption of ties with the United States, stating that since 1990 the circumstances had changed considerably and that he now rejected any form of talks with the United States.[61] This was insufficient, however, to appease his critics. *Jomhuri-ye Islami* wrote that the ministry of Islamic guidance was 'the command staff of the cultural forces' in the confrontation with the enemy's cultural onslaught in a 'war without frontiers'. It was not expedient, therefore, to leave it in the hands of 'intimidated' people who lacked sufficient 'hatred toward America' in their hearts. Those who did not consider America 'the enemy', and even proposed 'direct talks', could not be assigned to manage the country's 'Islamic guidance', to which 'the political fate of the system' is strongly tied.[62] The newspaper feared that with Mohajerani's nomination 'we will have to seek God's help to

save the culture in this country'.[63] (For the conservatives' attempt to impeach Mohajerani in 1999, see below.)

(2) Nuri (Interior), a staunch Khatami supporter throughout the campaign and a vehement critic of the conservatives, and of Nateq-Nuri personally, openly castigated the conservatives for monopolizing power.[64] He maintained that the interests of the revolution required endorsing more liberal policies. Although an exponent of radical views in the 1980s, Nuri became a resolute supporter of liberalism in the 1990s. (For his removal from the cabinet in 1998, under pressure from conservatives, see below; he was sentenced to five years in prison in November 1999.)

(3) Kharrazi, a former ambassador to the United Nations and director of the Islamic Republic News Agency (Foreign Affairs), was criticized for having spent too much time in the United States as a student and later as ambassador, and thus being overly influenced by American culture. 'It is not fitting', *Jomhuri-ye Islami* typically wrote, that someone who has lived there [the United States] so long should be in charge of the foreign policy of a nation that considers the United States 'its greatest enemy'.[65] The newspaper described Kharrazi as only a 'miniature model' (*nemuneh-ye kuchak*) of the out-going foreign minister Velayati.[66]

That all his ministers, even those whose appointments were most contentious, were approved marked a substantial show of strength for Khatami. In fact, in debates over all previous governments, except for Rafsanjani's 1989 cabinet list, the Majlis had always rejected some of the nominees. This achievement provided Khatami with a significant degree of leverage at the outset of his presidency. His main task, however, remained to overcome the conservatives' opposition and to follow his own preferred policies. More importantly, he faced the challenge of promoting actual change and thereby meeting the expectations that had led him to the presidency.

IN SEARCH OF AUTHORITY

Notwithstanding Khatami's remarkable electoral success, the basic framework of the Islamic governmental system (*nezam*) and the pivotal tenets of its creed remained unchanged. Khatami's presidency, while harboring the potential for a policy change, did not constitute a new political system; rather it signified a fresh approach within the Islamic regime – an attempt to fulfill revolutionary aspirations in a somewhat modified fashion. It was a call to reform policy, not to change the regime; to save the revolution, not altogether to abandon dogma. That Khatami's credentials were approved by the screening committee testifies to his perceived loyalty to basic revolutionary tenets.[67] Belittling the importance of the new presidency, *Kayhan International* termed it merely an 'orderly transition of power', not even 'a change of policy'.[68] It was probably more than that. In many ways, this was 'a vote for new ideas, new people, [and] more responsive government',[69] suggesting that the political scene was becoming more pluralistic, and possibly more flexible. Nevertheless, Khatami does not represent 'the opposition in Iran'[70] and the election of the new president cannot be viewed as a vote for a full-scale change. Three years after the elections, the degree of change that Khatami envisaged – or believed possible – remains unclear due to constraints that continue to limit his ability to pursue his preferred policy.

Both during and after his election campaign, Khatami emphasized his commitment to working within the system. Khomeini's vision and the concept of *velayat-e faqih* constituted 'the basis of our political and civil system', he said, pledging to 'defend the values of the revolution'.[71] The view that his election signified a momentous change, *Kayhan* noted, ignored the fact that Khatami was a devout disciple of Khomeini. Choosing to stress his revolutionary convictions rather than his more current pragmatic posture, the newspaper pointed out that 'for a long time he has been recognized as an anti-American figure', and many of his supporters had 'anti-American records'. How then, it asked, could he possibly 'ignore the path and aspiration' of Imam Khomeini, or initiate a compromise 'between the revolution and its main enemy', the United States?[72] To be sure, most pragmatists remained loyal to basic revolutionary principles and the difference between the main trends, although significant, was one of degree only. As one of Khatami's ministerial nominees said, Iran should 'leave the door open to allow a breeze through' but 'not to let in a destructive storm'. Another fundamental debate, therefore, was over the degree of openness that turns a 'breeze' into a 'storm'.[73]

The massive vote for Khatami in itself was insufficient to promote unqualified change. For one thing, the vote seemed more to reflect dissatisfaction with the 'old guard' rather than support for Khatami's distinctive world-view and particular programs, which at that stage at least were not widely known. No less importantly, policy-making continued to be determined by laborious negotiation between the various power centers, of which the president was only one – and not the most powerful, either constitutionally or in practice. The religio-political structure and the multiplicity of power centers constituted an additional obstacle to substantial changes. Furthermore, in the absence of Ayatollah Khomeini's commanding authority, factional rivalries at the highest echelons of power hampered decision-making. Most decisions also tended to conform to the more extremist line, led by the conservative forces. State, clerical, and a range of vested interests 'embedded in Iran's complex structure of parallel policy-making and policy-vetting institutions' appeared to fight Khatami 'tooth-and-nail', further limiting his ability to modify, or even fine-tune policy.[74] Khomeini's first prime minister, Bazargan, had once complained that his government had only held 'a knife without a blade'.[75] Khatami's election provided him with a mandate for a guarded change, but not a carte blanche to pursue unfettered reform or retreat from the basic revolutionary creed. It is not yet clear how much 'blade' his 'knife' carries.

The Majlis, a stronghold of conservatism, continued to aim for dominance and to stifle fresh initiatives. Since the early stages of the revolution it has proven a strong power center, and appears determined to preserve its prominence in the hierarchy of power. While the president took pride in the popular support that carried him to the presidency, the Majlis also represents the people. Its vote in favour of Khatami's government did not mean an automatic acceptance of its policies. As Majlis deputy Ahmad Ma'ruf Samadi said during a Majlis debate: 'I am against the cabinet', but nevertheless, 'will vote for all of them.'[76] There is no doubt that there was a strong pro-Khatami and pro-reform nucleus in the Majlis following the 1996 elections. (See Chapter 2.) Nevertheless, it remained one of the main bastions of conservatism and a significant arena of power struggles, which intensified with the approach of elections to the Sixth Majlis, held in early 2000. (See Chapter 5 and the Epilogue.)

Rafsanjani was another force with which Khatami had to reckon. After eight years as speaker and two terms as president, and with significant revolutionary credentials, political experience and personal prestige, he was still a considerable presence. His position as head of *shura-ye tashkhis-e maslahat* gave him key decision-making authority in disputes between the legislative and the executive. Interestingly, just before the presidential election on 17 March 1997, Khamene'i ordered the expansion of the *shura-ye tashkhis-e maslahat* to strengthen its centrality and effectiveness. The declared aim was to extend its function as an advisory body to assist the Supreme Leader in formulating general policy. It had previously included prominent figures from the three branches of government. (See Chapter 1.) The new roster of permanent members included 25 prominent figures appointed for five years.[77] Rafsanjani served as head of the council, in anticipation of an opportunity to return to a more dominant position in the administration.

Another aspect of the out-going president's influence related to the fact that many of Khatami's ministers and several of his vice-presidents had first been appointed to their posts by Rafsanjani. Some had also played a central role in the formation of the *kargozaran-e sazandegi*. His support, therefore, was significant for Khatami's success on assuming the presidency. In the first couple of years of Khatami's presidency, however, Rafsanjani appeared to opt in favor of sitting on the fence, failing to put his full weight behind any of the two main rival groups. With the approach of the 2000 Majlis election, his candidacy as deputy was supported mainly by the conservatives, who favored his return to the post of the Speaker. By then, however, he seemed to have lost much of his prestige and power. (See also Chapter 5 and the Epilogue.)

Although his reputation as an establishment 'outsider' was an asset during his campaign, Khatami's lack of an independent power base has presented a serious challenge to the extension of his reform programs after entering office. Much of his freedom of action depends on the other power centers. In addition to the Supreme Leader, the faction-ridden (fifth) Majlis and the former President Rafsanjani, Khatami has also had to reckon with other powerful revolutionary organizations. The judiciary, headed by Ayatollah Mohammad Yazdi (one of the staunch supporters of the conservative trend and of Khamene'i personally), has usually worked to block or slow down new initiatives. The Council of Guardians, the Council of Experts, and powerful foundations (such as *Bonyad-e Mostaz'afin* and *Bonyad-e Shahid*), and a range of vested interests and revolutionary bodies (like *Ansar-e Hezbollah*), have also resisted the president's new policies. The Revolutionary Guards made their position clear on several occasions, when they warned Khatami and his supporters against seeking reforms. Their commander Yahya Rahim Safavi was reported to have threatened to decapitate and cut out the tongues of political opponents (see below), while a group of commanders warned Khatami, following the student riots in July 1999, that their patience had run out. (See Chapter 5.) Whereas Mikhail Gorbachev succeeded in gaining control of the party and the state in the Soviet Union when he became president and secretary-general of the Communist Party, Khatami has had to share power. Eventually, the conservatives appeared to possess disproportionately more power in ruling institutions than in civil society, the main power base of the

president. In 1999, such popular support was still insufficient to achieve
a significant practical breakthrough.

In addition, the regime's previous deviation from major ideological
convictions made it even harder for Khatami to retreat from the revolutionary creed, especially on issues that might involve restricting the
independence of the *vali-ye faqih* in the day-to-day running of government, establishing ties with the United States or alter attitudes towards
Israel. In fact, such issues had become entrenched symbols of the
revolution, making a retreat appear as an open admission of failure,
or, as Velayati put it, signaling to the defeat of Iran's revolutionary
myths.[78]

No less important, were the formidable objective social and economic
difficulties facing the government, especially a government functioning
under such harsh political constraints and rigid dogma.

At the same time, while popular expectations provided Khatami with
decisive support they also imposed a heavy burden, as many Iranians
expected immediate action and instant results. Expectations 'are high'
commented one Iranian newspaper and jubilant Iranians who elected
Khatami expected him to make good on his promises instantly.[79] Faced
with a similar challenge, Bazargan had pointed out in 1979: 'I am not
another [Imam] 'Ali.' He was not 'a bulldozer', he had said, 'crushing
all obstacles in its path', but rather 'a delicate car' capable of traveling
only on good roads. 'You should pave the way for me', Bazargan had
pleaded.[80] Whether Khatami would attain the needed assistance
remained to be seen. As things appeared in 1999, the conservatives
seemed to watch his steps very carefully while the Supreme Leader as
the head of the conservative trend, stood firmly against his main reform
programs.

The final stumbling block to the president's effectiveness was the fact
that the head of state was the Supreme Leader (*rahbar*), Khamene'i, not
the president. Undoubtedly, Khatami's victory also constituted a setback
for Khamene'i. Not only had he come close to openly endorsing Nateq-
Nuri, but being deeply involved in politics he could not escape some
responsibility for the country's mounting difficulties. Moreover,
Khamene'i's lack of credentials to serve as *the marja'-e taqlid* increased
his vulnerability. (See Chapter 1.) Nevertheless, despite his failure to
gain supreme theological endorsement, the recognition he had achieved
as one of the prominent 'sources' (*maraje'*) and his status as Khomeini's
heir, sustained his authority and gained him the support of like-minded
revolutionaries. Khamene'i's position in the revolutionary hierarchy as
the Supreme Leader clearly limited Khatami's freedom considerably,

since he did not share many of Khatami's general convictions nor his actual policy preferences and, more often than not, identified openly with the presidents' rivals.

Khatami was not unaware of the limits of his powers, but was confident that his path was the correct one to follow, and believed that he had the support of the majority of the people. Shortly after his election, Khatami said: 'I am determined to fulfill my promises and I believe the atmosphere is conducive and will improve day by day.' While acknowledging that in Iran 'overall policies are determined by the eminent leadership [i.e., Khamene'i]', he still believed that he would be given the freedom to pursue his preferred policy. 'I feel there is no barrier along the way of the government's authority. . . . We will surely implement any policy that we formulate.'[81] Often the realities seemed very different.

During his first meeting with the new government on 24 August 1997, Khamene'i tellingly cautioned it to preserve revolutionary values and avoid hasty action. His statements thereafter, as for example, during the Islamic Conference Organization (ICO) meeting in Tehran in December 1997, attested both to the wide differences between Khamene'i and Khatami and to Khamene'i's determination to dictate the general policy himself. (See Chapter 7.) His appointment of former foreign minister Velayati as his adviser for international affairs (August 1997) further illustrated his commitment to continuity. Even if Velayati's appointment failed to guarantee continuance of Iran's basic policy, it was certainly intended to guard against significant change. During the student riots in July 1999, Khamene'i once again made clear his stance against the president's soft policy. (See Chapter 5.) In August 1999, he challenged Khatami on the issue of civil rights and urged him to deal, instead, with the real problem: the ailing economy. (See Chapter 5, the Conclusion to Part Two and the Epilogue.)

Notwithstanding the enormous difficulties in introducing meaningful change, Khatami's elections undoubtedly harbored the potential for reform. Like Khomeini in 1979, Khatami had become a symbol for hope and a harbinger of change. He provided the people with renewed expectations that he would achieve the hitherto unfulfilled promises of the revolution. This gained him the support during the elections of an increasingly dissatisfied Iranian public, and remains an important asset.

Moreover, the revolution has by now matured, and has grown much more aware of the limits of its message. People grew more dissatisfied while objective conditions also called for greater pragmatism, even at the expense of a retreat from established dogma. Many Iranians, including a growing number of aging revolutionaries, seemed to have realized that fundamental reforms were essential to solve the country's mounting problems and to assure the stability and the longevity of the regime. Khatami was aware of the need for it and had a degree of latitude to carry it out. His election campaign and his statements since taking over also suggest his determination to make good on his pledge. He seemed confident that his platform was the best program – if not the only feasible path – to advance the goals of the revolution and to improve the realities of life for the Iranian people. His nomination of highly con-troversial candidates to several key posts also attested to his determina-tion to blaze his own trail, while the initial approval by the Majlis of all of his cabinet nominees strengthened further his mandate. Finally, following his election, Khatami made several courageous doctrinal state-ments that, although often fenced in by conditions and declarations of dogmatic devotion, reflected a persistent commitment to change. Although moving in slow motion, and often appearing hesitant, he has so far not retreated.

About three years later, with no substantial improvement in social and economic fields, domestic rivalries have continued even more fiercely, with the pressure from conservatives inhibiting the drive for greater pragmatism and reform.

The domestic rivalries intensified significantly around the first anniversary of the presidential elections, as demonstrated by the severe accusations and harsh terms used by the rival camps to denounce each other. The conservatives equated Khatami's rule to that of former president Bani Sadr, who was ousted in June 1981.[82] Ayatollah Khaz'ali alluded to his tenure as chicken pox. 'The revolution', he said, 'has been inflicted with a chicken pox, which will cool down quickly.'[83] Domestic rivals branded each other as Yazid (the notorious Caliph charged with the massacre of Imam Hosein in Karbala, in AD 680), and similar defamatory labels.[84] Yahya Rahim Safavi, the commander of the Revolutionary Guard, called Khatami's supporters 'diseased people' whose plague, he said, was well known to the authorities. He reportedly went as far as to state, that the Revolutionary Guards were ready to even decapitate and cut out the tongues of political opponents.[85] In a demonstration in May 1998 supporters of the president reiterated harsh slogans such as: '*Monafeq* be Ashamed (*haya kon*)', 'Leave Khatami Free (*raha kon*)'; 'Death to Despotism' and 'Death to Monopolism'.[86] That domestic rivals are mutually depicted as Yazids or *monafeq* (hypo-crites) best illustrates the depth of the animosity.

One dramatic manifestation of the domestic struggle was the conservatives' attempts to drive out of office or limit the influence of the president's men.

The first such attempt was the arrest in April 1998 of the popular mayor of Tehran, Gholamhosein Karbaschi, a supporter of the president (and a close associate of Rafsanjani). The mayor, in office since 1989, had angered Islamic hard-liners when he embarked on a campaign to modernize the city, setting up modern art galleries and cultural centers . Karbaschi further antagonized the conservatives for his decisive role in the formation of the *kargozaran-e sazandegi* and his active role in the 1996 Majlis elections, and the presidential campaign. Karbaschi then became the target of attacks by conservatives, who demanded his arrest for alleged mismanagement, embezzlement and misconduct.[87] The Supreme Court on 23 July 1998 sentenced Karbaschi to five years imprisonment, a suspended sentence of 60 lashes, a substantial fine and a ban from state employment for 20 years. (In December a court of appeal reduced Karbaschi's prison sentence to two years and the ban from state employment to ten years, and imposed a lesser fine.) In May 1999 Karbaschi began his jail sentence. The arguments for and against his case revealed the widening gap between the two camps.

His opponents insisted that an official charged with corruption had to stand trial regardless of his rank, past services or political affiliation, and that Karbaschi's achievements as mayor did not justify waiving the charges against him.[88] They accused his supporters of politicizing the case to tarnish the authenticity of the trial.[89] Majlis deputy Mohammad Reza Bahonar asked the pragmatists, who often chanted slogans about the rule of law, to be tolerant of its application in the case of the mayor.[90] His colleague 'Ali Zadsar added that the mayor's superiors 'are also guilty'. If one were to review the performance of those politicians who advocated democracy, he added, one would realize that they were, in fact, absolute dictators. 'Karbaschi and his gang are an example of these authoritarian politicians.'[91]

Supporters of Karbaschi argued that charges against him were leveled because of his role in the *kargozaran-e sazandegi* and in Khatami's election, and that the trial was organized by 'the right wing' to avenge its electoral defeat. They maintained that the mayor, who in less than a decade had transformed the appearance of Tehran, deserved praise not punishment. Unwilling to relinquish power, they argued, the conservatives had turned against Karbaschi, tried to bring down Nuri, and were likely next to target Mohajerani – all pillars of the Khatami administration[92] who were later also to become the targets of conservative attack. Karbaschi's supporters found it strange that 'one of the strongest and

dedicated' managers in the country had been accused of mismanagement.[93] Similarly, Fa'ezeh Hashemi, Rafsanjani's daughter, said that by
bringing Karbaschi to trial, the faction that had lost the election was
seeking revenge.[94] 'This affair has a political colour to it', she said,
adding that 'Karbaschi's arrest is a blow to democracy, [and to] political and cultural reform in Iran'.[95] 'Abdollah Nuri, the minister of the
interior, said that the arrest, instead of bringing Karbaschi under question, had put the judiciary under question. People should be tried for
their offenses, he said, not for their competency, merit, boldness, and
courage. He called Karbaschi a 'national hero', with his audience
responding: 'free the Amir Kabir'.[96] Ayatollah Seyyed Jalal al-Din
Taheri, the Friday prayer leader of Isfahan (known for his support for
Khatami), maintained that Karbaschi's detention was directly related
to 'the Epic of the Second of Khordad' and 'is 100 per cent politically
motivated'.[97] (Karbaschi was released from jail before the Majlis
elections.)

The conservatives then moved on to target the 'Abdollah Nuri. On 10
June 1998, 31 Majlis deputies demanded his interpellation, claiming
that his tenure in the interior ministry was 'detrimental to tranquillity
and stability in the country'.[98] Nuri was an even more important target
than Karbaschi, because of his sensitive post as minister of interior (in
charge of elections, political activities, and licensing demonstrations),
his unequivocal endorsement of liberalism, his support for Khatami, and
his open backing for Karbaschi. Nuri's supporters also pointed to the
factional motivations behind this move. The leader of the *Majma'-e
Hezbollah* faction in the Majlis, Majid Ansari, called the conservatives
the interpellation's main architects.[99] A *Salam* commentary argued
that the 31 Majlis members, having failed to grasp the message of the
popular vote, were 'lining up' against the 'creators of the epic of Second
Khordad' – that is, 'the people'. Who should be interpellated, the newspaper asked, a person who has issued a permit for a political gathering,
or those who have kept silent 'in the face of the ruthless attack waged
against the gathering by a notorious gang wielding clubs, wearing
knuckle-dusters and even carrying tear gas canisters?'[100] *Mobin* added:
'It is not the interior minister alone' who is being attacked, but 'the
president himself, the entire cabinet, all the forces and groups who
support Khatami and all those millions who created the epic event of
Second Khordad.'[101] Khatami, vowing to respect the Majlis decision,
still considered Nuri's service in the cabinet 'beneficial and useful'. He
thanked Nuri and his colleagues at the ministry who 'have bravely taken
important actions to further the security and political development of

the country', vowing that whoever Nuri's successor might be, he would follow Nuri's path. He promised that the government would make good use of Nuri's capabilities and experience[102]. He later acted on his word by appointing Nuri vice-president. (For his trial, see Chapter 5.)

The next among the 'president's men' to be targeted by the conservatives was Mohajerani – which was expected. The motion to impeach Mohajerani in May 1999, was also prompted by conservative-oriented Majlis members who opposed the cultural reforms advocated by Khatami and advanced by Mohajerani. Mohajerani's contribution to a free press and the relaxation of cultural Islamization, were viewed by the conservatives as manifestations of Western cultural influence. This was in addition to accusations of Mohajerani's soft policy towards the USA. (See Chapter 6.) Mohajerani barely escaped impeachment.[103] However, criticism against Mohajerani has continued since then, with calls to remove him from his ministerial post being repeated systematically, mainly during the students' riots in July 1999 and the publication of a satirical article by students in September 1999 which offended religious feelings. (See Chapter 5 below.)

While these developments were clear setbacks for the pragmatists, they had their own victories too. One such success, was their resounding victory in Iran's first municipal elections since the revolution, in February 1999, which testified to continued popular support for reform. The local elections were regarded by many as 'the most democratic' elections held in Iran. This time the conservatives' intent to disqualify leading pro-reform candidates, many of them supporters of the president, including Nuri, Jamileh Kadivar and Ebrahim Asgharzadeh, has generally failed.[104] Nuri led by a significant majority in Tehran – a short time after being impeached by the Majlis. Women constituted one-tenth of the estimated 400,000 candidates and many were, indeed, elected. The election generated heated political debates in larger cities like Tehran, Isfahan, Shiraz, and Tabriz. One candidate even presented his pictures wearing a tie – a symbol of Western culture. Khatami's supporters won an absolute majority throughout the country.[105] *Salam* examined the results in the city councils. It classified the contending groups as supporters of the Second of Khordad movement including Iran's Islamic Participation Front (*Jebheh-ye Mosharekat-e Iran-e Islami*) and other pro-reform groups and individuals, the conservatives ('the right') and independents. The results show, that from 815 seats in the cities examined, 579 (71%) were won by pro-reform groups, 119 seats (14.6%) went to the conservatives and 117 (14.3%) to independent candidates. In Tehran, the reformist candidates won 13 out of

the 15 seats, in each of the municipalities of Tabriz, Isfahan and Shiraz
eight seats (out of 11), in Meshhed six (from 11), and all the five seats
in Khomeini's own home town, Khomein, and the seven seats of
Montazeri's home town, Najafabad. Only in Qom the conservative won
a majority (eight of the nine seats).[106] The elections, many believed, were
an important step toward turning over responsibility to the people.
However, this was not sufficient to define Iranian politics.

All in all, Khatami's election attests to growing disillusionment and
a popular demand for change. His election may be viewed as a stiff
warning to the leaders of the revolution, but it also provided renewed
opportunity to prove that the revolution possessed the cure for Iran's
basic problems, the persistence of which had led to the revolution in the
first place. The fierce struggle for power has continued, the social and
economic difficulties remain as pressing as before, and the atmosphere
of relative openness and freedom of expression have only intensified the
growing demand for freedom. (See Chapters 4 and 5.) Developments
since his election as president in 1997 testify to Khatami's awareness of
the challenge and his determination to bring about significant change.
But they also attest to the strength of opposition to any major departure
from the revolutionary stance.

These tensions came to the fore recently with major tenets of the
revolution being put in question. The first was the challenge – implicit
or explicit – to the basic concept of *velayat-e faqih* and the general idea
of clerical rule. The second concerned the (economic and national)
advantages to be gained through relations with the United States. For
the first time, such concepts are being discussed more or less openly.
Such views, it should be stressed, were considered a taboo until
recently, and the public debate about them, in itself, constitutes a major
innovation. Yet, since assuming the presidency, Khatami has made no
major breakthrough in important policy areas nor are the practical
results of his policies any clearer. The popular vote was clear. What it
meant in terms of politics is more difficult to discern.

Khatami was thus caught in the middle of the two opposing trends:
for the hard-line conservatives, he was advancing reforms too fast; for
many people, mainly the youth and students, he was moving too
slowly. The results of the elections attest to popular demand for change,
with the mood among the youth exceeding far beyond what Khatami
viewed as desirable or conceivable. Khatami could not, as yet, advance
even his own – more limited – aims. The political debate turned much
more heated in the second year of Khatami's presidency while domestic
rivalries have intensified further. (See Chapter 5.)

Judged by their active role in recent Iranian history the people of Iran seem determined to shape their own path and destiny. Iran has gone through two major revolutions in the twentieth century – the Constitutional Revolution and the Islamic Revolution. The goals of neither have fully materialized, but the vision has not been abandoned. The main stimulus for change seems to rest in growing domestic difficulties, rather than any ideological conviction. More than two decades after the revolution, the stability of the regime seems to depend less on the degree of its return to Islam than on the degree to which it resolves the social, economic and political problems that initially fueled popular discontent. While in 1997 people voted primarily *against* the policies of the conservative elite and the harsh realities established under the clerical rule, since the elections they have signaled what they were opting *for*: above all, social and economic betterment and greater freedom.

NOTES

1. See, for example, *Iran Times*, 30 May 1997.
2. *Wall Street Journal*, 26 May 1997.
3. *Al-Riyad*, 8 June 1997. For other, similar references to Khatami as an intellectual, see Bahman Baktiari, 'Iran's New President', *Middle East Insight*, 13/1, (November–December 1997), p. 20; *International Herald Tribune*, 28 May; *Washington Post*, 25 May 1997.
4. *Washington Post*, 25 May 1997.
5. *Financial Times*, 23 August 1997.
6. Shaul Bakhash and Patrick Clawson, 'Iranian Presidential Elections: A Preview', in *Special Policy Forum Report* (Washington Institute for Near East Policy), 23 May 1997.
7. Laila Danesh, 'A Breathtaking Victory', *Civil Society*, 6/66, (June 1997), pp. 8–9.
8. *Washington Post*, 25 May 1997.
9. *Kayhan-e Hava'i*, 29 July 1992 – DR, 25 August; Agence France Presse (AFP), 18 July 1992 – DR, 20 July 1992.
10. Lamote, 'Iran's Foreign Policy', p. 12.
11. See Mohammad Khatami, *Zamineha-ye Khizesh-e Mashruteh* [The Circumstances Behind the Emergence of Constitutionalism] (Tehran: Paya, n.d.); *Bim-e Mowj* [Fear of the Wave] (Tehran: Sima-ye Javan, 1995); *Az Donya-ye 'Shahr' ta Shahr-e 'Donya'* [From the World of the City to the City of the World] (Tehran: Nashr-e Ney, 1997); *Hope and Challenge: The Iranian President Speaks* (Binghamton, NY: SUNY, 1997); *Mutala'at fi al-Din wal-Islam wal-'Asr* [Studies on Religion, Islam and the Era] (Beirut: Dar al-Jadid, 1998).
12. Khatami, *Mutala'at*, p. 21.
13. Khatami, *Bim-e Mowj*, p. 139.
14. Ibid., pp. 52, 172.

15. Khatami, *Mutala'at*, pp. 121, 139.
16. Tehran TV, 10 May 1997 [DR]. See also, Tehran TV, 19 May 1997 [DR].
17. Tehran TV, 20 May 1997 [DR].
18. Tehran TV, 10 May 1997 [DR].
19. Tehran TV, 14 May 1997 [DR].
20. *Gozaresh*, 21 May 1997 [DR].
21. *Hamshahri*, 6 March 1997, as cited in S. C. Fairbanks, 'Theocracy versus Democracy: Iran Considers Political Parties', *Middle East Journal*, 52/1 (Winter 1998), p. 18.
22. Banuazizi, 'Faltering Legitimacy', p. 571.
23. *Akhbar*, 8 June 1997, cited in Fairbanks, 'Theocracy versus Democracy', p. 18.
24. Baktiari, 'Iran's New President', p. 21.
25. Khatami's interview, *Middle East Insight*, 13/1 (November–December 1997), p. 31.
26. IRNA, 22 February 1997 [DR].
27. *Iran*, 17 March 1997 [DR].
28. Tehran TV, 14 May 1997 [DR].
29. *Iran*, 17 March 1997 [DR].
30. Tehran TV, 20 May 1997 [DR].
31. Tehran TV, 10 May 1997 [DR].
32. *Al-Riyad*, 8 June 1997.
33. IRNA, 21 September 1998 [DR].
34. Tehran TV, 18 May 1997 [DR].
35. Baktiari, *Parliamentary Politics*, p. 222.
36. *Ettela'at*, 3 November 1993.
37. Tehran TV, 20 May 1997 [DR].
38. IRNA, 7 February 1997 – SWB, 8 February 1997.
39. Tehran TV, 19 May 1997 [DR].
40. *Iran News*, 22 December 1996 [DR].
41. Radio Tehran, 14 May 1997 [DR].
42. *Iran Times*, 30 May 1997.
43. Ibid.
44. To compare, in 1993, 128 candidates put forward their candidacy and four were allowed to run; in 1989, 80 candidates applied and only two were approved; in 1985, there were 45 candidates and three approvals; in 1981, 45 candidates and four approvals; again in 1981, 71 candidates and four approvals; and in 1980, the first presidential elections, 124 candidates and eight approvals.
45. Tehran TV, 28 April 1997 [DR]. See also Baktiari, 'Iran's New President', p. 18.
46. Previously, establishment candidates had gained higher support: Rafsanjani had won 94.5 per cent of the vote in 1989, and Khamene'i had won 88 per cent in 1985 and 95 per cent in 1981.
47. *Iran Times*, 30 May; *Iran News*, 2 June 1997.
48. *Iran Times*, 30 May 1997.
49. *Washington Post*, 25 May 1997.
50. *Iran Times*, 30 May 1997.
51. *Kayhan* (Tehran), 4 August; *Tehran Times*, 5 August 1997.
52. Tehran TV, 13 August [DR]; IRNA, 19 August 1997 [DR].

53. *Salam*, 6 July 1997 [DR].
54. *Salam*, 17 August 1997 [DR].
55. *Akhbar*, 16 August 1997 [DR].
56. *Jomhuri-ye Islami*, 10 August 1997 [DR].
57. Tehran TV, 19 August 1997 [DR].
58. *Salam*, 9 August 1997; *Mobin*, 11 August 1997 [DR]. They were particularly angered by Khatami's failure to appoint Hojjat ul-Islam Mohammad Musavi Kho'iniha as minister of intelligence.
59. Fallahiyan was accused by a German court for master-minding the murder of the Kurdish opposition leaders at the Mykonos restaurant in Berlin in September 1992. *Die Welt*, 11 April 1997; *Frankfurter Rundschau*, 12 April 1997. Qorban 'Ali Dori Najafabadi was not one of Khatami's own choices for the post, but he was supported by Khamene'i. He was replaced by 'Ali Yunesi after the assassination of Daryush and Parvaneh Foruhar. (See Chapter 5.)
60. *Iran News*, 13 August 1997; IRNA, 12 August 1997.
61. *Iran*, 16 August 1997 [DR]. See also, IRNA, 16 August 1997 [DR].
62. *Jomhuri-ye Islami*, 4 August 1997 [DR].
63. *Jomhuri-ye Islami*, 10 August 1997 [DR].
64. *Salam*, 15 April 1996.
65. *Jomhuri-ye Islami*, 12 August 1997.
66. *Jomhuri-ye Islami*, 10 August 1997.
67. It is possible that his license to run was based on the false assumption that he would not pose any real challenge to the establishment candidate and would be devastatingly defeated, *Salam*, 8 June 1998.
68. IRNA, 5 August 1997, quoting *Kayhan International* [DR].
69. *Washington Post*, 26 May 1997.
70. Azar Nafisi, 'The Veiled Threat', *New Republic*, 22 February 1999, pp. 24–9.
71. Tehran TV, 10 May 1997 [DR].
72. *Kayhan* (Tehran), 17 December 1997 [DR].
73. Thus, while supporters of reform approved dialogue with other civilizations, the conservatives viewed it as a major threat. Majlis deputy Ahmad Nejabat, quoting Khomeini, made this point clear, while discussing Mohajerani's nomination in the Majlis: 'Cultural onslaught is like a storm which will destroy even an electronic door.' Tehran TV, 19 August 1997 [DR].
74. *Financial Times*, 23 August 1997.
75. Radio Tehran, 28 February 1979 – DR, 2 March; *Newsweek*, 19 March 1979; *Daily Telegraph*, 2 September 1979.
76. *Iran Weekly Press Digest*, 16–22 August 1997, Vol. 10, No. 34.
77. *Salam*, 18 March 1997.
78. *Kayhan* (Tehran), 16 February 1998 [DR].
79. *Kayhan International*, 5 August 1997 [DR].
80. *Kayhan International*, 10 February 1979.
81. Khatami's interview on CNN, broadcast by Iranian TV, 8 January 1998 [DR].
82. See, for example, *Salam*, 18 June 1998.
83. *Ettela'at*, 1 June 1998. See also *Kayhan International*, 30 May 1998; IRNA, 28 May 1998 [DR].
84. See, for example, *Salam*, 27 January 1998. For other similar accusations see *Kayhan* (Tehran), 3 May 1998, and *Resalat*, 3 May 1998.

85. *Kayhan* (Tehran), 28 May 1998 and *Mobin*, 2 May 1998; AFP, 29 April 1998 [DR].
86. *Kayhan* (Tehran), 30 May, 2 June 1998.
87. *Iran News*, 11 November 1997. See also statements by Mohammad Yazdi, *Jomhuri-ye Islami,* 22 November 1997.
88. In fact, 146 out of 270 Majlis deputies signed a petition addressed to Khamene'i requesting him to pardon Karbaschi. *Iran News* (Internet database), 12 May 1999 [DR].
89. *Kayhan International*, 17 June 1998 [DR].
90. IRNA, 14 April 1998 [DR]. Majlis member Morteza Nabavi argued that claiming that the detention of officials weakened the government was tantamount to providing them with immunity. IRNA, 5 April 1998 [DR].
91. *Iran News*, 13 June 1998 [DR].
92. *Kayhan International*, 17 June 1998 [DR].
93. Majlis deputy Mohammad Baqer Musavi Jahanabad, in IRNA, 5 April 1998 [DR].
94. IRNA, 5 April 1998 [DR].
95. *Tehran Times*, 9 April 1998 [DR].
96. IRNA, 11 April 1998 [DR]. Amir Kabir, Qajar prime minister, was a modernizer. He was assassinated in 1851.
97. *Hamshahri*, 6 April 1998 [DR].
98. IRNA, 10 June 1998 [DR].
99. IRNA, 17 June 1998 [DR].
100. *Salam,* 18 June 1998 [DR].
101. *Mobin*, 20 June 1998 [DR].
102. IRNA, 21 June 1998 [DR].
103. The impeachment motion against Mohajerani was defeated by 135–121 votes, with 7 abstentions. *Kayhan* (Tehran), 2 May; *Kayhan International*, 3 May 1999.
104. *Ruzegar-e Now*, no. 205 (February–March 1999), pp. 19–22; *Frankfurter Rundschau*, 9 March 1999 [DR].
105. *Ruzegar-e Now*, no. 205 (February–March 1999), pp. 19–22; Radio Free Europe/Radio Liberty (RFE/RL), Iran Report, 2/10, 8 March 1999.
106. *Salam*, 16 March 1999.

4

Social and Economic Difficulties and Political Repercussions

GOVERNMENT POLICY: VISION AND REALITY

The economy was undoubtedly one of the most pressing challenges facing the Islamic regime in its first two decades in power. To begin with, the acute social and economic hardships experienced by ordinary people under the monarchy were among the principal reasons for the discontent which led ultimately to a change of regime. The coming to power of the new regime further raised expectations of an improvement in living standards. After two decades of Islamic rule, however, such expectations remained largely unfulfilled. In the 1990s, social and economic distress has been the main cause of popular discontent, often leading to harsh criticism – even by devout revolutionaries – and sporadic disturbances, in urban centers as well as in the periphery (mainly in the regions inhabited by ethnic minorities). Economic policy became enmeshed in fierce doctrinal and political disputes, with rival domestic camps differing intensely over the priority that economic reconstruction should have as against political liberalizations, the goals to be pursued and the means to achieve these. Such grievances and the demand for greater reform were also behind the massive support for Khatami. Consequently, his election engendered renewed hopes for significant change and a brighter future.

Objective conditions, the magnitude of the problems and political controversies over economic policy, further hindered the government's efforts to resolve them. The programs that were executed successfully were not wide-ranging enough to address the growing needs of a fast-growing population and to meet the rising expectations. Some experts went as far as to maintain that such difficulties had accelerated the Islamic regime's delegitimization.[1] Khatami himself was openly critical of the economic situation, describing the economy as 'sick'. Evidently, the government, and Khatami personally, faced the daunting task of economic restructuring and improving living conditions. In 1999 – half way through his term – Khatami and his government became the targets of fierce criticism for their failure to resolve the economic crisis. Khamene'i, who met with Khatami and his cabinet on 24 August 1999 made it clear: 'The most important problem of the country today is the economic problem.'[2] Yet, eventually, this was also the most difficult problem to resolve.

This chapter does not intend to analyze the roots of Iran's economic difficulties, nor to discuss in detail the social and economic policy under the Islamic regime. In line with the main theme of this book, the discussion here limits itself to establishing the main social and economic difficulties and their effects on the regime and its policy, and their impact on the people in the second decade of the revolution.[3]

The Islamic regime assumed power equipped with a general vision of the ideal Islamic state, including a very general economic theory, but with no detailed programs for immediate action in the management of the economy. Some general theories of an 'Islamic economy' have been outlined in the decades preceding the Iranian Revolution by such thinkers as Ayatollah Muhammad Baqir al-Sadr (in Iraq) and Ayatollah Mahmud Taleqani, and to a degree, also by Abul-Hasan Bani Sadr.[4] These, and many of Khomeini's own writings and declarations prior to taking power, stress the general goals of social justice; reducing social disparities; easing the lives of the *mostaz'afin*; and improving basic social services, especially for the underprivileged. They also stress economic independence and self-sufficiency, as well as reducing Iran's dependence on oil revenues. But such general ideals were not accompanied with programmatic plans for action. Moreover, objective conditions also hindered the government's efforts to remedy these grave problems.

The conditions under which the new regime assumed power were difficult. The rapid modernization witnessed in the 1960s and 1970s, land reforms under the Shah, and Iran's growing dependence on the outside world – in addition to a long period of revolutionary upheaval – left a heavy burden on the government. Rapid population growth and accelerated urbanization which began under the monarchy, were exacerbated under the Islamic rule, which also triggered the flight of many professionals (and their capital) and a drop in foreign investment. The war with Iraq added new difficulties, including costly expenditures, destruction of infrastructure near the front lines, and growing numbers of refugees from war-ravaged areas in Iran and neighboring Afghanistan following the Soviet invasion of 1979 and the resulting civil war. The tension in relations with the West, mainly the United States, as well as the United States' 'dual containment' policy and its economic sanctions, also added to the difficulties. (See Chapter 6.) Finally, the drop in oil income further hindered efforts to remedy the mounting difficulties. Aside from the controversies generated by some measures adopted in response to these problems (programs such as land redistribution and taxation, the acceptance of foreign loans and privatization, or incentives for Iranian expatriates to return home), there were also ideological and political differences. Under such circumstances, the resolution of basic economic problems and the easing of hardships experienced by common people was a Herculean task.

In the first decade of the revolution, with Khomeini at the helm and war raging on Iran's borders with Iraq, popular expectations were limited. Thereafter, however, they grew considerably, often with the government's encouragement. Unlike Khomeini, who avoided making pledges to deliver economic prosperity and consistently labored to lower expectations, his successors promised to eliminate poverty (*faqr*) and privation (*mahrumiyyat*) and serve the barefoot (*paberahnegan*),[5] thus fueling expectations. Opposing pressures thus buffeted Rafsanjani when he first became president in 1989. To effectively address the root problems of the economy, the regime had to adopt new policies, which often deviated from basic ideological convictions and generated controversy. To meet popular expectations and advance the economy Rafsanjani had to implement major reform programs (e.g., privatization, elimination of subsidies, improving ties with the West), which infuriated the doctrinaire elements in the leadership. At the same time, he also had to lay down the foundations for solid, long-term economic growth (such as investing in infrastructure), which incurred large expenses and entailed immediate hardship for the poor but that did not show instant results. The same dilemma faced Khatami who was also expected to lay down the foundations for a strong economy and provide immediate results; to adopt new, pragmatic policies and remain 'politically correct' to gain the support of the ideological purists, at the time that he seemed preoccupied with advancing political reforms.

The popular demand for social and economic welfare was noticeable especially after the Iran–Iraq war (and the death of Khomeini soon after). Rafsanjani who was then Majlis Speaker and later the president regarded economic reconstruction as one of the government's major aims. Striving to 'maintain ideals' but also to 'meet the needs of the people',[6] he supported the expansion of the private sector and encouraged expatriate professional and foreign firms to return to Iran. He approved foreign borrowings, and – slowly and gradually – adopted other similarly controversial measures. Initially, at least, Khamene'i (first as president and later Supreme Leader) generally supported this policy (though occasionally after some hesitation). Thus, immediately following the cease-fire with Iraq, he agreed that since reconstruction could not be prolonged 'for decades', Iran needed 'financial resources and technology' from foreign sources as well as the involvement of its private sector in the economy.[7] But whatever reforms were adopted, they did not lead to any substantial improvement in the lives of the *mostaz'afin*. Objective constraints, doctrinaire and political disputes and economic mismanagement also curtailed efforts to address properly existing problems. As one Iranian economist observed, regardless of objective constraints, 'We have a sick economy because of bad policies.'[8]

The government's policy to remedy economic problems was soon enmeshed in a fierce doctrinal and factional disputes which made decision-making arduous and practical improvements inadequate. Thus, the conservatives (and with them the 'radicals') opposed cooperation with international monetary agencies and foreign investment, and strongly resisted proposals to normalize relations with the United States. Iran's Central Bank, leading economists and President Rafsanjani personally supported privatization and foreign enterprise.[9] But such plans provoked harsh dogmatic objections. Mohtashami typically characterized supporters of privatization as having been 'deceived by America'.[10] *Jahan-e Islam*, viewing such schemes as tantamount to 'handing over' Iran's economy to foreign firms, argued that they would not resolve Iran's problems but merely allow foreigners 'to pillage' its national wealth.[11] Yet, the underlying difficulties were not merely, or even primarily, doctrinal or political.

Iran's main source of external revenue was, and still is, oil. Yet the drop in production in Iran, the world oil glut and the resultant decline in prices in the international market made it difficult to finance Iran's growing needs, let alone provide the necessary capital for over-ambitious reconstruction programs initiated by the government and put into motion in the early 1990s.

Iran's oil production dropped below pre-revolution levels as prices – forecast at around US$20 per barrel at the outset of the first economic plan (1990–94) – fell to between US$16–$17 by the end of 1994, far below the roughly US$40 per barrel in the early 1980s. Oil continues to be Iran's leading export commodity, yet in the first half of 1377 (the year beginning on 21 March 1998), for example, revenue was down US$3bn compared with the same period in the proceeding year. This was the result of the decrease in exports, increased domestic consumption and the weakening of Asian markets.[12] Indeed, Iranian ministers have unveiled 'grandiose' plans for the rapid growth of non-oil exports. These expect non-oil exports to rise in future.[13] The government has also invested in copper extraction and called for foreign investment in the oil sector, but in other sectors, agriculture for example, reform remains a distant goal.[14] Iran continues to depend on oil income, and revenues up to 1999 remained low (see below).

Notwithstanding the drop in income, the government 'which kept a tight rein on consumption' throughout the Iran–Iraq war continued to overspend.[15] Thus imports rose from US$8bn in 1988 to US$23bn in 1992 – a total of US$72bn over the four years, of which roughly 40 per cent was financed by debt. After Rafsanjani's election to the presidency, foreign debt stood at a mere US$6bn, but subsequently skyrocketed as a result of the government's large-scale borrowing and investments in infrastructure. Although reports were inconsistent, most sources estimated that Iran's total debt at the end of Rafsanjani's first term in the presidency (1993) stood at almost US$30bn, with US$8–10bn overdue.[16] Thus having emerged from the war with virtually no foreign debt problem, Iran found itself falling behind schedule on its repayments on short-term loans in the early 1990s.[17]

Although Iran was eventually able to cut its annual imports, it could not escape the heavy burden and severe consequences of earlier, and still high, consumption. The radical faction censured both the government's main policy guidelines and the practical results of its policy. Mohtashami grumbled in 1993 that debt repayment was 'breaking our backs'.[18] *Jahan-e Islam* also voiced concerns that 'an important part of [Iran's] national income' was being 'devoured by debts'.[19] Other officials acknowledged the existence of the problem, but not its dimensions and certainly not its possible destabilizing influence. Questioned in 1993 about the debt problem 'bedeviling the country', Rafsanjani stated that the situation was 'under control'.[20] Iran's creditors, however, exhibited 'anxiety that Tehran [had] over-reached itself'.[21] Iranian officials admitted in 1993 that 'few banks are . . . willing to take Iranian risk' until the delays in repayment are rectified.[22] The main means of easing the burden was debt rescheduling, which removed the most immediate burden but created future difficulties.[23] Whereas in the aftermath of the war with Iraq Iranians had argued about whether to accept foreign loans, in the mid-1990s they wondered how to repay them and who would provide them with additional loans.

Reduced oil revenues and the pressure of foreign debt continued to pose a problem under Khatami. The Governor of the Central Bank, Mohsen Nurbakhsh, in his annual report on the economy for the year ended 20 March 1999 confirmed that the economy faced fundamental problems. He mentioned, among others, a drop in the economic growth rate; the low level of (foreign and domestic) investment; foreign debts repayment and 'soaring inflation'. The government had managed to reduce its foreign debts from US$30.3 billion in 1992 to as low as US$12.8bn by mid-1999, he said, adding that meanwhile, the fall in oil prices, the Asian economic crisis and the increase in the government's foreign debts had complicated the repayment of the loans. During 1997–98 and 1998–99 the price of crude oil had slumped and reached levels that were unprecedented in the last two decades. Consequently Iran's oil income had dropped to just US$9.9bn, i.e. US$5bn lower than forecast. To compensate for the loss of oil revenues the government had taken the initiative of encouraging the export of non-oil goods, which was still insufficient to cover payment of outstanding foreign debts commitments, Nurbakhsh said. (The rise of oil prices in the international markets in 1999 was a significant relief, and if prices remain high and exports unchanged, they could help the government to advance its program. Interestingly, according to Iranian official sources, there was a steady decline in the share of oil revenues in government income. While in 1993–94 some 75 per cent of the government income was from oil, in 1998–99 it totalled less than 37 per cent.[24] See below also on Khatami's third five-year development plan). The drop in oil revenue was not the only problem, however.

Economic pressures were also exacerbated by rapid population growth, which hampered government efforts to provide essential services. Iran's population, estimated at 38m in 1979, had risen to around 65m by the late 1990s. The high population growth continues to pose a serious challenge to the government.[25] Studies estimated that some 44 per cent of Iran's population in the early 1990s were less than 15 years old and more than half under 20. The population was, thus, young and demanding. Rapid population growth began to occupy the minds of policy-makers mainly after the 1988 cease-fire with Iraq (and the publication of the 1986 census, the first after the revolution). Since then, however, Iran's family-planning program has made impressive gains. United Nations experts praised it as one of the world's most successful population control programs for 'melding religion and *realpolitik*'.[26] Fertility declined in the 1990s and population growth was 'beginning to moderate'.[27] Although this was a significant change with important long-term consequences, in the short-run the earlier (and still high) growth is hampering government economic and social planning, and making it difficult to supply essential services. (See below.)

The repercussions of inflation were felt mainly by the lower social strata which led to popular discontent. It was in this realm that common people felt the economic problem most directly and painfully. Soaring prices put many commodities beyond their reach, while the black market boomed and speculators prospered. Official statistics showed only a marginal rise in the rate of inflation, compared with popular perceptions. Thus, the official inflation for the year 1993–94 was set at 22 per cent (the same as 1992–93), although economists viewed these figures with skepticism.[28] The 'undeniable truth', declared *Kayhan International*, reflecting popular sentiments, was that prices were rising 'at a crazy rate'.[29]

As a result, the purchasing power of vulnerable groups had 'dropped sharply'[30] and the poor were showing growing signs of irritation. As prices rose, *Kayhan* noted in 1982, the 'irritation [*a'sab*] index' was moving upward as well. If this continued, it added, 'economic malaise' would likely 'undermine the political success of the revolution'.[31] Mocking the government's customary appeal for 'revolution-inspired patience', Hojjat ul-Islam Ahmad 'Ali Burhani noted cynically that an hungry *mostaz'af* 'cannot buy bread with patience'.[32] *Abrar* added that the price rises 'made people lose hope in their future' and 'put psychological and nervous pressure on society'.[33] When in 1993 Rafsanjani's supporters solicited votes with the slogan 'every vote is a bullet fired in the heart of the revolution's enemies', his rivals retorted that each additional percentage of inflation was a bullet fired into the stomach of the hungry *mostaz'afin*.

Faced with growing popular resentment, the government occasionally launched initiatives to fight inflation and profiteering. In 1994, for example, a committee was formed under the president's supervision to combat high prices and coordinate the distribution of essential goods.[34] The ministry of justice announced severe measures against profiteers and hoarders, including fines, confiscation, imprisonment, and even execution.[35] But previous similar efforts had yielded no meaningful results and people had little hope that such new measures would prove any more successful. The *Tehran Times* typically depicted such economic measures as a 'tranquilizer', that was unlikely to cure the illness itself.[36]

Added to this were growing unemployment (particularly among the young), shortages of basic utilities, the shrinking value of the riyal, and many other problems – all pressing hard primarily on ordinary people.

Yet, while the poor suffered, the rich continued to lead pleasant lives.

Among the *mostaz'afin* there was a growing sense that the revolution
had abandoned, if not betrayed them. In addition, official misconduct
(sometimes involving clerics), gave economic privation a moral dimension. Aware of the cynicism and skepticism that had long governed
popular attitudes towards the statements and personal conduct of
officials, Khamene'i repeatedly urged them to avoid excessive consumption (*esraf*) and ostentatious lifestyles (*tajammolgara'i*). He admonished
those who traveled in expensive cars, held lavish marriage ceremonies,
and occupied the luxurious houses that once belonged to the Shah's
former dignitaries.[37] Yet, even according to some Iranian sources, the
problem was so deeply rooted that it was unlikely to be removed by
'superficial affectation' because 'some government officials and MPs are
the prominent examples' of such conduct.[38] *Kayhan* asked rhetorically,
why government agents traveled in expensive cars, and how Majlis
members could justify their lavish lifestyles.[39] Citizens complained, 'You
never see a Revolutionary Guard or a *mullah* having to queue for anything'.[40]

These social disparities were highlighted by a series of corruption and
fraud scandals involving prominent officials. The 1995 Bank Saderat
affair was one such scandal that became known as 'the theft of the
century'. Morteza Rafiqdust (brother of Mohsen Rafiqdust, the head
of the *Bonyad-e Mostaz'afin*) and seven others were charged with
embezzling nearly US$450m from the Bank.[41] Majlis member
Mohammad Baqer Tavakkoli described the culprits as 'economic
terrorists' who should be declared 'corrupt of the earth' (*mofsed fil-arz*)
and severely punished.[42] Eventually, one offender was sentenced to
death and two (including Morteza Rafiqdust) to life imprisonment; one
was acquitted and the rest given shorter terms. There were many other
cases in which clerics and officials were found guilty of fraud.[43]
Ayatollah 'Ali Meshkini, the head of the Council of Experts, tapped into
the popular sentiment arguing that those involved in the scandal had
not only harmed the economy but also tarnished the 'dignity of the
system'.[44] Nateq-Nuri expressed concern that if such acts of corruption
are not stopped, they may even threaten the revolution.[45]

The government also found it difficult to supply basic welfare services.
Meeting the growing demand for education was one such a challenge.
As under the Shah, pre-university education expanded rapidly but
remained largely limited to instruction of the curriculum. In many
respects, this instruction was lacking in quality. Many schools operated
two and sometimes three shifts, with classes often overcrowded. Though
facilities for higher education expanded significantly under the Islamic

regime, capacity continued to lag behind demand and some of the main qualitative deficiencies persisted. The ratio of applicants to admissions remained wide, no less than in the late 1970s (about 10:1), with the number of rejected applicants growing rapidly. There was a large exodus of veteran professors (mainly following the 1979 revolution and during the Iran–Iraq war) and shortages of classroom space and basic teaching materials, such as laboratory equipment and even books. Professors were in high demand, often travelling to different cities to teach in various academic centers. They thus became known as 'flying professors' (*ostadha-ye parvazi*). Some taught 30 hours per week, others also had jobs in the government. (The Free Islamic University absorbed many students, but was not considered sufficiently prestigious for university aspirants, nor capable of providing the necessary skills and the diversified expertise needed by industry, nor even of meeting the growing demand for higher education.)

Housing was as much of a problem in the 1990s as it was in the 1970s. According to official statistics contained in a 1983 survey, there was a shortage of 3.7m housing units in the mid-1980s, causing rents to rise faster than incomes. Families in Tehran often spent most of their incomes on rent.[46] In the early 1990s, officials predicted that 'the current [difficult] situation would prevail' for the next two decades. As a result of growing demand and rising inflation, rents spiraled out of control and became yet another major cause of public disillusionment.[47]

Similarly, ordinary Iranians had to search frantically for affordable healthcare, often turning to the black market for basic drugs. *Kayhan International* described medical services as 'a mess, and the system, if any . . . at best chaotic'. The newspaper advised the government to take the issue 'very seriously', lest it creates 'public resentment and discontent'.[48] The situation deteriorated further in mid-1995, after a health ministry decision to limit the import of many drugs.[49] These are only few examples, mentioned briefly here, of a much wider problem.

Ethnic groups, living on the periphery and less developed parts of the country, continued to suffer even greater economic difficulties than their compatriots in the center, adding to their ethnic-based grievances.

Notwithstanding the myth of Iran as a unified entity, ethnic diversity is a problem. Iran has always been a multicultural society, divided into a number of ethnic minorities inhabiting mainly the peripheral areas: Azeri Turks in the northwest, Kurds in the west, Arabs in the southwest, Baluchis in the southeast, and Turkomans in the northeast. About half of Iran's population is made up of minority groups.[50] Although they were integrated in varying degrees into the social, economic and political system, many felt discriminated against and continued to feel so after the revolution. They sought greater autonomy than the Shah's regime (basing itself on national concept), was willing to grant. Soon they realized that the new regime (from its Islamic perspective), was also unwilling to grant them the kind of local autonomy they sought. Neither regime addressed their particular economic problems in any meaningful way.

The ethnic minorities differ in their history, sectarian affiliation, strength and degree of political organization although several common features make them all a challenge for Tehran. They are concentrated mainly in peripheral areas, with ties to parallel ethnic groups, including Azeris, Kurds, Arabs, Baluchis, Turkomans, across the border. They have fostered separatist movements in the past, some of which led to autonomy for short periods, such as the Kurdish Republic of Mahabad and the Autonomous Government of Azerbaijan. Many of them feel social and economic deprivation and are indignant because the process of development has bypassed their areas. The modernization process of the last century has accomplished no more than a surface integration and, generally speaking, has not prevented continued backwardness in their regions.[51] Their unfulfilled expectations of at least cultural autonomy, coupled with their sense of economic deprivation, added to their disillusionment, posing yet another challenge to the Islamic regime.

Finally, the experience of 20 years of Islamic rule led many Iranians to feel that in some respects the clerics in power were not so different from the regime they had replaced – a devastating feeling for a people who had supported the Islamic Revolution in the hope of bringing about a significant change. An observer noted that the reports of widespread corruption 'prompt comparisons between the rule of the *mullahs* and the last days of the Shah'.[52] Hashim added that ruling clerics 'abused [their] power and amassed great wealth, which contributed to the growing chasm between themselves and the traditional clergy' and debased 'the spiritual value of the clerical establishment' by their 'corrupt behavior'.[53] Religion, another scholar added, 'has become a cover for greed' and corruption. The regime's inherent contradiction – wealthy *mulla*-bureaucrats preaching virtue to the poor – 'engendered rampant anger and cynicism'.[54]

However, it is undeniable that under the circumstances, the government had some significant achievements which ought not be overlooked. The basic infrastructure when the clerics assumed power, and the consequent developments in Iran (such as population growth) as well as the international developments (the war, the drop of oil price, sanctions), made it difficult to address the mounting difficulties. The government (mainly under Rafsanjani's first term as president), launched important reconstruction programs and invested in a number of significant infrastructure projects. Notable achievements were observed in rural areas. Yet, the basic difficulties could not appropriately be addressed. The heritage of pre-revolutionary realities and initial difficulties including the Iran–Iraq war, tension with the outside world, declining oil income, negligence by the regime of important sectors (agriculture, private sector, tourism) and economic and administrative mismanagement, were among the long list of problems and difficulties. Domestic rifts and the fact that the government's hands were often tied when it sought to adopt a more pragmatic line were also obstacles. More importantly, even allowing for some achievements, the regime fell significantly short of the rising expectations of most Iranians by failing to meet the essential needs of a rapidly expanding population.

On 15 September 1999 Khatami presented the government's bill on the third five-year development plan (2000–04) in the Majlis, and said that it was a 'highly important' means to realize revolutionary aims. Because Khatami viewed economic reconstruction in a wider political, cultural and international context, his plan emphasised the rule of law, and the creation of a safe and stable atmosphere to protect the rights of all people. He also stressed the 'promotion of Islamic thoughts and ethics', preservation of human dignity, care for people's rights and the protection of 'legal freedoms and social security'. Finally, Khatami underlined the need for comprehensive and fundamental reforms of the country's economic structure. Yet, most of the major aims and policy directions remained similar to those of the early days of the Islamic regime. Reducing dependence on oil, reforming the structure of social welfare, curbing inflation, expanding employment and encouraging the private sector were among the significant aspects of the plan. Oil, Khatami said, should be viewed as 'the asset of the present and future generations'. Spending this capital for 'consuming purposes is tantamount to maintaining [the] welfare of [the] present generation at the expense of poverty for generations to come', he said. However, the achievement of these economic goals, Khatami said, would depend upon 'national determination', and the cooperation and convergence of all institutions and masses of the society.[55] Above and beyond pure economic problems and political and ideological constraints were concurrent factional rifts, which posed a significant challenge to Khatami and his government. (See the conclusion to Part One.)

At this stage, however, people were expecting tangible improvements, not promises and eloquent speeches. The urge for more concrete and effective policies ultimately led to growing popular pressure and the election of Khatami. These were preceded, however, with harsh criticism of the government's economic failures and a series of riots in different parts of the country.

POPULAR RESPONSE: GROWING IMPATIENCE

These severe economic difficulties notwithstanding, the government customarily portrayed the economic situation sanguinely, promising even brighter prospects for future. Thus, on the fourteenth anniversary of the revolution in 1993, President Rafsanjani said that he was 'greatly satisfied' with the government's economic performance.[56] Iran had followed the revolutionary path 'to perfection', he added, with 'no dark spots' on its 'performance record'.[57] Khamene'i similarly said in 1994 that Iran had managed 'to overcome the obstacles' and advance 'in all spheres', promising a 'bright and glorious' future.[58] Although President Rafsanjani often reiterated the view that Iran was 'traveling on a satisfactory path in all fields', he conceded occasionally that things could have been better. 'We want construction . . . material progress, and economic progress', he said, 'so that we will no longer have any poor . . . [the] deprived classes will no longer feel deprived . . . [and the] difference between the rich and the poor will be less every day.'[59]

When officials did admit difficulties, they inevitably blamed the Shah's policies, the revolutionary process, the war with Iraq, Western imperialism or their regional allies, and advised people to demonstrate 'revolutionary patience'. In the 1990s they focused primarily on blaming the West, particularly the United States and its regional allies for their hostility to Iran and Islam. They blamed the United States for lowering oil prices,[60] and accused Saudi Arabia of overproducing oil[61] – all to harm Iran. Rafsanjani's government (and subsequently Khatami's) also accused the more doctrinaire factions at home of hindering its efforts to remedy the situation, and as will be shown, the hard-liners at home often blamed, first President Rafsanjani and then President Khatami.

The government continued to rely on well-worn themes, advising people to demonstrate revolutionary patience and support the government and, thus, defend Islam. It advised businessmen – as Rafsanjani did – 'to be fair' and 'mindful' of the economic situation and warn that they would deal severely with profiteers.[62] He blamed an unholy alliance of producers, middlemen, and retailers for creating 'a poisoned climate',[63] with the aim of adding to Iran's economic problems. In rhetoric reminiscent of the Shah's pledges, he promised to solve remaining problems by the end of the second economic plan in 1999.[64] Even while acknowledging these problems, officials continued to castigate the West for magnifying them in an attempt to 'ignite psychological maneuvers' against Iran.[65] This 'propaganda ploy', Khamene'i said, was aimed at 'creating despondency and despair'.[66] Officials expressed confidence that people who had risked their lives for the revolution would not abandon it just 'for the sake of a few shortages or high prices'. Such imaginary 'threats', they often argued, existed only in the minds of Iran's enemies who 'continue wallowing in their foolish concepts', unaware of the strength of the revolution.[67] In fact, the people had proved to be patient and willing to accept hardships. Nevertheless, especially after the cease-fire with Iraq, they had expected at least some improvement in their living conditions. Clearly, there was growing sense of disillusionment and greater expectation of real change.

For their part, the *mostaz'afin* felt that although they had borne the main burden of the revolution and the war, they were discriminated against by the very regime that claimed to be 'the government of the *mostaz'afin*', while allowing the rich to become even richer. Montazeri had already pointed to the paradox during the Iran–Iraq war. 'Today', he said in 1983, 'the heavy burden of the revolution, the war and the resultant shortages [are] pressing far more on the lower strata'. The upper strata 'enjoy a large share' of the services and commodities but 'contribute precious little at the front lines of the revolution and war'.[68] The *mostaz'afin*, he added, are the 'main owners' of the revolution,[69] yet the rich, whose children 'avoid going to the front' are its primary beneficiaries.[70] This was not fair in principle and contradicted basic Islamic values. Majlis economic committee spokesman, Mohammad Khaza'i, also concluded that it was unacceptable to an Islamic regime that 'one part of the population walks around with stomachs bloated from malnutrition, while the stomachs of another part are bloated from over-eating'.[71] Khomeini himself spoke with much distaste of the gulf separating shanty-dwellers (*kukh-neshin*) from palace-dwellers (*kakh-neshin*) in Islamic Iran, and warned that if the mentality of the latter prevailed, the revolution would be in real danger.[72]

But the gap has persisted and even widened since Khomeini's death, and criticism of the clerical regime has intensified. The government's domestic critics painted a dark picture of the economic situation and projected gloomier future prospects. While criticizing the government's general policy, they focused on its failure to serve the underprivileged. Mohtashami, and the radical faction in general, used such failures to censor the government in the early 1990s. Mohtashami foresaw 'extremely dangerous consequences' arising from the government's economic failures.[73] Rafsanjani, he said, had made 'lavish promises' of extensive welfare schemes, but 'not even one' of them had so far materialized. Instead, prices had 'spiraled enormously', foreign exchange rates had 'started a swift upward trend', the affluent had become wealthier than before, and the social gap wider. The government's policy, he said, was tantamount to 'letting the economy run amok'. If this situation continued, Mohtashami predicted a 'catastrophe'.[74] He accused the government of serving the rich only,[75] and complained that soaring inflation had wiped out the value of salary raises for the poor. In this sense, he went as far as to suggest that the situation in Islamic Iran was even worse than in some capitalist countries. There, governments secure that the purchasing power of the people rises proportionally with the rise in prices, he said. Yet, in Iran, they are being 'crushed under the burden of debilitating inflation'.[76] Clearly, Mohtashami added, 'there is greater welfare . . . for the rich', but all people 'unanimously agree' that the life of the poor in Iran is 'significantly more difficult today than yesterday'.[77] Similarly Sadeq Khalkhali maintained that under Amir 'Abbas Hoveyda (the Shah's hated prime minister), prices were at least stable, whereas they were now rising by the hour.[78] These derogatory comparisons with the capitalist West and the Shah's reign were the harshest possible indictments for the Islamic regime, especially when they came from devout revolutionaries. (For the economic philosophy of the radicals and the pragmatists, see Chapter 2.)

The press was similarly critical of the government's economic policy and prevailing realities. The harsh tone adopted by prominent revolutionaries (mainly in the Majlis and also among some government officials), was taken as a license openly to censure the government's economic failures. They often exceeded the milder official tone and – more often than not – reflected the radical-pragmatist dichotomy. The picture they painted was gloomy, reflecting growing hardships and impatience. Thus, *Kayhan International* wondered who was really responsible for this 'state of chaos'. Galloping inflation, mismanagement and indifference towards the lower strata had made life for them 'intolerable and miserable', it wrote in 1993. Social justice, at one time a major ideal of the revolution, seemed to be the government's last priority and 'if current trends are any indication . . . [its turn] may never come'.[79] People's trust in government policy, it added, was 'decreasing daily along with their purchasing power'.[80] Six years after the end of the war with Iraq, it wrote, 'at best . . . the situation had deteriorated'. It dismissed policies such as displaying price tags on goods (one method used by the government to curb inflation), as gimmicks, likely to meet the same fate as hundreds of previous similar efforts. 'Rhetoric has far outstripped reality', it wrote, adding that in addition to people's purchasing power, their 'morale and tolerance' were also in decline.[81]

Salam reminded its readers that every basic textbook of Islamic economics stressed that an Islamic system is free from poverty and hunger. Yet, 'with the prevalent deep economic crisis, given the poverty and suffering of the masses', is it possible at all to refer to Iran as 'an Islamic society?'[82] *Jahan-e Islam* (owned and edited by Khamene'i's brother, Hadi, who often express independent views), was bitterly critical. No serious effort had been made to block spiraling prices, it wrote, and whenever the regime did formulate a policy, it failed completely in its implementation.[83] Referring to a renowned *hadith* (a saying attributed to the Prophet) – '*al-mulk yabqa' ma'a al-kufr wala yabqa' ma'a al-zulm*' ('a regime can survive blasphemy but not injustice') – a reader queried whether the discrimination, favoritism, price-hikes, nepotism, shortages, and socioeconomic gaps were not all clear signs of injustice.[84]

Some critics even targeted President Rafsanjani personally, mainly in his second term in office. Referring to one of his sanguine statements, *Salam* castigated those whom it labeled as 'dreamers', who are happy with the situation and care only about criticizing the press for reporting problems,[85] or attributing their own failures to foreign foes and local capitalists.[86] Mohtashami ridiculed Rafsanjani for imagining that he could solve problems through delivering articulate sermons or instigating people against foreign or domestic foes.[87] *Payam-e Daneshju-ye Basiji* argued that neither Iran's external nor its domestic enemies could possibly have contributed even one per cent to prevailing hardships. It attributed such problems instead to the government's policies and its incompetence, and charged Rafsanjani personally with the responsibility.[88] His officials had made 'all of the decisions that led to the current [difficult] situation', it remarked.[89] *Omid* mocked the government's tendency to attribute all the failings to the Shah or foreign powers, absolving itself of the responsibility. 'The blows that we have inflicted on our economy are harsher than the conspiracies of the East and the West combined', it wrote. How was it at all possible, the paper said mocking another typically official line, to cite national independence as a major gain of the revolution and to claim at the same breath that 'we don't have a say in what is going on in our "independent" state?'[90]

Popular discontent did not find its expression solely in Majlis speeches, scholarly discussions and critiques in the press. There were numerous strikes, assassination attempts on officials, and riots in some of the main urban centers.

Occasional demonstrations, strikes, and acts of violence have been a repeated occurrence since 1979. Yet, the series of popular riots in the early 1990s proved extremely worrying for the government, because the participants were primarily ordinary – mostly young – people whose grievances touched upon some of the basic failures of the government and whose attacks were aimed against some of the defining symbols of the regime. Although the connection between riots in various cities is not clear, there was a sense of a chain reaction. Rafsanjani typically dismissed such occurrences as 'small incidents', that were 'blown way out of proportion'. Compared with the 1992 riots in Los Angeles, he said, these were 'very small'. He was confident that in Iran 'the people are with the government'.[91] But the regime was nonetheless concerned.

Large-scale riots began in Shiraz on 15 April 1992 with a demonstration by disabled war veterans protesting against the mismanagement of funds by the *Bonyad-e Mostaz'afin*. It soon widened and turned into demonstrations against the government's general policies. A month later, citizens in Arak protesting against the government's treatment of residents in the city's shanty town clashed with security forces, setting fire to and destroying parts of the City Hall and government offices. Attempts to prevent illegal housing construction triggered similar riots in Meshhed on 30 May, when participants set fire to a number of government vehicles and buildings. Riots, albeit on a lesser scale, were also reported in other cities. Echoing the government's customary refrain – and his favorite allegation – Khamene'i blamed the incidents on foreign conspiracies.[92] Although some citizens may be discontented, he admitted, 'they are not ruffians'. Rather, the fact that the revolution has turned Iran into 'a very big power' led its enemies to employ 'harassment and mischief' to confront its rising power.[93] The Iranian opposition, going to the other extreme, maintained that these were 'only some' expressions of a much wider popular disillusionment with the clerics in power.[94]

Riots were triggered in Qazvin on 3 August 1994 by the rejection in the Majlis of a bill to recognize the region as a province, thereby depriving it of larger government allocations. Officials again claimed that the events were 'exploited by opportunists',[95] and blamed 'anti-social elements' for instigating them.[96] Rafsanjani dismissed the unrest as lacking any political basis adding that, 'all of these events are distorted by the

West'.[97] There were further signs of popular resentment in 1995. On 14 January, a sporting event in Meshhed turned into a clash with the authorities. Four days later, a clash between rival soccer fans developed into a political protest. Local press reported 'acts of vandalism'.[98] Opposition sources stressed the political implications of the rioters' 'anti-regime slogans' and clashes with Revolutionary Guards, claiming that they were yet another expression of public rage. A joint statement by some opposition movements said that the young generation faces a 'rotten life today and feels concern over its uncertain future'.[99]

Riots spread to Islamshahr and Akbarabad (near Tehran) in April 1995. It was the first major unrest to reach the outskirts of the capital. The immediate cause was a reduction in the water supply and a rise in public transport fares. Rioters armed with clubs and stones damaged public buildings and vehicles, as well as gas stations and banks. They disarmed police officers before Revolutionary Guard anti-riot units intervened and sealed off the area. Slogans of 'Down with the Islamic Republic' and 'Down with Rafsanjani – Down with Khamene'i' were then reportedly raised.[100] The government imposed a news blackout on the riots, but gave extensive coverage to subsequent pro-government demonstrations. It resolved not to give the opposition credit for being able to organize such riots (particularly because it had long claimed to have practically eliminated the opposition), nor to present the riots as a 'popular movement' or politically motivated. It stressed, instead, the limited nature of the disturbances and the supposed role of foreigners in inciting riots. Tehran also blamed the disturbances on anti-revolutionaries and hooligans, and accused foreigners of highlighting them to advance their propagandist schemes.[101] There was a similar response by the government to student riots in 1999. (See Chapter 5.)

Yet the regime was genuinely concerned by the popular nature of the riots and the grievances (e.g. inflation, unemployment, housing) that inspired them. *Jahan-e Islam* warned that when people's legitimate wishes are ignored, an 'abscessed tumor' evolves.[102] Typically, it quoted 'the man in the street' as wondering why the government 'fails to accept the truth' – that the patience of the people had been totally exhausted (*tamam shodeh*).[103] *Sobh* added that instead of dismissing the riots as arising from isolated issues (like water supply), the authorities should examine the wider context of growing popular disenchantment, such as inflation, that press so hard on the lower strata.[104]

The riots were thus a warning signal, reflecting popular displeasure with domestic, mainly socioeconomic realities. The scale of the disturbances, the predominance of young people among the participants, and the grievances they voiced pointed to the perilous nature of the situation. The government proved sensitive to the potentially grave nature of popular discontent and took strong measures to suppress any such occurrences before it acquired threatening dimensions.[105] It also set up special Revolutionary Guard forces known as '*Ashura* battalions (rapid-deployment forces specializing in anti-riot tactics), to combat domestic unrest while the minister of the interior was given wider powers to enforce security within the country.[106] Overall, the government managed to prevent these outbursts from assuming threatening proportions. Yet, it did not address the roots of growing disenchantment.

Signs of unrest were evident also in the periphery, primarily in regions inhabited by ethnic minorities. The Kurds and the Azeris presented the most crucial challenge. Both groups had links with similar movements across the border: the Kurds with their compatriots in Iraq and the Azeris with the newly independent Republic of Azerbaijan. The government also faced a serious challenge from other regions inhabited by ethnic minorities such as: in the Arab-inhabited region close to the Gulf, especially in the initial stages of the Iran–Iraq war, and the less developed regions of the southeast inhabited by the Baluchis. Compared with the early years of the revolution, violent opposition in these regions had subsided. Nevertheless, given the profound social and economic difficulties – in addition to their expectations for autonomy – signs of unrest continued among such groups too.

Although the struggle of many of these ethnic groups in the early stages of the revolution was violently suppressed, the government still viewed developments in regions inhabited by these groups with caution. Generally, these minorities demanded cultural autonomy and economic betterment rather than secession. At the outset of the revolution, for example, the slogan of the Kurdistan Democratic Party (KDP) was democracy for Iran, autonomy (*khod-mokhtari*) for Kurdistan. Yet, whatever hopes the Kurds may initially have entertained, faded significantly by the time the regime had stabilized. After two years of active struggle following the coming to power of the new regime, the balance in Kurdistan – as on other ethnic fronts – shifted in the government's favor. Already in 1980, to quote 'Abdul-Rahman Qasemlou, the Kurds no longer had 'any illusions about Khomeini'.[107] Qasemlou then added that Kurdistan was worse off under the Islamic rule than under the monarchy.[108] The challenge of the ethnic minorities was not removed, but the actual violence which typified the early days of the revolution has been somewhat mitigated since then. It seems that while the initial expectations have largely evaporated, what antagonized ethnic minorities most in the 1990s was socioeconomic deprivation.

In 1994, disturbances were reported in Zahedan, where 'plotters' smashed windows of residential buildings and damaged vehicles, including those belonging to the security forces. Again, the government blamed foreign elements who aimed 'to make the active presence of the people look pale' on the anniversary of the revolution.[109] This was followed by other violent incidents: the bombings of Zahedan's City Hall and the Jum'ah Mosque on 2 March, an explosion in mid-town Tehran on 19 April, an attempt on the life of the jum'ah imam in Meshhed on 22 April, and a blast at Iran's most important mosque, the Imam Reza mausoleum in Meshhed on 20 June 1994. Observers highlighted both the sectarian aspects of these incidents, and their link to economic difficulties in the Baluchi-Sunni areas.[110] (It is not yet clear, however, who carried out such actions.) The Azeris, who were much better integrated into the Iranian state, presented the most serious challenge in the 1990s. Whatever unrest was evident in the early days of the revolution in Azerbaijan was suppressed by the government's law-enforcing units and frustrated by Ayatollah Shari'atmadari's instructions to his Azeri disciples to stay calm. Yet, the emergence of an independent Azerbaijan and growing national sentiments in that country were potential influence of nationalist sentiments among Iranian Azeris. In the spring of 1996 (during elections to the Majlis), there were several demonstrations in Tabriz (mainly at the university).

The expectations of these ethnic groups also rose with Khatami's election. Khatami, for his part, was aware of their difficulties and led an extensive election campaign in their regions (some statements of support for him were published in Azeri). Khatami's official campaign stated that despite 'religious, ethnic, and linguistic variations' Iran enjoys 'a particular solidarity and unity'. The recognition of these 'varieties and differences', he added, is 'necessary for social solidarity and consensus'.[111] In his view, 'every Iranian', irrespective of religion or ethnic affiliation, should have a chance to progress. Kurds, Lors, Baluchis, Sunnis and Shi'is 'are all Iranians and all must strive [towards the] making [of] a developed and powerful Iran'.[112] Minorities had overwhelmingly voted for Khatami expecting some improvement in their condition. Among minorities also the government managed to maintain stability, but failed to address the more fundamental problems: their ethnic and cultural aspirations, and social and economic grievances.

Encouraged by growing signs of popular disenchantment, the opposition depicted the regime as increasingly unstable and expressed renewed optimism that it would be soon overthrown. The head of the National Resistance Council (NRC), Mas'ud Rajavi, called the 'heroic uprising' in Zahedan, in 1994, a manifestation of the illegitimacy of the 'crisis-stricken clerical regime' and an 'indicator of the extent of public rage and aversion against the regime'. He blamed 'the *mullas*' regime' for having 'discredited freedom, democracy, and Islam' and promised soon to 'bring [NRC leader] Maryam [Rajavi] to Tehran'.[113] The (clandestine radio) Voice of Iranian Kurdistan said that the 1995 riots reflected the 'rebellion of a generation that has been deprived' by the Islamic regime. Popular dissatisfaction, it said, had turned into 'an active volcano'.[114] Some even viewed the riots in the different cities as the harbinger of a new revolution.[115] Similarly, foreign observers predicted that Iran was heading for a 'civil war', a 'coup', or a deep economic crisis.

Although the opposition may have over-rated the significance of the unrest, the government – at least in its public statements – underestimated them. Despite evidence of growing unrest, the regime expressed confidence in popular support and viewed its vigilance as an effective tool to quell its enemies' designs.[116] President Rafsanjani depicted his government as 'stronger and more stable than any other regime in the world'.[117] The revolution enjoyed even greater support than in its early days, he maintained, and although certain ignorant people (i.e., his domestic rivals), provided foreigners with 'grist for propaganda', most people acknowledged the achievements of the revolution and would continue to support it emphatically.[118] The regime had 'reached such political maturity', Khamene'i added following the Qazvin riots, that 'no power can bully Iran'.[119] Yet, domestic developments – mainly economic difficulties and the restriction on individual freedom (see Chapter 5) – led to growing popular disillusionment while the popular riots gave the regime cause for concern.

Easing the social and economic burdens of the people – mainly the *mostaza'afin* – constituted one of the main reasons for the anti-Shah revolution and was one of the major aims of the leaders of Islamic regime and of the people who supported it enthusiastically. Expectations of an improvement in living conditions was high, but as far as the disadvantageous class was concerned, no meaningful change had so far been achieved.

Long-term social and economic goals, such as self-sufficiency, diminishing dependence on oil income, or bridging social gaps have not yet materialized. Other important social and economic aims, such as blocking the population growth and influx of people into the large cities (mainly to Tehran), have not been accomplished. Major programs (privatization) were delayed because of domestic controversies. Official preference for agriculture rather than industry have similarly failed to be translated into reality, and the aim of building firm infrastructure – which began forcefully under Rafsanjani's 'decade of reconstruction' – could not be completed due to the lack of financing. Gradually, signs of growing alienation between the haves and the have-nots became evident. This turned politically dangerous as the *mostaz'afin* came to believe that an improvement in their condition was 'their right' – earned by their contribution to the revolution and sacrifices in the war with Iraq.

Several factors, some tangible some not, have contributed to the government's success in preventing economic difficulties from reaching dangerous proportions. To begin with, Iran's oil income, although lower than before, was still large enough to finance the purchase of staple commodities. Khomeini's systematic discouragement of material expectations and his strictures against consumerism have been at least initially convincing, and the still zealous support of many Iranians for the revolution continued to serve as an important asset. The weakness of the opposition was another asset. Yet, at the end of the second decade of the Islamic Revolution, there were clear signs of growing disillusionment and disenchantment, with patience in short supply.

The election of Khatami seemed a real opportunity to ameliorate the system from within. Much like Khomeini in 1979, Khatami has turned into a symbol of change in 1997. Yet, three years after Khatami's election, no meaningful breakthrough has been registered under his presidency. Khatami seemed preoccupied with the political rifts, and, while focused on the struggle for civil rights he did not seem to have a free hand in advancing his preferred policies. At the end of 1999, with no breakthrough in sight to heal economic wounds, popular expectations for change became more demanding and criticism harsher. Following the student riots and with the reformists' accent on questions of freedom and liberalism, the conservatives turned to use such difficulties against the president. This was eventually meant to achieve several goals simultaneously: to divert attention from questions of freedom to the economy, and to put the blame on Khatami for failing to address economic problems. Popular disaffection was the fertile ground on which he made his way to the presidency. Khatami's rivals were accusing him of generating the same disaffection. (See Chapter 5.)

While economic distress was the most immediate difficulty facing the people, the restriction on freedom was another major arena of popular discontent. For some Iranians it was the prerequisite to major economic reform. Whether the issue was political (civil rights) or economic, for most Iranians the problem was primarily domestic. The major discontent expressed by young people in the riots of the mid-1990s and student protests of 1999, was related to domestic issues inside Iran.

NOTES

1. Kaveh Ehsani, '"Tilt but Don't Spill": Iran's Development and Reconstruction Dilemma', *Middle East Report*, 24/191 (November–December 1994), p. 20.
2. Tehran TV, 24 August 1999 [DR].
3. For a discussion of the Iranian economy see Jahangir Amuzegar, *Iran's Economy under the Islamic Republic* (London: I.B. Tauris, 1993); Anoushirvan Ehteshami, *After Khomeini The Iranian Second Republic* (London: Routledge 1995), mainly Ch. 5; and Eliyahu Kanovsky, *Iran's Economic Morass: Mismanagement and Decline Under the Islamic Republic* (Washington, DC: Washington Institute for Near East Policy, 1997).
4. See, for example, Seyyed Muhammad Baqir al-Sadr, *Iqtisaduna* [Our Economy], 4th edn (Beirut: Dar al-Fikr, 1973,); Seyyed Mahmud Taleqani, *Islam va Malekiyyat* [Islam and Ownership] (Tehran: Entesharat-e Masjed-e Hedayat, 1954); and Abul-Hasan Bani Sadr, *Eqtesad-e Towhidi* [Economy of Divine Unity] (n.p.: Ettehadiye-ye Anjomanha-ye Islami dar Orupa, 1978).
5. Khamene'i's address to the Majlis on 28 May 1992, in *Salam, Abrar* and *Jomhuri-ye Islami*, 30 May 1992.
6. Radio Tehran, 9 October 1988, in *SWB*, 11 October 1988.
7. *Ettela'at*, 17 September 1988; Radio Tehran, 16 September 1988, in *SWB*, 19 September 1988.
8. Jamshid Pajuan (referring specifically to Iran's fiscal policy) in *Time Magazine*, 22 March 1993.
9. *Jahan-e Islam*, 27 November 1994 – DR, 13 December 1994; IRNA, 10 May 1993 – DR, 12 May 1993; *Ettela'at*, 8 June 1994.
10. *Jahan-e Islam*, 1 November 1994 – DR, 9 November 1994.
11. *Jahan-e Islam*, 27 November 1994 – DR, 13 December 1994.
12. Economist Intelligence Unit (EIU), *Country Report - Iran*, no. 1 (1999), pp. 3, 5, 9, 20.
13. Eliyahu Kanovsky, 'Iran's Sick Economy: Prospects for Change under Khatami', in P. Clawson *et al.* (eds), *Iran Under Khatami: A Political, Economic and Military Assessment* (Washington, DC: Washington Institute for Near East Policy, 1998), p. 57.
14. Economist Intelligence Unit (EIU), *Country Report - Iran*, no. 1 (1999), p. 19.
15. *Financial Times*, 8 February 1993.
16. *Salam*, 2 December 1993. See also Agence France Presse (AFP), 2 December 1993 – DR, 3 December 1993; A. Hashim, *The Crisis of the Iranian State* (London: Oxford University Press, 1995), pp. 13–14. *Salam* estimated the debt in the early 1990s at over US$36bn, whereas Mohtashami cited a figure of around US$40bn (*Jahan-e Islam*, 19 October 1993 – DR, 10 November 1993). Rafsanjani stated in 1994 that it was only US$17bn, of which US$10bn had been scheduled to be repaid at an annual rate of US$3bn, with the goal of solving the problem by 2000 (Radio Tehran, 31 May 1994 – DR, 1 June 1994).

Referring to these 'vague and sometimes contradictory' figures, *Jahan-e Islam*, 22 May 1994 – DR, 2 June 1994, observed that 'a clear picture' of the actual debt 'cannot be obtained'.

17. Patrick Clawson, *Business as Usual?*, pp. 12, 32–3.
18. *Jahan-e Islam*, 19 October 1993 – DR, 10 November 1993.
19. *Jahan-e Islam*, 22 May 1994 – DR, 2 June 1994.
20. *Time*, 24 May 1993.
21. *Financial Times*, 8 February 1993.
22. *Echo of Iran*, no. 62 (March 1993), p. 17.
23. In March 1994 Iran signed credit agreements with Germany and Japan that along with similar agreements signed subsequently with other creditors, rescheduled a total of some US$14bn in debts: Radio Tehran, 12 March 1994 – DR, 14 March 1994; *Iran Times*, 22 and 29 April 1994; EIU, *Country Report – Iran*, no. 3 (1995), p. 23.
24. Nurbakhsh's statement is brought in *Iran Daily* and IRNA, 13 September 1999. For the share of oil income between 1993–94 and 1998–99, see IMF, Staff Country Report, No. 99/37, Islamic Republic of Iran – Statistical Appendix in the IMF Internet database.
25. Official statistics are inconsistent. The government's Plan and Budget Organization estimated annual population growth at 3.36 per cent for the first decade of the revolution and 2.95 per cent from 1987 to 1992 (*Ettela'at*, 12 July 1993). According to a World Bank study, Iran's annual population growth exceeded 3 per cent during the 1980s and peaked at 3.8 per cent between 1976 and 1986. See Rodolfo A. Bulatao and Gail Richardson, *Fertility and Family Planning in Iran* (Washington, DC: World Bank, 1994), p. 4. In 1992, the interior ministry estimated annual population growth at 2 per cent. In 1993 Vice-President Hasan Habibi estimated growth at 2.3 per cent. See Tehran TV, 3 June 1993 – DR, 4 June 1993. Health Minister 'Alireza Marandi cited a similar figure in September 1993. See *Ettela'at*, 11 September 1993. The government's Statistics Center put it at 3.17 per cent. See *Kayhan* (London), 22 July 1993.
26. *Jerusalem Post*, 8 July 1995. See also, *Financial Times*, 1 September 1994.
27. Bulatao and Richardson, *Fertility and Family Planning*, pp. 2, 13, 20–2, 31–2.
28. *Iran Times*, 22 April 1994.
29. *Kayhan International*, 1 March 1993 – DR, 5 March 1993.
30. *Kayhan International*, 15 April 1993 – DR, 23 April 1993.
31. This unsigned editorial, published in five instalments, contained extremely harsh criticism. See *Kayhan* (Tehran), 17–20 and 24 October 1982.
32. *Ettela'at*, 1 November 1982.
33. *Abrar*, 1 May 1993, in Joint Publication Research Services (JPRS), 8 June 1993.
34. Tehran TV, 9 October 1994 – DR, 14 October 1994.
35. *Kayhan* (Tehran), 15 October 1994.
36. *Tehran Times*, 26 May 1994 – DR, 26 May 1994.
37. *Ettela'at*, 15 August 1991; *Echo of Iran*, no. 43 (August–September 1991), p. 12.
38. *Echo of Iran*, no. 43 (August–September 1991), p. 12.
39. *Kayhan* (Tehran), 18 August 1991. A cartoon in the satirical magazine *Gol Aqa* typified such sentiments: an old car and two people on motorcycles driving into the Majlis as a luxury car drives out; the cartoon is described in *Al-Safir*, 10 June 1992 – DR, 25 June 1992.

40. *Financial Times*, 6 March 1990.
41. See Menashri, 'Iran', in *MECS* 1995, pp. 288–9.
42. *Salam*, 27 February 1995. *Mofsed fil-arz* is a term for those who transgress Islamic law and thus spread 'corruption on earth'.
43. *Kayhan* (Tehran), 5 February, 22 July, 16 August, 18 September 1995; *Salam*, 6 March 1995; *Ettela'at*, 22, 30 July 1995; *Iran*, 7 February 1995.
44. *Akhbar*, 22 July 1995. See also *Sunday Telegraph*, 6 August 1995; *Jerusalem Post*, 16 August 1995.
45. *Kayhan* (Tehran), 5 February 1995.
46. *Iran Press Digest* (Economic Bulletin), 14 July 1987. According to 1981 statistics, 1.4m families in Tehran shared only 900,000 apartments; see *Kayhan* (Tehran), 25 April 1983.
47. *Iran Times*, 31 December 1993. See also *Kayhan* (London), 29 July 1993 – DR, 6 August 1993; *Kayhan* (Tehran), 3 June 1995.
48. *Kayhan International*, 21 October 1993.
49. *Jomhuri-ye Islami*, 4–6 and 9 September 1995; *Kayhan* (Tehran), 10 September 1995.
50. Different, often contradictory statistics on ethnic minority groups are found in the literature. At the outset of the revolution, Keddie writes, scholarly literature was in agreement that the Persian group is 'approximately 45 per cent of 40 million', making it thus 'a country without a compact majority'. See Nikki R. Keddie, *Iran and the Muslim World: Resistance and Revolution* (New York, NY: New York University Press, 1995), pp. 134–5. Ervand Abrahamian maintained that the Persians constituted 45 per cent of the population; see Ervand Abrahamian, 'Communism and Communalism in Iran: The Tudah and the Firqah Dimukrat', *International Journal of Middle East Studies*, IV (October 1970), 292–93. Hunter, claiming that only 'about 35 percent of Iran's population is composed of other linguistic groups', still held that 'Iran's ethnic and linguistic diversity undermines its national unity'. See Shireen Hunter, *Iran and the World: Continuity in a Revolutionary Decade* (Bloomington, IN: Indiana University Press, 1990), p. 11. For a rough estimate of their numbers on the eve of the revolution, see Patricia Higgins, 'Minority–State Relations in Contemporary Iran', *Iranian Studies*, 17 (Winter 1984), p. 48.
51. For a historical review of the monarchy's failure to integrate minority groups and their sense of deprivation, see Akbar Aghajanian, 'Ethnic Inequality in Iran: An Overview', *International Journal of Middle East Studies*, 15 (1983), pp. 211–24. See also Leonard M. Helfgot, 'The Structural Foundations of the National Minority Problem in Revolutionary Iran', *Iranian Studies*, 13/1–4 (1980), pp. 195–214.
52. *Sunday Telegraph*, 8 August 1995.
53. Hashim, *Crisis of the Iranian State*, pp. 7, 24.
54. Shirley, 'Fundamentalism in Power', p. 39.
55. *Tehran Times*, 16 September 1999.
56. *Echo of Iran*, no. 61 (February 1993), p. 12.
57. Radio Tehran, 19 March 1993 – DR, 22 March 1993.
58. Radio Tehran, 2 November 1994 – DR, 3 November 1994.
59. Tehran TV, 20 March 1993 – DR, 22 March 1993.
60. Nateq-Nuri in *Iran Times*, 17 December 1993. See also his similar contention

in *Iran Times*, 25 March 1994. Rafsanjani claimed that the United States had 'created [the slump in oil prices] to harm' Iran. See IRNA, 18 December 1993 – DR, 20 December 1993 and *Iran Times*, 14 January 1994.

61. IRNA, 14 March 1994 – DR, 14 March 1994.
62. Radio Tehran, 7 October 1994 – DR, 11 October 1994.
63. Radio Tehran, 26 October 1994 – DR, 7 November 1994 and 4 November 1994 – DR, 7 November 1994.
64. *Le Figaro*, 12 September 1994 – DR, 13 September 1994. See also Radio Tehran, 5 February 1993 – DR, 8 February 1993.
65. *Kayhan* (Tehran), 11 October 1993 – DR, 20 October 1993.
66. Tehran TV, 9 January 1994 – DR, 10 January 1994.
67. Nateq-Nuri in *Resalat*, 26 August 1994 – DR, 13 September 1994.
68. *Kayhan* (Tehran), 24 November 1983. See also his speech quoted in *Kayhan* (Tehran), 7 November 1988.
69. *Jomhuri-ye Islami*, 21 November 1984.
70. *Kayhan-e Hava'i*, 22 May 1985; *Kayhan* (Tehran), 1 May 1985.
71. *Kayhan* (Tehran), 8 January, 1983. For similar remarks by Ayatollah Mohammad Mo'men Qomi, Rafsanjani and Khamene'i, ibid., 10 April, 26 February, 30 March and 31 March 1983, respectively.
72. Radio Tehran, 21 March 1983 – DR, 24 March 1983.
73. *Salam*, 16 and 17 May 1993. See also, DR, 28 May 1993.
74. *Jahan-e Islam*, 27 May 1993 – DR, 15 June 1993. See also *Salam*, 27 July 1994.
75. *Al-Majallah*, 18 March 1992.
76. *Salam*, 27 July 1994 – DR, 11 August 1994.
77. *Salam*, 5 May 1992.
78. *Kayhan* (London), 16 April 1992.
79. *Kayhan International*, 25 November 1993.
80. *Kayhan International*, 15 December 1993.
81. *Kayhan International*, 26 May 1994 – DR, 7 June 1994.
82. *Salam*, 31 January 1995.
83. *Jahan-e Islam*, 5 July 1994 – DR, 11 July 1994.
84. *Jahan-e Islam*, 31 January 1995.
85. *Salam*, 28 January 1995.
86. *Salam*, 30 January 1995.
87. *Salam*, 8 February 1995.
88. *Payam-e Daneshju-ye Basiji*, 25 January 1995.
89. *Payam-e Daneshju-ye Basiji*, 14 March 1995.
90. *Omid*, 12 March 1995.
91. Interview with Rafsanjani, *Middle East Insight*, 11/5 (July–August 1995), pp. 7–14.
92. Radio Tehran, 10 June 1992 – SWB, 12 June 1992; see also *New York Times*, 11 June 1992.
93. Radio Tehran, 12 June 1992 – SWB, 15 June 1992.
94. Voice of Iranian Kurdistan, 2 June 1992 – DR, 3 June 1992. Foreign observers also viewed the riots as a sign of serious disaffection, see *Financial Times*, 12 June 1992 and *New York Times*, 1, 11, and 12 June 1992.
95. IRNA, 4 August 1994 – DR, 5 August 1994; *Hamshahri*, 4 August 1994 – DR, 12 August 1994.

96. Agence France Presse, 5 August 1994 – DR, 5 August 1994.
97. *Le Figaro*, 12 September 1994 – DR, 13 September 1994.
98. *Kayhan* (Tehran), *Jahan-e Islam* and *Resalat*, 21 January 1995.
99. Voice of Iranian Kurdistan, 5 February 1995 – DR, 6 February 1995.
100. *Independent*, 5 April 1995; Agence France Presse, 4 and 5 April 1995 – DR, 5 and 6 April 1995; *Ha'aretz*, 5 April 1995; Voice of Mojahed, 5 April 1995 – DR, 6 April 1995.
101. *Tehran Times*, 8 April 1995; *Salam*, 8 April 1995; Agence France Presse, 5 April 1995 – DR, 6 April 1995.
102. *Jahan-e Islam*, 8 August 1994 – DR, 12 August 1994. See also *Resalat*, 8 August 1994.
103. *Jahan-e Islam*, 31 January 1995.
104. *Sobh*, 10 April 1995.
105. Asef Bayat, 'Squatters and the State: Back Street Politics in the Islamic Republic', *Middle East Report*, 24/191 (November–December 1994), p. 11; *Economist*, 13 June 1992.
106. *Ha'aretz*, 10 June 1992; Voice of Mojahed, 10 June 1992 – DR, 11 June 1992; Michael Eisenstadt, *Iranian Military Power: Capabilities and Intentions* (Washington, DC: Washington Institute for Near East Policy, 1996), p. 41; Lamote, 'Iran's Foreign Policy', p. 10; *Ettela'at*, 11 September 1995; *Jomhuri-ye Islami*, 12 September 1995; *Jomhuri-ye Islami* and *Salam*, 18 September 1995.
107. *Le Monde*, 13 December 1980; *al-Hawadith*, 3 April 1981.
108. Voice of Iranian Kurdistan, 16 November 1980 – DR, 19 November 1980. See also Voice of Iranian Kurdistan, 9 October 1981 – SWB, 10 October 1981. See, similarly, 'Izz al-Din Hoseini in *Le Monde*, 14 January 1982.
109. *Kayhan* (Tehran), 1 February 1994; Radio Tehran, 1 February 1994 – DR, 3 February 1994.
110. Agence France Presse, 2 February 1994 – DR, 2 February 1994. On the Sunni challenge, see Lamote, 'Iran's Foreign Policy', pp. 15–17.
111. For the text of the statement issued by Khatami's office see *Salam*, 25 March 1997 [DR].
112. *Abrar*, special supplement on elections, 23 April 1997.
113. Voice of Mojahed, 5 August 1994 – DR, 5 August 1994. See also *Famiglia Cristiana* (Rome), 10 August 1994 – DR, 4 August 1994.
114. Voice of Iranian Kurdistan, 5 February 1995 – DR, 6 February 1995.
115. *Al-Majallah*, 16 April 1995 – DR, 21 June 1995.
116. Radio Tehran, 2 February 1994 – DR, 2 February 1994.
117. Radio Tehran, 3 February 1994 – DR, 3 February 1994.
118. Radio Tehran, 11 February 1995 – DR, 14 February 1995.
119. Radio Tehran, 31 August 1994 – DR, 31August 1994.

5

The Quest for Freedom and Intensified Struggle for Power

SIGNS OF FREE EXPRESSION AND GOVERNMENT POLICY

The quest for freedom was one of the most exalted ideals for which Iranians had long struggled. It was the main goal of the Constitutional Revolution, one of the prime objectives of the Mosaddeq era, and one of the stimuli of the anti-Shah movement. In fact, many Iranians viewed the Constitutional Revolution as their country's greatest achievement in modern history, at least until the Islamic Revolution. Similarly, the ideals of freedom and constitutionalism featured as major aims of the Islamic Revolution. Yet, while there was general agreement on their importance, there were significant differences among various domestic trends regarding their centrality and priority in the framework of revolutionary politics, and about the meaning and limits of the freedom under the new regime.

Iranian intellectuals upheld freedom as a sacred goal. The first recipients of a modern education, who experienced Western realities at first hand since the early nineteenth century, had been fascinated by the Western concepts of freedom and liberalism. They viewed them as the main cause for the progress and strength of the West and gradually advocated their application in Iran. Western-educated intellectuals were the driving force behind the first newspapers (in the nineteenth century), defended new schooling (which many of them viewed as a prerequisite for a democratic system) and supported parliamentarianism and constitutionalism. Increasingly, graduates returning from abroad felt an urge to make public their new-found views on political freedom. Although they were no more than 'inexperienced youngsters', the chronicler Mehdi Qoli Hedayat then wrote, 'each holds under his arms a thesis (*resaleh*) about the French Revolution and wishes to play the role of Robespierre or Danton'. They were 'extremely enthusiastic and fiery', he observed.[1] While Arab intellectuals at the turn of the century were primarily concerned with questions of nationalism and political independence, their Iranian counterparts – living in an independent state – focused their criticism on internal decadence and foreign encroachment, and fought for a constitution and the protection of civil liberties. True, their ability to approach the public at large, winning its support for their cause, was severely limited. In fact, when it came to the point of mobilizing mass support, it was the *'ulama'*, not Western-educated intellectuals, who were the main driving force. Yet, when political change was imminent and revolutionary forces searching for an ideology to unite their otherwise divergent camp, it was the intellectuals who offered their vision – constitutionalism – as the cohesive element. However, they were less powerful in guaranteeing a parliamentary and democratic system in action – as Pahlavi rule attests.

The consolidation of Pahlavi rule led to the adoption of more markedly autocratic and paternalistic methods. Freedom of expression and political organization was curtailed, the Majlis was reduced to a mere rubber-stamp assembly, the separation of powers laid down by the constitution was totally ignored, and all manifestations of disloyalty to the Shah were harshly repressed. This became more evident under Mohammad Reza Shah's White Revolution which began in 1963. In fact, the political restrictions added to the ferment in the late 1970s, and for many Iranians this was the prime source of discontent and rebellion. The desire for freedom was also a major ideal for clerics, as was reflected in numerous statements, on the eve of the Islamic Revolution by Ayatollah Khomeini, Ayatollah Shari'atmadari, Ayatollah Taleqani and other leading clerics. It was, of course, a major aim of the liberal and centrist movements, such as the Freedom Movement – as its name indicates – and numerous other organizations (including leftist parties). Yet, the liberal movement could not claim as much as its predecessors at the turn of the century. The end-result of the revolutionary movement – the Islamic regime's basic philosophy and actual politics – did not correspond to their liberal ideal.

The new political realities under the Islamic regime did not meet the expectations of those who had joined the anti-Shah movement in anticipation of greater liberties. Soon enough they were forced to acknowledge that the new regime was almost as intolerant of dissent as the Shah's government had been.

By equating the Islamic regime with Islam, the clerical establishment succeeded in denouncing the opposition as 'enemies of Islam' and 'hypocrites', engaged in apostasy, whose suppression was a sacred duty.

To make clear to the believers where their obligations lay, the ruling elite made sophisticated use of Shiʻi sentiments and symbols. Thus, by labeling the Shah, Saddam Husayn and later some of their domestic adversaries (from within the revolutionary camp) as 'Yazid', the regime channeled religious–historical sentiments of frustration against them. Similarly the opposition movement *Mojahedin* (literally, fighters for the cause of God, a term with positive Islamic connotations) was labeled *Monafeqin* (hypocrites, with a negative historical connotation). The Kurdish religious leader, ʻIzz al-Din ('glory of religion') Hoseini, was nicknamed Zed al-Din ('anti-religion'). Loyalty to the revolution was presented as a religious obligation of true believers. The nation was, therefore, endowed with a religious mission: the destiny of Islam and the Islamic regime were portrayed as 'identical'; the defeat of the revolution – as the clerics in power often asserted – was the defeat of Islam. If the present generation failed to grasp the historical opportunity to restore the glories of Islam, history and Allah will not forgive it, they often re-iterated.[2] Typically, Khameneʼi stressed in 1994, that those who 'dearly love' the Qurʼan and the Prophet (Muhammad) must have a 'commitment to the Islamic Republic'.[3]

Since its early days in power, the Islamic regime has been extremely sensitive to criticism by intellectuals. As in many other policy areas, it was Khomeini that led the way. Warning against the dangers of 'verbal violence', Khomeini claimed that 'the clubs of tongues (*chomaq-e zaban*) and the clubs of pens (*chomaq-e qalam*)' were much more dangerous than any other form of association.[4] The government's indoctrination machinery (including the educational system, the media and the mosques) were mobilized to enlist and preserve people's support for the revolution, while security forces were occasionally used to intimidate and suppress dissidents.

Upon coming to power, Khomeini made it clear that the press must conform to the principles of the Islamic Republic which had been 'endorsed by an overwhelming majority' of the people. Addressing journalists on 15 May 1979, he said: 'The press must write what the nation wants.' He left no room for doubt that 'the nation wants newspapers that conform with its views'.[5] Addressing journalists on another occasion, Ayatollah Khomeini explained: 'Your duty today is the pen in your hand . . . If the pen slips the nation will slip.' Guiding the people by means of the pen, he went on, was even 'more acceptable that prayers'. He spelt this out as follows: 'Your publication must be in line with Islamic ideology and must be useful to the people as a teaching material. Your paper must be a school of teaching and should satisfy those who believe in God . . . Take heed!! An Islamic country must have an Islamic press.'[6]

Papers that did not conform to the general outlook of the regime were banned. Those that were essentially loyal, but subsequently failed to adjust their policy in an appropriate way were also banned. Those who conformed were occasionally cautioned so that, as Khamene'i put it, they understood that their freedom of expression has a limit which is 'defined by Islam'.[7] Such limits were actually decided, as a matter of course, by the government. Speaking at the conclusion of his tenure as the supervisor of *Kayhan*, in 1982, Mohammad Khatami defined the role of the press as a sounding-board for the views of the people. The people's views, he went on, 'are identical to those of Islam and Imam Khomeini'.[8] Prime Minister Mir-Hosein Musavi declared that anyone 'could think' what he wants 'in his heart' but, whoever spoke out, or acted against the revolution, would see the regime fighting him 'with all [its] strength'.[9] The calls supporting freedom of expression proliferated on the eve of Khatami's election although hard-liners warned against crossing the limits.

Ayatollah Jannati was among those opposed to the current wave of fast-expanding publications (mainly following Khatami's election, but also earlier). They are growing rapidly, he said in 1998, like mushrooms. Yet, the contents of some of them could lead ultimately to the total abandonment of faith. In line with Khomeini's past exhortations, and in keeping with the conservative approach in general, he claimed that defending the boundaries of Islamic values is 'hundreds of times' more crucial than the defense of the country's territorial borders. This is because 'the boundaries of Islamic values are the borders of God'.[10] Ayatollah Naser Makarem Shirazi reiterated the conservative approach stating that freedom does not include the right to withdraw from values for the sake of which so many martyrs had shed their blood.[11] *Kayhan* passionately criticized the prevailing tendency among some intellectuals to issue 'all sorts of ridiculous statements' that serve as grist for propaganda by foreign enemies. It went as far as to equate such statements with the bombing of a mosque by the opposition during the Iran–Iraq war.[12] Such an attitude legitimized, of course, any harsh steps against those voicing decent.

Following student riots in July 1999 Ayatollah Mohammad Taqi Mesbah Yazdi (a member of the Council of Experts) went into great detail to provide the doctrinaire justification for the suppression of dissident voices. He dismissed the spirit of leniency and indulgence, and advocated the use of violence against those who were considered enemies. (See below.) In 1998, Rahim Safavi, in his capacity as commander of the Revolutionary Guards, warned that violence would be used if necessary to purge the unfaithful elements in the press who, he said, were known to the authorities. He said that segments of the press had turned into the nests in which anti-revolutionaries flourished. If necessary, the Guards would introduce them to the people. Viewing the West's cultural onslaught as the main threat to the regime, and recognizing the dangers of free expression, he said that the Guards would not allow anyone to inflict blows on the most precious ideals of the revolution.[13] He reportedly said that the Guards were ready to decapitate and cut out the tongues of political opponents. (See Chapter 2 and Conclusion to Part One.)

The government occasionally banned papers that crossed a certain (undefined) line, and restricted the freedom of intellectuals to express dissent. (See below.) Yet, compared with the realities before the Islamic Revolution and in the early 1980s, as well as with most neighboring countries, there was some measure of free expression in the 1990s, especially on the eve of, and immediately after, Khatami's elections. They reached an unprecedented peak before the Majlis elections of 2000. (See Epilogue.)

By regional standards, the government allowed its domestic critics some freedom of expression, albeit within narrow limits. (This did not include banned opposition movements such as the *Mojahedin-e Khalq*, or those who challenged the basic tenets of the ruling system.) The radical press of the early 1990s – such as *Salam, Bayan, Jahan-e Islam, Payam-e Daneshju-ye Basiji* – voiced harsh criticism of the realities established under the clerical regime and bluntly pointed to the country's numerous problems. Some journals (e.g. *Kiyan, Goftogu*) also carried penetrating discussions and critical debates on various – although not all – issues facing the nation. To this long list, were added numerous other newspapers which emerged more recently, such as *Jame'eh, Zan, Tous, Neshat, Mobin, Khordad, Akhbar-e Eqtesad*, and *'Asr-e Azadegan* (all were subsequently proscribed) which voiced harsh criticism and expressed independent views. More recently, some of them have even engaged in questioning basic revolutionary principles, hitherto considered taboo, such as pointing to the advantages of relations with the United States and criticizing the way in which the concept of *velayat-e faqih* was applied and practiced. As the arguments quoted in this study demonstrate, the regime allowed or tolerated an impressive degree of free expression.

Clearly, 'there are signs of resilience and even vitality' in Iran's vibrant intellectual life.[14] At the same time, there is no doubt that criticism and statements by the licensed press were often ruthlessly suppressed. Cases of banning newspapers, restricting the freedom of expression of clerics such as Shari'atmadari, Montazeri or Azari-Qomi, or limiting the freedom of intellectuals, such as Soroush and Kadivar, to propagate their ideas were abundant. Many of the government's critics were arrested and some intellectuals killed. Freedom of expression was denied even to a revolutionary (such a Mohtashami). The restrictions placed on the freedom of clerics was discussed in Chapter 1; that of the students will be detailed below. Here only a few examples are provided of the measures taken against intellectuals and the media up until the fall of 1999. (The opposition, of course, was denied any right to propagate its views.)

The attitude to Soroush is most revealing. As one who had supported the revolution he deserved certain rights, but the regime could not tolerate the propagation of his ideas, which it viewed as negating the basic principles of the ruling system. (See Chapter 1.) The hard-line elite deemed his philosophy blasphemous and was vehemently opposed to his thinking. Ayatollah Jannati, for example, called to eliminate what he termed 'harmful freedoms'.[15] Nateq-Nuri, referring to Soroush rhetorically asked: 'Should we obey irreligious people and delegate the governing of society to them?'[16]

Naturally, the universities were the hub of fierce struggle. In July 1995 hard-line students physically assaulted Soroush at Isfahan University, where he had been invited to lecture. *Kayhan* wondered why the university would invite a speaker who advocated a philosophy hostile to the basic tenets of the revolution.[17] In October, students again attacked Soroush, this time at Tehran University, shouting 'Death to fascism' and 'Death to anti-*velayat-e faqih*'.[18] Even more worrying were the threats by the *Ansar-e Hezbollah* (Champions of the *Hezbollah*).[19]

However, there were other more tolerant voices. Tehran University's Islamic Society, condemned the attack on Soroush, arguing that a university was a venue for the clash of opinions and that debating new ideas is part and parcel of freedom of speech.[20] Similarly, the Islamic Society of the Amir Kabir Technical University urged the interior minister in a letter, to safeguard the cultural realm and security of the universities: 'What need is there to guard the country by night when the law is breached in daylight? What meaning do claims of power have when the cultural realm of a university is violated by some while the law-enforcement forces act as mere spectators?'[21] In July 1995, pro-Soroush students at Tehran University held a demonstration to protest at the brutal behavior of the *Ansar-e Hezbollah* – the first implicitly anti-government demonstration of such scale on a university campus since 1981. Unrest spread to other universities, including Shahid Beheshti (or National) University and the Technological University of Isfahan. In response to the growing climate of political repression, over a hundred academics urged President Rafsanjani to ensure the citizens' constitutional rights and guarantee the freedom of expression.[22]

Criticism of Soroush gathered greater momentum as his views gained support. Foreign Minister Velayati went as far as to claim that Soroush's opinions had inflicted a serious blow to Iran's independence and to its national cohesion, and that they had thereby weakened the regime. He said that Soroush's views were as harmful as those of Ahmad Kasravi – a nationalist author and thinker who was assassinated by Islamic activists in 1946.[23] Khamene'i regarded Soroush's ideas as seditious and warned that the Islamic system 'will slap' those who express such views 'in the face'.[24] Responding, Soroush wondered how someone who lacked access to the media and was constantly accused of spying, treachery and of being Rushdie, Kasravi, and Malkom Khan (a leading intellectual at the end of the nineteenth century who supported reforms and Westernization), could weaken the pillars of the regime. Comparing him with Kasravi, he said, was essentially a threat to his life.[25] *Salam* denounced the regime's restriction on freedom. It claimed that whoever challenged the regime's basic perceptions risked sharing the fate of Rushdie and Kasravi – awaiting an assassin.[26] Soroush became very popular among Iranian students (as well as academics in the West), although his access to public opinion at home has been limited and he was banned from teaching at Tehran University.

The conservatives were even more deeply opposed to Kadivar and his thinking. (See Chapter 1.) They claimed that his views, if propagated in society could 'shake the bases of the concept of *velayat-e faqih* and the very rule of religion'.[27] Kadivar was therefore arrested on 27 February 1999, apparently on charges of 'acting to weaken' the Islamic system and undermining the regime. He was accused of insulting Khomeini and Khamene'i, misleading public opinion, supporting Montazeri and advocating the separation of religion from politics.[28] Students staged a rally in Shiraz, outside Kadivar's family home on 28 February to show him their 'support and solidarity'.[29] In an open letter to Khatami, a number of newspaper editors urged him to defend Kadivar's constitutional right to express his thoughts. His arrest, they wrote, showed 'disrespect for the law' and 'inflicted severe damage on the legitimacy of the system and weakened reformist thought'.[30] Hojjat ul-Islam 'Ali

Mo'allemi (a Majlis deputy), on the other hand, believed that 'new thinking' should be discussed only 'within the framework of the system and the constitution'. But Kadivar went beyond such boundaries by bringing 'the concept of *velayat-e faqih* under question', which 'cannot be tolerated'.[31]

The very expression of such thinking, and the support it received, was a manifestation of some freedom. Yet, the regime's suppression of new ideas attests to the limits that the system had set for such freedom. Thus, many Iranians claimed that it would be hard to speak of freedom when people were brought to trial in Special Courts for the Clergy (SCC), in a special court for the press, or in revolutionary courts – for political offenses not even defined by law. In fact, *Hamshahri* (supporting reform) complained, that no judicial or political institution had furnished any binding definition of what constituted a political crime in Iran. In any case, it noted, the charges for which Kadivar has been detained – expressing criticism – 'is not a crime'.[32] Majlis deputy Qodratollah Nazariniya complained that the SCC did not even provide an explanation for the arrests,[33] while the *Tehran Times* charged that the SCC 'sometime acts quite irrationally'.[34] Some intellectuals known for their harsh criticism of the government policy were even assassinated. In late 1998, several prominent figures disappeared and were later found dead, among them were Daryush and Parvaneh Foruhar, who were brutally murdered at their home in November 1998. The writers, Mohammad Ja'far Puyandeh and Mohammad Mokhtari (who founded the writers' association), were also found dead after being violently assaulted.

Repression was not limited to those who challenged the regime or questioned basic revolutionary principles. Articles in sections of the press (such as *Bayan*, *Jahan-e Islam* and *Payame-Daneshju-ye Basiji*), and speeches by devout revolutionaries who argued that the government was not radical enough or had deviated from Khomeini's line, were also thwarted.

The experience of *Bayan* (a radical monthly edited by Mohtashami in the early 1990s), is instructive. Mohtashami, although careful not to overstep the limits, blamed the government for obstructing free expression. 'The atmosphere of our mass media' Mohtashami said in 1993, 'is not favorable [or] healthy'. *Salam's* interviewer was no less critical. He inquired about the existing 'poisonous atmosphere' and wondered if it was disseminated by certain 'power centers'.[35] Elsewhere Mohtashami claimed that the political climate had prevented the continuation of *Bayan*. No one had actually closed the magazine down, but 'the forces that cooperated with us' were treated in such a way 'in society [and] in government institutions', and the problems the magazine 'faced in printing and in enjoying certain facilities, all helped to stop the publication'.[36] In fact, Human Rights Watch observed, 'a large part of the government's mechanisms of control and censorship falls outside the law', with the regime employing various methods to intimidate its critics into silence.[37] 'Some groups in society', *Salam* then charged, could not 'tolerate journalistic criticism' and therefore 'resort to every possible means' to prevent a newspaper from carrying out its duties.[38]

There are numerous other examples of government interference with the freedom of expression. In 1993, *Salam* editor and vocal government critic, 'Abbas 'Abdi (one of the students who occupied the US embassy in 1979 who later advocated reform), was arrested on a warrant by the Revolutionary Court.[39] *Salam*'s publisher, Kho'iniha, was also summoned to the SCC in 1993 to face charges of slander against government officials.[40] In August 1995 a Tehran publishing house, Morgh-e Amin, was set on fire by armed Hezbollahis who threatened the publisher, beat, and detained him after claiming that a book he had published, *God Only Laughs on Mondays*, contained sex scenes, attacked Islamic values and contained criticism of the war against Iraq.[41] Ayatollah Jannati, *Jomhuri-ye Islami*, and *Kayhan* all supported the attack, claiming that it was the implementation of Khomeini's will. Mohajerani, by contrast, lamented that an entire bookstore had been set on fire in order to show disapproval of one book, which had already been removed from the shelves anyway.[42] *Salam*, arguing that this only added to the book's popularity, questioned how Jannati – a theologian member of the Council of Guardians – could defend criminals who set bookstores on fire.[43] A report by the New York-based Human Rights Watch states that repression 'gathered pace' in 1995, 'encouraged by state officials and religious spokesmen', and that 'intrusive restrictions on everyday life continued'.[44] Iran's thriving film industry also came under fire. More than 200 filmmakers petitioned for an end to government interference in script, production, funding and the distribution of films; in response the government banned the export of any film conveying a 'negative image of Iran'.[45] There were many other restrictions, from censorship of movies and periodicals, through attempts to prevent the use of satellite dishes.

The government's attitude hardened as the expression of independent views became more widespread. But proponents of such views continued their struggle. Before long, *Salam* became a target for the government's fury because of its penetrating criticism. Just before the

1996 Majlis elections, it was suspended temporarily. In July 1999, the newspaper was shut down, triggering student protests. Prior to that several other newspapers were closed down, including *Jame'eh*, *Zan* and *Tous*; in September 1999 the government banned *Neshat* and put its editor to trial. The case of *Jame'eh*, which began publication in mid-1998, was especially interesting. Following its closure, its editorial board published *Tous*, when that was closed down, the editors moved on to publish *Neshat*. With its closure on 4 September 1999 they began publication of *'Asr-e Azadegan* and *Akhbar-e Eqtesad* – all the while retaining the same editorial team, the same format and similar line.

On 7 July 1999, the Majlis went a step further in approving the general outlines of tough new press restrictions which threatened to undermine the free press. Proposed changes in the new bill included compelling journalists to reveal their sources, barring opposition journalists and editors from 'any form of press activities', and strengthening conservative influence over the media. Other proposed measures effectively limited government subsidies to reformist publications and institutionalized the right of the Revolutionary Court to intervene in complaints against the media. The changes were justified as important means to defend revolutionary values from a Western-inspired cultural invasion.[46] Following the student riots in July 1999 (which were triggered by such a decision and the subsequent closure of *Salam*), the ministry of intelligence and the judiciary made new and grave threats against the media, stressing that there would be no more patience shown towards publications which acted in line with the desires of the enemies. On 2 August, the judiciary submitted a 25-point draft bill defining political offenses. A political offense was considered to be any measure taken against the established system and the sovereignty of the Islamic Republic, or against the political and social rights of citizens. Some examples of political offense were revealing, and included: any act violating the country's independence by the attempt to intensify differences among the people; the spreading of lies and rumors; any form of communication and exchange of information and collusion with foreign embassies detrimental to the interests of Iran.[47]

The question of freedom of expression subsequently turned into a major issue in domestic politics and inter-factional rivalries. This was not only a clash between conservatives and reformists but also one between the clerics in power and the youth, especially students. The regime was determined to suppress any independent act they regarded – rather broadly – as detrimental to Islam. Supporters of freedom, and with them prominent pragmatists in government, were determined to fight back. This gained much more prominence in the light of two major recent events: the student riots of July 1999 and – initially a more trivial issue – a satirical play in the student newspaper, *Mowj* (The Wave).

The Islamic Republic thus remained 'an anomaly amid revolutionary regimes, an authoritarian government with some elements of licensed pluralism'.[48] Although it is true that 'compared with some countries in the region', the Iranian press 'presents a range of views', the scope of permissible dissent or criticism was still, in the mid-1990s, narrow and 'limited to partisans of the ruling movement',[49] and to them only. The Western image of 'increased openness' in Iran – as symbolized by the election of Khatami – was therefore somewhat misleading, wrote Azar Nafisi. In many ways, in fact, 'the new openness that characterizes Khatami's rule has been accompanied by increased repression'. The 'brief spring' that followed his electoral victory, 'during which freedom of speech flourished' was soon brought to an end 'with an abrupt crackdown', wrote Nafisi. The result has been 'a kind of chaos, a period marked by the arbitrariness of its events'. New newspapers were closed, progressive clergymen arrested, members of the Baha'is repressed and nationalist opposition leaders brutally murdered.[50] Indeed, as Bazargan observed shortly before his death in 1995, the regime relentlessly eliminates all viable alternatives. 'They have not allowed the people to breathe', he said. 'They have nipped all efforts toward freedom in the bud. The prospects for the future are extremely frightening.'[51]

Whatever signs of relative political openness exist, they should not be mistaken for genuine freedom, wrote Bakhash in the early 1990s.[52] The 'apparent intensity of public debate, variety of publications, and wealth of artistic achievements' create only 'an illusion of unrestricted discourse', the Human Rights Watch then observed.[53] In fact, freedoms 'are allowed only as long as the inviolability of Islamic tenets, the irreversibility of the revolution, and the absolute sovereignty of the *faqih* are not questioned',[54] added Amuzegar, and even this only selectively and to a degree. Newspapers not aligned with the clerical regime have found it increasingly difficult to steer a viable course between reliance on the government's avowed adherence to free expression and compliance with the arbitrary limits it has placed on such expression. Even more menacing, the boundaries between what is permissible and what is forbidden have never been clearly defined. Also 'laws are applied selectively and inconsistently'.[55] Under such circumstances, *Salam* suggested in 1993 that 'less freedom but quite clearly defined is better than more freedom which is unclear and undefined', as was the case in Iran.[56] Prime Minister Mehdi Bazargan recalled that when, in the early days of the revolution, he complained to Rafsanjani about the lack of freedom, Rafsanjani replied: 'When the Shah gave us freedom, we drove him out of the country. We shall not repeat this mistake.'[57] The regime certainly seems to have learned the lesson it taught the Shah in 1979, as its re-action to the student riots would demonstrate.

While the reformists' main struggle had hitherto been to prevent the regime from exceeding the law, there are growing voices against the law itself. Be that as it may, the threats directed towards the pragmatic trend – itself composed of loyal revolutionaries – was even harsher than before, with hard-liners threatening to decapitate and cut out the tongues of their political opponents. (See Chapter 3.) Ultimately, it was the conservatives in power – and often a handful of the most hard-line elements among them – who decided upon the limits of permissible criticism. It was they who arrogated to themselves the right to determine what Islam was and what constituted an anti-Islamic act as many of the student leaders and intellectuals were later to remark. Still, the spring of 1999 marked a new peak of free expression and liberalism in Iran. The reformists proved determined to continue the struggle for civil rights and gained significant achievement in their struggle.

During Khatami's first three years as president, there were in fact some signs of unprecedented criticism and free expression. At the same time, however, political repression also reached new heights. This appeared to be a genuine *Kulturkampf*, with rival camps fighting vigor-ously to determine the future course of the country. The universities – students and faculty – took the lead in this campaign.

STUDENT RIOTS AND THE CONSERVATIVES' RESPONSE

During the past century, students and graduates of institutions of higher learning have always been at the forefront of the struggle for indi-vidual freedom. The graduates (then mostly of foreign universities) were a significant force on the eve of the Constitutional Revolution, playing an active role in the protest movements of the early 1950s led by Mosaddeq and, again, in the movement of the early 1960s, headed by Khomeini. They had a significant role in the Islamic Revolution (in fact, large-scale demonstrations began at Tehran University in October 1977 – before other sectors stepped up their involvement in active opposition). Consequently, institutions of higher learning became important centers of political activity following the revolution, and played a significant role in the early stages of the new regime (which led the government to shut down the universities as part of its program of 'cultural revolution' and Islamization). While initially loyal to the hard-line trend (note their role in the occupation of the US embassy), students have always harboured a diversity of attitudes. Although their voice was not always heard, professors and students gradually grew more critical of the realities at home and were extremely resentful of restrictions on freedom. Within their narrow circles and occasionally in public, they expressed displeasure with the prevailing realities under Islamic rule and advocated reform. Signs of discontent among the younger generation emerged more forcefully on the eve of the 1997 presidential elections and have continued ever since.

The riots of July 1999 – the most extensive student unrest since the Islamic Revolution – presented the regime with a severe challenge. The criticism voiced by the students exceeded mere dissatisfaction with policy to encompass basic dogmatic conceptions and revolutionary practice. In doing so, they not only went further than what many hard-liners deemed tolerable but also beyond what Khatami himself could endorse.

The quest for freedom was at the core of their riots. Beginning as demonstrations against the closure of a newspaper (*Salam*), the protests touched upon wider areas of contention (including criticism of the functioning and the very concept of the *vali-ye faqih*). They soon spread to universities nationwide and gained further momentum and some support among other sectors of the populace. The pragmatists regarded a measure of liberalization as essential and initially at least lent the demonstrators their open support; the conservatives viewed them as a threat to the very basic foundations of the regime. Their suppression (and the consequent campaign against permissiveness in political and cultural realms) attests to the regime's determination to repress such demands and to maintain a tight grip on power. But the students and their backers within Khatami's government demonstrated their determination to continue the struggle for freedom, although they may have differed among themselves about the exact aims of the movement.

Unrest began at Tehran University on 8 July after police and hard-line vigilantes attacked students protesting the ban on *Salam*. The most violent confrontations took place in the university dormitories, which triggered a wave of protests that culminated in six days of street riots in central Tehran and spread to other academic centers in the country. (According to official sources, one person was killed, several injured and some 1,500 students were arrested.[58])

Generally speaking, the students, most of whom were born in the wake of the change of the regimes, regretted that the movement their

parents had supported over 20 years ago had failed to provide them –
parents and children – with a meaningful freedom and security and economic improvement. Conspicuously, the students' grievances focused on
internal politics – signaling that, in their view, the main problems were
domestic.

Some of the student leaders – whether expressing their own particular
world-view or representing wider circles – made their grievances public
mainly since the mid-1990s. They used unprecedently harsh language to
denounce realities at home, the conservatives in power and even some
basic revolutionary tenets. Gradually, some of them also revealed displeasure with President Khatami and his government's hesitant steps
towards reform.

Early in 1999, the Islamic Union of University Students and
Graduates (led by Heshmatollah Tabarzadi), issued a strongly worded
statement alleging that since Khatami's elections, the defeated conservative faction had 'lost its legitimacy to rule'. It suffered from 'intellectual
infertility' and had 'no theoretical capacity' to analyze Iran's problems,
'let alone to come up with [a] practical solution'. Abusing its hold on
the instruments of power, it strove 'to compensate' for its 'intellectual
sterility' and incompetence by 'resorting to social misbehavior', the
Union claimed. By contrast, the reformist movement of the Second of
Khordad (i.e. 23 May, the date Khatami was elected in 1997), was the
source of dynamism and intellectual curiosity, that gave the young
generation the opportunity of free expression and possessed the means
of solving Iran's problems.[59]

Tabarzadi (the founder and editor of *Payam-e Daneshju-ye Basiji*)
also engaged in harsh criticism. Two of his brothers were martyrs of the
Iran–Iraq war, and he himself had served in this eight-year war, which
made it difficult for hard-liners to doubt his revolutionary credentials and devotion. Tabarzadi regretted that the initial vision of the
Islamic Republic – based on democratic principles and the concept of
republicanism – had failed. He resented the way in which the concept
of *velayat-e faqih* was being practiced in Iran and its application in
opposition to the idea of republicanism (rule of the people). In an open
letter in February 1999, Tabarzadi emphasized that 'some people' failed
to realize that the Supreme Leader was only 'a common man', who
gained his 'power and legitimacy' on the strength of popular will. He
was not a prophet who was 'immune to error and wrongdoing' nor 'a
holy and innocent man, or God!' Criticism against the *vali-ye faqih*
should not be confused with polytheism, nor should his dethronement
'mean apostasy'. The Supreme Leader was 'answerable to the people'

and clerics 'must accept' that if even the Prophet had led society today, he would not 'exclude himself from criticism, objections, and protests'. The application of 'absolute *velayat*' by the conservatives, he said, '[leads] to monocracy' of the kind that 'no society' would accept, 'unless they want[ed] to impose it by force of the knife, the lash, the Revolutionary Court, [or] the Special Clerics' Court'.[60] In interviews with foreign radio services in Persian during April 1999, Tabarzadi reiterated that the initial ideal of the Islamic Republic had, over time, gradually transformed into the idea of *velayat-e faqih*, then into *velayat-e motlaqeh-ye faqih* (an absolute *velayat-e faqih*), and ultimately, into *velayat-e motlaqeh-ye fardi* (an absolute *velayat-e faqih* ruled by one person). The Supreme Leader was regarded as standing above the law, and even viewed almost as God, he charged. Rather than republicanism, the *velayat-e faqih* had turned into despotism. Was all the blood shed in the last two decades meant only to replace the Shah with someone with even wider authority? But Tabarzadi was not pleased with Khatami either. The expectations from him have not materialized, he said, and the new president had failed to advance his own policies. In an open letter to Khatami on 31 May 1999, Tabarzadi reiterated similar harsh charges castigating what he called the prevalent despotism in Iran.[61] Tabarzadi elaborated his charges in an article in *Mehregan* (published in Washington). The aim of the Islamic Revolution, he reminded the readers, was not to substitute one absolute rule with another, but to bring about a democratic system. If it aimed only at 'a mere replacement of the Shah with a *faqih*, to substitute the absolute rule of the Shah (*saltanat-e motlaqeh-ye Shah*) with the absolute rule of the *faqih* (*velayat-e motlaqeh-ye faqih*),' i.e. a system that operates in the name of one person or a certain group, but against the will and the interests of the people, 'there was no need for a revolution, for so many martyrs and such grave losses'. The real aim was to establish a government that operates in line with the will of people, according to the 'progressive principles of Islam', and not to bring about a new system also based on absolutism. Tabarzadi went on to criticize the politics of President Rafsanjani and the prevalent injustice under the Islamic Republic, the 'widespread violence and terror' in Iran, as well as the functioning of the Supreme Leader.[62] (For similar criticism by Kadivar, see Chapter 1.) Tabarzadi was arrested in June 1999 but was released on bail before the end of the year.

Manuchehr Mohammadi, another of the students' leaders, proposed to delete the term 'Islamic' from the title of their movement – The Islamic Union of University Students and Graduates – and replace it with 'National'. This, he said, was in recognition of the view that national interests should have priority in dictating Iran's politics. Similarly, in a series of interviews with Persian-language radio stations broadcasting from the West, he castigated the wide authority exercised by the Supreme Leader, which he termed dictatorial. If what people desired (democracy) was not guaranteed, he maintained, it would be necessary to consider changing the regime altogether. (Mohammadi was arrested in July 1999 and sentenced to 13 years in prison.)

It is not clear to what degree such views were popular or widespread among the students at the time of their riots in 1999, or how far they wished to go. The regime, however, viewed the riots with great concern. In one way or another they were linked with the ongoing struggle between Khatami's reform movement and the old guard among the religious hard-liners. The composition of the movement ('the true children of the revolution'), the focus of their indictment (lack of freedoms) and the wider connotations of their charges (the conduct of the conservative elite and the Supreme Leader and the very concept of *velayat-e faqih*), made the struggle even more challenging. The delicate political realities (their assumed links with the Khatami camp), and the convergence of some of their views with those of dissident thinkers (Montazeri, Soroush, Kadivar), served as an additional alarm signal. There was also the fear that their arguments would gain greater support among wider sections of the society, or that they would encourage other discontented groups to join or lead their own struggle.

The charges voiced by the students exceeded mere academic grievances and the demand for greater freedom. Their banners and slogans challenged the basic philosophy of the regime and the Supreme Leader personally. In fact, at one stage, it was not clear if the students were protesting against the revolutionary system, the Supreme Leader, or against the politics and actual failures of the ruling elite. Their charges combined them all. Some of their slogans were pointedly targeted at the undemocratic nature of the regime, and Khamene'i personally: '*marg bar estebdad*' (death to despotism); '*Ansar* [of *Hezbollah*] committing crimes, the *Rahbar* provides [them] support'; '*Majlis* made to obey [*farmayeshi*] should be annulled.' Others were more specifically aimed at the lack of freedom under the regime and conveyed determination to struggle for it: '*ya marg ya azadi*' (freedom or death); '*azadi-ye andisheh; hamisheh, hamisheh*' (freedom of thought; always, always); '*azadi-ye matbu'at, salamat-e jame'eh* (freedom of press [is] the health of society). They appealed for popular support ('students, people, unity, unity'), suggesting that freedom cannot be attained under the rule of the clerics.

Among other revealing slogans were: 'Khatami, Khatami, [show] reaction, reaction' and, even more revealingly, 'Khatami, Khatami, where
are you?' – a call that remained unanswered.

Many professors and intellectuals supported them, as did segments
of the more reformist press, mainly at the start of the protests. The
minister of higher education, the chancellor of Tehran University and
the deans of its various faculties, offered their resignation in protest.
Montazeri, too, issued a statement in support of the students, in which
he described the demonstrators as 'the true children of the revolutions',
and 'the eyes and the light of the nation'. He condemned their suppression by those who only 'pretend to defend Islam' and the values
of the revolution, but in fact manifest a violent image of Islam, thus
gambling with the dignity of Islam and the clerics. Those who ordered
action against the students, he said, 'betrayed the religion and the
nation'.[63] Most center movements, such as the Nation Party (see below),
also lent their support to the students.

Khamene'i signaled the harsh tone of the official response on 12 July,
by typically portraying the rioting students as the emissaries of foreign
enemies. The unrest, he said, was planned 'by true enemies' of the
Islamic system and financed by the United States. Warning the students
to beware of such plots, he called upon the people to resist them with all
their might. He regretted the violence used against the students in the
university dormitories and promised an official investigation. He vowed
to unveil what had transpired on campus and to punish the saboteurs,
whom he denounced as *mohareb* (those fighting God) and *mofsed*
(those spreading corruption) – charges that commonly carried the death
penalty.[64] The sharp reaction by the hard-liners in the regime and by
security officials (see below) was supplemented by an impressive show
of popular support, in a rally organized by the regime on 14 July.
Hundred of thousands of supporters of the hard-line faction reclaimed
the streets, expressing support for the Supreme Leader.

On 12 July, 24 top commanders of the Revolutionary Guards wrote a
strongly worded letter to Khatami, demanding immediate action to
suppress the riots, lest it be too late. Astonished at the compromising
attitude and simple-mindedness of his officials, they warned against such
events which 'made our enemies dance in joy'. The attack on the university's dormitories, they admitted, 'was wrong, ugly and vile', but
insisted that 'the violation of sanctities and insulting the principles of this
system' should also be investigated. Is the sanctity of the *vali-ye faqih*,
they asked, less sacred than the university dormitory? The officers
regretted that the enemies, disguised as students, were entering the fray

in droves while 'hostile and short-sighted insiders' were further 'exacerbating the situation'. They have the power in their hand, they said, but
'our hands are [still] tied'. How long, they continued, should we 'suffer
in silence and practice democracy through creating chaos?' How long
should we maintain 'revolutionary patience while the system is being
destroyed?' Expressing 'utmost respect' for Khatami, they urged him
to deal with the case promptly, because tomorrow may be 'too late'.
They concluded: 'our patience has run out. We cannot tolerate this
situation any longer'.[65] The paramilitary forces, *Ansar-e Hezbollah*, also
demanded to be armed to prevent the recurrence of such 'bitter events'.
Their weekly publication promised that if the *Hezbollah* had the authority to confront hard-handedly the violators, 'the snakes [would] return
to their hiding places'.[66]

While the security forces provided the regime with the power of arms,
hard-line clerics offered moral justification for violent suppression. The
main theme was that Islam not only approved the use of violence
(*khoshunat*), it also urged its followers to act mercilessly against its
opponents. The message for the students and their supporters was clear.

Ayatollah Mesbah Yazdi set the harsh tone. In a Friday sermon
delivered on 23 July, he stated that the heads of those acting against the
Islamic regime, or speaking out against its basic tenets, chanting slogans
against the Supreme Leader, should be cut by a sharp sword. Dismissing
leniency (*tasahol*) and indulgence (*tasamoh*), he asked: should those
who want to seize the people's lives, property, chastity and religion be
treated with negligence? 'Where do these fallacies (*ghalatha*) stem
from?' Those who claimed that Islam did not approve violence did not
understand Islam at all. Moreover, any government which endorsed
freedom and liberty without limits would quickly end in anarchy. Islam
directed us to remove the weed which obstructed its path, and we were
duty-bound to act vigorously against hooligans, traitors and heretics,
and against the mercenaries acting on behalf of foreigners. He advised
that we should use 'first exhortation (*nasihat*)', then, if necessary,
'the sword (*shamshir*)'.[67] These themes were repeated in subsequent
sermons, and evoked strong reactions – both for and against. At one
stage, Mesbah Yazdi deemed it appropriate to tone down his statements,
but even then he did not withdraw his basic arguments. In addition
to kindness, goodwill and tranquillity, he explained, Islam also has
injunctions regarding hostility, harshness and severity. To subvert
the regime and deceive our youth, the enemies presented leniency and
indulgence as absolute values, and violence as a non-value. He felt, he
said, 'that the taboo – that every act of violence is bad and every act of

tolerance is good – must be broken'. The enemies, he added, 'must also feel the harshness and violence of Islam'.[68]

While this was seen by many as 'theorizing violence', many others supported his attitude. Thus, Majlis deputy Ahmad Rasulinezhad maintained that Mesbah Yazdi only cited divine rules regarding punishing belligerents. In his view, the real proponents of violence were the reformists. He asked them: 'Why did you defend violence? Why do you defend the belligerent? Why do you support those who intended to overthrow the regime? Is insulting sacred beliefs not a crime?' For some time, he said, posing questions had been sanctified [among intellectuals]. It is time for them to listen to our firm 'answers'.[69] The conservatives were now on the offensive. Their leaders, their press and most of the Jum'ah *imams* set out sternly against the students.

Ayatollah Taheri, the imam Jum'ah of Isfahan, known for his support of Khatami, was the exception. He claimed that the brutal acts against the students were perpetrated by hard-line elements in order to undermine Khatami. The *Majma'-e Ruhaniyyun-e Mobarez* warned against the Revolutionary Guards becoming a party to factional disputes and betraying its sacred mission, and claimed that publication of their letter was tantamount to inciting a coup. It also warned against the pretension of any particular group 'to represent' true Islam. The concept of *velayat-e faqih*, it said, could not be damaged by 'freedom and democracy', but by monopolism (*enhesar talabi*), use of violence (*khoshunat*) and the devaluing of sanctities (*hormat shekani*). Interestingly, *Neshat* published an article claiming that justification of violence contravenes the values of human society – and was subsequently banned.[70]

In a different version Akbar Ganji rejected the interference of the armed forces in the political process as undemocratic and against the initial will of the Imam. The military, Ganji added, are not suited to engage in politics, since their logic is one of force, not one of choice. Khomeini, he wrote, not only forbade the armed forces from engaging in politics, he even viewed it as being as harmful as opium consumption. Why then, he asked, do the Revolutionary Guards interfere in politics? If they claim to follow the Imam, why do they not follow his strict instruction in this regard too?[71]

As always, and not unrelated to the broader context of the power struggle, attention was focused on Rafsanjani's assertion on the issue, which was viewed as a signal of his position in the wider contest for power, between reformists and the conservatives. In fact, Rafsanjani backed the conservatives and seconded Khamene'i. While advocating public 'debates, discussion, argument, [and] criticisms', he believed that the students had exceeded the limits of constructive criticism. They delighted the enemies, he said, and 'the snakes that were in their winter hibernation, were moving these days'. The United States had become 'hopeful [of] returning to Iran' and openly supported 'this sinister move' by the students. Echoing Khamene'i, he said that the existence of many enemies abroad and their agents inside Iran made 'sedition of this kind dangerous.' He regretted the attack on the clergy, which was 'absolutely unprecedented' in Iran's contemporary history. Even under the Shah, he said, the sanctity of senior religious authorities '[was] never violated like this'. This was 'a disgraceful page in the history of the Islamic Republic'.[72] Rafsanjani's position on the issue helped reveal his stance in the wider domestic debate – moving more closely and openly to identify with the conservatives. (See also the next section.)

Khatami found himself in an awkward situation. After what had been said by the Supreme Leader, and the warning given by the Revolutionary Guards, he could not support the students, which may have gone too far anyway, in his view. What started as a peaceful protest by students, Khatami said, had degenerated into a riot led by people with 'evil aims' who intended 'to foster violence in society'.[73] He then appeared to have been intimidated into an embarrassing silence and did not make public statements for some two weeks.

Finally on 27 July Khatami reiterated his determination to pursue his reform program and lend the students some – indirect – support. The Islamic Revolution, he contended, was a revolution of compassion and freedom, in line with the lofty ideals of Islam, which aimed 'to undo the shackles of bondage from the hands and feet of humans'. The revolution aimed to form a government 'of the people' which is 'responsible to the people'. He said that the attack at the university dormitories was a crime 'that pained the hearts of all', and promised that those responsible for such actions would be severely punished. Stating that his reform programs were endorsed by Khamene'i, he pledged to 'renew my covenant with the entirety of the Iranian nation' to defend the principles and values for which he was elected.[74]

Harsh action was taken against the student leaders and the political groups that were believed to have supported or incited them. 'Exclusive reports' were published, revealing individuals and groups which 'were behind the disturbances', and who had allegedly aimed to undermine the regime. They included well-known individuals in veteran national organizations, including Dr Mohsen Pezeshkpur (Pan-Iran Party); Dr Parviz Varjavand and Dr 'Ali Ardalan (both from the National Front) and his son, Dr Amir Ardalan. They were blamed for aiming to 'take advantage of the disturbances for political purposes'. The reports also blamed Iran's Nation Party, and the *Mojahedin-e Khalq* for their active role in the events. The 'exclusive reports' dwell at length on the role of the student leaders, particularly Manuchehr Mohammadi and the leaders of the Bureau for the Strengthening of Unity in the disturbances.[75] Leading student activists and members of the party of Iran's Nation Party had been arrested. The head of Tehran Revolutionary Court, Hojjat ul-Islam Gholamhosein Rahbarpur, disclosed on 12 September that four students had been sentenced to death and that two of these sentences have already been approved by the Supreme Court.[76] Pro-reform newspapers voiced dismay that a Revolutionary Court had met in secret to sentence the students, while public opinion has been 'kept uninformed about the court proceedings', the charges and even the identity of the students.[77]

The riots appear to have been a genuine and spontaneous movement by the 'children of the revolution', to attain the hitherto unachieved goals of the revolution, mainly freedom. They testified to the primacy of domestic problems as people's main concern. Yet, they also attested to the limits of the students' power at the time by demonstrating the lack of organization and leadership. Moreover, the main focus of their protest – freedom of expression – seemed to have a limited appeal among wider segments of the society, which failed to lend massive support. Finally, it was not clear what precisely the movement demanded. The hard-liners, on the other hand, were determined to suppress such voices before they got out of control. Although the riots have been suppressed and many of their leaders arrested, the controversies continue.

The riots also unveiled the gap between the initial ideals and the prevailing realities after two decades of Islamic rule. Similarly they brought to the fore the gap between the youth and the ruling establishment as well as the widening differences between existing domestic trends. (See the Conclusion to Part Two.) They also revealed growing popular resentment of the conservative leadership (including possibly Khamene'i himself). Yet they also testified to some elements of strength in the conservative establishment and the inherent weaknesses in Khatami's presidency. Above all, they attested to the difficulties in advancing fundamental reform. The contest between the two main rival trends intensified further following the student riots, with the pro-reform faction seemingly gaining force in the second part of 1999.

Explosive Political Atmosphere

In the summer of 1999, tension on the domestic scene grew with the conflict between the different trends becoming excessively grave and forceful. The debate centered on major questions on the revolutionary agenda at the time, mainly ideological controversies, the struggle for freedom and the economic difficulties. While such disputes had represented major challenges since the revolution, the approach of the Majlis elections (held in early 2000), heightened their relevance to the parliamentary contest. Both sides viewed the contest – in general and the parliamentary election in particular – as decisive for future course and destiny of revolution, as well as for their own standing in the hierarchy of power, and their role in shaping future policy.

Faced with the multiple challenges of running the state and pursuing their dogma and aware of the threat posed by Khatami and the champions of reform, and mindful of the growing popular disenchantment – the conservatives viewed their victory as crucial in determining the revolutionary path and their own share in command. They were keen to maintain their influence in the Majlis and prevent further setbacks, such as those that followed their devastating defeat in the 1997 presidential elections and the 1999 municipal contest. The reformists, viewing the control of the legislative as a prerequisite for advancing reforms, also resolved to use their earlier electoral gains to advance their goals. Given the experience of previous contests and the flexibility of political alignments the exact configurations are difficult to determine. At this stage, however, the two major trends could be still typified into two broad categories – the pragmatic–reformists and the hard-line conservatives. (See also the Epilogue.)

To illustrate the depth of the domestic dichotomy, the inter-relatedness of the various issues in public debate, and the fluidity and flexibility of the domestic politics that prevailed in the fall of 1999, our discussion will focus on a number of relevant concerns. Each has a wider implication and relates to different aspects of the domestic debate, and all are – in one way or another – inter-related.

First was the debate over the priority that political issues – including the quest for freedom, civil society and human rights – should have at this stage of the revolution. As has been stressed, Khatami and his government attached much significance to the issue, giving it priority and making it the focus of attention. The conservatives picked up this issue to attack the government for over-stressing political questions and thus neglecting the 'main problem' – the economy. Their objectives, in the service of their overall cause, were to blame Khatami for a serious misjudgment in assigning his priorities; to charge his government with mishandling the economy, and to distract the attention of the public from the political scene to the economy. By doing so they trivialized and ridiculed the over-emphasis on civil society and the political aspects of the domestic problems, while also holding Khatami responsible for the economic malaise.

Meeting Khatami and his cabinet on 24 August 1999, Khamene'i blamed them for having 'imposed on us' a 'secondary problem' which only 'obscures the major problem' (the economy). He said that suddenly 'the serial killings [of writers]' had become the country's 'major problem'. Is this truly Iran's major problem? he asked. People 'are facing so many problems', he added shifting the onus to the president and his government, but they are all 'pushed aside' only to discuss 'secondary and minor issues'.[78] The *Jame'eh-ye Ithargaran-e Enqelab-e Islami* (Association of Self-Sacrificers for the Islamic Revolution) attributed Khatami's economic failures to his focus on political development at the expense of the economy. It also castigated him for making empty promises and charged his associates with corruption, ignoring religious values and defying loyal revolutionary elements that threaten to lead to a national crisis.[79] Ayatollah Mesbah Yazdi, while referring to Khatami's eloquent promises for a 'civil society', warned him that, according to Islam, 'misleading people and giving false promises is wrong' and even regarded as a sin.[80] This is not a new debate, of course. Yet, while in the past the 'traditional left' (the radicals) raised such arguments against Rafsanjani and also against the conservatives (see Chapter 2), the conservatives now used them against the 'left' and against Khatami personally. The stress on his unfulfilled pledges during the campaign was another major element in their criticism.

After criticizing his lack of judgment in comprehending the real priorities of the revolution, the conservatives set out on a more pointed campaign to charge Khatami with the responsibility for economic failures. They even allowed themselves to portray a very gloomy picture of the economy, which on other occasions they had been unwilling to accept. (See Chapter 2.) While Khatami's associates stressed that he was only two years into the presidency, that his powers were limited and that his reforms were often frustrated by the conservatives, the conservatives reminded him that he was the president and had been in office for two years – more than half his term. While such accusations had already been levelled in the past, their recent tone placed an astonishing accent on Khatami's failures.

Majlis deputy 'Ali Zadsar asked Khatami bluntly in March 1999 'whether he prefers the enemies of the Revolution over the loyalists of the regime'. To imply, as did Khatami's associates that his hands were tied and incapable of realizing his promises, were 'enormous lies'. Terming Khatami's supporters as hooligans and 'wolves in the guise of sheep', he called for their arrest and warned them that Iranians did not elect Khatami to bring about the revival of Mosaddeq, whom Khomeini had termed a non-Muslim. He reminded the people that Khatami had promised to curb inflation and resolve economic problems; instead his government had wasted its time 'on so-called political problems'. Did Khatami know 'that the majority of the people are in mourning because as the Nowruz [New Year] approaches, they have nothing to eat?' The 'silence of the people', he warned, 'is not eternal'.[81]

Khamene'i's exhortation, in his meeting with the cabinet on 24 August signaled the beginning of an offensive. He warned that people did not trust empty promises any more, and – two years after Khatami's election – they rightly expected results. 'The most important problem of the country today', he said, 'is the economic problem', which should have been pursued more seriously. He, also, reminded Khatami: 'fifty per cent of your term has gone'.[82] Although Khamene'i complimented the president in the same speech, his charges gave the green light for harsh accusations against the government's economic failures. *Kayhan* appealed to Khatami to cease focusing on political development and take care instead of the ailing economy and social disparities.[83] Similarly, Majlis deputy Seyyed Ahmad Rasulinezhad urged Khatami to take the economy more seriously. With the government entering its third year, 'what answer does it have for the economic needs of the people?' he asked.[84] Interestingly, similar charges were also raised by Rafsanjani, who appeared increasingly to be closer to Khamene'i and the conservatives. A day after Khamene'i's speech to the cabinet, Rafsanjani claimed that the lack of attention given to the economic problems constituted a serious threat to the regime and was causing irrevocable damage to Iran. For a country that strives to avoid dependence on foreigners, the negligence of production, investment and economic growth would have harmful consequences, he warned.[85]

The next stage of the conservative attack was to denounce cultural and political permissiveness, and with it Khatami and his team. A short satirical play published in the campus journal *Mowj* (The Wave) by two students at the Amir Kabir Technical University, a hotbed of pro-reformists, turned into a major contentious issue when the story was disclosed by the conservatives on 24 September 1999. In the play, a student ('Abbas) uses his 'meeting' with the (twelfth) Imam to voice harsh criticism of the experience of Iran under clerical rule. Clearly the two young students, writing in a journal with limited circulation, were not the main issue for the government. However, their satire in *Mowj* certainly contained harsh criticism, touching upon highly sensitive issues. It soon turned into an occasion for conservative offensive against unrestricted freedom of expression and the government's leniency on questions of culture. Numerous charges were combined, with the focus being on the need to limit harmful freedoms, the importance of cultural purity, and the legitimacy of suppressing anti-revolutionaries. The political aspects were evident: the responsibility of Khatami (and mainly of Mohajerani) for encouraging dangerous moral decadence among Iranian youth in general and students in particular.

Rahim Safavi attributed such publications to Iran's foreign enemies and their emissaries, who aimed to weaken faith and spread discord among believers. Mohammad Reza Naqdi, head of the police security and intelligence division, warned that if relevant organizations would not perform their duty, 'I would implement the divine law myself'. Making it clear that this should not be dealt with as an independent case, he vowed to act also against those 'who support those responsible for the insult'.[86] Ahmad Jannati directly blamed liberal cultural officials for fostering attacks on Islamic values: 'Those who are giving the students a green light are responsible', he stated. 'They openly and overtly insulted the Imam of the Age', he said in a Friday sermon, breaking down in tears.[87] The conservative again charged Mohajerani with direct responsibility, blaming him for the open and permissive atmosphere that had allowed people to mock sacred Islamic values. Mohajerani's recent support for the banned *Neshat* was also raised against him. Turning to target another one of the president's ministers, *Abrar* asked why the minister of culture and higher education, who offered his resignation during the July riots, tried to downplay this case of the play which insulted the twelfth Imam.[88]

Khatami went out of his way to denounce those who had blown the story out of proportions. In his words, 'a small wave was turned into a huge storm in order to create unrest and tension throughout the country'.[89] Others argued that, in fact, those who publicized the article were to be blamed. Had they not made this an issue, only a few students would have read it, as was the case with Salman Rushdie. But for the conservatives, at this crucial stage – probably as Rushdie in 1989 did – the satire served wider interests, most importantly, to censor the government and the reform programs.

Finally, directly related to the Majlis elections, in 1999 Rafsanjani's associates worked vigorously to prepare for his comeback to a more prominent and official position – probably as the next Speaker, and preferably without him even resigning his post as the head of the Expediency Council, as was required by election law.

On 16 August the Culture and Islamic Guidance Committee of the Majlis approved an amendment to the Majlis election law (endorsed by the conservatives), absolving the head of the Expediency Council (Rafsanjani) from the obligation to resign if he stood as a candidate in Majlis elections. Supporters of Khatami, reformists and the 'traditional left', viewed this move as an alliance aimed to weaken their camp, and attacked Rafsanjani and the backers of the amendment on legal and ethical grounds. Some even accused Rafsanjani of adopting his positions primarily out of competition with or jealousy of Khatami. As in the case of earlier repeated attempts during 1995 and 1996 to amend the constitution to allow Rafsanjani a third term in the presidency (see Chapter 2), it is unclear whether the latest amendment was initiated by the conservatives or encouraged by Rafsanjani. Yet, there was a clear change in political alignments: while in 1995–96 the pragmatists had led the campaign (to block Nateq-Nuri), this time the idea was advanced by their adversaries – to hinder the campaign of the reformists and Khatami. This is yet another of the peculiarities of the Islamic revolutionary system: Rafsanjani, who was believed to support a measure of pragmatism and was behind groups who were, and still are, close to Khatami, denied him any significant support and has recently even joined his adversaries. This was a 'new coalition', *Neshat* observed, whose existence would be 'as amazing as bringing night and day together'.[90]

If Rafsanjani 'is exempted' from such a restriction, it was claimed, he would be accorded more prominence and placed above the president who was constitutionally required to resign if he stood for the Majlis. 'It seems that some gentlemen are getting their wires crossed', one observer wrote.[91] *Neshat* censored Rafsanjani's 'uninvited entry' to the race, suggesting that the amalgamation of the two high-ranking posts aimed to place Rafsanjani 'way above' senior officials. Perhaps, it wrote cynically, Rafsanjani imagines that such a return befits him only. 'The left' believed that such methods had passed their 'sell-by date'. Suddenly, however, 'the gears in Hashemi's haggling wheel sprang into motion'. The conservatives, who are currently 'thinking more in terms of defeating their rivals than their own victory', had given him a hand and Rafsanjani, who always regarded it as 'his duty' to support the weaker faction to maintain a balance, had now joined the conservative camp. However, the paper notes, if he reverts 'to the old method of covert diplomacy, it will perhaps be his last game'.[92] *Arzesh* advised Rafsanjani, for his own dignity, to avoid competing with Khatami and serving his rivals. The conservatives, it wrote, instead of searching for a substantial analysis of the country's problems, have turned to tranquilizers – the 'Rafsanjani project'. Running on such a ticket, the paper warned, would be political suicide for Rafsanjani.[93] Rafsanjani lost much of his popularity thereafter. Leading the campaign against him was Akbar Ganji. (See the Epilogue below.)

The pragmatists' immediate concern until then was to prevent a massive disqualification of their candidates for the Majlis. Ayatollah Montazeri took the lead in opposing the Council of Guardians' right to disqualify candidates. In an open letter to seminary students on 7 June 1999 he accused the Council of overstepping its authority to protect Islam and interfering in the democratic rights of the people. He said that the task of the Council was 'to supervise the elections' and not to 'supervise the candidates'. In fact, the Council had in effect created a two-tier electoral system, in which they first selected the candidates and then allowed the people to choose among those who had survived 'the filter of their preferences' and fitted its own particular world-view. As one of the initiators of the law, Montazeri claimed that this was not its original intention. Moreover, the authority for guaranteeing free and fair elections, he said, lay with the ministry of the interior and not with the Council of Guardians.[94] Going on the offensive on behalf of the Council, Ayatollah Khaz'ali said that the people had no more right to challenge the Council than to question the Prophet Muhammad.[95]

The developments discussed above all form part of an attempt by the rival trends to dictate the path of the revolution. The reformist camp, faced with the recent offensive by the conservatives but encouraged by the growing popular support for their cause, seemed determined to fight back. Thus, by the end of 1999 the domestic debate had escalated and the confrontation between the two camps reached a new peak.

'Abdollah Nuri (then in jail) became a major symbol of the reform movement. He led the campaign with determination and a sense of mission. The core of the campaign was upholding freedom (and, thus, also criticizing the lack of sufficient freedoms under conservative rule). At his trial, Nuri upheld the people's right to express criticism, maintaining that only 'through reform and political criticism' would it be possible to uphold justice and defend people's rights. People, he said, may accept injustice, 'but would not tolerate humiliation [*tahqir*] and apostasy [*takfir*]'. According to the constitution, and to God's will, 'sovereignty belongs exclusively to the people [*mardom*]'. All citizens (*shahrvandan*) 'regardless of color, race, religion [*mazhab*], occupation, wealth or designation' should be 'fully equal' before the law with no discrimination (*tab'iz*) or difference (*tafavot*) between them. Nuri particularly denounced the methods used by the special court for the clergy and the court for the press as contradicting civil rights and the constitution.[96] He argued that the Islamic Revolution, led by Ayatollah Khomeini, constituted a 'golden opportunity [*forsat-e tala'i*] for liberating people from suppression, tyranny and despotism [*estebdad*]'. Although this had not yet been attained, he added, Iranians now had another opportunity to achieve this sacred goal. They should not be forced to miss the chance, just because of the 'personal and factional greed' (*matame'-e shakhsi va jenahi*) of a few individuals and interest groups.[97]

Ganji supported him in his customary style, using an even harsher tone and even blunter language. He denounced the prevalent inquisition (*taftish-e 'aqa'ed*) in Iran and urged the granting of greater freedoms.[98] While acts of violence and terrorism existed before Khatami's presidency, he argued, they were now being aimed not only at the enemies but also against the president. He compared the terror of intellectuals (see above) with the massacre of the native Americans and to buffalo hunting in the US.[99] He denounced the methods used by the special courts of the clergy and the supra-constitutional (*fara-qanuni*) rights assumed by the *velayat-e motlaqeh-ye faqih*.[100] The title of his book, *Talaqqi-ye Fashisti az Din va Hokumat* (The Fascist Interpretation of Religion and Government), illustrates his harsh tone. In a lecture in Shiraz (June 1997), Ganji used the term 'Islamic Fascism' and called extremist factions in Iran as '*jonbesh-e fashisti*' (fascist movements). While answering questions on the same occasion, he admitted, 'I stated explicitly that in my opinion', groups like *Ansar-e Hezbollah*, *Ya le-Tharat* [*al-Hosein*], and the newspapers *Shalamcheh* and even the *Sobh* and *Kayhan*, 'are the symbols [*sombolha*] of the fascist movement in Iran'.[101] Ayatollah Khaz'ali (who said that even if 30 million people had voted for something, it would have to await the Leader's approval) and Jannati (who maintained that people need custodianship), best reveal the conservative approach – that the view of a few theologians is superior to that of the populace. Such attitudes, Ganji maintained, fully contradict Khomeini's view that people do not need a guardian (*qayyem*), and that the 'yardstick [*mizan*] is the will of the people'.[102]

This latter phrase has become one of the main slogans of the pro-reform faction in the Majlis elections. (See the Epilogue below.)

NOTES

1. Mehdi Qoli Hedayat, *Khaterat va Khatarat* [Memories and Dangers] (Tehran: Rangin, 1950/51), p. 150. They viewed themselves, wrote Mangol Bayat, 'as the new apostles', spreading the message of reason, science, liberty and progress. See Mangol Bayat-Philipp, *Mysticism and Dissent: Socioreligious Thought in Qajar Iran* (Syracuse, NY: Syracuse University Press, 1982), p. 134.
2. Words to that effect by Khomeini in: *Kayhan* (Tehran), 4 December 1982, 4 August 1983; *Jomhuri-ye Islami*, 12 March 1983; by President Khamene'i, *Kayhan* (Tehran), 4, 9 August, 10 September; by Mahdavi-Kani, *Kayhan* (Tehran), 7 May 1983; and by Montazeri, *Kayhan* (Tehran), 21 August 1983.
3. *Jahan-e Islam*, 1 February 1994.
4. *Ettela'at*, 24 February 1981.
5. *Ettela'at* and *Kayhan* (Tehran), 16 May 1979.
6. *Ettela'at*, 1, 2 June 1981.
7. *Tehran Times*, 27 November 1980.
8. *Kayhan* (Tehran), 24 November 1982.
9. *Ettela'at*, 5 September 1983.
10. *Kayhan* (Tehran), 30 May 1998.
11. *Kayhan* (Tehran), 28 May 1998.
12. *Kayhan* (Tehran), 31 May 1995.
13. See interview with Safavi in *Kayhan* (Tehran), 1 June 1998.
14. Banuazizi, 'Iran's Revolutionary Impasse', p. 2.
15. Radio Tehran, 25 August 1995 – DR, 29 August 1995.
16. *Resalat*, 29 August 1995 – DR, 13 September 1995.
17. *Iran*, and *Kayhan* (Tehran), 25 July 1995.
18. *Salam*, 16 October 1995.
19. *Salam*, 30 October 1995. In the wake of such threats, Soroush's wife expressed concern for the safety of her family.
20. *Salam*, 16 October 1995 – DR, 31 October 1995.
21. *Salam*, 16 October 1995 – DR, 31 October 1995.
22. *Iran*, 25 July 1995.
23. *Salam*, 26 October 1995.
24. *Los Angeles Times*, 30 December 1995.
25. *Salam*, 2 January 1996.
26. *Salam*, 28 January 1995.
27. *Ruzegar-e Now*, no. 205 (February–March 1999), pp. 31–3.
28. *Hamshahri*, 2 March 1999 [DR].
29. *Iran News*, 2 March 1999 [DR].
30. *Hamshahri*, 3 March 1999 [DR]. The signatories included the managing editors of *Khordad, Jahan-e Islam, Hamshahri, Sobh-e Emruz, Iran News, Akhbar, Neshat, Arya, Kar va Kargar* and *Ettela'at*.
31. IRNA, 8 March 1999 [DR].
32. *Hamshahri*, 2 March 1999 [DR].

33. IRNA, quoting *Iran News*, 8 March 1999 [DR].
34. *Tehran Times*, 7 March 1999 [DR].
35. *Salam*, 17 May 1993; DR, 28 May 1993.
36. *Jahan-e Islam*, 19 October 1993 – DR, 10 November 1993.
37. Human Rights Watch, *Guardians of Thought: Limits of Freedom of Expression in Iran* (New York, NY: Human Rights Watch, 1993), pp. 5, 39–49, 111–13, 128.
38. *Salam*, 25 September; DR, 6 October 1993.
39. *Salam*, 28 August 1993; Agence France Presse (AFP), 27 November 1993 – DR, 29 November 1993. 'Abdi was sentenced to a year in prison with a suspended sentence of 40 lashes of the whip: *Salam*, 25 December – DR, 27 December 1993; Agence France Presse, 25 December 1993 – DR, 27 December 1993.
40. *Salam* and Agence France Presse, 28 and 29 August 1993 – DR, 30 August 1993; *Iran Times*, 20 August and 3, 10, and 17 September 1993
41. See *Salam*, *Akhbar*, and *Kayhan* (Tehran), 24 August 1995; Agence France Presse, 24 August 1995 – DR, 25 August 1995.
42. *Ettela'at*, 24 August 1995. *Ettela'at* on 26 August 1995 joined in rejecting the action, claiming that it was unacceptable that 17 years after the revolution, unidentifiable groups of armed Hezbollahis would take the liberty to carry out such actions.
43. *Salam*, 28 August 1995. *Salam* was in turn criticized for supporting corrupt authors: *Salam*, 3 September 1995.
44. Human Rights Watch, *World Report 1996* (New York, NY: 1995), pp. 276–79.
45. Human Rights Watch, *Guardians of Thought*, pp. 94–102; *Los Angeles Times*, 30 December 1995.
46. Reuters (quoted from CNN website), 7 July 1999.
47. *Tehran Times*, 3 August 1999.
48. Fred Halliday, 'An Elusive Normalization: Western Europe and the Iranian Revolution', *Middle East Journal*, 48/2 (Spring 1994), p. 321. See also Anoushirvan Ehteshami, 'After Khomeini: The Structure of Power in the Iranian Second Republic', *Political Studies*, 39/1 (March 1991), pp. 148–57.
49. Human Rights Watch, *Guardians of Thought*, p. 125.
50. Azar Nafisi, 'The Veiled Threat', 22 February 1999.
51. *Frankfurter Rundschau*, 12 January 1995 – DR, 13 January 1995.
52. Shaul Bakhash, 'Iranian Politics Since the Gulf War', in Robert Satloff (ed.), *The Politics of Change in the Middle East* (Boulder, CO: Westview Press, 1993), pp. 78–9.
53. Human Rights Watch, *Guardians of Thought*, p. 1.
54. Jamshid Amuzegar, 'Islamic Fundamentalism in Action: The Case of Iran', *Middle East Policy*, 4/1–2 (1995), p. 25.
55. Human Rights Watch, *Guardians of Thought*, p. 2.
56. *Salam*, 1 September 1993 – DR, 4 October 1993.
57. *Frankfurter Rundschau*, 12 January 1995 – DR, 13 January 1995.
58. *Tehran Times* and *Washington Post*, 13 September 1999, quoting the head of the Revolutionary Court of Tehran, Hojjat ul-Islam Gholamhosein Rahbarpur.
59. *Jahan-e Islam*, 3 January 1999 [DR].
60. *Jahan-e Islam*, 14 February 1999 [DR].

61. An interview with Tabarzadi broadcast over Radio Israel (in Persian), 6 and 7 April 1999. Tabarzadi reiterated the students' displeasure with Khatami and his 'undue silence': *Kayhan* (Tehran), 22 June 1999. See also an open letter to the president, 31 May 1999. (The author has a copy of the letter.)

62. Heshmatollah Tabarzadi, 'Nagofteha-ye Enqelab: Rah-e Halli Bara-ye Sakhtar-e Siyasi-ye Ayandeh-ye Iran' [The Unspoken Words of the Revolution: A Solution for the Future Political Structure of Iran], *Mehregan*, Spring 1999 (Internet edn).

63. The author has a copy of the statement.

64. Meshhed Radio, 12 July 1999 [DR]; *Neshat*, 15 July 1999.

65. *Jomhuri-ye Islami*, 19 July 1999 [DR].

66. *Ya le-Tharat al-Hosein* (Hail the avengers of [Imam] Hosein), 24 July 1999.

67. *Neshat* and *Iran Daily*, 24 July 1999. Connotations of *khoshunat* include use of force, harshness, rudeness, violence. Given the context and usage of the term in current Iranian discourse, and in line with translations in Iranian and Western sources, I have used 'violence' for *khoshunat*.

68. IRNA, 6 August 1999 [DR].

69. *Resalat*, 19 August 1999 [DR].

70. *Neshat*, 21 July 1999; *Iran News*, 27 September 1999, quoting *Hamshahri*.

71. Ganji, *Talaqqi-ye Fashisti az Din va Hokumat*, pp. 224–7, 270–5.

72. Tehran TV, 15 July 1999 [DR]; *Neshat* and *Iran Daily*, 24 July 1999.

73. *Neshat*, 13 July 1999.

74. Iran, 28 July 1999; IRNA (Internet database), 27 July 1999 [DR]; *Mid-East Mirror*, 29 July 1999.

75. *Jomhuri-ye Islami* and *Kayhan* (Tehran), 19 July 1999.

76. *Jomhuri-ye Islami*, 12 September; *Tehran Times* and *Washington Post*, 13 September 1999.

77. *Akhbar-e Eqtesad* quoted by Reuters, 13 September 1999.

78. Tehran TV, 24 August 1999 [DR]. See similar charges below.

79. *Ettela'at*, 26 August 1999.

80. *Neshat* and *Iran Daily*, 24 July 1999.

81. *Kayhan* (Tehran), 7 March 1999.

82. Tehran TV, 24 August 1999 [DR].

83. *Kayhan* (Tehran), 28 August 1999. For similar charges see *Resalat*, 11 August; *Jomhuri-ye Islami*, 10 August 1999. Similar accusations were also raised during Friday sermons in different cities on 27 August 1999. See, for example, the statement by Ayatollah Ebrahim Amini in Qom in *Jomhuri-ye Islami*, 28 August 1999.

84. *Resalat*, 19 August 1999 [DR].

85. *Tehran Times*, 26 August 1999.

86. *Iran News*, 27 September 1999, quoting *Qods;* for criticism of such harsh statements, see, *Khordad* and *Payam-e Azadi*, 29 September 1999.

87. Reuters (quoted from CNN website), 24 September 1999.

88. *Iran News* (Internet database), 27 September 1999, quoting *Abrar*.

89. Tehran TV, 29 September 1999 – SWB, 2 October 1999.

90. *Neshat*, 28 August 1999 [Gulf2000].

91. *Neshat*, 26 August 1999 [from Gulf2000]. Critique entitled 'In the eyes of the law all are equal, but some are more equal than others', by Arash Sadeqiyan.

92. *Neshat*, 28 August 1999 [Gulf2000].
93. *Arzesh*, 2 September 1999.
94. The author has a copy of Montazeri's letter.
95. Reuters, 13 June 1999.
96. Nuri, *Showkaran-e Eslah*, pp. 11–12, 22, 28, 43.
97. Nuri, *Showkaran-e Eslah*, pp. 267–72.
98. Ganji, *Naqdi Bara-ye Tamam-e Fosul*, p. 12.
99. A. Ganji, *Tarik-Khaneh-e Ashbah: Asib-shenasi Gozar be Dowlat-e Demokratik-e towse'eh-gara* [Ghosts' Darkhouse: Pathology of Transition to the Developmental Democratic State] (Tehran: Tarh-e Now, 1999), pp. 16–21.
100. Ganji, *Tarik-Khaneh-e Ashbah*, pp. 78–87.
101. Ganji, *Talaqqi-ye Fashisti az Din va Hokumat*, pp. 313–20, 379–82. Ganji was sentenced to jail and 'paid the price' but he regretted that his warning had not been taken seriously. Ganji was arrested again in April 2000.
102. Ganji, *Tarik-Khaneh-e Ashbah*, pp. 239–43.

Conclusion:
A Tentative Appraisal

The Islamic Revolution was a major turning point in the modern history of Iran. Carried on a wave of popular support, the revolution represented a new prototype of power seizure, a new political system (known as *velayat-e faqih*) and leadership, with a new ideology and a vision of the ideal society. More than a mere replacement of governments, the revolution aimed entirely to restructure the Iranian political system and to implement its new doctrine in order to advance the country and combat the severe problems facing Iran. The revolution embodied a promise – and the expectation – of a brighter future for the country and the people.

Yet, more than 20 years on, the Islamic regime is still searching for an appropriate path to cope with the challenge of governance while adjusting its idealistic vision to evolving realities. All this, at a time of domestic upheaval, severe social and economic difficulties, and a perpetual struggle for power between competing tendencies, each attempting to decide the direction of the revolution and establish its own supremacy. At the same time, Iran continues to be influenced by the changing patterns of regional politics. Some of these have opened new opportunities, but others have confronted Tehran with grave challenges and serious policy dilemmas. The same could be said for domestic developments, which have aggravated the situation and brought about fierce differences among the conflicting tendencies in Tehran.

At the end of 1999, the political atmosphere seemed more heated than at any other time since the new regime consolidated its rule (in the early 1980s). This makes any attempt to come up with definite conclusions about Iran's policy direction and the balance of power within the leadership extremely difficult. This brief conclusion, therefore, is no more than a tentative appraisal of the situation in Iran as it appears after two decades of revolutionary rule. (See also the Epilogue.)

In its 20 years in power the new regime has demonstrated an impressive measure of political resilience and continuity. The clerics in command have managed to assume exclusive power and to keep the Islamic system intact (regardless of ideological retreat and perpetual struggle for power), dislodging all the other groups within the broad coalition that had led Khomeini to power, from any share in government. Until now, the clerics in power have succeeded in keeping a tight grip on power and maintaining a measure of political stability – regardless of the numerous difficulties that have plagued the country.

Yet, for the Islamic revolutionaries, the change of regime, *per se*, was not the ultimate goal, but the means to implement their dogma and to establish an ideal Islamic state. In this regard, despite some meaningful achievements, popular expectations and the expectations of various revolutionary factions have so far remained largely unfulfilled.

It is clear that the regime's efforts to advance its programs in its first two hectic decades in power was hindered by many difficulties – some objective, others the result of its own making. The domestic distress at the end of the Shah's rule, the period of revolutionary upheaval and conflicting tendencies within the revolutionary camp, were some aspects of the burdensome starting point. New difficulties were subsequently added, most profoundly the war with Iraq, hostile relations with the United States (and with many other Western countries and neighbour-ing states), and the drop in oil income. Rapid population growth, accelerated urbanization, the flight of professionals and capital and the government's own mismanagement, were some of the more pressing hardships in the decade of war and revolution that followed the dramatic takeover by Islamic revolutionaries in 1979. The death of Ayatollah Khomeini and the absence of his charismatic leadership made it even more difficult for the regime to shape new policy and hindered its efforts for post-war reconstruction at a time when crucial decisions were needed. The laborious decision-making process combined with domestic strife in a period of fierce factional in-fighting further com-pounded the regime's difficulties. The changing world order; the United States' 'dual containment' policy and sanctions against Iran; the con-tinued drop in oil income and fast growing population – presented the country with additional difficulties. Yet, popular expectations have risen markedly over time and the domestic rifts have intensified. The riots in the early 1990s (motivated primarily by social and economic griev-ances), and the unrest at Iranian universities in 1999 (mainly in the quest for greater personal freedom), testify to the urge for change, though they also demonstrated the government's power to suppress dissent.

Ideologically, the most important historical change was the unification of religion and state and the concentration of all authority, spiritual and temporal, in the hands of the prominent religious authority, the *vali-ye faqih*. Yet, it was in this very realm that the revolution was forced to make its most painful retreat. Following the death of the founding father of the revolution in 1989, Iran ceased to be ruled by the most prominent theologians or governed by purely dogmatic considerations. (See Chapter 1.) Over time, the regime seems to have abandoned many of its basic dogmatic tenets while others are being openly challenged. Public debates have recently questioned the application and sometimes the very concept of *velayat-e faqih*; the advantages of renewed ties with the United States are also being discussed quite openly. (See Chapter 6.)

Those seeking reforms (*eslah-talab*) through greater dogmatic flexibility have clashed sharply with the dogmatic dedication of the conservatives. This was a conflict between those who believed that revolutionary ideals could not be attained with the same old slogans, and those who viewed full dogmatic adherence as the only way to secure the initial goals of the revolution. By the end of 1999 domestic rifts had intensified further and the atmosphere had become more tense and harsher in tone. With the Islamic system fairly stabilized and the rival opposition factions seemingly less active, differences over domestic policy presented the regime with its most immediate political challenge. Asked in 1994 about the major threats facing the regime, the secretary of the SNSC, Hojjat ul-Islam Hasan Ruhani, said that the primary threat was domestic: 'If we maintain our unity at home, I don't think that any foreign enemy can create problems for us.'[1] Bemoaning the fierce rifts and power struggles, the hard-line *Jomhuri-ye Islami* wrote in early 1999 that whatever the enemies of the revolution wished for in two decades, and invested fortunes to accomplish, is unfortunately being achieved with the help of forces from within the country.[2] In a way, domestic rifts were the symptom of much wider problems.

The considerable retreat from dogma notwithstanding, the government did not manage to resolve – or even significantly lessen – pressing problems. The results of the revolution certainly fell far short of meeting rising expectations, particularly the pursuit of social and economic welfare and the quest for greater individual liberty. The economy, which Khamene'i described in August 1999 as the country's 'most important problem', continued to be the main cause of popular disenchantment and discontent. Even statements by Iran's leading officials confirmed that economic difficulties continued to press hard on the people (as shown in Chapters 4 and 5). Consequently, for many, patience seemed to run out.

While the revolutionary goal of social justice remained unfulfilled, political freedom – another major ideal of the revolution – has not been guaranteed either. For many, most notably students, intellectuals and segments of the press, as well as the clergy – this was no less a cause for resentment.

Foreign observers have often combined these multi-faceted difficulties to portray a gloomy picture of the situation.[3] Iranian observers were no less critical. The unflattering comparisons between the situation under the Shah and the realities under the Islamic rule – in both economic and political realms – were the harshest possible indictments of the new regime, particularly as they came from devout revolutionaries. (See Chapters 4 and 5.) The effect of such failures, many Iranians feared, could extend far beyond Iran's borders and discourage Islamists elsewhere. Khomeini's first prime minister, Mehdi Bazargan, went as far as to warn in 1993 that the main threat to Islam in Iran then was the experience of the people under the Islamic government.[4] Seyyed Mahmud Qomi (currently living in Europe) gave rise to similar concerns. He claimed in 1995 that the outcome of the revolution had only earned Islam and the clergy a bad reputation. Clerics are now identified with 'terrorism, torture, bombing, explosions, and hostage-taking', which 'have no place in Islam'. The world perceived Iran's politics as representing Islam, and their example had brought nothing but disgrace to true Islam. Even judging by practical results, Mahmud Qomi maintained that the Islamic government has failed to secure 'anything' for the oppressed, who are 'even more oppressed now' than they were before the revolution.[5] (See Chapter 4.) Similar charges were brought by Mehdi Ha'iri in his letter to the UN Secretary-General. (See Chapter 1.) The essence of such a challenge was encapsulated in a penetrating question put to President Rafsanjani by a Turkish journalist who argued that although Iranian policy was based on Islam the situation in Iran was no better than in other developing countries. How is it possible then, he asked, to regard Islam as the best guide to solve the country's problems?[6]

No doubt, the retreat from dogma did not necessarily portend the imminent demise of clerical rule. Paradoxically, the greater the deviations from dogma (and the concomitant adjustment to new realities), the better the government was able to deal with pressing difficulties. Yet, the more flexibility it exhibits, the further the revolution distances itself from the original ideology and the greater the domestic strife.

In 1997, the Iranian people, by electing Khatami, signaled their preference for greater openness and reform. Khatami's election was, in many ways, the result of growing difficulties and looming popular discontent. Khatami offered renewed hope that the revolution carried the cure to end the country's malaise, and that the Islamic system could be reformed from within to fit the new realities in Iran and face the challenge of the modern world. It was a severe warning to the Iranian leadership, but also another opportunity. Khatami, while still minister of Islamic guidance, expressed the fear that the realities established under the Islamic regime endangered Islam. (See Chapter 3.) As president it has been his mission to avoid such a scenario.

It would be difficult, of course, to weigh Khatami's success after three years in office. Yet, it seems that Khatami was entrusted, to use Bazargan's phrase, with 'a knife without a blade'. The dire economic and social difficulties, the political structure and basic elements inherent in the Islamic republican system made the introduction of significant change an extremely arduous mission. One Iranian source wrote early in 1998, that ever since entering office, Khatami has hardly had 'a crisis-free week'.[7] In this sense, the realities of 1999 were even more difficult, with domestic rivalries reaching a new peak. Moreover, Khatami's 'peer reviews' are clearly unsatisfactory: both the conservatives and the more reformist elements blame him for serious misjudgment and, even worse, for actual failures. (See Chapter 5.) The hard-liners, who 'see true reform as their own doom and the end for all practical purposes of the Islamic Republic', are determined to oppose reform and to prevent merely a 'virtual theocracy'.[8] Supporters of reform are disappointed both by the narrow scope of reform and by the slow pace of change. More than that, what they seek is much more than Khatami seems capable of endorsing. Even reforms pursued by Khatami have been confronted with harsh conservative opposition. Hard-liners generally believed that Khatami was going too far and too fast; reformists believed that he was advancing too slowly and setting only limited goals for himself. While in 1999 Khatami maintained that he had held office for *only* two years, both hard-liners and reformists constantly reminded him that he had *already* been in office for two years – more than half the length of his term. Both domestic camps have another point in common; they agree that the situation is bad and worsening. Before Khatami, Iran seemed to many like 'a country of broken promises'.[9] Khatami provided the hope, inspired growing expectations, and – compared with his predecessors – striving for greater reform. The ideas raised were sufficient to arouse the hard-liners' fury; the results are still insufficient to satisfy the pro-reform camp. Yet, for many Iranians, Khatami remains the symbol of hope for reform.

Twenty years later, the Islamic Revolution seems much more mature, but has not yet resolved the many paradoxes and conflicts inherent in the revolutionary system. People's patience seems to have been exhausted, and the demand for practical solutions is weighing harder on the government. After two decades, people appear to judge the revolution not by the expectation and hope that it initially excited, but by actual results. Consequently, there is a sense of exhaustion, over-saturation with revolutionary excess, and a concomitant 'loss of zeal'.[10] Moreover, Islam is now seen as the 'official ideology' and the clergy are no longer viewed 'as the savior of the people', but rather as 'the state's agents'. Thus the widening gap between the clergy and the population led to the 'obvious failure of political Islam'.[11] *The Failure of Political Islam* was, in fact, the title of a scholarly book by Olivier Roy, published in 1994. Most devastating of all is the fact that the revolution that came to power on a wave of popular enthusiasm, has lost much of its initial support. 'Abbas 'Abdi, to cite one example, bemoaned the fact that, in his view, the gulf between the people and the government was as wide as it was during the days of the Shah.[12] In 1999, this was probably one of the main problems facing the regime.[13]

Nevertheless, in 1999, the Islamic regime was still in control of the main apparatus of power, and the system as such – regardless of fierce conflicts and domestic strife and considerable dogmatic retreat – remained intact. The revolution may have lost its way, but not its muscle nor its determination to struggle for survival. Unlike the Shah, the Islamic regime is aware of the threats it faces and is fighting for its existence. This was demonstrated most dramatically in the way that the student riots were put down in 1999, and by the consequent offensive against the reformists. The regime's repeated threats to use violence and its rejection of leniency and indulgence best exemplify its determination. In more and more cases, thus, the regime seems to rely on force – or the threat of force – to maintain the acquiescence of the people. This has involved the closure of newspapers and threats by military commanders, such as by Rahin Safavi or Naqdi, or by clerics, such as Mesbah Yazdi.

Finally, recent events also attest to the widening divide between the ruling establishment and emerging civil society – mainly the youth. In one sense, this is a generational crisis – a struggle between young people on the one hand, and the conservative elite and the institutions of power at their service, on the other. An interesting manifestation of this dichotomy can be found in an article in *Jame'eh*, published in May 1998. Responding to an appeal by Hojjat ul-Islam Mohammad Javad Hojjati-Kermani, who asked the youth not to exceed the boundaries of true Islam, one student wrote passionately: how many Islams are there? And who decides which is the true Islam? The main question, he continued, was not of violating this or another law, but that 'in a one way street' a certain group – the conservative clergy – 'drive against the flow of traffic', and restrict the thought (*andisheh*) of the entire society within a 'narrow and dark alley'.[14] In fact, in 1999, 'the children of the revolution', many of whom had not yet been born when Khomeini returned from exile, signaled their determination to achieve the goals which had led their parents to join the Islamic Revolution 20 years before.

Two decades after the Iranian Revolution, the stability of the regime seems to depend less on the degree of the return to Islam than on the government's ability to satisfy the expectations that initially brought it to power. This is the main challenge facing the revolution, and it is in this area that significant progress has yet to be achieved.

The Iranian ship of state continues therefore to drift from course to course in constant search of a proper equilibrium, between dedication to its revolutionary convictions and the importunate demands of governance, between religion and state, and between Islam and the West.

NOTES

1. *Hamshahri*, 4 September 1994.
2. *Jomhuri-ye Islami*, 11 January 1999.
3. Iran faces 'an existential crisis', one scholar observed, that includes acute threats to 'its political legitimacy, domestic stability and national security'. It is 'ideologically bankrupt, economically and morally exhausted, militarily weak, increasingly unpopular domestically . . . and friendless abroad'. See, Hashim, *Crisis of the Iranian State*, p. 3. It is becoming 'ideologically rigid, economically unstable, politically repressive, and internationally isolated', noted another. See Banuazizi, 'Iran's Revolutionary Impasse', p. 2. The domestic difficulties threaten to 'bring down' the regime. See Lamote, 'Iran's Foreign Policy', pp. 6–8, 24. It 'has failed', added another observer. For the poor, 'the revolution and its utopian hopes are dead'. See Shirley, 'Fundamentalism in Power', pp. 35, 39; see also Shirley, 'The Iran Policy Trap', *Foreign Policy*, 96 (Fall 1994), p. 93.
4. Interview with Bazargan in *Kiyan*, 11 (March–May 1993).
5. *Kayhan* (London), 15 December 1994 – DR, 20 January 1995.
6. *Ettela'at*, 8 June 1994.
7. *Iran Daily*, 11 June 1998, quoted by IRNA, 11 June 1998 [DR].
8. See Azar Nafisi in *The Washington Post*, 15 July 1999.
9. *International Herald Tribune*, 31 May 1995.
10. Chubin, *Iran's National Security Policy*, p. 67.
11. Lamote, 'Iran's Foreign Policy', pp. 7–9.
12. *Christian Science Monitor*, 20 April 1995.
13. *Salam* noted sarcastically that the ruling elite has so wronged the people and lost popularity in the eyes of the public, that no matter what position it takes, people feel an urge to take exactly the opposite line: *Salam*, 9 July 1998.
14. *Jame'eh*, 19 May 1998.

Part Two:
Iran, the West and the
Middle East Peace Process

Introduction

The Islamic Revolution led to a dramatic change in Iran's foreign outlook and its international relations. By all accounts, Khomeini's worldview presented a mirror image to the creed of the Shah. While the previous regime had made a determined drive towards Westernization and rapid modernization, the Islamic Republic saw Western influence as a major threat. In terms of Iran's relations with the superpowers Khomeini seemed to believe – as he often put it – that 'all infidels belong to the same camp'. The attitude towards the two world blocks was encapsulated in the revolutionary creed 'Neither East nor West', which rejected them both. Similarly, in contrast to the Shah's close ties with the United States, Khomeini viewed that country as 'the Great Satan'. In clear contradiction to the Shah's stress on Iranian nationalism, Khomeini's theory also ignored the existence of political boundaries within the Muslim world community (*umma*). Similarly the revolutionary doctrine obliged Iran to view all Muslims as one family, to seek their friendship and to extend to them Iran's support. Initially, Khomeini had declared all governments in Islamic countries, to be illegitimate in principle. As against the Shah's striving to expand foreign ties, the Islamic regime wished to expand its influence among the peoples. Only through isolation could Iran become truly independent, Khomeini said.[1] Yet, over time, realities have forced Iran to conform to some accepted norms in international relations.

The Islamic revolutionary doctrine, as outlined by Ayatollah Khomeini in exile, was by no means intended for the people of Iran alone, nor for Shi'is or even Muslims. Its ultimate goal was to launch an 'ideological crusade' aimed at bringing the genuine message of Islam to all peoples everywhere. In fact, Khomeini often compared the movement that brought him to power with the advent of Islam,[2] and with its overall message extending to humanity at large. Typically, Ayatollah Mahmud Taleqani viewed the revolution (just prior to the revolutionary takeover), as carrying a message for the whole of mankind, 'offering a world tired of all the teachings of East and West a new way'.[3] Although the revolutionary aim was not usually described in such general terms, most domestic trends seemed initially to agree that eventually the Islamic revolution would offer salvation to the *mostaz'afin* of the world – an issue where religious duty fades into social ideology. The idea was so powerful at the outset of the revolution that it seemed worthwhile for the foreign minister, Mir-Hosein Musavi, to declare in 1981 that, one of the 'objectives of Iran's foreign policy' was to 'carry the message of Iran's Islamic Revolution to the [entire] world'.[4]

Some statements pointing to the centrality of such a worldwide mission continued to be made in subsequent years. One such was the assessment of Mohammad Javad Larijani who said following the fall of the USSR, that 'the cresting of the Islamic movement will soon transform the face of the world' in the same manner as the Renaissance changed Europe.[5] Just as the Renaissance 'brought new fundamentals' of legitimacy, freedom, and scientific progress to the West, so Islamism – launched from Iran – would have a similar impact: 'We shall be the watchmen of this immense ideological political movement. We shall pave the way for the expansion and deepening of contemporary Islamism.'[6] Ayatollah 'Abdul-Qasem Khaz'ali (member of the Council of Guardians) spelt out this general vision in 1998: 'Today, Islam does not know borders.' In line with Islamic doctrine, he said that 'Arabs, non-Arabs and Afghans are [all] the same nation'.[7]

But such an approach – typical of revolutionary movements in history – always had a ritual rather than a programmatic ring to them. More importantly, as with basic trends in Iranian domestic politics, ideology was gradually subordinated to interests while actual policy combined ideological conviction with a healthy dose of regard for Iran's national interests.

The change was already noticeable under Khomeini, but became more marked following his death. Within five years of the revolution, Khomeini announced that Tehran wanted to establish 'relations with all countries,' with the sole exception of the United States, Israel and South Africa. Not to do so, he said, would be 'against reason and Islamic law'.[8] And although the revolutionary regime shared the belief that Iran should assume the leadership of the Muslim and non-aligned worlds, Rafsanjani implied in July 1988 that Iran's anti-Western version of non-alignment had harmed its interests. Rafsanjani added, in a note of criticism aimed at earlier revolutionary practices, that 'by the use of an inappropriate method . . . we have created enemies for our country'. Those who might have remained neutral (in the Iran–Iraq war) were led to transform their neutrality into hostility, he said, and Tehran did not labor to attract the friendship of those 'who could have been our friends'. He added that the foreign ministry had been instructed to 'tread the correct path' – the path 'we should have always followed'.[9] Even the generally hard-line *Kayhan* editorialized that, unlike the practice of the past, 'the breaking of diplomatic ties should not be seen as a principle'.[10] The urgency of forging ties, even with countries that did not fit Iran's revolutionary criteria, had become evident even earlier, such as with Iran's purchase of US arms during the war with Iraq, but gathered momentum in the early 1990s. Generally speaking, Rafsanjani's 'conception of world politics' proved 'more geopolitical than ideological'.[11] Clearly, then, beliefs were seen to be subordinate to national interests. This became even more evident following Khatami's election. (See the next chapter.)

Profound international and regional changes in the 1990s, including the disintegration of the Soviet Union, the Gulf War, the Middle East peace process, and the spread of Islamism, offered Iran new opportunities but also presented it with severe challenges and serious dilemmas. In addition to the general dilemmas involved in formulating and putting in place new revolutionary politics, these changes combined with intense domestic strife to redefine Iran's interests and hence also its politics. The urge to respond to such changes often seemed likely 'gradually, but surely, [to turn] the doctrines and practices of Iranian foreign policy on their heads'.[12] It soon became a major issue in domestic rivalries, further embroiling the formulation and directions of Iran's foreign policy.

In fact, in contrast to the period of the Shah's rule, Islamic Iran made policy 'in a more untidy and altogether less consistent manner'.[13] After Khomeini, Iran's 'two-track foreign policy'[14] became still more puzzling, coalescing with domestic disputes during a period of fierce factional strife and indecisiveness. Much like the differences over domestic politics, some hard-line revolutionaries continued to stick to the original revolutionary dogma all along, viewing it as the only way to secure the genuine aims of the revolution. Pragmatic and reformist elements, on the other hand, proposed more realistic means to advance the revolutionary goals. In addition, like the dynamics of Iran's domestic politics, decision-making was subject to contradictory pressures and laborious bargaining which often emerged in apparently conflicting tendencies.

The result was vague and unclear, indicating an attempt on the part of the regime to be all things to all people: revolutionary to hard-line ideologues yet 'moderate and reasonable to European and Asian countries whose trade and investment' was sought by Tehran. It remained unclear which of its often-contradictory statements represented new policy, which was really 'a smoke screen', and which merely 'simple confusion'.[15] That outsiders had difficulty discerning Iranian priorities is not surprising, given that Iranians themselves had similar difficulties. Thus *Jahan-e Islam* regretted that Iran's regional policy had been 'plunged into ambiguity and it is impossible to portray a clear picture of it'.[16]

The government's blurred and dualistic approach came under fierce fire in the early 1990s from both ends of the political spectrum. Some critics questioned the advisability of pursuing doctrine to the point of damaging the interests of the state; others blamed the government for abandoning pure doctrine and following too 'soft' a policy, unfit for a revolutionary and powerful state like Iran. The former group argued that the days when Iran could 'offer a mixture of sloganeering' as 'an attractive pattern for oppressed movements' had long passed.[17] It suggested, instead, a more realistic attitude to foreign policy issues. Revolutionary purists, on the other hand, advocated even stricter adherence to dogma, regardless of changing realities. Castigating the government for lacking 'a correct analysis of the regional situation', they advocated greater activism, reflecting Iran's 'powerful and righteous stance'.[18] Hojjat ul-Islam Mohtashami, who was the figurehead of the more radical trend in the early 1990s, censured the government for abandoning the 'pure stances of the revolution'. He blamed 'certain elements' in the government for failing to comprehend 'the depth of the revolution's strength' and 'the honor and prestige of the Iranian system', claiming that they were 'overwhelmed with intense fear'. He accused the architects of Iran's foreign policy of 'political impotence' and dismissed their policy as totally 'unsuccessful'.[19] The conservative *Jomhuri-ye Islami* also regretted that the Islamic government remained a passive spectator of events, in a manner unsuitable for a revolutionary nation like Iran.[20] With its self-imposed silence and policies 'swathed in ambiguity', the paper queried, 'are there not . . . eyes that see and ears that hear' Khomeini's vision any longer?[21] And indeed, the revolution had deviated considerably from its fundamental dogmatic convictions and adapted its politics to suit emerging realities in most policy areas.

Although questions of foreign relations were marginal to the 1977 presidential election campaign, the general world-view outlined by Khatami at that time signaled a possible relaxation in Iran's foreign relations. His stress on dialogue between civilizations and the need to reduce regional tension, his accent on the importance of Iran's expanding co-operation with the outside world and the goal of mitigating domestic difficulties, all led to a similar conclusion.

Following the election of Khatami, the gaps between the rival domestic tendencies became much deeper, touching upon some of the most delicate issues of foreign policy. While Khamene'i became the main bastion of conservatism, Khatami has become the symbol of hope for change and reform. (Interestingly, many of those critical of the government's pragmatic policy in the early 1990s, supported President Khatami.) Yet, as in domestic politics, while the president raised new and more moderate ideas on foreign relations, the ideologue-purists labored to block such attempts at change.

At the level of principle, Khamene'i continued to view foreign policy as generally within the framework of the early thinking of the revolution. In 1996 he declared that the message of Islam was the message of unity, security and fraternity, and 'those who undermine this correct movement [deserve] severe action [as it says in the Qur'an]: Be severe with the infidels'.[22] This approach was well articulated by 'Ali Akbar Velayati, former foreign minister from 1981 to 1997, and since then Khamene'i's adviser for international affairs. Reiterating the orthodox dogma, Velayati noted that 'the foundations' of Iran's foreign policy had remained 'relatively constant' since the early days of the revolution. They stemmed, he said, 'from the precepts and principles of the holy ruling system' and included the defense of Islamic values and of Muslims all over the world. For revolutionary Iran, he said, the interests of Islam and Iran have always been 'intertwined'. He maintained that wherever the interests of Muslims and Islamic values were in danger, Iran viewed it as its sacred duty to 'defend them', whether in Bosnia, in Lebanon, or among the Palestinians.[23] In practice, however, in many cases Iran has already moved away from its pure, dogmatic convictions.

By 1997, growing numbers within the Iranian political establishment came to realize that the policy of the early days of the revolution alienated foreign countries, isolated Iran and harmed its national interests. Here, too, Khatami led the pragmatic line.

Upon his confirmation as president, Khatami vowed that, based on the 'three strong pillars of wisdom, integrity, and expediency', Iran would 'shake the hands of all countries and nations' who believed in 'mutual respect' and who would not undermine Iran's independence and interests.[24] He pledged to resist the expansionist policies of domineering superpowers and to withstand aggression by outsiders, stressing that only mutual respect and common interests could lead to a fruitful dialogue. Revolutionary principles, he said, led Iran 'to maintain good relations with all nations except Israel' – a country which also elicited satanic associations from Khatami. He considered 'dialogue between civilizations' an essential tool, and pledged to 'avoid any action or behavior causing tension'.[25] He reiterated that 'the world needs peace

and tranquility', adding that Iran 'seeks neither to dominate others nor
to submit to domination'. Dialogue would open the way to mutual
understanding and genuine peace 'based on the realization of the rights
of all nations'.[26] As humankind enters the twenty-first century, he said,
'it should take inspiration from the past and build a world full of
dignity, peace and honor'. Instead of using the 'language of force',
people should use 'the language of reason and logic to speak to each
other', he suggested.[27] Some prominent officials, taking their cue from
the president, followed suit. Foreign Minister Kamal Kharrazi stated
that with the world 'becoming transpolar, countries should abandon
their former hegemonic policies that sought to dictate to other societies
and influence the fate of other nations'.[28] The deep difference in
approach was manifested in the December 1997 Islamic Conference
Organization (ICO) summit in Tehran, which put on 'display the widening political divisions' between the 'dogmatic clerics' and their 'more
pragmatic rivals'. While Khatami endorsed dialogue between civilizations to achieve 'deep-rooted understanding', Khamene'i delivered 'a
fiery speech that boiled over with hostility toward the West, especially
the United States'.[29]

   Gradually, the moderate voices have become more conspicuous and
daring. The basic arguments used by the pragmatists to justify reform
in domestic politics (see, mainly, Chapter 1) were also employed to
justify moderation in Iran's foreign outlook. Most importantly, such an
approach maintained that the principles of the past – even those outlined
by Ayatollah Khomeini – should not necessarily define the current politics, nor should criticism of current policy and suggesting an alternative
approach be viewed as criticism of past practices or of Imam Khomeini.
Policy, such logic maintained, should be permanently reconsidered –
as Khomeini himself, and his disciples after him, had done. Thus,
Khomeini promised to continue the war with Iraq 'until victory', Nuri
said in 1999, but endorsed the cease-fire. Had the Imam passed away a
few months prior to the cease-fire, should we have continued the war
indefinitely? he asked.[30] From the same premise, Ganji pointed to the
conflicting tendencies in Khomeini's own policy and that of the conservatives themselves, to justify further adaptation of dogma to the
emerging realities. Thus, following the killing of Iranian pilgrims in
Saudi Arabia in 1987, Khomeini said that even if Iran were to change its
policy towards Iraq and Israel, it should not forgive Saudi Arabia.
Should we, therefore, put Nateq-Nuri on trial for visiting there and kiss-
ing King Fahd?[31] In addition to stressing the need to reconsider past
policies, such an approach also advocated departing from the old phi-

losophy, which viewed the entire world as Iran's enemies. Thus, Nuri stated, it would be wrong to think that 'the entire world has taken up sword against us' (*shamshir-e doshmani ba ma basteh*).[32] Iran, such logic went on, should reconsider its politics and adjust them to the new realities, striving to serve best the interests of the country, regardless of dogma and past politics.

Much as in the case of its domestic policy, the government's actual foreign policy generally tended towards increased pragmatism, although some domestic political factions continued to adopt extremist positions from time to time. As in other areas of Iranian politics, hard-line ideologues often managed to counterbalance whatever pragmatic initiatives were proposed by the pragmatists and to confine the scope of change. (See Chapter 6.) The dispute over the appropriate path to be followed has not yet been resolved, and this has led to ambiguity, dualism, and contradiction in Iran's actual foreign policy. Nevertheless, at the time of Khatami's election, the attention of most Iranians was focused primarily on domestic issues. The main division between pragmatists versus conservatives centered on questions of domestic politics; foreign policy issues were marginal to the election campaign and as during the student riots of 1999, not the major concern of the Iranian people.

Finally, the Islamic Revolution attracted the world's attention to the centrality of religion in the fabric of Iranian society. However, the experience of the revolutionary regime demonstrates that one cannot detach Iran altogether from its attachment to its distinctive cultural and national traditions, nor from the influence of its encounter with the West over the last two centuries. Can Iran's specific national legacy and its Islamic heritage coexist? A hundred years ago, proponents of the national creed in the Muslim Middle East did not regard their vision as necessarily opposed to their Islamic identity. *Al-wajeb al-dini* (roughly, religious obligation) and *al-wajeb al-watani* (national obligation) seemed complementary rather than contradictory. Nor did the proponents of Iran's Constitutional Revolution see the two as necessarily in disagreement. Iran's unique identity – ethnic (Persian) and religious (Shi'i) – and its distinctive history also allowed for a workable balance. The Shah and Khomeini, each in his own way, attempted to upset this equilibrium. Yet the Shah could not totally separate Iran from the tradition of Imam 'Ali, much as Khomeini could not totally break Iran's links with its pre-Islamic history and traditions. Likewise, both ideology and national interests remained powerful components in shaping Iran's external orientation. (See also Chapter 7.)

In the first two decades of the revolution the result of such conflicting pressures has been a 'dual policy' wherein the logic of 'state interests and of the revolution coexist uneasily'[33] in a mixture of national considerations and revolutionary ideology. However, with very few exceptions, whenever ideological convictions have clashed with the interests of the state, state interests ultimately triumphed over dogma, in foreign relations as much as in Iran's domestic politics.

This part of the book will focus on three major areas in Iran's foreign outlook – the West (and the United States in particular), Iran's immediate neighborhood (mainly in the Gulf region) and the Arab–Israeli peace process (especially Iran's attitude to Israel). While reviewing Iranian policy in the three regions, an attempt will be made to discern the interplay between domestic policy and foreign relations, between revolutionary ideology and national interest in Iran's policy and between dogma and praxis. There will also be an attempt to discern elements of continuity and change, and – as much as possible – differences over time and between various domestic camps.

NOTES

1. Khomeini's speech broadcast on Radio Tehran, 3 November 1981 – *SWB*, 5 November 1981.
2. This was especially conspicuous in his interview with Muhammad Hasanayn Haykal, in *al-Mustaqbal*, 13 January 1979.
3. *Kayhan* (Tehran), 22, 23 January 1979.
4. *Ettela'at*, 23 August 1981. A few weeks later (as prime minister) he reiterated, that Iran's struggle would continue 'until the region and the world are rebuilt upon new foundations'. *Tehran Journal*, 7 October 1981.
5. *Resalat*, 14 December 1992 – DR, 21 December 1992.
6. *Ettela'at*, 31 December 1992 – DR, 22 January 1993.
7. IRNA, 28 May 1998 [DR].
8. *Kayhan* (Tehran), 29 October 1984. For a similar view expressed a year later, see *Kayhan-e Hava'i*, 11 November 1985.
9. *Ettela'at*, 3 July 1988.
10. *Kayhan* (Tehran), 2 July 1988.
11. Ramazani, 'Iran's Foreign Policy', p. 405.
12. Ibid., p. 393.
13. Chubin, *Iran's National Security Policy*, pp. 65–6.
14. Banuazizi, 'Iran's Revolutionary Impasse', pp. 4–5.
15. *Iran Times*, 1 October 1993.
16. *Jahan-e Islam*, 2 June 1993 – DR, 16 June 1993.
17. *Hamshahri*, 9 February 1993 – DR, 23 February 1993.
18. See, for example, an editorial advocating greater activism entitled 'Foreign Policy Needs Reform', in *Jahan-e Islam*, 2 June 1993 – DR, 16 June 1993.
19. *Jahan-e Islam*, 20, 24 May 1993 – DR, 1, 4 June 1993; *Iran News*, 9 February

1995 – DR, 17 February 1995. See also Clawson, *Alternative Foreign Policy Views*, pp. 27–48.

20. *Jomhuri-ye Islami*, 2 November 1994. For the official response of the foreign ministry, see *Jomhuri-ye Islami*, 6 November 1994.
21. *Jomhuri-ye Islami*, 11 September 1994 – DR, 20 September 1994.
22. Radio Tehran, 9 October 1996 – DR, 11 October 1996.
23. Tehran TV, 22 August 1996 – DR, 27 August 1996.
24. *Jomhuri-ye Islami*, 4 August 1997 [DR].
25. *Iran News*, 5 August 1997 [DR].
26. IRNA and *Kayhan* (Tehran), 9 December 1997.
27. IRNA, 14 December 1997.
28. Tehran TV, 15 January 1998 [DR].
29. *Los Angeles Times*, 11 December 1997.
30. Nuri, *Showkaran-e Eslah*, pp. 126–9.
31. Ganji, *Talaqqi-ye Fashisti az Din va Hokumat*, pp. 143–51.
32. Nuri, *Showkaran-e Eslah*, p. 126.
33. Hashim, *The Crisis of the Iranian State*, p. 45.

6

Iran, the West and the United States

'Neither the East nor the West' had epitomized Iran's revolutionary approach to the two world powers – the United States and the former Soviet Union. The attitude expressed the belief that Iran should curtail the reach of domineering superpowers which, it was claimed, had interfered over long decades with Iran's independence, exploited Iran's resources and influenced the minds of its people. While the doctrine rejected both superpowers, animosity to the United States turned into one of the main symbols of the revolution. However, the impact of some two centuries of contact with the outside world could not easily be wiped out, nor could Iran ignore the need for ties with the West, even – as acknowledged by many revolutionaries – the United States.

In fact, the impact of the West on Iran had become increasingly noticeable since the early nineteenth century. The progressive deterioration of Iran's internal situation under the Qajar dynasty and expanding contacts with the West had contributed to the growing awareness of the country's weakness as compared with the West – particularly in economic, military and technological terms. This, in turn, promoted – much as it did at the same time in the Ottoman Empire and in semi-independent Egypt under Ottoman rule – the twin processes of imitation and change. The West provided both the impetus for change and the model for imitation, generating the characteristic and conspicuous tension between the urge to reject and the desire to emulate.[1] While some traditional forces (such as clerics, *bazaar* merchants and landlords) preached adherence to the old system, support for change in Iran (mainly from Western-educated intellectuals and segments of the political elite), gradually won out. As in other Muslim countries of the region, the indifference which had generally characterized the attitude to the West, has come to an end. As Bernard Lewis has observed, although it has not yet been replaced by an 'anxious emulation', the Middle East was no longer able to ignore the threatening presence of the West and has sought to 'discover and apply the elusive secret of its greatness and strength'.[2]

Jamshid Behnam, a professor of demography and sociology in Iran, offers a penetrating depiction of Iran's dualistic approach to the West in a recent study. After 150 years of Westernization, he suggests, 'apart from a relatively small group, the rest of us have learned [from the West] only technology (*fan*) and science (*'ilm*), but have not stretched out our hand towards western thought (*andisheh*)'. For the common (*'adi*) people, the West has remained primarily the 'land of the infidels' (*sarzemin-e Kuffar*) and later on 'it turned into a synonym for imperialism and arrogance (*estekbar*)'. Yet, in all this time, the West was also 'the land of wealth (*thervat*) and happiness (*khoshbakhti*)'. The West was, thus, both 'the promised paradise' (*behesht-e mow'ud*) and 'the kingdom of Satan' (*sarzemin-e sheytan*). This basic paradox is all the more forceful, since the West seemed to pose a challenge to Islam, and the return to Islam seemed to many to contradict modernity. Nevertheless, Behnam argues, Islam is a real and valid model, and Islamic tradition (*sonnat*) is not affected by the passage of time. Therefore, the return to Islam should not be construed as a retreat. According to Behnam, the terms 'new' and 'old', and time in general, have different meanings for different societies. For Iranians, the term 'old' (*qadim*) signifies something which is fundamental, permanent and lasting (*asasi, da'em va mostamar*), even noble (*asil*), while modern and new (*jadid va now*) are fleeting (*gozara*), transient (*napayedar*) and artificial (*masnu'*). The terms 'old' and 'new' are not contradictory, and the difference between tradition and modernity unlike the contrast between black and white. Tradition has its place in modern society, and modern society can also benefit from tradition. Moreover, science and technology belong to the West today, as once they belonged to China, India and in certain periods also to Iran. What is seen today as Western industrial civilization is, in fact, the total sum of the achievements of the human race.[3] Nevertheless, as Khatami has also stressed – science, technology and wealth are today concentrated in the West, a fact which Iran cannot ignore. Here too the revolution which began by totally rejecting the West, had gradually to come to terms with reality.

From the early nineteenth century, Iranian intellectuals, especially those educated in the West and captivated by its impressive progress, wished to promote the process of change and imitate some of its achievements. However, while they clearly were fascinated by Western civilization, they did not wish to imitate it in its entirety. Impressed by what they witnessed, such intellectuals generally wished to borrow,

selectively, some elements of it. This desire became even more conspicuous in the late nineteenth century. For many of these intellectuals
progress, freedom, modernization and strength became synonymous
with Westernization.

Such a tendency to regard Westernization as the remedy for Iran's
problems was reversed in the 1960s, with the emergence of a new
generation of Iranian intellectuals who viewed the West as the cause,
rather than the cure, of Iran's malaise.[4] Some of those who had become
disappointed with Western theories and disillusioned by the experience
with Westernization, then turned to Islam for a solution. The most
influential among them were Jalal Al-e Ahmad and 'Ali Shari'ati.
Al-e Ahmad's *Gharbzadegi* ('Weststruckness') came to represent this
approach most fully. It portrayed the West as the source of all evil and
the symbol of all misery. The West is seen as repressive, unjust and keen
to perpetuate Western supremacy and maintain its status as the master
and to keep the East in servitude. Shari'ati, and to a degree Bani Sadr,
expressed similar anti-imperialist views. Khomeini and like-minded
clerics also stressed the same philosophy, making anti-imperialism one
of the main unifying elements in their opposition to the Shah's regime,
with Khomeini's theory pleading more forcefully and directly for a
return to Islam. Thus in the 1960s it was 'the Western Other that was
set against the Iranian Self'.[5] The West, which had once been the
symbol of hope, had in the eyes of many Iranians, become the main
cause of Iran's regression and the prime reason for its decline.

A typical essay in a school textbook on Iranian history, civilization
and culture published under the Islamic regime, portrays this new image
of the West. Dealing with 'the reasons for the decline of the Muslims', it
begins by describing attacks against the Muslim world by the Crusaders
and the Mongols, before turning to the modern assault by the West,
viewing this last challenge much more severely. In its inhumanity and
cowardliness (*namardi va namardomi*), the essay continues, the West is
worse than the Mongols. For while the Mongols lacked a specific culture
of their own to impose on others, the West attacked Muslims with its
weaponry and also initiated a 'cultural war' against them.[6] Similarly in
the introduction to his book, *Iran and the Question of Palestine*,
Velayati argues that from the early nineteenth century, the West has
been 'launching all-out cultural onslaughts' on the lands of Islam. It
has strived 'to promote secularism, to encourage extreme nationalism
against Islamic brotherhood, [to promote] permissiveness in religious
matters, and a western way of life as against traditionalism'. This has
been done, Velayati maintains, with the aim of 'weakening the identity

roots' of the Muslim peoples. Such policies, he continues, have been even 'more detrimental than occupation of lands', since they 'have paved the way for the destruction of Islamic solidarity and dignity.' Thus, while 'the gift of the East to [the] West', was 'based on God's revelations', that of the West to the East has been 'devil-centered'.[7]

The Iranian loathing for Western imperialism has deep roots in historical memory and was reinforced by the harsh realities in Iran prior to and since the revolution. Iranians accused Western imperialists of using the Shah as a 'mask', backing his policies and supporting his autocratic regime. Foreigners, this logic went on, were exploiting Iran economically and using its natural resources for their own benefit. Imperialism, declared Khomeini, had also introduced the concept of the separation of religion and state as a tool to weaken Islam and advance its malicious aims in Muslim lands. Khomeini told his students: 'If you do not interfere with the imperialist polity, but concern yourselves with religious study only . . . they will not care what you do . . . They want your oil, what do they care about your prayers?' He asserted: 'They want to keep us from rising to the level of human beings.' Khomeini also blamed imperialism for dividing the 'Muslim motherland' into numerous 'fictitious states' governed by 'lackeys' whose true function was to serve the interests of imperialism, to prevent the 'liberation of the Muslim people' and impose an 'atmosphere of despair' on them.[8] In a message directed at Muslim students in North America on 10 July 1972, Khomeini warned that the agents of imperialism 'engage in sabotage and try to prevent the resplendent visage of Islam from showing itself by poisoning and polluting the minds and the thoughts of the young'.[9] Similarly, *Kayhan* attributed support for the separation of religion and state to foreign enemies and their domestic agents. They always wished to prevent an active religion, to prevent the *maraje'* from influencing politics, with an aim of eliminating the rule of Islam and the *'ulama'* in the society.[10] The liberal and national movements that joined the Islamic Revolution were no less critical of imperialism, viewing the Shah similarly as a 'servant of imperialist interests'. But they had a different point of departure. The concept of nationalism, which Khomeini thought of as an 'imperialist plot against Islam', was for them an ideal. While Khomeini believed that Islam provided a bulwark against imperialism, for nationalist movements such as the National Front that bulwark lay in nationalism. (See also Chapter 7.)

More often than not, the charges against the West were harsh and multifaceted. 'The West was criticized for its past colonialism and present imperialism, its excessive admiration of technology and rampant irreligiosity, its materialism and consumerism, and its abandonment of moral conviction and justice.'[11] For many revolutionaries the critique of the West remained generally ethical and moral. For Velayati, as for many of the revolutionaries, the West was staging a 'war of values' against Iran and its revolution.[12] The West's main threat, they alleged, was its 'cultural onslaught' (*tahajom-e farhangi*). The United States, which in the past had been less involved in Iranian affairs compared with the European powers (mainly Britain and Russia), has since the early 1950s become a symbol of imperialism and was regarded by Iran's Islamists as Iran's arch enemy. (See below.)

President Khatami has sought to balance the unqualified anti-Western approach. 'Having deep knowledge of the West' was 'very important' to him, he said: 'I think the West has a superb civilization, which has influenced all parts of the world.'[13] Moreover, in a world of 'computers, communication networks, satellites, and sound waves', Khatami asked what was wrong in 'utilizing the experience of other human communities'. He did not recommend 'imitating them blindly' nor abandoning our 'own identity', but he did advocate borrowing 'the good points of other cultures' in order to 'enrich our own culture'. Even if it were possible to 'distance' the young generation from Western influence for a while, it would prove impossible in the long-run, he predicted.[14] Since the road to development undeniably goes through the West, he said, Iran 'will not [attain] development unless we correctly identify the positive and negative aspects of western civilization'. Iran 'should study the West', which is 'a fountain of all [current] transformations', he said, but it should also analyze the developments 'according to Islamic values'.[15] In both material and moral (*ma'navi*) realms, he added, Iran could appreciate positive and negative impacts of Western influence. Thus, for example, the students sent abroad in the early nineteenth century 'were all brain-washed by imperialism', he wrote in one of his books.[16] But he did not ignore the positive elements of Western civilization. Not unaware of the danger of a Western 'cultural onslaught', he advocated 'the principle of immunizing ourselves', i.e., strengthening Islamic values, mainly among the young generation.[17] Nevertheless, it was necessary to borrow selectively from what was worth borrowing.

Even in this major revolutionary principle – as will be shown below – there were some significant nuances and differences in accent, between various individuals and in different phases. Although no breakthrough has so far been registered in relations with the United States, significant change has been noticed, mainly since Khatami's election.

The United States Remains 'The Great Satan'

Since gaining power, the Islamic regime has perceived the United States as the 'Great Satan' (*sheytan-e bozorg*). Animosity to the United States has remained one of Iran's most forceful symbols, raised 'to a near religion'.[18] Washington has turned into the main symbol of arrogance, the prime cause of all evils in the world and the main source of Iran's misery. It is believed to have harmed Iran domestically, such as by imposing economic sanctions, supporting the opposition against the Islamic regime and conducting a 'cultural onslaught'. It is also seen to have harmed Iran regionally, for example, by its support for Iraq during the war, its policy in the Gulf, its backing of the Middle East peace process, its support for Israel and its hostility towards Islamist movements. Animosity to the United States has almost become 'an article of faith'. But Khomeini promised that 'America can't do any damned thing' (*hich ghalat*).

The hard-liners (both conservatives and radicals) set the tone of the debate. They perceived US policy as aimed at dismantling the Islamic regime altogether, weakening the world of Islam and harming Iranians and the Muslims worldwide – the USA was the arch-enemy of Iran and Islam and 'the mother of all corruption'. Retreat from such an entrenched attitude proved extremely difficult and the mere suggestion of rethinking policy and adopting a more accommodating view was politically risky. Under the circumstances, those who 'call for a rational dialogue' run the risk of being labeled Islamic apologists or supporters of Western imperialism.[19] Here, too, a significant change in rhetoric became evident following Khatami's election. While in the past even suggesting the advisability of renewing ties with the USA was taboo, the possible benefits of such ties are now being openly discussed. Nevertheless, some major obstacles have impeded more practical steps towards the re-establishment of formal ties.

Khomeini presented the confrontation with the United States as a struggle between Islam and infidels – between all Muslims and all infidels. This typified his approach from the earliest days of his appearance on the public scene, through the 1960s, and his exile abroad, until after his triumphant return to Iran. In 1979 he appealed to Muslims everywhere to come to the aid of Iran against the United States, declaring that 'all Muslims must bear in mind that it is not only our [Iranian] fate which is caught between existence and annihilation; it is the fate of Islam and all Muslims'.[20] He said: 'America is the number one enemy of the deprived and oppressed people of the world. There is no crime

America will not commit in order to maintain its political, economic, cultural and military domination of those parts of the world where it predominates.'[21] He viewed the United States as a 'defeated and wounded snake', with whom Iran did not need relations 'at all'. He said: 'Our relations with them are those . . . of a ravaged victim with a plunderer. We do not need America; it is they who want us.'[22] Khomeini made it clear that Iran was 'determined' to have no relations with the United States 'unless they turn themselves into human beings and refrain from injustice'.[23]

After Khomeini's death, and with the disintegration of the Soviet Union, a more accommodating approach gained force, but this was still insufficient to produce meaningful and actual change. Rafsanjani and Khamene'i – the two leading figures at the time – demonstrated noticeable differences in their public statements regarding the meaning and implications of the collapse of the Soviet Union.

Khamene'i represented the uncompromising approach, emphasising the Islamic regime's hostility to the United States. He believed that 'in the confrontation between Islam and global arrogance', the latter would soon 'be brought to its knees'.[24] Western power, he believed, was based on two main pillars – US capitalism and Soviet communism, one of which had just collapsed, while the other was unlikely to last long. Concerned primarily with cultural considerations, Khamene'i maintained that the slogan, 'Death to America', emanated from 'the depths of the being of each and every' Iranian. He excoriated the United States for being arrogant, greedy, insolent and contemptuous of the Iranian nation, and for ceaselessly hatching conspiracies against Muslims worldwide. Hatred, he said, 'comes from our side, while mischievous enmity emanates from their side'.[25] For Khamene'i, the Western cultural onslaught led by the United States was 'a cultural night raid, a cultural act of plunder, a cultural massacre'.[26] Suspicious of US intentions, Khamene'i warned that even when '[Americans] appear with a deceitful smile . . . [they] have a dagger hidden behind their backs and the other hand is ready to plunder'; this is 'their true nature'.[27] Therefore, Iran has 'nothing to talk to them about' and 'no need for them'.[28] Enumerating examples of US misconduct, Khamene'i declared that the United States 'invites people to use arms [and] sets brother against brother'. It awakens 'animal instincts in people', and 'war, bloodshed, destruction, [and] annihilation are the results of [its] satanic behavior'.[29]

Rafsanjani's approach was somewhat different. Following the disintegration of the Soviet Union, he complained that the defeat of 'one side [i.e. the Soviet Union] in the Cold War' had encouraged 'the other side [the United States] to devise means to . . . ensure [its] absolute dominance'.[30] And although he did not deny Iran's interest in economic ties with the United States and considered 'popular sensitivity' to the issue inappropriate,[31] he opined that the United States needed to prove its goodwill first – through deeds.[32] 'Everything depends on America correcting her policies', he said.[33] The United States, Rafsanjani re-iterated, should 'prove its good intentions so that the road [to better relations] can be paved'.[34]

On the whole, the general tone was dictated by the hard-liners, and it was usually harsh and uncompromising. Ahmad Jannati, in a 1995 Friday sermon, made the unyielding conservatives' approach clear, depicting the United States as the wolf and Iran as the innocent sheep (as Khomeini himself often typified the relationship). 'Showing mercy to the "wolf"', he said, is only a sign of weakness. It is unlikely either to satis-fy the wolf or rescue the sheep.[35] Similarly, Deputy Foreign Minister Hosein Shaykh ul-Islam added in 1996: 'The Americans want the relations of a wolf with cattle, as they have with the rest of the world.' More generally, Shaykh ul-Islam characterized the differences between Iran and the United States as being between 'belligerence, materialism, corruption and worldliness,' on the one hand, and 'the spirituality and exaltation of the barefoot oppressed masses', on the other. The United States holds that the 'future of the world will be determined' by the 'clash of ideas', he said. Clearly, he added, 'this contention will result in the victory of pure Islam', of which Iran is the flag bearer. Due to the conduct of the United States, he said, 'there is no future' for bilateral relations; Iran 'will never permit the United States to speak to [it] in a threatening tone'.[36]

The opposition to the Western 'cultural onslaught' forged a 'nexus', between those who were ideologically opposed to relations with the West and those who wanted economic ties but feared the consequences for Iran's Islamic identity.[37] In addition to seizing Muslim territories and exploiting Muslim resources, the West was now being accused of attempting to capture the minds of young Iranians. School textbooks systematically denounced the endeavor by Western imperialists to encourage the imitation of their culture, in the service of economic, political and military ambitions.[38] Among the main and most recent weapons of the Western cultural onslaught, it was claimed, were com-munications, satellites, the media and the Internet. As Nateq-Nuri main-tained: a 'foreign culture is launching an onslaught against the cultural foundations of our nation in order to dominate this nation'. While in the past foreign powers had dispatched their armies to capture new territories and enslave other nations, today 'they dominate other nations' by 'attacking their thoughts and ideologies and promoting 'the culture of corruption, decadence, and idleness'.[39] Starting from a similar premise, Ahmad Jannati urged the government to limit access to the Internet except for scholarly use, comparing it to 'poison poured into the mouths of the people'. The Internet, and the Western cultural onslaught in general, he warned, was even more dangerous than other forms of poison, for if someone poisons the water, or if schoolchildren are poisoned by infected ice cream, people could complain and the problem is immediately identified. However, the poisoning of thought, behavior and the intellect went unchallenged: 'The child who has been poisoned is taken to the hospital and treated', but this kind of poisoning by the West 'is not so easy to remedy ... even with 100 doctors at the bedside'.[40]

Yet, throughout the 1990s, some officials wished to leave the door open for some kind of dialogue with the United States, at least to allow some economic ties. At the same time they wished also to see the United States taking practical steps to satisfy their expectations.

Iranians were infuriated by the United States' failure to understand them, their revolution and their grievances, even after a decade of Islamic rule in Iran. This was demonstrated, in their view, by the US policy of 'dual containment', that was announced on 20 May 1993 by Martin Indyk, then the special assistant to President Bill Clinton and senior director for Near East and South Asian affairs.[41] The 'dual containment' policy signified the abandonment of the 'balance of power game' toward Iran and Iraq that had characterized US policy during the Iran–Iraq war, and continued until the 1991 Gulf war. Foreign Minister Velayati viewed it as just another blatant attempt by the United States to intervene in Iran's internal affairs, and expressed confidence that 'independent countries will not submit' to US 'pressure and bullying'.[42]

The Islamic regime was also infuriated by the subsequent laws and regulations which were regarded as further means to harm Iran. They included the banning of US investment in Iran's energy sector (March 1995); a ban on trade with and investment in Iran ('the trade ban', in May 1995); and the 'Iran and Libya Sanctions Act of 1996', which imposed sanctions on making certain investments in Iran (August 1996). Referring to the latter, President Rafsanjani said 'this idiotic thing' was aimed at punishing companies that had dared to act against US policy. The United States was 'adopting laws to impose [its] will on the whole world' in what was clearly 'tyrannical, aggressive, [and] monopolistic' behavior.[43] Rafsanjani emphasised that Iran would resist the United States' aggressive policy and would not yield to pressure; nor, he maintained, would Iran be threatened, as its eight years of war with Iraq had demonstrated. 'Iran today is strong enough to defend itself', he declared, warning that, 'if Iran becomes insecure, the whole world will become insecure'. Although he acknowledged that Iran 'had economic contacts' with the United States before the sanctions were imposed, 'they have dropped [such contacts] and we [now] have better alternatives'.[44] Moreover, Rafsanjani claimed, 'we do not feel threatened by the embargo at all'. In fact, he noted, the embargo harmed mainly the United States,[45] while its effect on Iran 'has been practically nil'. The sanctions were 'a mistake' by the United States, which lowered that country's own dignity. Nevertheless, by the mid-1990s, Rafsanjani seemed to believe that a dialogue between the two countries was not impossible, provided that, as a gesture of goodwill, the USA released Iran's assets frozen there since the 1979–81 hostage crisis.[46] Questioned about reports that Iran and Washington were communicating behind closed doors, he confirmed then that they had exchanged messages occasionally through the Swiss Embassy in Tehran and were engaged in 'a debate' at the International Court of Justice in The Hague. As far as President Rafsanjani was concerned, the main obstacle to a dialogue was the lack of confidence. If, however, 'the United States proves its goodwill, we are prepared for a dialogue', he reiterated late in 1996.[47]

In a similar combination of determination to resist the United States and to encourage US gestures, UN Ambassador Kamal Kharrazi claimed late in 1996 that 'any change in our position' depended upon the attitude of the United States. If it would recognize 'Iran's importance in the region and its role in achieving stability, peace, and development, Iran will, in the future, be ready to cooperate with the United States'. Washington, however, 'must change its attitude' first. The United States 'must respect us and respect our ideas', he stressed repeatedly. The issue of respect 'is very important for us'. The problem was not whether to have a dialogue in secret or in the open, Kharrazi maintained, but 'whether this is the right time' (which he doubted), and whether the United States was sincere in its appeal for a dialogue (which he also doubted). The United States' interpretation of dialogue, he argued, 'is to impose [its] control on us'.[48] According to Kharrazi, dialogue can be 'useful and meaningful' only 'in an atmosphere of trust and confidence', which is currently missing. The United States 'has to take some practical steps' to gain Iran's trust and confidence and 'establish its sincerity and good faith'. Moreover, Washington should view its relations with Iran as 'based on mutual respect', demonstrate that it 'abides by the principle of non-intervention' and make some gestures 'to show its sincerity and to bring about that trust' (such as releasing frozen Iranian assets).[49] Yet Kharrazi believed that 'the real quarrel [of the United States] is with the nature of this [Islamic] government, this system'[50] – which prevents a breakthrough. That many Iranians believed that this was, and still is, the ultimate goal of the United States made a breakthrough even more difficult.

Notwithstanding these problems, some elements within the establishment viewed Iran's continuing hostility towards the United States as harmful to Iranian interests, and pointed – more directly – to the advisability of keeping some kind of dialogue going between the two countries. The prevalence of such views can be deduced mainly from the repeated denials of their existence and the warnings against them by hard-liners. Voices proposing greater pragmatism in the Iranian approach were discernible even before the 1988 cease-fire with Iraq, becoming more pronounced since the death of Ayatollah Khomeini. They acquired additional momentum following the disintegration of the Soviet Union, and reached a peak following the election of Khatami. Yet, until now, they have not been powerful enough to produce a policy change.

In the past, Rafsanjani took the lead in advocating some compromise between the old radical ideology and new realities. His approach was more complex than that of other prominent figures, and at times less belligerent towards the United States. In 1983, he addressed 'the Americans', noting that, in principle, Iran was ready for relations with all countries (with the exceptions of Israel and South Africa only) that were willing to have 'correct [*sahih*] relations' with Iran.[51] Given the broad consensus of anti-US opinion within the Iranian leadership at that time, this was a refreshing innovation. In fact, Rafsanjani had often expressed his appreciation of US-made weapons and the necessity of buying US arms, especially as long as the war with Iraq continued.[52] Thus in April 1986 he said: 'We will buy American weapons wherever they are available for us.'[53] (Such attitudes also lay behind the Iranian initiative to purchase US-made weapons in 1985–86, known as the Iran–Contra affair.) Rafsanjani clearly did not wish altogether to close the doors to rapprochement, even when he and his associates appeared to criticize it harshly.[54] Although Tehran was as yet unwilling to admit this, by the late 1980s many Iranians recognized the need for a dialogue. In December 1988, in an attempt to justify the improvement of relations with the outside world, Rafsanjani explained the general logic, although he did not refer explicitly to relations with the United States. It was 'impossible in today's world to be totally independent', he said. Even

Japan was dependent on other countries, such as the United States. In an indirect reference to the need to reconsider Iran's policy towards the United States, Rafsanjani made it clear that, as Iran set out to reconstruct the country after its war with Iraq, 'there is so much machinery in the country which depends on foreigners to a large degree . . . There are many projects which cannot be completed with the country's [own] resources.'[55] But he stopped short of advocating ties, or even a dialogue.

The sobering realities of the damage caused by the mutual hostility of Iran and the United States had led some intellectuals – and probably Iranian officials – to reconsider this attitude and try to change the policy, although such views were rarely exposed publicly. Still, the occasional criticism of individuals advocating rapprochement attested to their existence. Thus, in October 1988 Khamene'i (then Iran's president) set out to deny speculation that Tehran was seeking to 'compromise with the superpowers' by making 'concessions on the revolution's principles'. He pledged that revolutionary Iran will 'preserve its principles under all conditions'. However, he too admitted that some 'writers and orators' write and say things that might be so interpreted.[56] This trend was powerful enough to lead *Abrar* to call upon the government not to set aside the revolutionary ideology in its search for foreign ties. The newspaper emphasized that the idea that Iran should 'stretch out a begging arm to anyone and any country' in order to end its isolation must be cleansed from the minds of Iran's policy-makers. It cautioned that some foreign countries had only changed the appearance of their policy in an attempt to make their way into Iran like 'wolves in sheep's clothing'.[57] While such negative statements attest to a general hostility to the USA, more moderate views were expressed from time to time, even in public. Such statements were rare, but still important, especially as they came from prominent officials and in public.

In a 1990 article in *Ettela'at*, Vice-President Mohajerani advocated some kind of dialogue with the United States. As far as can be established, this was the most moderate public statement by a prominent Iranian official to support dialogue, almost explicitly. Not to engage in dialogue, Mohajerani wrote, was against the interests of the Islamic Revolution. He justified his stance by pointing to the strength of the United States in the world. This was also important, he added, in order to regain Iranian assets frozen in the United States and to secure the release of Iranian citizens and some leading Lebanese citizens (notably Shaykh 'Abd al-Karim 'Ubayd), who were held by groups under the influence of the United States and by Israel. Mohajerani also mentioned Iraq's continuous efforts to build up its military power as another reason to justify such a policy change. Such a change, he maintained, was also the prerequisite to Iran's post-war economic reconstruction. 'These are the opportunities', he wrote, adding tellingly, that the great leaders of Islam in its early days had also negotiated with the enemies of God and the Prophet Muhammad. Finally, he reminded his readers that Iran had never sought to construct a wall around its people, or desired to isolate itself totally from the outside world. He mentioned the Syrian dialogue with the United States as an example: Damascus did not altogether reject dialogue with Washington, but used it to advance Syria's national interests. Mohajerani thus concluded: 'In my view, if under the existing special circumstances we do not give priority to the interests of the state and the revolution, we will end up losing the opportunities open [now] for our revolution, for our state and for the people.' Failing to grasp the opportunity now, he warned, would mean that more long and precious years would pass with Tehran continuing only to 'play with slogans'.[58]

In 1994, aware that such an idea was still 'strongly rejected' and that the Supreme Leader Khamene'i had repudiated it altogether, Mohajerani reiterated that direct dialogue was, in fact, necessary.[59] During the Majlis debate over Khatami's proposed cabinet, Mohajerani – the nominee for minister of Islamic Guidance – was castigated for his 1990 article. Mohajerani denied advocating resumed ties with the United States, adding that in any case 'the situation has [since] changed and under the current circumstances I reject even holding talks with the USA'.[60] This was insufficient to appease his critics, although it did not prevent his election. (In 1999 he barely escaped impeachment by the Majlis, and later became a target of the conservatives' fury, although this was mainly because of his lenient attitude to press violations and student unrest. However, the 1990 article has often been held against him.)

A letter by Majlis deputy Sa'id Raja'i Khorasani to Ayatollah Khamene'i on 29 November 1992, advocating a change of policy towards the United States, generated much public furor when it was disclosed a year later.[61] Raja'i Khorasani admitted that he had written such a letter, adding that he had devoted months of study to the issue, and that in his letter he had, in fact, proposed a new policy. Unfortunately, he added, the Supreme Leader had rejected his advice. Nevertheless, he maintained, it was his Islamic duty to express his opinion, which was he believed, in the best interests of Iran and Islam. Any believer had the right to express his views, he maintained, and 'no one has the right to interfere in the *umma*'s direct relation with Imam'. Raja'i Khorasani said that he continued to support the policy he had advocated to the

Supreme Leader. Yet this could only become policy with the Leader's blessing, he concluded.[62] Typically, such moderate statements came from people who were believed to be close to President Rafsanjani, although he did not endorse them. (See below.) These were certainly not the only proposals.

Just before US President Bill Clinton entered office in January 1993, the *Tehran Times* proffered him an olive branch. 'Any sign of goodwill will be responded to by goodwill from the Iranian side', it declared, adding that it hoped that the new US president would 'take advantage of this golden opportunity'.[63] It went on that the wide ideological differences should not mean 'that we intend to be in permanent strife' with the United States, and pointed to the recent Iranian–Soviet reconciliation as a 'possible solution' for US–Iranian tension. Reminding Washington that 'Iran had used its spiritual influence' to win the release of Western hostages in Lebanon, the *Tehran Times* added that Iran was still waiting for an appropriate US response to this gesture of Iranian goodwill. The paper suggested that lifting the freeze on Iranian assets in the United States would be 'a proper gesture'.[64]

Such mild utterances did not go uncontested, however. If there were prominent figures supporting such overtures they did not dare to make this fact public, while denunciation of them was unequivocal and abundantly evident. The tone and wording used by the opponents of a policy change revealed, however, that these views were just some of many positions widely held among certain groups in Iran even in the early 1990s.

Public criticism of such 'unprincipled voices' came from all sides of the political spectrum, mainly from conservatives and radicals. Responding to Mohajerani's proposal, Mohtashami stated that such a blatant deviation from Khomeini's doctrine was a 'mistake that will never be forgiven'. He condemned such views, which, he said, 'penetrated the body of the Islamic regime like a scourge'.[65] Mohtashami blamed President Rafsanjani for supporting 'deviationist ideas'[66] such as those expressed by Raja'i Khorasani. He wondered whether someone who had lived in the United States for such a long time, could at all comprehend the real essence of the Islamic Revolution.[67] *Salam* saw in Raja'i Khorasani's letter a reflection of the United States' 'miraculous ability' to influence people's minds.[68] Ayatollah 'Abdul-Karim Musavi Ardabili (former president of the supreme court), similarly censured such ideas, and totally dismissed 'compromise' (*mosaleheh*) or 'reconciliation' (*sazesh*) with the United States as utterly 'anti-revolutionary'.[69] Relations with the United States, he said, were contrary to the interests of 'the religion, the revolution and the state'.[70] *Kayhan* responded to overtures such as those expressed in the *Tehran Times* by censuring those who 'naively believe' that ties with the United States would 'solve all of our problems' and who attempt to disguise the enemy's true nature.[71]

Referring to the larger phenomenon that stimulated such an idea, Mohtashami castigated those officials seeking to change Iran's policy as simple-minded and gullible. They were, he declared in 1994, 'bankrupt Westernized [and] selfish' elements, who were 'bereft of intelligence and understanding'. He bemoaned the penetration of the Islamic system, under President Rafsanjani, by 'westernized elements' with leanings toward the West. Mohtashami argued that as economic relations and political ties were 'closely interlinked', even economic relations with the United States were a threat to Iran's 'identity, revolutionary prestige, and image'. He also dismissed the customary argument that only the United States could resolve Iran's problems as 'a major error'. Commercial ties were unlikely to solve Iran's problems, and would only add to them. Therefore, rather than seeking to develop such ties, Iran should 'vaccinate' itself against the West's economic viruses, he said.[72] More than that, to argue that Iran's problems would disappear with the renewal of ties with United States, Mohtashami argued, was tantamount to considering the United States as 'God on earth'.[73] The conservative *Resalat* similarly dismissed the 'theory' – then being raised in some circles – that Iran should assimilate into the world-system as a *sine qua non* for advancing its own economy.[74]

Faced with such harsh criticism, whatever hopes Rafsanjani had entertained for a rapprochement with Washington were, in the words of one Iranian source, 'destroyed'; his 'Westward-looking' policy had 'completely failed', and he was forced to retreat.[75] If he did support a policy change, he did not express this openly and explicitly. Even when such proposals were raised by his close associates, he did not endorse them. When Mohajerani wrote his article, Rafsanjani asked his associates to deny that Mohajerani's proposals reflected the president's views.[76]

Moreover, when anti-US sentiment ran high, even those considered to be more pragmatic joined in voicing harsh criticism against the United States. In May 1989, after Khomeini's *fatwa* against Salman Rushdie, Rafsanjani called upon the Palestinians to retaliate against Israel by attacking Westerners and their interests worldwide. 'If, in retaliation for every Palestinian martyred in Palestine, they kill . . . five Americans or Britons or Frenchmen', Rafsanjani said, the Israelis 'would not continue their wrongs'. His choice of targets was based on the 'pragmatic' observation that 'it is a bit difficult to [kill] Israelis', but 'it is not hard to kill Americans or Frenchmen' because there are so many of them 'around the world'. He also advised the Palestinians to hijack planes, blow up factories in Western countries, and threaten US interests 'throughout the world'.[77] Similarly, on the fifteenth anniversary of the seizure of the US embassy in Tehran in 1994 – an anniversary when anti-US sentiments often run high in Iran – Rafsanjani joined the hard-liners by using derogatory language to chastise the United States. He pointed out that when the Americans were still 'savages and eating fruit from the trees in the jungle', Iran already had a great civilization; thus Iran could not be forced to 'surrender' to US demands.[78]

Khatami was certainly right in observing shortly after assuming the presidency that 'a bulky wall of mistrust' existed between the two states. He added, however, that such mistrust was 'rooted in the improper behavior of American governments'. Among US policies held responsible for the current state of affairs, was US involvement in the 1953 coup d'état against the Mosaddeq government and the attitude of the United States after the victory of the Islamic Revolution which Khatami said 'has not been a civilized one'. The United States had 'adopted a hostile policy toward Iran,' he added. 'They have tried to inflict economic damage on us', which is the 'continuation of cold war mentality'. Another example of hostile US policy, Khatami said, was the allocation of US$20 million 'to topple the Iranian government'. All these led to 'grave mistrust', Khatami observed. US foreign policy, he suggested, should 'stop considering others as objects'. The United States should 'respect the rights of others and adopt an approach based on communicative rationality which is inherent in American civilization'. This should be a first step towards making 'a crack in this wall of mistrust'. Unfortunately, the behavior of the US government in the past 'has always exacerbated the climate of mistrust', Khatami noted.[79] (For more moderate views of Khatami, see below.)

As far as Iran was concerned, the main question was not merely whether prominent Iranian figures genuinely wanted some change, but the degree to which they were capable of leading Iran in that direction. The harsh criticism of those advocating some kind of rapprochement attests to the existence of such voices, but with hard-liners setting the tone and making hostility toward Washington a major element of Iran's foreign policy, the supporters of change found it extremely difficult to promote their ideas. The issue was imbued with ideological rejection of the United States and was rooted in deep anti-American sentiments and mistrust, rather than on logic and rational calculations.

To some degree, emotions and misconceptions have also characterized the approach of the United States. Khomeini's zealous anti-US
stance, the hostage crisis (1979–81), the Iran–Contra affair (1985–86)
and the experience of US citizens held hostage by pro-Iranian groups in
Lebanon (in the early 1980s), were among the issues that have deeply
hurt the feelings of most Americans – much more than the Iranians
seemed to have realized. The wide political and cultural differences
between the two countries also made it difficult for Washington to comprehend Iran's revolutionary rhetoric and its blurred and inconsistent
policies. For its part, the United States also seemed to be sending mixed
signals to Tehran, from hostility to the revolutionary movement upon
the fall of the Shah; its anti-Iranian stance during the Iran–Iraq war; its
'dealings' with the Iranian regime over the Iran–Contra affair; and the
pursuit of its 'dual containment' policy concurrently with expansion of
economic ties with Iran in the early 1990s.

Despite strong public statements in the USA and the 'dual containment' policy, economic ties between the two countries actually
expanded. In fact, in the early 1990s, the United States (including
foreign subsidiaries of US companies) became one of Iran's leading trade
partners. In 1994, US oil companies and their subsidiaries reportedly
purchased about a fifth of Iran's total oil exports.[80] These mixed signals
confused both Iran and allies of the United States – whom Washington
had pressured into not conducting business with Tehran – and lent further credence to one of Khomeini's chief slogans: 'America can't do any
damned thing.' According to this view, expanding economic ties
amounted to an admission by the United States of its failure to contain
Iran; one could chant 'Death to America' and still do business with it.
This not only made it difficult for Washington to demand that its allies
act to contain Iran, but it gave them a 'license' to expand contacts further, rendering the 'dual containment' policy a leaking sieve.
Interestingly, Iran did not even attempt to refute reports of its trade with
the United States. As President Rafsanjani cynically remarked, it was
beneficial to Iran's global policy 'to make Western countries wonder
why the United States, which keeps telling them not to have relations
[with Iran], has so many dealings' with Tehran itself.[81] The *Economist*
referred to US–Iranian 'relations' at that time as 'a convenient marriage',[82] while the *New York Times* columnist Thomas Friedman called
it 'feel-good containment – a policy that makes us feel good but doesn't
make Iran feel bad enough to change its behavior'.[83]

US rhetoric against Iran was no milder than Iranian discourse. Iran
was often referred to as an 'outlaw nation' and 'the world's leading

sponsor of terrorism'. Thus, US Secretary of State Warren Christopher typically stated, 'They have projected terror throughout the region . . . Wherever you look, you find the evil hand of Iran in this region.'[84] But US hostility was not restricted to verbal denunciations only.

In a series of rulings and regulations in 1995–96, the United States imposed sanctions on trade with and investment in Iran as the means to convince the Iranian government to modify its policy. More specifically, it was stated that Washington wished to pressure Tehran to end its involvement in international terrorism and to deprive the government of money that could be used in the service of Iran's armament program.

The executive orders of 1995 and 1996 banned all US trade with and investment in Iran, including the purchase of Iranian oil by US companies abroad. US Assistant Secretary of State for Near Eastern Affairs, Robert Pelletreau, said that the new sanctions, in conjunction with the existing set of restrictions on trade with Iran, were 'the culmination of a painstaking review' of 'our Iran policy'. They were 'chosen carefully', he said, to advance US strategic interests 'challenged by Iran's outlaw activities'. Their impact, he believed, 'will be strong'. Although such steps 'will result in some costs' to US 'firms and workers', Washington was convinced that it was 'the most effective way' to make Iran pay 'for flouting the norms of law-abiding nations' and to cause its leadership 'to review its policies'.[85] Under Secretary of State for Political Affairs, Peter Tarnoff, added that the US embargo complemented 'long-standing American determination' to counter Iran's 'rogue activities'. He noted, however, that US policy was not aimed at the government of Iran, but against specific Iranian policies, 'which we judge to be unacceptable to law-abiding nations'. He too believed that 'making Iran pay' is 'the best way to convince' the Iranian leadership to change its policy.[86] In May 1996, Pelletreau noted that Washington did not aim at overthrowing or reverse the Islamic Revolution. Moreover, he said, the United States 'recognize[d] Iran's importance as a regional state' and 'remain[s] ready for an authorized, out-in-the-open dialogue when Iran's leaders are willing to discuss our differences face-to-face'.[87]

Among other more specific US indictments of Iranian policy were its 'active support for and sponsorship of terrorism', its support of opposition groups seeking to subvert secular regimes in the Muslim world, its opposition to the Middle East peace process and support for Palestinian rejectionist movements. Iran was also blamed for pursuing the development of weapons of mass destruction and the missile systems to deliver them, and for being engaged in a conventional military build-up that threatened regional peace and stability (mainly in the Gulf). At home,

Iran was castigated for abuses of human rights, particularly of political dissidents, women, and religious minorities. Pelletreau noted: 'None of these activities is called for in the tenets of Islam. All represent leadership choices of a human, not divine character and can thus be changed by human reconsideration.'[88] US officials explained the policy as an attempt to encourage Tehran 'to make a strategic choice'. Washington is 'still willing to engage in a dialogue with authoritative representatives' of Iran, said one such source. 'We believe that pressure and dialogue can go together.'[89] Tehran continued to view the attitude of the United States as arrogant and uncompromising. The Iranians expected practical gestures of good intentions, not sanctions and threats.

Analysts believe that the direct effect of US sanctions on the Iranian economy may have been only slight owing to the fact that the United States 'is no longer a vital trade partner'. Foreign oil companies benefited from the absence of US companies in Iran, as did some foreign countries. Indeed, US companies are now lobbying their government to ease the restrictions and to allow them to compete for Iranian contracts.[90] Had Washington's allies joined in its efforts to contain Iran, Rafsanjani conceded, they could have had 'some effect' on Iran's economy.[91] But he was confident that they would not. The main effect, therefore, was mainly political and psychological.

Publicly, Tehran played down the effects of the 1995 US executive order and focused on their advantages for Iran. Pragmatists and conservatives argued similarly. Velayati declared that it had 'failed at birth',[92] while Rafsanjani claimed that it 'bore no fruit but defeat and shame' for the United States,[93] and 'further strengthened the Iranian economy'.[94] *Jomhuri-ye Islami* believed that US trade sanctions would ultimately benefit Iran by demonstrating Washington's failure to organize an anti-Iranian front and dealing the final blow to Iranians who had entertained ideas of improving relations with the USA.[95] Yet US sanctions did raise concerns and harmed Iran's program of economic reconstruction. They inflicted a psychological blow on the economy and triggered a crisis of confidence in Iran, at least for some time. This was perhaps best exemplified by the sharp decline in the value of the riyal, which shrank from around US$1.00=IR2,500 in January 1995 to between US$1.00=IR4,300 in April and US$1.00=IR6,500 in May 1995. Overall, the absence of a concerted sanctions effort meant that Iran could, in fact, get what it needed from other countries. Nevertheless, many Iranian economists viewed the improvement of ties with the United States as an essential step to rehabilitate the economy, while Rafsanjani still seemed to regret that President Clinton had passed up opportunities to improve ties. Iran's business deals with US firms, he maintained in 1995, were 'a message' that Washington had not correctly understood.[96] In 1996, it seemed, neither country was willing to budge from its policy; and each was still waiting for actual signals by the other side, which did not come.

Domestic observers of US policy have argued that given Iran's geopolitical importance and the evolving internal political and economic situation, the United States would be wise to 'keep the door open' to contacts.[97] '*Iran is Ripe for a Peaceful Overture*' was the title of one such article by Gary Sick, who dismissed as 'a pipedream' the 'notion that we are going to drive Iran into bankruptcy and thereby bring down the Islamic government'.[98] Washington's 'obstruction of international development credits for Iran will neither transform nor bring down' the Islamic regime, he wrote.[99] 'Economically, Iran is not going to be hurt' by the sanctions, argued another commentator; 'and politically, they will strengthen the regime' by becoming 'a rallying cry for the government'. This, in turn, could also discredit the pragmatists in Tehran and bring 'more hard-line attitudes and leaders to the fore'.[100] Indeed, the European Union (EU) and Japan have justified their alternative approach to Iran on the grounds that the clerical regime 'is not made up only of radicals' and it is 'necessary to support the moderates'.[101] According to proponents of this view, 'if Iran is not economically successful, it will become more radical'.[102]

Although the difficulties of unilateral US sanctions are self-evident, a more accommodating approach like the EU policy of 'critical dialogue' with Iran, was equally problematic. Overall, 'critical dialogue' has failed to produce any significant breakthrough or change in Iranian policy (e.g., in its attitude toward the West, the Middle East peace process, the *fatwa* against Salman Rushdie, or support for militant Islamists). The former French Prime Minister Edouard Balladur made it clear that France's desire 'to respect human rights' is mitigated by the fact that it has 'an economic position to defend' in Iran and seeks 'a good balance' between the two.[103]

The EU approach turned much more critical in the spring of 1997, following the Mykonos trial. (See Chapter 3.) At that time the EU presidency asked all EU member states to recall their ambassadors to Tehran for consultations on the future of relations between the EU and Iran, and the suspension of the EU's 'critical dialogue' with Iran.[104] The call was answered by all the EU member states, except Greece.[105] Iran reacted by harshly attacking Germany and the trial, which several spokesmen described as 'political' and 'biased'.[106] Khatami, then a presidential candidate described the German court's verdict as a 'puppet show that was being held by the global arrogance'.[107] EU attitudes softened further following Khatami's election. (See below.)

Generally speaking, the anti-US stance taken by Khomeini at the outset of the revolution did not produce a pro-Soviet turn in Iran's policy. In fact, the Soviet Union was as unattractive a partner as the United States in the foreign policy calculations of the Islamic regime. Khomeini reminded the nation repeatedly that Iran was fighting against 'international Communism' just as it was fighting 'the Western World devourers'.[108] For the Iranian revolutionary, 'Neither the East, Nor the West', was a genuine ideal, and it rejected both the United States and the Soviet Union.

Iran resented Moscow for its record of intervention in Iran, loss of the territories in Caucasia and the humiliating treaties of Golestan (1813) and Turkmanchay (1828) imposed on it by Russia, and for its intervention in Iran during both world wars. It also criticized Moscow for its exploitation of Iranian resources as well as its ties with the Shah (mainly since the mid-1960s). The religious foundations of the Islamic regime also stood in marked contrast to the anti-religious elements inherent in communism. Additionally, the Soviet Union's ties with leftist groups within Iran (mainly the pro-Moscow Tudeh Communist Party) and with Iranian ethnic minorities struggling against the central government (mainly Kurds), were held against Moscow at the outset of the revolution. Two significant events further inflamed tension in the 1980s: the Soviet invasion of Afghanistan, and its support for Iraq during its war with Iran. An especially critical approach was adopted by Khomeini in his message to Soviet leader Mikhail Gorbachev a decade after the revolution. In his message on 4 January 1989, Khomeini criticized communism and Soviet policy and advised Gorbachev to begin *perestroika* by revising the Soviet state's policy of banning religion. He said that 'from now on communism should be sought only in museums' and advised Gorbachev 'to turn to truth', to religion, and to the study of Islam. Islamic Iran, he offered, could easily fill 'the ideological vacuum (*Khalla'-e e'teqadi*) in your system'. Yet, he concluded, 'as in the past, our country believes in reciprocal relations and good neighborliness, and respects them'.[109]

In fact, expediency dictated the advisability of not straining relations with both great powers at once, and of having regard for the fact that Iran shared a long border with the Soviet Union. Thus, while Iran's vociferous anti-US stance did not produce a concurrent pro-Soviet tilt, political considerations still made Moscow almost as repugnant as Washington to Tehran's Islamic regime. After the Iran–Iraq war, and particularly following the disintegration of the Soviet Union, however, there was a significant relaxation in mutual relations between Tehran and Moscow. As the deputy foreign minister Mohsen Aminzadeh put it recently, 'the dreams of a strong superpower' to the north of Iran 'have turned to dust'. This development, he said, is 'a positive point for us'.[110]

A new relationship was established but the two countries continued to be separated by deep disagreements. Although Russia no longer shared a common border with Iran, it still considered its borders with the new Muslim replublics of Central Asia and Transcaucasia as 'security borders' that served its vital interests. For Iran, the breakup of the Soviet Union 'replaced one stable border' with 'unstable borders', leaving Iran to contend with the threat of refugees and blocked trade routes as the byproducts of conflict in the region.[111] Following the dissolution of the Soviet Union, Russia and Iran also vied for lucrative trade deals with the new states of Central Asia on which Moscow once had a monopoly. In the international arena, too, Iran and Russia have often shown fundamental differences, such as over the war in Bosnia (where Iran backed Bosnian Muslims against the Serbian regime supported by Russia) and the Arab–Israeli peace process which Russia supports and Iran does not. Despite these areas of contention, the two countries found that they had much in common. Russia did not support the US policy of containing Iran and was willing to expand trade. President Yeltsin's spokesman, Sergei Yastrzhembskii, stated – rather like the EU – that Russia believes that isolating states such as Iran 'will only make them more radical'.[112] They also had many areas of common interest, in the security, economic and political arenas. Overall, Moscow seemed a lesser threat to Iran than Washington, and Tehran could not overlook Russia's interests and power.

The demise of the Soviet Union, however, led rival factions in Iran to similar conclusions: Iran should strive to fill the void left by the collapse of the Soviet Union by leading the Islamic world, the non-aligned movement, or the South bloc. Alternatively, deputy foreign minister 'Abbas Maleki suggested, Russia should now 'view itself as being part of Asia, or at least as a Euro-Asian country', in order to 'establish a solid and strong economic and political front against the West'. He added: 'We have the oil, Japan the technology, China the labor and Central Asian countries the agriculture; therefore, an intermingling of these economies could bring prosperity to the continent.'[113] Although this was a far-reaching vision, clearly Tehran was by then looking increasingly to the East.

Japan, and the East in general, had been a region of major Iranian interest long before the revolution, but it gained further centrality in Iran's foreign policy calculations after 1979, and even more so after the demise of the Soviet Union.

Both from the ideological and the practical point of view, Tehran viewed Japan as an 'ideal' partner: it had no 'imperialist record' and no political aspirations or commitments in the region; and it symbolized the potential ability of eastern nations to modernize and surpass the superpowers. Moreover, it possessed the advanced technology Iran required and needed the oil Iran wished to sell. All this provided a solid basis for improved relations.[114] Most revealingly, Khatami, in his book *Zamineha-ye Khizesh-e Mashruteh,* devoted a chapter to Japan's victory over Russia (1904–05). Nuri pointed out that while in the nineteenth century, Mirza Taqi Khan Amir Kabir and Meiji began from a similar point in their quest for reform and restoration, Iran failed to match Japan's achievements.[115] The rapid progress of Japan in the late nineteenth century, in fact, had fired the imagination of Muslim intellectuals and given them confidence in the ability of the East to equal, and eventually outpace, the West. Ignoring what was unique to the Japanese experience, Iranians used it as a paradigm.[116]

After the Islamic Revolution, Iran signaled its profound interest in forming close ties. In 1985 Speaker Rafsanjani paid a state visit to Japan (and China), making it the first such visit by an Iranian official of his rank to a non-Muslim country since the revolution. There were, however, two points that delayed practical implementation of closer links with Japan. One was a legacy from the past: the 1973 joint venture to build the huge petrochemical complex in Bandar Shapur (now Bandar Khomeini). The other was an imbalance of imports and exports between the two countries. Furthermore, given Japanese relations with the United States, and Japan's interests in the Gulf region (and later its failure to meet Iranian expectations for loans), bilateral relations did not always meet Iran's expectations. During the Iran–Iraq war Iran argued that Japan received 'dollars from Iran' (stemming from its huge sales in the country) which it had 'passed on' to Arab countries in the Gulf, where Japan shopped for oil, which were hostile to Iran.[117] Iran sought Japanese participation – and loans – to an extent greater than Japan was willing to provide. While Japan agreed to reschedule Iran's debts (see Chapter 4), Iran regarded Japan as being increasingly susceptible to US pressure to withhold further loans to Iran. Yet, Japan continued to be an important business partner for Iran and bilateral relations seemed to have improved further since Khatami became president. Iran also worked to improve its relations with China. As result of Iran's financial difficulties and US sanctions, as well as China's growing need for oil as a source of energy, China gradually became a major supplier of arms, technologies and equipment.[118]

The advantages in relations with Europe, Russia, the Far East, and other countries notwithstanding, given the unique stature of the USA – economically, politically and strategically – the pragmatists believed that there still seemed to be no substitute for improved relations with the United States.

Despite the hostile exchange of accusations, the advisability of some kind of dialogue was stressed occasionally, mainly by intellectuals and in the media. With all the hostile statements of 'Death to America', a significant measure of appreciation was increasingly noticeable (mainly among Iranian youth), not only for US products and commodities, but also for some symbols of American culture (such as rock music and cinema).[119] Similarly, the collapse of the Soviet Union has left its imprint in the reaction of many Iranians, who were aware of the dominant power of Washington in the world. The growing economic difficulties in Iran were another factor encouraging reductions in bilateral tension. The peace process in the Middle East and Syria's relations with Washington have also left their mark. Although such opinions were expressed on occasion during the last decade, they gained greater force and were voiced more openly after the election of Khatami in May 1997.

THE KHATAMI FACTOR

The most significant steps towards smoothing the atmosphere between Iran and the United States were made after Khatami's election. The new realities – in Iran and on the international scene – had not yet led to a resumption of formal ties, but signs of an improved climate were increasingly evident. Moreover, greater segments of Iranian society seemed tired of the old slogans and opted for change. Khatami seemed to have internalized the need for change and – at least in his first three years in the presidency – looked set to lead the way. Washington, for its part, was also sending more encouraging signals. Although the resolute opposition by the conservatives did not allow a breakthrough, support for a dialogue was no longer taboo in Iran. Discussion of its benefits and liabilities became a legitimate issue for public debate. President Khatami took the lead in stressing the positive aspects of Western culture, and by extension the advisability of removing tensions between Iran and the West. Even though this was not yet sufficient to lead to a breakthrough, there were more signs of change, on both sides.

President Khatami acknowledged frequently that in the modern world Muslims lived under the dominant impact of Western civilization. He expressed profound appreciation for the achievements of Western culture and deemed it totally impossible, and also unwise, to cut Iran off from the outside world. He also recognized the central role the USA plays in international affairs at the end of the twentieth century. Khatami thus prepared the background for a possible change, but did not yet move directly to support formal relations.

The West is the birthplace of the new civilization, he wrote in one of his books, and civilizations influence each other.[120] This is an age of 'the dominance and entrenchment' of Western civilization, 'intellectually, morally, and technologically'. The West has 'made great strides in science, politics, and social regulation', he added, although it is already 'worn out and senile'. Iran should understand the West 'correctly and comprehensively', in order to 'judge it fairly and objectively' and to 'use its strengths', while at the same time 'staying clear of its defects by relying on our revolution's values'.[121] Living in the age of technology, Iran 'can no longer remain isolated', he believed. In addition, given the 'immense progress in technology', the world today 'is interconnected'.[122] Moreover, Iran should not ignore the fact that in addition to its political 'face', the West also has an intellectual (*fekri*) dimension, with liberalism as one of its cornerstones.[123] Khatami rejected both the conservatives (who, he said, wished to return to the past), and those intoxicated by the West (*mabhurun*). He suggested instead an 'intellectual approach', i.e., selective borrowing from the West.[124] 'Give-and-take among civilizations', in his view, 'is the norm of history'.[125] Knowledge of Western culture and civilization, he said, was a historical necessity (*zarurat-e tarikhi*).[126] Muslims should look at the West 'with a neutral outlook', devoid of sentiments, to avoid its dangers but benefit from its profound human achievement (*injahatihi wa-mo'tayatihi al-insaniyya*). They should also strive to re-establish their great civilization, not by remaining in the past, but by straining forward to new horizons.[127]

Moreover, in Khatami's view, 'foreign policy does not mean guns and rifles', but utilizing all legitimate 'international means' to convince others.[128] Iran, he said repeatedly in his election campaign, wants relations with all the nations 'which respect our independence, dignity, and interests'. If Iran does not have relations 'with an aggressive and bullying country' such as the United States, this is because of that country's failure to 'respect those principles' and because it put itself 'at the head of the aggressors and conspirators against us'.[129] The United States 'must change its policy and [its] view of Iran'. Yet, Khatami added that 'we must try' and establish a dialogue. 'Informed theoreticians and experienced politicians can start the dialogue. This is the only way we can bring about coexistence without enmity.' In his view, 'Any country that recognizes our independence and does not have an aggressive policy toward us can be our friend.' Iran's arms, he said, 'are extended to shake hands with all the countries of the world'.[130]

Khatami's plea for a 'dialogue between civilizations', was supported by some Iranian intellectuals, who had long acknowledged such a need. Together, they provided the philosophical background for such a general change in approach. Thus, Soroush's argument that religious science could grow only when engaged in an 'intimate dialogue' with the non-religious sciences also provided the foundation for such an intercultural dialogue. Advances in one country, he believed, should transcend their country of origin to influence the greater body of international scholarly thought, and this could only be achieved through interaction with the wider scholarly community. In his view, it was both possible and necessary to borrow selectively from the West, without succumbing to a wholesale imitation of Western culture. Developing nations should avoid general, non-descriptive, dogmatic labels, and interact rationally, selectively and consciously with foreign cultures and concepts.[131] According to Kadivar, the issue of relations between Iran and the United States was beset with concrete difficulties and not by any religious obstacle. Khomeini, he stressed, did not altogether reject relations with the United States, but only demanded that they 'should be based on respect'. If Iran felt strong and able to 'attain our goals on the basis of expediency and prudence, we will be able to have relations with that country, whether at the civil or [even] the political level'. Moreover, he added, the revolution possessed a spiritual message, which the world was eager to hear: 'What other path do we possibly have for conveying this message except through talks?'[132] Shabestari advocated a dialogue between Islam and Christianity. This, he said, is not only 'recommended' (*mostahab*), but 'a necessity' (*zarurat*) for Iran. Relations between Islam and Judaism were even easier, he pointed out, because the historical contact between these two faiths was divorced from political dimensions.[133] Human rights, he believed, emanated from the philosophical concept of equality and were based on the principle that the humanity of a person has priority over his beliefs, rather than on the idea of defining people in purely religious terms.[134] By 1997, many others, while recognizing the strength of the United States in the new world order, pointed to the benefits promised by improved relations with Washington and viewed such an improvement as serving Iran's national interests. (See below.)

Reducing tension in ties with the United States was probably one of the most important areas in which a change was expected in Iran's foreign relations after Khatami's election. This, however, was also one of the most difficult aspects of the revolutionary agenda to change, pitting Iran's competing ideological camps against each other. With Khatami's election the two main domestic trends continued to confront each other fiercely on the issue.

After being formally sworn in, Khatami reaffirmed his campaign pledges, offering dialogue as a mechanism for removing misunderstandings between nations. Only mutual respect and common interests could lead to a fruitful dialogue, he reiterated. He added: 'My government considers dialogue between civilizations . . . essential, and will avoid any action or behavior causing tension.'[135] Although speaking in general terms, he did not exclude dialogue with the United States within the framework of a 'dialogue between civilizations'. In his speech at the ICO on 9 December 1997, he acknowledged that the 'replication of the old [Islamic] civilization' was neither possible nor desirable. In his words, we are living in 'the era of predominance' of Western civilization, 'whose accomplishments are not few, and yet whose negative consequences, particularly for non-Westerners, are plentiful'. Through dialogue Iran should open the way toward mutual understanding and genuine peace, 'based on the realization of the rights of all nations'.[136] Appealing to the American people in unprecedentedly moderate language, Khatami expressed the hope for 'a philosophical and historical interchange', based on the belief that 'whenever intellectual interchanges go ahead, the world will achieve peace'. He castigated US statesmen for seeking to go backwards and regretted that the United States was still trying 'to impose its objectives on other nations'. This, he said, was a sign of its backwardness. Iran, for its part, he pledged, was 'ready to have sports and even economic relations with all states', except for Israel.[137]

Khatami went on to signal Iran's willingness to open a new chapter in its relations with the United States – more explicitly and specifically – in his interview with CNN television in January 1998. The issues he raised, the terminology used, and the overall approach, were unusually moderate.

In his interview Khatami appealed directly to the American people, expressing respect for 'the great American people' and praising their civilization, which he said was founded 'upon the vision, thinking, and manners of the puritans', who 'desired a system, which combined the worship of God with human dignity and freedom'. This civilization had even abolished slavery, he added. 'There were numerous martyrs who gave their lives for this cause, the most famous of whom was Abraham Lincoln.' Moreover, the American nation 'was the harbinger of independence struggles', and the initiator of efforts to respect human dignity and rights. With Iran 'experiencing a new phase of reconstruction of civilization', Khatami said, it is as if 'what we seek is what the founders of American civilization' pursued centuries ago. 'This is why we sense an intellectual affinity with the essence of American civilization', he added. Nothing should prevent 'talk and understanding between two nations, especially between their scholars and thinkers'. He therefore recommended 'the exchange of professors, writers, scholars, artists, journalists, and even tourists'. Yet, he made clear that the 'dialogue between civilizations and nations is different from political relations', which depended on resolving the 'factors which led to the severance of relations'.

Khatami regretted that US policies over the past half century had been incompatible with American civilization which was 'founded on democracy, freedom, and human dignity'. This 'flawed policy of domination' had its setbacks, among which was the severe damage that it inflicted upon deprived nations, including Iran. He expressed the hope, however, that US politicians would 'adjust themselves' to the standards of American civilization, 'and at least apologize to their own people' for their past politics. Yet, regrettably, US foreign policy was still based on 'a cold war mentality' and tried 'to create a perceived enemy', with 'certain circles' in Washington 'targeting progressive Islam'.

Khatami also expressed regret that 'the feelings of the great American people have been hurt', by revolutionary events in Iran. Yet, in his view, this was no different from the time 'when bodies of young Americans were brought back from Vietnam'. Just as Americans then had 'blamed their own politicians for dragging their country' into 'the Vietnam quagmire', so should they now look at the case of Iran. The 1979–81 hostage crisis, he explained, was 'the crying out of the [Iranian] people against humiliations and inequities imposed upon them' by the policies of foreigners. Today, he went on to say, 'our revolution has matured', the government is strong, and there is no longer any need for such 'unconventional methods'. Now, he promised, we 'fully adhere to all norms of conduct that should regulate relations between nations and governments'. Continuing his conciliatory tone, Khatami advised the American people not to be overwhelmed by anti-US slogans in Iran. In his view, even those chanting such slogans 'do not harbor any ill will for the American people'. Such slogans only 'symbolize a desire to terminate a mode of relationship' that had once existed between the two states.[138]

Although Khatami repeated some anti-US accusations, and pointed to the difficulties involved in removing tension, this was undoubtedly the most moderate appeal to the United States, suggesting that the doors for reconciliation were open. To speak about the 'great American culture', to refer to Lincoln as a *shahid*, and of the American people as the defenders of lofty ideals, had deep meaning, not only for the American people, but also for Iranians. Khatami's statements became an issue of fierce argument in Tehran. While the hard-line camp reiterated its original position, there was much innovation – in magnitude, tone and contents – in the pragmatic discourse. Their general approach and tone testified to the considerable change within the ranks of the revolutionaries.

Foreign Minister Kharrazi seconded his president. Reiterating that the ball was in the US court, he said that 'we are ready to work with all nations', which are prepared to base their relations with us 'on mutual respect'.[139] *Salam* (hitherto known for its fierce anti-US stance) published its readers' penetrating comments in favor of dialogue and voiced a more moderate tone. Thus, one reader asked whether it would be more difficult to change the anti-US line than it was to retreat from anti-Iraqi slogans earlier? Another reader asked why relations with Britain were acceptable while dialogue with the United States was not? If the United States had usurped Iran's rights, another reader queried, was it not better to engage in dialogue to regain these rights?[140] Reiterating such questions, *Salam* itself wondered: Is there any doubt that many Iranians support a dialogue, and that their numbers are constantly growing?[141] Iran, the paper suggested, should not be terrified by an offer of dialogue.[142] Such statements represented a swerve from the line taken by the paper just a few years ago. One reader appealed to Kho'iniha (the editor of *Salam*, who was one of the mentors of the students who occupied the US embassy in 1979, and has since changed his attitude considerably): What did Iran achieve by raising the slogan 'Death to America'? In fact, 'Japan was attacked by nuclear bombs, but has never set fire to American flags. What have you achieved so far by [promoting] animosity to the USA? If you are right, do something. Clearly, by shouting "Death to America" problems could not be resolved.'[143]

Jame'eh openly censured Iran's isolationist policy, wondering why it lay down conditions for renewing ties with the United States while no similar conditions were imposed on other former foes of Iran. Based on such logic, the paper wrote, Iran should have requested the return of its northern cities from Russia, or Herat from Afghanistan. Similarly, Iran should have insisted on compensation from Iraq and Saudi Arabia for the damage of the war, which was much more severe than the damage inflicted on Iran by any of the superpowers. Iran still sticks to an extremist approach, the paper explained, out of fear of losing its 'last card'. In fact, even if the United States were to accept all Iran's conditions, the paper noted, Iranian officials would refuse to retreat from their approach, since animosity to the United States had become an issue of prestige for Iran. Enmity towards the United States, the paper added, has turned into 'an instrument (*vasileh*) with which to settle domestic infighting' and to put spokes in the wheels of other factions.[144]

Taking their clue from Ayatollah Khomeini, the hard-liners generally used the metaphor of the 'wolf' and the 'sheep' to characterize the relationship between the United States and Iran. (See above.) More recently, the supporters of dialogue, while still viewing the United States as the 'wolf', have tended to present Iran as the 'lion' (rather than as 'sheep', 'cattle' or a 'lamb'). Such a metaphor is used to justify a dialogue from a position of strength, not weakness.

Hojjat ul-Islam Mehdi Karubi (Secretary-General of *Majma'-e Ruhaniyyun-e Mobarez* and former Majlis Speaker) also used the metaphor of the 'wolf' and the 'lion'. In a lecture at the University of Ahvaz, Karubi, although refraining from a direct call for negotiations with the United States, supported Khatami's policy of defusing tension (*tashannoj zada'i*; détente). He mentioned three different accommodating approaches: support for full relations, dialogue, and defusing tension. While he supported the latter, he believed that only experts could determine the advantages and disadvantages of such relations. In some regions – such as Afghanistan, Pakistan and Central Asia – both Iran and the United States have interests, he said, and it would be logical to discuss such issues with the United States to protect Iran's interests. In his words, the metaphor of the 'sheep' and the 'lion' was 'interesting'.[145] Karubi later denied the wording of the report of his talk, admitting only to have said that 'the issue of resumption of relations with the United States is not new' and that it had been raised after the death of Khomeini. At that time, he added, some figures maintained that the metaphor of 'the wolf and the sheep' was only true in the early years of the revolution. 'We are like a lion now.'[146] That Karubi, one of the leading radicals of the early 1990s, would even entertain such ideas reveals how profound the change had been. 'Abdollah Nuri put his weight behind the moderate approach. Even countries which had wars with each other maintain ties. Having relations with the USA does not mean giving up Iranian identity or betraying their own interests. Had all the countries that currently have relations with the USA given up their identity? In addition, one cannot ignore the central role of the USA in the world today. While Iran does not have relations with the United States, its economic partners do, and they are not very different from the USA. In addition, Nuri warned that the question of Iran's policy towards the USA should not be used as a tool in the ongoing factional rifts.[147]

On 8 May 1999, Tehran University held a conference, focusing on the question of whether relations with the United States were a taboo or a national necessity. Professor Qasem Sho'leh-Sa'adi said that the initial Iranian policy was good in the given situation of crisis, but it did not address any of Iran's long-term problems. The decision on the issue, he said, should be based on 'our national interests'. He regretted, however, that the issue had become an instrument in domestic rivalries. 'Abbas 'Abdi said that those who viewed relations with the United States as taboo were acting against their own homeland.[148] The paper *Iran* initiated a series of interviews with experts on the issue. Economist 'Ali Rashidi argued that relations with the United States would benefit Iran's economy and praised Khatami's policy of encouraging foreign investment. Other interviewees seemed equally forthcoming, although they were 'waiting' for America's signaling of good will first.[149] 'Ali Rashidi stressed elsewhere that relations with the United States were, in fact, inevitable, and pointed to the damage done to the Iranian economy because of the absence of such relations. Another expert, Mohammad Tabibiyan, said that while in relations between people there are issues like hate and love, they should not have a place in relations between countries: only national interests are important.[150]

Hojjat ul-Islam Mohammad Javad Hojjati-Kermani, a former advisor to President Khamene'i, in an article in *Ettela'at*, commented on President Clinton's highly respectful references (12 April 1999) to Iran and Islam. (See below.) For the first time, he said, the US president had gone so far as to criticize the United States and the West for mistreating Iran, in 'an apologetic tone of voice'. This was the result, he said, of Khatami's political wisdom, which was 'in accordance with the instructions' of Ayatollah Khamene'i. He regretted, however, that some people in Iran 'believe that they should never climb down from their [uncompromising] stance'. This, he said, contradicted 'wisdom, the *Shari'a*, [and] the tradition of our Prophet', which approved of a 'highly lenient' approach 'in their treatment of adversaries and opponents'. Such a hostile attitude is 'a big mistake'. He observed pointedly that questions of 'war or peace are not strategies, rather they are [only] tactics'.[151] Yet, even more important than the arguments raised above was the very public discussion on the issue, stressing the need constantly to reconsider policy.

Nevertheless, those supporting full relations, dialogue, or the removal of tension expected Washington to take the first – and practical – step. Kharrazi complained that the United States was still behaving 'as if its interference in the affairs of other countries is permissible'. Asked in 1998 if there were signs of change in the United States' attitude towards Iran, he said: 'Not in practice.' The tone of their statements has changed, but 'this is not enough'. Practical action, he insisted, should come from Washington: 'Let them not interfere in our domestic affairs . . . [and] not impede Iran's positive role in the region.'[152]

Occasionally, however, especially when addressing domestic audiences, Khatami sounded as extremist as his conservative rivals. Immediately after being elected, he said that the key to the problem 'is in their hands', but unfortunately 'we have not seen' any encouraging sign from the United States so far. US policy 'has always been hostile to our revolution'.[153] Addressing schoolchildren on the eighteenth anniversary of the seizure of the US hostages, he castigated 'misguided and expansionist' US politicians who 'place their nation's resources and interests against other nations'. Making a distinction 'between our objection' to US policies and 'our [positive] opinion of the American nation', he added, typically, that to 'make up for the past', US politicians 'must apologize' to the Iranian nation first. Unfortunately the enmity of the United States had continued 'in a terrified and mindless way', as if it 'considers fighting the Iranian nation' as its 'main mission'.[154]

Notwithstanding the harsh statements occasionally voiced by Khatami, his general tone remained milder than that of any of the leading figures since the revolution. Intellectuals, students and segments of the media reiterated such mild statements, thus creating an unprecedentedly calm atmosphere for the debate on bilateral 'relations'. Significantly, during the student riots at Iranian universities in 1999, the focus of the students' fury and the slogans raised touched upon the difficulties on the domestic scene. Conversely, the rally arranged by the conservative establishment, centered on the customary allegations, namely, that the uprising was a conspiracy by the enemies of the revolution to harm Iran, the Islamic regime and Islam, and by extension the Iranian people. (See Chapter 5.)

In fact, whatever pragmatic statements were made by Khatami were offset by the hard-line messages sent out by Khamene'i and the conservatives. Not only has their position not softened, but the moderate expressions voiced by the reformists seem to have triggered even harsher statements by the conservatives. As in many other policy areas, there was a wide gap between different Iranian positions, and, on this important question too, the supreme authority was with Khamene'i.

The gap between the views of Iran's two top leaders was best manifested when they both spoke at the ICO summit in Tehran in December 1997. In contrast to Khatami's mild attitude Khamene'i used harsh words to denounce the West. He blamed Western civilization for 'directing everyone towards materialism while money, gluttony and carnal desires are made the greatest aspirations'. The West, in 'its all-rounded invasion', has 'targeted our Islamic faith and character'. It has 'intensively and persistently exported to our countries the culture of laxness and disregard for religion and ethics'.[155] Stressing one of the main charges of the conservatives, Nateq-Nuri's election platform presented Western policy as focused on the 'cultural onslaught'. According to him, such an onslaught was the West's vehicle for attacking the Iranian nation's ideology, religious thinking, national identity and revolutionary values.[156] He continued to make similar charges later as Majlis speaker. Similarly, Velayati continued to pursue the radical line of his 16-year tenure as head of the foreign ministry, pointing out that the mere talk of dialogue only served the interests of the enemy. Branding the advocates of such a policy 'stupid', or 'dependent on foreigners', he warned that such an approach could lead to the dissipation of the revolutionary legends of Islamic resistance.[157] In his view, 'no intelligent person ('*aqel*) could accept negotiating with the USA', nor could a dialogue with the United States lead to the results that Iran sought. Therefore, he asked rhetorically, why should Iran retreat from its principles if it is clear that negotiations with the United States 'are useless'.[158]

In a similar vein, the conservative press dismissed supporters of a dialogue as misguided, superficial and naive, and failing to perceive the enemy's real intentions.[159] Commenting on President Clinton's expressed hope that Khatami's election would 'bode well for the future', *Iran News* noted that had he and his aides studied the basics of the Islamic Revolution 'they would not have found' Khatami's presidency so 'intriguing' and 'fascinating'. The paper warned that 'a nightmare awaits' foreign countries which assume that with Khatami's presidency 'a new era has opened' for the resumption of ties with Iran in order to dominate it and usurp its wealth. The Iranian and US governments, the paper added, were 'treading on contrary paths that will never meet'.[160]

Jomhuri-ye Islami, Resalat and *Kayhan*[161] echoed this line repeatedly, particularly when Khatami made more accommodating statements. Khatami's interview with CNN television, *Resalat* observed, had taken place in circumstances where various individuals 'are overtaking each other in the race to resume ties'. They were 'eager to taste America's forbidden fruit', and 'lose every means of self-control just to babble in praise of America'. They stressed 'the miracle' that resumption of ties would perform while totally overlooking the 'negative consequences'. The result was to reduce 'the level of Muslim hatred against the arrogance of America' and replace it with 'despondency among militant Muslims'.[162]

The US request that Khatami's mild words be matched by deeds further infuriated Iranians in both camps. 'What is most important are actions, not words', said US Secretary of State Madeleine Albright after Khatami's election. More specifically, the United States laid down benchmarks (see below) to test Iran's actual approach, stating: 'Everything depends on how the new government deals with those key issues.'[163] Responding, Iran's foreign ministry spokesman, Mahmud Mohammadi, said that it is the United States that 'should prove in practice' that it had 'modified its behavior'.[164] Washington's preconditions prove, *Kayhan* wrote, that the United States simply wanted to impose its 'arrogant conditions' on Iran. It wished to 'turn Iran into a submissive, useless, and abject entity'.[165]

Nevertheless, after Khatami's election, US officials sounded somewhat milder. They acknowledged a degree of change, among some (though not the most significant) elements of Iran's ruling establishment. They also noted Iran's importance and the significance of the change since Khatami's election. However, while expressing the will for authoritative dialogue, they refused to compromise on the pre-conditions they had set, and continued to criticize Iran's actual policy in extremely harsh terms. Clearly, the United States was unwilling to accept the words coming out of Tehran as proof of real change. In 1998 Iran was also named as one of seven countries designated by the State Department as state sponsors of international terrorism. Iran, it said, 'continues to plan and conduct terrorist attacks' and assassination of dissidents abroad. It also claimed that Iran supported groups, including several that opposed the Middle East peace process, that used terrorism 'by providing varying degrees of money, training, safehaven, and weapons'.[166]

Official statements therefore combined mild words with tough conditions and uncompromising benchmarks. Martin Indyk, Assistant Secretary of State for Near Eastern Affairs, acknowledged on 12

November 1997 that 'Iran is a major regional power', and that its people had 'made a choice' for change, and noted 'some toning down' of its rhetoric. Yet, given Iran's efforts to subvert its neighbors, its 'regional charm offensive', he noted, was 'ironic'. He assured Iran that the United States sought 'a change in behavior, not a change in the regime', and expected 'deeds, not words' from Tehran. To encourage such a change in Iran, the United States sought 'to raise the cost' to Iran of its actions, to make it choose between the economic aspirations of its people on the one hand, and the pursuit of weapons of mass destruction and the promotion of terrorism and instability in the region on the other.[167] On 14 May 1998 Indyk reiterated similar charges, stressing that the United States was determined to make it clear to Iran 'that there is a price to be paid for pursuing policies which violate international norms'. Washington believed that Khatami's election reflected a 'desire for change on the part of a large majority of the Iranian electorate' and since his inauguration, 'one surprise has followed another'. However, in Iran, the presidency typically does not control national security policy, nor critical Iranian institutions, which remain the domain of Khamene'i. Yet it is precisely in this realm 'that Iran is pursuing policies of greatest concern to us'.[168] Bruce Riedel also acknowledged on 6 May 1998 that Khatami's election 'obviously marked a milestone', and that Iranians had voted 'in impressive numbers for a change'. Moreover, since his inauguration, there had been 'many positive statements', and a marked 'decision to increase the level of interaction at the people-to-people level between our two countries'. Yet 'serious issues' still 'need to be changed' and Khatami's words 'must now be matched by deeds'. The United States, he said, is 'patient and prepared to wait'. In the interim, 'we will continue to do all we can to constrain Iran's actions' in those areas that threaten the interests of the USA and its allies.[169]

Nevertheless, there was great diversity and variety in the American statements. The harsh tone remained, but was accompanied by some soft words. Washington continued to wave the 'stick' but also showed the 'carrot'. Much like Tehran, Washington was expecting practical steps but it viewed the ball as being in the Iranian court.

It was exactly when the internal Iranian debate reached a new peak, in the summer of 1998 during Karbaschi's trial and the interpellation of Nuri (see Chapter 3), that Washington came out with extraordinarily mild statements – a speech by Madeleine Albright on 17 June and a statement by President Clinton two days later. They have thus turned into another issue in the domestic controversy.

Albright's reference to the Islamic regime (perceived as a hint that the

United States recognized the regime's legitimacy and was willing to negotiate with it) and her reference to security in 'the Persian Gulf', sounded positive to Iranian ears. She stressed the 'signs of change' in Iran since Khatami's election (his gestures of goodwill, steps taken against drug smuggling, and Iran's attempts at mediation in Afghanistan), and added that the United States 'fully respects Iran's sovereignty' and that the two countries 'are now focused on the future'. She added, 'We are ready to explore further ways to build mutual confidence and avoid misunderstandings.' Obviously, 'two decades of mistrust cannot be erased overnight', but she added that it is now 'time to test the possibilities for bridging this gap'. The speech lacked the customary reference to Iran as a rogue state and an outlaw. While stating that there is much more that Iran must do to prove its trustworthiness (e.g. on the issues of terrorism and human rights), Albright left the door open for improved relations.[170] Even so, no major breakthrough was expected instantly. As US State Department spokesman James Rubin said on 18 June 1998, the United States expects reaction 'over time', not 'overnight'.[171] Clearly, the timing of the US gesture, in the middle of growing tension between domestic camps, was somewhat problematic for Khatami and his colleagues. Nevertheless, this was another important step in the slow motion dialogue, helping to soothe the atmosphere between Khatami and the White House but simultaneously exacerbating the ongoing dispute within Iran. The Iranian response to Albright's speech was thus divided; some factions vehemently rejected any possible rapprochement,[172] others sounded more forthcoming.[173] Interestingly, however, supporters of rapprochement expressed their views more openly than ever before.

Whatever mild statements each side made seemed insufficient to satisfy the other party. On 12 April 1999, President Clinton went one step further, recognizing that Iran had been subject to 'quite a lot of abuse from various Western nations'. They 'have a right to be angry' at something that the United States or those allied with it 'did to you 50 or 60 or 100 or 150 years ago'. Clinton hoped 'to find some way to get dialogue'.[174] Yet, the conservatives combined their rejection of Clinton's offer of goodwill with harsh accusations against Khatami and his associates. The United States' attitude, *Jomhuri-ye Islami* wrote, was continuation of its old methods, though it now hoped that the companions of Satan (*hamsarayan-e sheytan*) within Iran would give it a hand. 'It is regrettable', it wrote, 'that a certain group' at home, for the sake of advancing factional and personal interests, had turned one of the most essential questions in Iran's foreign policy into a tool of factional rivalry.[175] Those who now embraced the United States were the same people who had failed to contribute or suffer for the revolutionary cause, it added. 'They are cowardly, wretched, and spies.' They did not even suffer a rebuke. They received everything free, and were therefore ready to put all on sale (*harraj*). They were motivated by greed and by the desire to satisfy the interests of a particular faction.[176]

While pragmatists and conservatives differed in their perception of the benefits of resuming relations with the United States and the possibility of a significant breakthrough, they were united in expecting the United States to make the first, and practical, move, and in rejecting US allegations of Iranian complicity in acts of terrorism and the acquisition of unconventional weapons. The pragmatists expected a more forthcoming response from US officials at this juncture. The conservatives had no illusions about US intentions, but used such allegations to expose what they believed was the anti-Iranian and pro-Israeli nature of US policy, and to censure the pragmatists.

Iranians were especially infuriated by accusations of Iranian support for terrorism. They accused the United States of itself being the instigator of numerous crises in the world, and planning wars, assassinations, conspiracies, the violent overthrow of regimes and various other crimes,[177] while Iran was only a victim of terrorism. Such fictitious US accusations were only meant 'to coordinate' hostility against Islamism, and particularly against Tehran, 'the Islamic metropolis'.[178] Khatami, who repeatedly rejected such accusations, condemned 'any kind of terrorist activity', but drew a distinction between terrorism and 'the legitimate right to defend the occupied territories [in Palestine]'.[179] Muslims, Khatami said, believed that 'the slaying of one innocent person is tantamount to the slaying of all humanity', and rejected categorically 'all these allegations'. In any case, he went on, 'supporting people fighting for the liberation of their land is not, in my opinion, supporting terrorism'.[180]

According to many sources, Iran continued its efforts to develop weapons of mass destruction. In recent years such plans have reportedly been accelerated, especially the plan for a long-range missile. Iran was proud of its successes, such as the experimental launch of the 'Shehab-3' missile. Iran repeatedly stated that it did not have plans to develop nuclear weapons, and that it was a signatory to the Chemical Weapons Convention (CWC) and the Nuclear Nonproliferation Treaty (NPT). Khatami's pragmatic declarations did not apply to Iran's weapons of mass destruction policy,[181] and in any case the issue was not within his direct responsibility. Khatami stated that his country was not planning to build nuclear weapons, but to employ nuclear energy exclusively for peaceful purposes. The charges against Iran, he said, were a pretext for imposing certain policies on Iran and for creating panic. 'We are not a nuclear power and do not intend to become one. We are an IAEA [International Atomic Energy Agency] member and our facilities are inspected by the Agency.'[182] Tehran also repeatedly maintained that it was itself a victim of chemical warfare, during the Iran–Iraq war. It also made the point that it was 'sandwiched' between countries around its borders that had acquired or were attempting to acquire nuclear status. Yet what Iran was actually doing in this regard is difficult to ascertain in a study such as this. Clearly, such questions further hindered attempts at reconciliation between Iran and the United States.

Practical steps towards a dialogue between the United States and Iran since 1997 have so far been hesitant, slow and limited in nature. With each side claiming that the ball was in the other's court, each was waiting for the other to take practical steps first. Nevertheless, some important strides were made, such as the visit to Iran of a US wrestling team in February 1998, a visit by Iranian wrestlers to the United States in April 1998, and the Iran–US World Cup soccer game in France in June 1998. Important statements by US Secretary of State Madeleine Albright on 17 June 1997, and by US President Bill Clinton on 12 April 1999, raised new hopes for a rapprochement. After Khatami's election, more US scholars visited Iran and students arrived for research and study.[183]

While some direct contacts had been maintained under President Rafsanjani (see above), they seem to have widened and became more extensive under Khatami. In 1999, both sides confirmed that they used to communicate messages through third parties. In September it was disclosed that President Clinton had sent a letter to Tehran through a high-ranking official of an Arab state which had close ties with Iran.[184] Iran's foreign ministry spokesman, Hamidreza Asefi, while confirming such a message added that, 'the two countries are constantly conveying their viewpoints to each other through official messages and notes'. He said that at certain times in the past, the United States had sent messages to Iran through relevant channels, and that Iran, from a position of dignity and power, had always given explicit, clear and decisive responses to these messages.[185] Similarly James Rubin noted: 'There are many opportunities for us to pass official messages, and they happen regularly.'[186]

Thus the atmosphere for expanding academic, economic and other ties was created, and for the first time, a breakthrough seemed possible. Although the wounds of the past and a lack of mutual trust continued to imperil mutual relations, a measure of change has been registered. For each side, however, a demonstration of dramatic change was complex. One remaining major obstacle is that both Iran and the United States use their lack of relations as an indication of their prestige.[187]

Iran's anti-US stance remained, in fact, a major symbol of the revolution, and deviating from it proved extremely difficult. In the past, some pragmatists, anxious to prove their revolutionary devotion and to demonstrate its strength raised the anti-US and anti-Israeli banners even higher. At one stage, it appeared that President Khatami was attempting to separate the two banners and lower the anti-US one. As far as Khatami is concerned, and much like on other key issues in domestic politics, the main question was not his aim but his ability to produce a breakthrough. Khamene'i and the conservatives, who controlled some of the key decision-making machinery in Iran may be able to do so, but they do not yet seem willing to take such a step. (See also the Epilogue.)

Notes

1. Gustav von Grunebaum, 'Acculturation and Self-Realization', in B. Rivlin and J. S. Szyliowicz (eds), *The Contemporary Middle East* (New York, NY: Random House, 1965), pp. 141–2.
2. B. Lewis, *The Middle East and the West* (New York: Harper & Row, 1964), p. 45.
3. Jamshid Behnam, *Iraniyan va Andisheh-ye Tajaddod* [The Iranians and the Thought of Modernity] (Tehran: Farzan, 1996–97), pp. 171–4, 178–80.
4. Hamid Dabashi, *Theology of Discontent: The Ideological Foundations of the Islamic Revolution in Iran* (New York: New York University Press, 1993); Mehrzad Boroujerdi, *Iranian Intellectuals and The West: The Tormented Triumph of Nativism* (Syracuse, NY: Syracuse University Press, 1996), pp. 52–76, 99–130; Afsaneh Najmabadi, 'Iran's Turn to Islam: From Modernism to a Moral Order', *Middle East Journal*, 41/2 (Spring 1987), pp. 202–17; Ayelet Savyon, 'Hostility and Attraction in Iran's Attitude towards the West: The Pahlavi Monarchy and the Islamic Republic' (unpublished MA in Hebrew, Tel Aviv University, 1999), pp. 56–79.
5. Joya Blondel Saad, *The Image of Arabs in Modern Persian Literature* (Lanham, MD: University of America Press, 1996), p. 14; Manucheher Dorraj, *From Zarathustra to Khomeini: Populism and Dissent in Iran* (Boulder, CO: Lynne Rienner, 1990), p. 111.
6. *Tarikh, Tamaddon va Farhang* [Textbook in History, Civilization and Culture], III year of high school, edition of 1365 (Tehran, 1986–87), pp. 152–61.
7. 'Ali Akbar Velayati, *Iran va Mas'aleh-ye Felestin* [Iran and the Question of Palestine] (Tehran: Daftar-e Nashr-e Farhang-e Islami, 1997), pp. III, VI, IX in the English Introduction.
8. Ayatollah Ruhollah Khomeini, *Al-Hukuma al-Islamiyya* [The Islamic Government] (in Arabic, n.p.: 1970), pp. 18–22, 34–7, 138–9. See also Khomeini's

interviews with *al-Mustaqbal*, 13 January 1979 and *al-Safir*, 18, 19 January 1979.

9. Hamid Algar, *Islam and Revolution: Writings and Declarations of Imam Khomeini* (Berkeley, CA: Mizan, 1981), p. 209.
10. *Kayhan* (Tehran), 8 May 1999.
11. Boroujerdi, *Iranian Intellectuals*, p. 135.
12. IRNA, 12 August – DR, 13 August 1993.
13. Bahman Baktiari, 'Iran's New President', p. 20.
14. Tehran TV, 19 May 1997 [DR].
15. *Salam*, 6 May 1997 [DR].
16. Khatami, *Zamineha-ye Khizesh-e Mashruteh* (Tehran: Paya, n.d.), pp. 67–8.
17. Tehran TV, 19 May 1997 [DR].
18. Robert Snyder, 'Explaining the Iranian Revolution's Hostility Toward the United States', *Journal of South Asian and Middle Eastern Studies*, 17/3 (Spring 1994), p. 19.
19. Vakili, *Debating Religion and Politics in Iran*, pp. 38–9.
20. Radio Tehran, 22 November 1979 – DR, 24 November 1979. Similar statements were made by Ayatollah Montazeri, Radio Tehran, 23 November 1979 – DR, 26 November 1979.
21. Algar, *Islam and Revolution*, p. 305, from *Jomhuri-ye Islami*, 13 September 1980.
22. Radio Tehran, 19 May 1979 – DR, 21 May 1979; *Ettela'at*, 20 May 1979; *New York Times*, 21 May 1979.
23. *Jomhuri-ye Islami*, 29 October 1984.
24. *Salam*, 23 August 1992; IRNA, 23 August 1992 – DR, 24 August 1992.
25. Radio Tehran, 2 November 1994 – DR, 3 November 1994.
26. *Iran Times*, 24 July 1992, cited in Baktiari, *Parliamentary Politics*, p. 223.
27. *Echo of Iran*, no. 62 (March 1993), p. 18.
28. AFP, 2 November 1994 – DR, 2 November 1994.
29. Radio Tehran, 9 October 1996 – DR, 11 October 1996.
30. Radio Tehran, 18 September 1992 – DR, 20 September 1992.
31. Tehran TV, 1 February 1993 – DR, 3 February 1993; AFP, 19 December 1993 – DR, 20 December 1993.
32. *Resalat* and *Ettela'at*, 8 June 1994. Similarly, Mohammad Javad Larijani, vice-chairman of the Majlis foreign relations committee, contended that it was 'the responsibility of our Western partners' to generate a change, see *Financial Times*, 8 February 1993.
33. Tehran TV, 1 February 1993 – DR, 3 February 1993.
34. Interview with Rafsanjani, in *Middle East Insight*, 11/5 (July–August 1995), pp. 7–14.
35. Radio Tehran, 27 January 1995 – DR, 30 January 1995.
36. *Kayhan* (Tehran), 12 November 1996 – DR, 2 December 1996.
37. Hashim, *Crisis of the Iranian State*, p. 46.
38. *Danesh-e Ejtema'i* [Social Sciences], textbook for fourth grade in high schools (1986/87 edition), pp. 120–5.
39. Tehran TV, 19 May 1997 [DR].
40. Radio Tehran, 20 December 1996 (DR).
41. Speech before the Near East Institute, 20 May 1993, by Martin Indyk,

Publications of the Center for Security Policy, no. 93–D 41 (Attachment), 21 May 1993.

42. IRNA, 30 May 1993 [DR].
43. Tehran TV, 24 August 1996 [DR]. For the US sanctions, see Kenneth Katzman, *US–Iranian Relations: An Analytic Compendium of US Policies, Laws and Regulations* (Washington, DC: Atlantic Council of the United States, 1999), pp. 37–119.
44. IRNA, 11 March – DR, 12 March 1996.
45. Interview with Rafsanjani in *Der Spiegel*, 14 October 1996 – DR, 17 October 1996.
46. IRNA, 11 March 1996 – DR, 12 March 1996.
47. Middle East Broadcast Corporation (MBC) TV, 22 December 1996 – [DR].
48. *Al-Majallah*, 8–14 December 1996 – DR, 12 December 1996; IRNA, 26 December 1996 – DR, 30 December 1996.
49. *Middle East Insight*, 13/1 (November–December 1997), p. 35.
50. *Middle East Policy*, 3/3 (1994), p. 125.
51. *Kayhan* (Tehran), 14 May 1983.
52. See his statements in *Jomhuri-ye Islami*, 19 July 1984; *The Guardian*, 9 September 1985; *Kayhan-e Hava'i*, 19 February 1986 and 30 April 1986.
53. *Kayhan-e Hava'i*, 30 April 1986.
54. See, for example, a Friday sermon by Rafsanjani, Radio Tehran, 25 November 1988 – SWB, 28 November 1988 and his letter to President Carter in November 1988, Radio Tehran, 28 November 1988 – SWB, 30 November 1988.
55. Radio Tehran, 17 December 1988 – SWB, 20 December 1988.
56. Radio Tehran, 14 October 1988 – SWB, 17 October 1988.
57. IRNA, 21 November 1988 – SWB, 24 November 1988.
58. *Ettela'at*, 26 April 1990.
59. *Al-Majallah*, 6 November 1994.
60. *Iran*, 16 August 1997 [DR]. See also IRNA, 16 August 1997 [DR].
61. *Salam*, 15 September 1993 – DR, 1 October; *Iran Times*, 5 November 1993.
62. *Kayhan International*, 2 November; *al-Safir*, 29 November; DR, 14 December 1993.
63. *Tehran Times*, 20 January 1993; *New York Times*, 21 January 1993.
64. *Tehran Times*, 13 January 1993 – DR, 21 January 1993.
65. *Kayhan* (Tehran), 29 April 1990. Yet, in 1997, Mohtashami supported Khatami, who has since appointed Mohajerani a minister.
66. *Jahan-e Islam*, 19 October 1993 – DR, 10 November 1993.
67. *Jahan-e Islam*, 19 October 1993 – DR, 10 November 1993. See also statements by Mohtashami in *Ettela'at*, 4 November 1993; *Jahan-e Islam*, 3 November 1993 – DR, 19 November 1993; *Iran Times*, 5 November 1993; AFP, 2 November 1993 – DR, 3 November 1993; *Kayhan* (London), 11 November 1993.
68. *Salam*, 28 and 30 October 1993.
69. *Ettela'at*, 20 November 1993.
70. *Ettela'at*, 9 October; *Iran Times*, 15 October 1993.
71. *Kayhan* (Tehran), 1 February 1993 – DR, 12 February 1993. Ibid., 28 January 1993 – DR, 10 February 1993.
72. *Salam*, 27 July 1994.
73. *Jahan-e Islam*, 19 October 1993 – DR, 10 November 1993.

74. *Resalat*, 4 November 1992 – *DR*, 20 November 1992.
75. *Echo of Iran*, no. 61 (February 1993), p. 12 and no. 62 (March 1993), pp. 8, 11.
76. *Jomhuri-ye Islami*, 1 May 1990, wrote that three of his close associates disclosed that they were asked by Rafsanjani to express his displeasure at the publication of the article.
77. IRNA, 5 May 1989 – DR, 5 May 1989.
78. Radio Tehran, 4 November 1994 – DR, 7 November 1994.
79. Interview with Khatami's on CNN, in Tehran TV, 8 January 1998 [DR].
80. Neal Sher, *Comprehensive US Sanctions Against Iran: A Plan for Action* (Washington, DC: AIPAC, 1995), pp. 27–8; 'Ban on Trade and Investment with Iran', Robert Pelletreau, Statement before the House International Relations Committee, Subcommittee on International Economic Policy and Trade, Washington, DC, 2 May 1995 (Internet database): Economic Intelligence Unit, *Country Profile – Iran*, First Quarter, 1995, pp. 3, 18.
81. Tehran TV, 9 May 1995 – DR, 16 May 1995.
82. *The Economist*, 25 February 1995.
83. *New York Times*, 29 March 1995.
84. Sher, *Comprehensive US Sanctions Against Iran,* p. 16.
85. Pelletreau, Statement before the House International Relations Committee, Subcommittee on International Economic Policy and Trade, Washington, DC, 2 May 1995 (Internet database).
86. Statement by Peter Tarnoff, before the House International Relations Committee, Washington, DC, 9 November 1995 (Internet database).
87. Pelletreau, at the Council on Foreign Relations, New York, 8 May 1996 (Internet database).
88. Ibid.
89. Ellen Laipson *et al.*, 'US Policy Toward Iran: From Containment to Relentless Pursuit', *Middle East Policy*, 4/1–2 (1995), p. 2.
90. Economic Intelligence Unit, *Country Report – Iran*, First Quarter 1999, p. 8; Second Quarter 1995, pp. 4, 15.
91. Tehran TV, 9 May 1995 – DR, 16 May 1995. See also Gary Sick, 'A Sensitive Policy Toward Iran', *Middle East Insight*, 11/5 (July–August 1995), pp. 21–2.
92. Radio Monte Carlo, 5 May 1995 – DR, 8 May 1995.
93. Radio Tehran, 26 July 1995 – DR, 27 July 1995.
94. IRNA, 27 July 1995 – DR, 27 July 1995.
95. *Jomhuri-ye Islami*, 3 May 1995.
96. *International Herald Tribune*, 17 May 1995.
97. Edward P. Djerejian, 'The Prospects for US–Iranian Relations', *Middle East Insight* 11/5 (July–August 1995), pp. 4–5.
98. Sick, 'A Sensitive Policy Toward Iran', pp. 21–2; and 'Iran is Ripe for a Peaceful Overture', *Los Angeles Times*, 17 November 1994.
99. Sick, *Los Angeles Times*, 17 November 1994.
100. *Los Angeles Times*, 2 May 1995.
101. Remarks by Japanese Prime Minister Tomiichi Murayama, *Middle East Economic Digest*, 27 January 1995; *Los Angeles Times*, 15 February 1995; *The Economist*, 25 February 1995. See also Clawson, *Business as Usual?*, p. 35.

102. Kazuo Takahashi, an expert on the Middle East, quoted in Clawson, *Business as Usual?*, p. 35.
103. *Financial Times*, 30 April 1994; Clawson, *Business as Usual?*, p. 30.
104. Rome ANSA (Ansamail database version), 10 April 1997 [DR].
105. Agence France Presse (AFP), 17 April 1997 [DR]; IRNA, 22 April 1997 [DR]; *Mideast Mirror*, 15 May 1997.
106. *Frankfurter Rundschau*, 14 May 1997; IRNA, 10 April 1997 [DR].
107. IRNA, 13 April 1997 [DR].
108. Message on the occasion of the Iranian New Year, *International Herald Tribune*, *The Times*, 22 March 1980.
109. *Ettela'at*, 9 January 1989; Radio Tehran, 8 January 1989 – SWB, 10 January 1989. See also Habibollah Abul-Hasan Shirazi, *Melliyatha-ye Asya-ye Miyaneh* [The Peoples of Central Asia] (Tehran: Daftar-e Motala'at-e Siyasi va Beynol-Mellali, 1991–92), pp. 321–3.
110. See Roundtable discussion in the new Iranian quarterly, *Discourse*, 1/1 (Summer 1999), p. 6.
111. Galia Golan, *Russia and Iran: A Strategic Partnership* (Discussion Paper no. 75; London: Royal Institute of International Affairs 1998), pp. 2–5.
112. Ibid., p. 53.
113. *Tehran Times*, 22 February 1993.
114. See announcement to that effect by Rafsanjani to the Japanese Ambassador in Tehran in *Kayhan* (Tehran), 15 September 1982. See also statements by Nabavi and Velayati to an economic mission from Japan, ibid., 1 November 1982 and *Ettela'at*, 2 November 1982, and by Musavi and Khamene'i at a press conference in *Kayhan* (Tehran), 4 and 9 November 1982.
115. Khatami, *Zamineha-ye Khizesh-e Mashruteh*, pp. 125–8; Nuri, *Showkaran-e Eslah*, p. 270.
116. See Menashri, *Education and the Making of Modern Iran*, pp. 42–3.
117. Radio Tehran, 7 March 1982 – DR, 8 March 1982; *Kayhan* (Tehran), 4 November 1982.
118. Plamen Tonchev, 'China and Iran: A New Tandem in World Energy Security', *The Iranian Journal of International Affairs*, 10/4 (Winter 1998/9), p. 485–94.
119. The Iranian monthly *Me'yar* (July–August 1995) wrote that many high school students deride the values of Islam and the revolution while expressing admiration for the symbols (e.g., movies, music, T-shirts) of Western culture.
120. Khatami, *Bim-e Mowj*, pp. 52, 172.
121. Khatami, *Hope and Challenge*, pp. 1, 19. See also his *Mutala'at*, pp. 21–2 and *Bim-e Mowj*, pp. 176–7.
122. *Middle East Insight*, 13/1 (November–December 1997), pp. 28, 32.
123. Khatami, *Bim-e Mowj*, pp. 185–91.
124. Khatami, *Mutala'at*, pp. 121, 139.
125. Khatami, *Hope and Challenge*, pp. 1, 19; *Mutala'at*, pp. 21–2.
126. Khatami, *Az Donya-ye 'Shahr'*, pp. 14–15.
127. Khatami, *Mutala'at*, pp. 41–2, 79; *Bim-e Mowj*, pp. 112, 176–7.
128. Tehran TV, 20 May 1997 [DR].
129. Tehran TV, 10 May 1997 [DR].
130. *Middle East Insight*, 13/1 (November–December 1997), p. 32.
131. Vakili, *Debating Religion and Politics*, pp. 39–41.

132. *Hamshahri*, 15 November 1998 [DR].
133. Shabestari, 'Islam va Masihiyat-e Orupa'i', pp. 409–15.
134. Shabestari, *Din Modara va-Khoshunat*, pp. 6–19.
135. *Iran News*, 5 August 1997 [DR].
136. IRNA, 9 December 1997.
137. IRNA, 14 December 1997.
138. Interview with Khatami by CNN, on Tehran TV, 8 January 1998 [DR].
139. IRNA, 23 December 1997 [DR].
140. See comments in *Salam* on 27 January and on 2, 25, and 28 February 1998.
141. *Salam*, 3 January and 2 February 1998.
142. *Salam*, 17 January 1998.
143. *Salam*, 28 December 1998.
144. *Jame'eh*, 28 June 1998. For harsh criticism of such statements see *Kayhan* (Tehran), 29 June 1998 (commentary titled 'More American Than the Americans'); *Jomhuri-ye Islami*, 1 July 1998 and *Salam*, 28 December 1998.
145. IRNA, 4 May 1999; *Salam, Kayhan* (Tehran), *Jomhuri-ye Islami* and *Neshat*, 4 May; *Jehan-e Islami*, 5 May 1999.
146. *Iran News*, 6 May 1999, quoting *Jahan-e Islam* [DR]. See also, *Jomhuri-ye Islami*, 4 May 1999. Karubi's statement as well as his subsequent clarifications were harshly criticized by the conservatives. *Resalat* on 5 May 1999, quoted his firm position in the past (when he served as Majlis Speaker), against relations with the United States to contradict them with his newly formed positions.
147. Nuri, *Showkaran-e Eslah*, pp. 129–36.
148. *Iran* and *Neshat*, 9 May 1999.
149. *Iran*, 15 May 1999.
150. *Jame'eh*, 27 June 1998.
151. *Ettela'at*, 18 April 1999. Israel, he added, is the exception to this rule, since its very existence is illegal.
152. Tehran TV, 15 January 1998 [DR].
153. IRNA, 27 May 1997 [DR].
154. Tehran TV, 4 November 1997 [DR].
155. IRNA, 9 December 1997.
156. Tehran TV, 18 May 1997 [DR].
157. *Kayhan* (Tehran) 16 February; *Iran News*, 17 February 1998.
158. *Jomhuri-ye Islami*, 4 April 1999.
159. *Jomhuri-ye Islami*, 10, 11, 17 January 1998.
160. *Iran News* , 8, 23 August 1997 [DR].
161. See *Kayhan* (Tehran), 30 December 1997, and 4, 8, 10, 11, 17 January 1998; *Resalat*, 11, 17 January 1998; and *Jomhur-ye Islami*, 10, 11, 17 January, 2 February 1998.
162. *Resalat*, 11 January 1998 [DR].
163. *Wall Street Journal*, 26 May 1997. See also statement by US State Department spokesman, James Rubin cited in IRNA, 21 August 1997 [DR].
164. IRNA, 21 August 1997 [DR].
165. *Kayhan* (Tehran), 17 December 1997 [DR].
166. US Government, State Department, *Patterns of Global Terrorism: 1998*.
167. Martin S. Indyk, at the Middle East Insight, College of William and Mary

Conference Williamsburg, VA, 12 November 1997 (Internet database).

168. Martin Indyk, Testimony before the Senate Subcommittee on Near East and South Asia Foreign Relations Committee, Washington, DC, 14 May 1998 (Internet database).

169. Bruce O. Riedel, Special Assistant to the President and Senior Director, Near East and South Asian Affairs, National Security Council. Remarks at the Washington Institute for Near East Policy, Washington, DC, 6 May 1998 (Internet database).

170. US Department of State, Office of the Spokesman, Press Statement, 17 June 1998.

171. US Department of State, daily press briefing, 18 June 1998.

172. *Jomhuri-ye Islami*, 20 June 1998; *Resalat*, 20 and 27 June 1998.

173. *Jame'eh*, 20 and 27 June 1998.

174. The White House, Office of the Press Secretary, 12 April 1999 (Internet database).

175. *Jomhuri-ye Islami*, 18 April 1999.

176. *Jomhuri-ye Islami*, 19 April 1999.

177. *Jomhuri-ye Islami*, 31 July 1994.

178. *Tehran Times*, 12 July 1994 – DR, 15 July 1994.

179. *Kayhan* (Tehran), 14 December 1997.

180. Khatami's interview with CNN correspondent Christiane Amanpour, on Tehran TV, 8 January 1998 [DR].

181. M. Eisenstadt, 'The Military Dimension', in Clawson, *Iran Under Khatami*, pp. 78–86.

182. Khatami's interview by CNN correspondent Christiane Amanpour, ibid.

183. A group of 13 US graduate students from the American Institute of Iranian Studies had been asked by Washington to hurriedly leave Iran in 1999. US officials confirmed the fact but did not provide details or the circumstances of their departure. See statement by James Rubin, US Department of State, daily press briefing, 13 September 1999 (Internet database).

184. *Iran News*, 12 September 1999 [Gulf2000]. Although such messages were not necessarily friendly, their very exchange was in itself important.

185. IRNA, 13 September 1999 (Internet database).

186. US Department of State, daily press briefing, 13 September 1999 (Internet database).

187. See article by Daryush Sajjadi in *Iran News*, 8 January 1998 [DR].

7

Iran and its Troubled Neighborhood

THE TRIUMPH OF NATIONAL INTERESTS

The Islamic regime viewed its victory as a stage in, and an instrument of, an overall change in the world of Islam – a model for imitation by other Muslims. 'Our movement is for an Islamic goal, not for Iran alone', Khomeini said upon taking power. Iran was only 'the starting point'. Muslims 'are one family', he added, 'even if they live in regions remote from each other'. This is 'the important and basic point, this is the strategy'.[1] Furthermore, even being Shi'i or Sunni 'is not the question'.[2] Carried on the wave of their dramatic victory, Khomeini and his disciples firmly expected a chain reaction in all Muslim societies. One of Khomeini's Paris aides told an Arab correspondent early in 1979: 'Be patient . . . we will both see the fate of Saudi rulers six months after our return to Iran.'[3] In this realm, too, the sobering realities of some 21 years in power forced a significant departure from the professed revolutionary creed in favor of more pragmatic – and national – considerations.

As long as he headed an opposition movement, Khomeini had depicted a 'new Iran' modeled on an Islamic design. Once in power, he – and even more so his disciples after him – realized they could not rule by means of revolutionary slogans alone. Thus, although national considerations were alien to Khomeini's general principles and theory of foreign relations, as they were formulated mainly in the 1970s, his regime nonetheless chose to conduct its regional policy primarily from a standpoint of Iran's national interests. How does Iran's assertion that there was no difference between Muslims – either in ethnic or in sectarian affiliation – accord with the article of the 1979 constitution laying down that only a Shi'i of Iranian origin can hold office as president?[4] How can one reconcile the abhorrence of national divisions within the world of Islam with the insistence that the Gulf must be called Persian?[5] Evidently, Khomeini did not exclude close relations with

Arab nationalist and Ba'thist Syria, which in fact has turned into Iran's main regional ally.

Khomeini was in fact in an awkward position from his very first days in power. His basic ideological creed prescribed full national independence and detachment from both world blocs. Yet, given the international realities and the country's needs, Iran could not totally detach itself from the outside world. Similarly, as head of state Khomeini could not 'disavow the idea of the nation-state', but as an Islamic leader he could not 'make his commitment to the national idea too strong or his commitment to the *ummah* ('community of believers') too weak'.[6] In fact, 'in so far as Khomeini chose to emphasize a purely Shi'i ideology, he alienated the Sunni Muslim world, in so far as he emphasized a universal language, he weakened the appeal of his vision to Iranian Shi'ites'.[7] Thus, in reality, while revolutionary and Islamic intent prescribed the new regime's general outward approach, actual realities often encouraged greater expediency and an emphasis 'on reasons of the state' as against a striving for the 'ideological crusade'.[8] Like other revolutionary movements in history, 'once having acceded to power', the leaders of Iran had 'to reconcile their revolutionary aspirations with the demands of statecraft'.[9] Eventually, 'the primary political arena, even for avowed Islamic "internationalists" who take over governments, soon becomes the existing nation-state'.[10]

In exile, Khomeini seemed to disregard the national, sectarian and ethnic differences that existed within the Islamic community of believers, as well as the fact that Shi'is were only a small minority within it. This new policy represented a clear deviation from his own earlier thought, as well as from the politics of his regime following his takeover.

In his book *Kashf al-Asrar* (Unveiling of the Secrets), written in the early 1940s, Khomeini still provided a cautious defense of Iranian nationalism. While maintaining that modern states are the 'products of man's limited ideals', and stressing that Islam intended to 'remove the borders' between states to create 'one general state' (*yek keshvar-e hamegani*),[11] this utopian vision hardly amounted to categorical denunciation of the nation-state.[12] At this stage, Khomeini even used some patriotic terminology, as when addressing his readers as 'dear compatriots' (*ham-mihanan*), 'young lovers of Iran' (*Irandust*) and 'Iranians who desire glory'.[13] *Kashf al-Asrar* also attests to the Shi'is' hostililty to Sunnis and their feeling of superiority. He denounced the Umayyad and 'Abbasid dynasties as the worst (*badtarin*) and most usurpatory (*zalemanetarin*) of regimes and accused their caliphs of killing the Shi'i Imams.[14] Such particular Iranian Shi'i views, expressed by Khomeini well into the 1960s, were in keeping with the attitudes then current among the mainstream Iranian *'ulama'*.

By contrast, from the late 1960s Khomeini expressed more ecumenical views. The concept of nationalism became alien to him, and he viewed it as a Western 'imperialist plot' to divide and weaken Islam. Nationalism, he then claimed, was no better than tribal solidarity (*'asabiyya*).[15] Khomeini further deplored the fact that the Muslim world, in a futile attempt to cure its ills, had embraced such alien ideologies as pan-Arabism, pan-Turkism and nationalism. He accused the imperialists of dividing the Islamic *umma* and 'artificially creating separate nations', and then each of these states 'was entrusted to one of their servants'. He called for the 'unity of the Islamic *umma*' and demanded the establishment of a single Islamic government 'to preserve the disciplined unity of the Muslims'.[16] Yet despite this and while the anti-imperialist rhetoric was beyond question, it is not clear whether he wished, in fact, to reverse history.

Khomeini's views on nationalism did not win much support at the time among leading Iranian *'ulama'*, especially those of the rank of *Ayatollah 'uzma* (grand ayatollahs). As in many other fields, the greatest ideological challenge at this stage in Khomeini's career was posed by Shari'atmadari. His point of departure was Iranian, and his views lacked pan-Islamic motifs. He seemed to regard Shi'i Islam as the cohesive element of Iranian nationalism and the main instrument in strengthening the country's national unity and sovereignty.[17] Shari'atmadari's views were closer to those espoused by centrist political parties than to those advocated by Khomeini. Thus, nationalism was an ideal for the National Front, which viewed the Islamic Revolution as a movement of national revival, and regarded Islam as an important instrument for forging Iranian nationalism.[18] One of their main slogans was: 'The entrenchment of national sovereignty is the goal of the National Front.' The Iranian people, the Front argued, had 'an Iranian national identity' as well as an Islamic identity.[19] Islam and nationalism were 'two sides of the same coin', complementary rather than contradictory.

Upon the coming to power of the new regime, however, it was Khomeini's doctrine that dictated the general goals. Yet, while the regime had striven to spread the message of the Islamic Revolution beyond Iran's borders, the priority and the means to achieve this goal have changed considerably over time and have had different meanings for various domestic trends. In a 1980 message to *hajj* pilgrims Khomeini stated: 'I extend my hand of friendship to all committed Muslims of the world and ask them to regard Shi'is as their dear brothers.'[20]

Ayatollah 'Ali Meshkini (the imam jum'ah of Qom) even said, in 1982, that the goal of the revolution was 'to impose the Qur'an over the entire world'.[21] A textbook used at Iran's high school typically enumerates 'the main principles' of Iran's all-Islamic policy. These include 'preparing the ground for the formation of a unified worldwide Islamic nation, through preservation and expansion of Islamic culture', striving to save people who are deprived (*mahrum*) and who suffer injustice (*taht-e setam*) throughout the world, and fighting 'world arrogance'.[22] The same general philosophy is also manifest in the 1979 constitution, which demonstrates the difficulty of its implementation. According to it, 'all Muslims' are 'one nation' and the government must exert 'continuous effort' to realize 'the political, economic, and cultural unity of the Islamic world' (Article 11). Yet the constitution also makes 'safeguarding of the independence and integrity of the Iranian territory' the basis of Iran's foreign policy (Article 152). Again, such general statements of brotherhood and fraternity were usually phrased in general terms, mainly to express a utopian vision and the religious and cultural bonds between Muslims, but lacked an operative and programmatic scheme.

Generally speaking, whatever radical expressions regarding the 'export' of the revolution were voiced in moments of enthusiasm in the early days of the revolution, were toned down over time. The course of history, Khomeini stressed in 1983, made the spread of the revolutionary creed inevitable and irreversible. Yet Iran need not 'worm its way' into other countries, rather it should walk in 'like an invited guest'.[23] Until that happened, it was Iran's primary duty to spread the word of Islamic ideology and to make the country's 'new realities' known, so as to encourage it being 'invited'.[24] President Khamene'i affirmed in 1984 that we 'will not give direct aid to [Muslim] movements . . . to help them or to force them to change their regimes. The Islamic Republic has a policy of not supporting such acts, and whatever is said about us to the contrary in this regard is untrue.'[25] The idea was to encourage the 'import' of the revolution, rather than actually 'exporting' it. Thus, prime Minister Mir-Hosein Musavi declared in 1984: 'We do not want to export armed revolution to any country. . . . Our aim is to promote the Islamic Revolution through persuasion.'[26] In 1985, he made an even more sober assessment:

> [Initially] our view regarding exporting the revolution was that the Islamic Revolution would spread within a year as a chain reaction. This idea is not altogether unrealistic in the long-run. But it seems that we were wrong in our initial assessments with regard to the fast spread of the revolution.[27]

Over time, thus, the plea for unity made room for vaguer appeals for brotherhood (*baradari*), 'unity of the word' (*vahdat-e kalam*) and 'unity of purpose' (*vahdat-e hadaf*). Khomeini called for solidarity, appealed to Muslims to 'avoid divisions' and preached for 'empathy with one another'. But he stopped short of demanding unity. On a more realistic note, President Rafsanjani, while acknowledging Islam's 'great potential', observed that the current divisiveness within the Muslim world 'is not that good'. He regretted that even within the Organization of Petroleum Exporting Countries (OPEC), where most members were Muslim, 'it is very difficult' to agree on appropriate policies. Similarly, owing to obstacles 'from within', the ICO could not 'resolve the problems facing its members'.[28] Clearly, over time the pragmatic–national interests of Iran triumphed over the ideological creed. In reality, thus, the Islamic regime gradually chose to act towards the neighboring Muslim world from the standpoint of Iran's national interest.

In fact, the concept of territorial nationalism is relatively new in the Middle East. Yet, in the twentieth century, as Majid Khadduri has suggested, after Islam, territorial nationalism despite 'Islam's tacit or expressed disapproval', 'dominated the minds of the Arabs to a greater extent than any other ideology'.[29] The case of Iran, however, long independent and a Shi'i state since the Safavid period, was somewhat different. Eventually, the adoption of Shi'ism in Iran led to the separation of the Sunni and Shi'i worlds on a territorial basis, making it easier for Iranian Shi'ism 'to become associated with [Iranian] nationalism, or rather to become the vehicle for the expression of nationalist sentiments'.[30] Moreover, in Iran, Shi'ism 'was lifted out of its purely Islamic context and merged with the Iranian historical tradition'. It offered 'a way of expression to this nationality' and 'the Persian idea was reincarnated in religious form'.[31]

Moreover, being Shi'i by faith (as against the predominantly Sunni neighboring states), and Persian in language and culture (as against the predominantly Arabic cultures of the Middle East), fostered the unique national character of Iran as a separate entity in the region. Khomeini 'in developing an ideology which sees the world in terms of an apocalyptic struggle between the forces of good and evil', has in many ways 'gone beyond traditional Ithna Ashari messianism'.[32]

In power, however, a greater balance was sought by the Islamic regime. The general direction was one of movement towards a national identity, although one not unrelated to Iran's firm Islamic convictions. In fact, as Cottam has observed, the 'nationalism of much of the liberal constitutional element [in Iran] was inextricably interwoven with devotion to Islam'.[33] Iran is a country 'with a basic tension between the national and religious poles of its culture', observes Hunter, 'politics based on either purely nationalist or purely religious premise have triggered popular reaction'. Religion and nationalism, thus, 'have always interacted in Iran and have shaped its national identity and character and, to varying degrees, its international behavior'.[34]

While in power, thus, the ecumenical assertions typical of opposition were gradually toned down. True, Iran continued to attribute Middle Eastern nationalism to imperialists' fear of Islam and to their attempt 'to prevent the emergence of one Islamic *umma*, based on Islamic culture'. Similarly its leadership maintained that Islam was intended for all nations, not for any particular people (*mellat*), race (*nezhad*), nation (*qowm*) or territory (*sarzemin*) and resolutely rejected 'any divisions – cultural, political, racist, economic, geographical' within the domain of the Islamic *umma*.[35] Yet nationalism, once viewed as a heresy by the Islamic Revolution, gradually re-emerged as an important ideal. No wonder then that during the war with Iraq Khomeini himself often used patriotic terminology, combined with typical Islamic pleas, while appealing to the Iranian people. Thus, a week after the war started Khomeini stressed that 'the honor and the glory of the *mihan* (homeland) and *din* (faith) are dependent on the war' and he vowed to 'fight the attackers of our beloved homeland (*mihan-e 'aziz*) until death'.[36] Not only are national poets (such as Ferdowsi, the author of the national epic *Shahnameh*) being taught in schools in Islamic Iran, but Iranian school textbooks under the Islamic Republic use unusually patriotic language in fostering pupils' national loyalties. One example is the following passage in an elementary school textbook. Under the title 'Love of Iran' (*Iran dusti*) it says:

> Iran is my home, Iran is the home of my brethren and sisters, the home of my fathers, my mothers and my ancestors. Iran is my great and precious home. Cherished Iran is my homeland. I love my country [*keshvar*]. . . . I love Iran and the free nation [*mellat*] of Iran with yearning and faith [*iman*]. . . . I study well so that when I grow older I can strive in the path of Iran and Iranians' advancement and progress and so that I can get to know better the ways to assist my compatriots. . . . Should it one day happen that Iran is in danger, what would my life be worth compared to it? At that time, I will defend my homeland like the 'victorious holy fighters' [*mojahedan-e piruz*]. That time I will repel the enemy, [leaving him] frustrated and defeated. I will devote myself to the assistance of my free nation. I will chose martyrdom [*shehadat*] for the sake of protecting the glory and the independence of my country and will give away my life wholeheartedly.[37]

Under the title 'O Iran, O the Land of the Fearless' (*sarzemin-e dali-ran*), another story in the fifth-grade textbook similarly combined national and Islamic motifs and vowed to defend Iran against all foes and conspiracies.[38]

In fact, an analysis of Iran's regional policies demonstrates the degree to which the regime's actual politics have been primarily shaped by pragmatic, national interests, rather than ideological, Islamic convictions.

This was clearly evident in Iran's lack of support for the Shi'i uprising in southern Iraq in 1991. Because of the rebels' sectarian–Shi'i affinity with Iran, their struggle against Saddam Husayn and the Ba'th regime (which Iran vehemently opposed) their attempts to form an Islamic republic, their anti-US attitude and their pleas for the *mostaz'afin*, the Shi'is of Iraq deserved Iranian support. Yet Tehran did not come unequivocally and substantially to their aid, and with good reason: it feared that they would ultimately fail and that Iran's support would harm its own interests – a clear sign of a preference for national interests over pure dogma. Thus, while deploring the suppression of the Shi'is in Iraq,[39] Iran preferred to view the events there as an exclusively internal Iraqi issue. Stressing the policy of expediency, Khamene'i, while wishing that 'an Islamic and truly popular government . . . will come to power [there],' maintained that Iranian intervention was 'not recommended'.[40] Prominent revolutionary figures, such as Mehdi Karubi, 'Abdul-Karim Musavi Ardabili and Mohammad Yazdi, also maintained that the future of Iraq should be determined by its own people alone.[41]

Iraqi Kurds – who were waging their own struggle against Baghdad and expecting to benefit from Iranian support – seemed to have a better chance of success. Yet Tehran had no incentive to help them realize their aims, fearing the 'negative influence' such success might have on its own Kurdish minority. The pragmatic interests of the state seemed more powerful than the dogmatic philosophy of the revolution – yet another clear sign of realpolitik. Later, in the struggle that evolved during August–September 1996 on the Iraqi Kurdish front, Tehran sided with the Patriotic Union of Kurdistan, led by Jalal Talabani, against the Barzani faction, which was supported by Iraq. From the Iranian perspective, there seems to be no ideological preference for the Talabani faction. In fact, the more tribal and traditional Barzanis may be closer to the Iranian doctrine than the Talabanis, with their more liberal pretensions. But the latter reside closer to Iranian territory and were willing to cooperate with Tehran – and, among other things, to contain their own brethren, the Iranian Kurdistan Democratic Party (KDP), in their bases inside Iraq.[42] The interplay between the Islamic regime and the Kurds – in Iran as well as in Iraq – was also based more on politics and national interests than on pure dogma.

Nor did Iran's policy *vis-à-vis* its Afghan neighbors show any marked ideological purity. Zalmay Khalilzad, writing about the first decade of the revolution, observed that 'the ideological factor' was 'insufficient as a guide for understanding Iran's Afghan policy'. More than 'Islamic internationalism it was Shi'i internationalism that has played an important role' in shaping Iran's policy there. Yet being Shi'i in itself 'was not sufficient to gain Iranian support'. Iran's strategic interests, Khalilzad observed, led it to 'follow a cautious policy designed to avoid a direct confrontation with the Soviet Union and pro-Soviet Afghan forces'.[43] This cautious and nationalistic approach has also been visible following the takeover by the Taliban in Afghanistan in 1996. On the face of it, the Taliban were ideologically closer to Iran than Rabbani: i.e., in their adamant opposition to the West and their support for strict Islamization. Yet, Iran blamed the Taliban for being under the influence of Pakistan and was engaged in fierce conflict with them.

Similarly, in dealing with the Muslim republics of the former Soviet Union, the main focus lay in expanding Iranian interests rather than winning souls and promoting the ideological creed. In line with its national interests, Iran was careful not to antagonize Moscow and to maintain good relations with the governments of the different republics. The fact that none of their leaders was an ideal Islamic ruler, and that they maintained close ties with Turkey, the United States and even with Israel, did not prevent close ties. This was very clear, for example, in Rafsanjani's tour to five of these republics in 1993 and 'the relative paucity of anything to do with Islam' as one of the main 'curiosities' of the president's trip.[44] (See also below.) Moreover, the drive to expand Iran's ideological influence in these republics was most visible in Tajikistan, the country closest to Iran culturally; Iran's most problematic relations emerged with Azerbaijan, the only Shi'i republic among them.[45] Iran's own large Azeri population was another significant consideration, for an independent Azeri republic across the border might have stimulated similar aspirations among Iranian Azeris who in the past had sought, and briefly enjoyed, autonomy. The Azeri nationalist vision of a 'greater Azerbaijan' held by some Azeri groups (north and south of the border) added to Iranian concerns, as did its worry that the opening of the borders would lead to population movements, mainly of Azeri refugees into Iran.[46] Needless to say, the 'inflammatory statements' by the president of Azerbaijan, Abulfaz Elchibey, regarding 'southern' Azerbaijan and his country's close relations with Turkey infuriated the Iranians. As early as his election (June 1992) Iran lashed out at Elchibey for his hostile stance against Iran, recalling his demands for the unification of the two Azerbaijans and his more 'recent irresponsible remarks'.[47] Here, too, Iran was primarily concerned with national and strategic interests rather than with any religious affinity or ideological convictions.

The Iranian approach to the Azeri-Armenian crisis best illustrates Iran's self-interested national attitude. While Iran officially adopted a neutral position and engaged in mediation, its policy was seen as amply pro-Armenian. Eventually, Iran served as an important supply route to Christian Armenia which was in direct conflict with Shi'i Azerbaijan.[48] The ensuing tension between Iran and Azerbaijan became visible during Foreign Minister Velayati's visit to Baku in March 1996, which ended in a tense press conference filled with mutual recriminations between Velayati and the Azeri foreign minister Hasan Hasanov.[49]

While in the Nagorno–Karabakh conflict Iran sought to mediate with a view to preventing instability, it already took a more active initiative in distant Bosnia in the early 1990s. But even in this regard, some Iranians warned that Islamic military support for the Muslims in Bosnia might backfire and harm the interests of Iran and the Muslims. Thus one citizen challenged Rafsanjani's call in November 1995 to support the Muslims of Bosnia on economic grounds. Such support, he noted, might have been appropriate had Iran enjoyed at least a minimum degree of welfare itself. How could one think of offering such help, he queried, when Iran could not supply its own children with even the most essential needs.[50]

The NATO attack on Kosovo, in 1999, essentially serving the interests of Kosovar Muslims posed a serious dilemma for Iran which found it difficult to applaud the move by NATO (and led by the United States), but was unable to oppose it. The result – much like Iranian policy *vis-à-vis* the 1991 American attack on Iraq – was ambivalence.

Because of its self-image as the leader of the Islamic front Iran saw it as its sacred mission to protect the rights of Muslim Kosovars. Iran sent food, medicine and shelter to Kosovar refugees in Albania and Macedonia, and established a clinic for refugees in Tirana. There were also reports that Iran had provided the Kosovo Liberation Army (KLA) with military aid. Yet Iran did not trust NATO as a peacemaker. Evidently Iranian policy was fuelled by its obligation to aid fellow Muslims, but was constrained by its antagonism towards the West and,

more specifically, the United States.[51] Thus Iran called on the UN
Security Council to intervene and issue a resolution to end the crisis.[52]
Khamene'i added that the objective of NATO attacks, contrary to what
was claimed, was a war between two power-hungry forces, the United
States and its allies against Yugoslavia, and was not intended to defend
the Muslims.[53] Challenged by such contradictions in Iranian foreign
policy, Kharrazi maintained that his country's policies were 'quite
fundamental and we see no contradiction in them, not at all'. He added,
revealingly, that the 'approach which we have adopted is very logical,
reasonable and consistent with the circumstances'.[54]

Similarly, the improved atmosphere in Iran's relations with Russia led
to less pronounced Iranian emphasis on the struggle in which Muslims
in Chechnya were engaged with Russia. Thus a reader of *Salam* observed that, while Tehran had often lauded Chechen Muslims' struggle
for independence, the signing of the agreement with Moscow (in
January 1995) over the Bushehr nuclear plant had allowed even the
killing (in April 1996) of Johar Dudayev (president of Chechnya) to go
unnoticed by the Iranian media. Iranian policy, the reader went on,
could be described as baseless, or unprincipled policy (*siyasat-e
napayedar*), a bad policy (*siyasat-e bad*) or, in the words of the Persian
phrase, *'nun ra be nerkh-e ruz khordan'* – a policy which fluctuates daily
with the change of interests.[55]

The Iranian move in 1992 to ascertain its sovereignty over the three
islands in the Hormuz straits – Abu Musa, and the Greater and Lesser
Tunbs – also confirmed that Iran's policy was motivated in the main by
realism and was more faithful to its national interests, rather than to its
professed dogmatic creed. Clearly, Iran wished to control the islands not
as a means to advance any ideological creed, but to advance its strategic
interests. Tehran claimed at the time – using transparently patriotic
jargon – that the islands 'are integral parts' of Iran's territories.[56] Iran
based its claim to sovereignty over the islands 'on historical, legal and
geographical facts'.[57] Islamic dogma did not have much to do with such
Iranian claims, or its actual policy.

In many ways, therefore, 'Iran is moved by the same impulses that
move other states, and it uses the same rationalizations'.[58] Clearly, in
the pursuit of its ideological aims Iran over the first two decades of the
revolution often operated within the constraints of realpolitik. This
became still more visible following the election of President Khatami.
His accent on 'proper governance' and on 'interest' inescapably led to
even greater deviations from the line of dogma.

In fact, Khatami's program combined faith and state and stressed the need to form a rational policy to secure Iran's national interests. On the eve of the elections, when asked to identify 'the most important issue' in his program, he noted that there are 'so many complicated issues' that it would be difficult to say which is 'the most important'. However, 'if you press me to select the most important issue, I would say that the most tangible gains of our revolution are our independence, our national sovereignty, and our national interests'.[59] Consequently, as a Tehran University professor observed, under Khatami Iranian leaders have made 'conscious adjustments to the reality of regional politics'.[60] The *Tehran Times* noted that since Khatami took over 'a new atmosphere has been created' in Iran's relations with foreign countries. His policy of 'détente', his accent on 'mutual respect' and his plea for 'dialogue between civilizations' bore fruit 'almost immediately'. The newspaper went on to state that Iran's credibility at the international level also had improved and a 'real process of rapprochement' had developed in its relations with the outside world, particularly with its Arab neighbors.[61] True, whatever pragmatic statements were made by Khatami were 'balanced' by more ideological and hard-line expressions by other officials, including the Supreme Leader. It is not yet clear what actual results Khatami's policy will ultimately bear. However, the atmosphere in Iran's neighborhood has undoubtedly improved. Although pragmatic tendencies in Iranian policy have been conspicuous from the early days of the revolution, Khatami's election and the philosophy he pursues attest more than ever before to the supremacy of national interests over the ideology of the revolution.

THE GULF STATES AND THE ARAB WORLD

For revolutionary Iran, the most natural arena for expanding foreign ties was among neighboring Muslim states, particularly in the Persian Gulf. Yet historical animosity, cultural distinctiveness (Persians *vs.* Arabs, Turks, Afghans), sectarian differences (Shi'is *vs.* Sunnis), and ideological and political differences, as well as strategic and economic interests made it difficult to promote such goals. Certainly the fact that Iran and its neighbors shared the same faith did not create mutual trust and fraternity between them (as the war with Iraq showed). The heritage of the past and the conflicting interests of more recent times led to tension with most Arab countries. However, along with major policy changes in Iran and while basic disagreements were not resolved, there have been signs of improving ties with Iran's Arab neighbors in recent years.

The relations between Iran and its Arab neighbors in modern times have been often marked by competition and hostility – initially as part of the Ottoman Empire and later as independent states. More recently, the dispute over the Shatt al-Arab led to an open conflict with Iraq (earlier part of the Ottoman empire), and the competition for hegemony in the Gulf region soared relations with its most immediate Arab neighbors and their more distant Arab supporters (mainly Egypt under President Gamal 'Abdul-Nasser). Under the Islamic Repulblic Iran had a long war with Iraq (1980–88), in which most of the Arab states supported Iraq, and tense relations with most of the Arab world.

Iranian attitudes towards the Arabs have at times been tinged with a mixture of mistrust and suspicion at one end, and disregard and disdain at the other. Typically, as in Ferdowsi's national epic, the *Shahnameh*, Arabs are portrayed as inferior to the Iranians, living on 'camel's milk and lizards'.[62] More recently, in their search for the roots of Iran's weakness, some secular intellectuals in the late nineteenth century tended 'to place part of the blame' on Islam, and to establish 'a more authentic definition of Iranianness based on pre-Islamic past'. Thus, Fath'ali Akhundzadeh and Mirza Aqa Khan Kermani exalted ancient Achaemenid and Sasanid Iran 'whose glorious civilization was destroyed' by 'savage Bedouins'. Kermani even regarded Islam as 'an alien religion' forced upon the 'noble Aryan nation' by 'a handful of naked barefoot lizard-eaters, desert-dwelling nomads, savage Arabs', which had brought nothing but the ruin of Iranian civilization.[63] In his view, Islam only suits such a 'barbaric nation' as the Arabs; it is not for the Iranians, with such a proud and noble history behind them.[64] Akhundzadeh also blamed Islam as the prime cause of the backwardness of the Muslims. In his words, 'there is no nation more disgraceful and despised than the Arabs'.[65]

Later, in the twentieth century, Sadeq Hedayat hated religious institutions as 'something alien, as part of the evil resulting from the Arab conquest which suppressed true Iranian ideals'. His treatise, *Karavan-e Islam*, reveals such sentiments in a very derogatory style.[66] In his view, Arabs and Jews, Islam and Judaism, all belonged to the Semitic race and were essentially the same. Similar nationalist views can be found in the writings of intellectuals, such as Ahmad Kasravi, Sadeq Chubak and Nader Naderpur.[67]

In this realm too, there was a significant change in Iranian attitudes in the 1960s. While Iranian intellectuals since the late nineteenth century had generally supported Westernization and often expressed anti-Arab sentiments, neo-revolutionary intellectuals (like Al-e Ahmad and 'Ali Shari'ati) were anti-Western and pro-Islamic.[68] Yet even this basic approach did not reverse the deep-rooted hostility toward the Arabs among some Iranians.

Iran's Islamic tendencies had, in fact, a more particular Shi'i characteristic. Dorraj has maintained that, 'In pursuit of self-assertion, many Iranians reached deep within and revived their cultural identity' as Shi'is.[69] Imam 'Ali became Persianized, Iranian culture 'Ali-ized, and Imam 'Ali's Arab origins barely discussed.[70] Al-e Ahmad's desire to de-Arabize Shi'i Islam, added Saad, was motivated by deep anti-Arab prejudice, as was evident in his early writings. In his *Al-Gomarak va al-Makus* (Customs and Excise), published in 1949, he stressed their deceit, greed and crude language and his own discomfort in an inhospitable, foreign, Arab environment.[71] Arabs deserved scorn, and true Islam emerged only when it reached the Persian Empire. Only then did 'it become the true Islam. Before that there was merely the nomadism and *jaheliyyat* (period of ignorance) of the Arabs'.[72] For Al-e Ahmad, Islam is a tool against the West, and Shi'ism an essential component of Iranian national identity.[73] Ultimately, even the 'return to Islam' did not necessarily lead to greater affinity between Iranians and their Arab brethren. (For Al-e Ahmad's attitude in the 1960s, see Chapter 8.)

The Islamic Revolution was supposed to mark a turning point, leading to greater fraternity and closer mutual ties between Iran and the Arab and Muslim world. Yet, some aspects of the revolutionary regime or the regional politics of the Islamic Republic pitted Iran against most of its Arab neighbors. The very nature of the clerical regime, Iran's striving for Islamic and regional leadership, its close ties with Islamist movements, the Islamic regime's animosity towards the United States and Arab rulers, led to growing tension. Soon enough, other fundamental differences became evident. The Iran–Iraq war, and the fact that most Arab states sided with Saddam Husayn, maintained close ties with the United States, and supported the Arab–Israeli peace process, sharpened these differences.

After the initial stage of the revolution, however, Iran became more active in expanding its international ties. Expressing pride in Iran's centrality in the region, Velayati declared in 1996 that there were only 'very few issues' in the world in which Iran 'has not participated'.[74] Without Iran, he added, it would be impossible to do 'anything serious' in the Middle East.[75] His successor in the foreign ministry, Kamal Kharrazi, stated in 1998 that Iran 'plays a role at the highest level of international relations today' and is likely to play an even greater role in the future.[76] The Arab world in general and neighboring Arab states in particular were the main countries to be considered for expanding mutual ties and regional alignments. In forming actual policy, priority was given to Iran's particular national interests. In fact, the improvement in bilateral ties derived, to a great degree, from Iran's willingness to tone down its ideological creed.

Because of its Islamic revolutionary ideology and specific geo-strategic and economic interests, the main focus of Iran's attention lay in the Gulf region. Yet the first decade of revolutionary rule was overshadowed by the Iran–Iraq war. For Iran, the war symbolized the intertwined path of Iran and Islam, the faith and the homeland. That the Arabs, particularly the coastal states, supported Iraq was a major cause of tension in the 1980s.

After the war, Tehran proved more flexible in dealing with its neighbors. Rafsanjani was openly critical of his country's past policies towards some Arab states. 'If Iran had demonstrated a little more tactfulness' in its relations with Saudi Arabia and Kuwait, he said late in 1988, 'they would have not supported Iraq'.[77] He added that his country saw 'no obstacles' to expanding relations with Arab countries in the Gulf region.[78] The deputy foreign minister 'Ali Mohammad Besharati stressed Iran's desire to 'turn over a new leaf' in its relations with Arab countries after the Iran–Iraq war. He used the Qur'an to support his view that 'bygones are bygones'. Referring to Saudi Arabia, he said: 'We are prepared to sit down, talk and overcome the great misunderstanding between us.' Using arguments which revealed great realpolitik, he reminded his audience that 'neighborhood is unchangeable' and that 'our holy shrines . . . and our Ka'ba are there'. The Prophet, too, is buried there. 'Can we ignore it?'[79] Although the more doctrinaire elements within the Iranian political establishment stuck to their hard-line dogma, the statements of top officials generally reflected a significant change both in tone and in content, but some major difficulties prevailed.

The initial Iranian hostility to Saudi Arabia related both to the nature of the Saudi regime and to its politics, which Iran viewed as 'anti-Islamic'. Tehran charged Saudi Arabia with turning into Washington's watchdog in the Gulf, and adopting policies against the interests of Islam and the Saudi people in particular.[80] King Fahd's 1981 plan to resolve the Arab–Israeli conflict,[81] like the Saudi acceptance of the Middle East peace process, was criticized by Iran as intended to serve the interests of US imperialism. More specific allegations of Saudi hostility to Iran included Saudi support for Iraq, Saudi backing for a cut in oil prices (depriving Iran of income), and Saudi backing for domestic opposition to the Islamic regime in Iran. Obviously, the competition for the leadership of the Muslim world remained a constant issue in souring bilateral ties.

Islamic dogma continued to influence Iran's policy after the Iran–Iraq war. This was seen mainly in the attitude of the more doctrinaire Iranian factions. Tehran still wished to prove to the Gulf littoral states, to the outside world, and to its own people, that although Ayatollah Khomeini was dead, the revolution continued along the same lines. The statements made in Tehran (mainly on the occasion of the *hajj*) attested to the leadership's attempt to echo Khomeini. This was particularly true with Khamene'i, whose messages to *hajj* pilgrims were designed to resemble those of the late Ayatollah. Thus in his first message to the pilgrims, on 6 July 1989, shortly after assuming the Leadership Khamene'i condemned the Saudis for having 'blocked the path of God' to the Iranian pilgrims. He blamed the rulers of Riyadh for being 'the sinful idols of arrogance and colonialism' and 'ignorant of God'. In line with Khomeini's previous statements, Khamene'i also described Saudi clerics as 'court preachers' and termed the type of religion they followed, 'American Islam'.[82] Other Iranian leaders followed suit, calling for an end to Saudi rule over the holy shrines in Mecca and Medina and questioning Saudi faithfulness to 'true Islam'. Ardabili (president of the supreme court) prayed to God, that 'the corpse of Meccan *taghut* [idol-worshippers]' would be removed from Saudi Arabia.[83] Majlis Deputy Speaker (and former representative of Khomeini on the *hajj*) Mehdi Karubi termed Saudi rulers 'disqualified to administer the holy sanctuaries'.[84]

Subsequent Iranian statements aimed at Saudi Arabia combined threat and appeasement, ideology and self-interest. Gradually the main issue on the agenda became their rival strategic and economic interests, particularly the security of the Gulf and oil – which revealed basic differences on major questions. This became evident during the 1991 Gulf war (and the Saudi role in it), and following the war, with the defense system agreed upon by the six Arab littoral states as well as Egypt and Syria, with the support of the United States.

Notwithstanding its past hostility towards Kuwait (and despite Kuwait's support for Iraq in the Iran–Iraq war), Iran nevertheless supported the sovereignty and territorial integrity of Kuwait after the Iraqi invasion of 1990. Although Kuwait's independence was of strategic interest to Iran, it preferred to stress humanitarian and ideological arguments to justify its stance. Throughout the Gulf crisis Iran let it be known that it wished to play a key role in any consequent strategic arrangement in the region. Iran believed that the Gulf's coastal states –

including Iran – should be responsible for security in the Gulf and that the Gulf should be free of foreign interference. Iran insisted on having a share in the security of the Gulf proportional to its power and its long border along the Gulf. While there were significant changes in Iranian politics, it is noteworthy that these precepts were adhered to throughout the revolutionary era and gained the unanimous assent of all domestic groupings.

Against this background, the issuing of the Damascus Declaration on 6 March 1991 by the 'six-plus-two' states infuriated the Iranians. It stated that Egyptian and Syrian forces should constitute the 'nucleus for an Arab peace force' that would safeguard the security of the Arab states in the Gulf region, as well as serve as 'an example that would guarantee the effectiveness of the comprehensive Arab defense order'.[85] Rafsanjani said that although Iran did not wish to become a hegemonic power and was willing to be friendly with all regional states and 'together' create 'a new security system', it was determined to be a principal partner in maintaining the region's security.[86] There can be no workable security plan for the Gulf, he said, if Iran – one of the most powerful states in the region – was not a party to it.[87] The hard-liners were even more assertive on the issue. According to *Jomhuri-ye Islami*, any arrangement excluding Tehran would be 'meaningless'.[88] The exclusion of Iran from the security programs in the Gulf remained a major issue of contention.

While Tehran seemed willing to soften its revolutionary slogans, it proved unwilling to compromise on issues of national interest. Tension in its relations with the Gulf littoral states re-emerged in 1992 following the Iranian move to ascertain its sovereignty over the three islands in the straits of Hormuz – Abu Musa, and the Greater and Lesser Tunbs. Given their strategic location, control of these islands was vital to advance Iran's regional aims and to project an image of Iranian power and success. The weakening of Iraq and tension among the Arab states provided the opportunity to advance such aspirations. The three islands were seized by the Shah in November 1971. Since then, Abu Musa has been jointly administered by Iran and Sharjah although Iran has never acknowledged the sovereignty of the United Arab Emirates (UAE) over the islands. In August 1992, Iran turned back a UAE-registered ship carrying passengers to the island, claiming it had entered Iranian territorial waters without obtaining the necessary authorization.[89] In Iran's view the islands 'are integral parts' of Iranian territory, and it has only 'strengthened control and supervision' over Abu Musa.[90] In sum, Iran initiated the move from a sense of strength. Although it declared a willingness to negotiate, it proved unwilling to compromise.

Iran's firm position on the islands did not change much even after Khatami's election. Tehran maintained that 'The Tunbs were non-negotiable', simply because 'no country can negotiate about its sovereignty'.[91] Yet during the 1990s, tension between Iran and neighboring Gulf states gradually reduced, becoming less marked before Khatami's elections and warming up further since 1997.

Once again, while the hard-liners wished to keep to revolutionary dogma, those who were more pragmatic (including members of government) favored greater realism aimed at better relations and closer ties with the Arabs. Iran labored to prevent the explosion at the US military base in Khubar in June 1996 from souring bilateral ties. Ambassador Kharrazi noted that not only did Iran not pose a threat 'to any country', but that it 'regards the Persian Gulf littoral states as members of a unique family'.[92] In a similarly conciliatory tone, the *Tehran Times*, in an article entitled 'Time is Ripe for Iran–Saudi Rapprochement' wrote that both states [Iran and Saudi Arabia] were 'influential countries in the Muslim world' whose interaction 'can pave the way for multilateral cooperation among Muslim countries' and improve regional relations. Iran, it declared, was the most powerful country in the region, while Saudi Arabia was the world's largest exporter of oil and the custodian of the holy sites of Mecca and Medina, wielding 'considerable influence among regional countries'. Smoother relations between the two countries, therefore, 'will increase the maneuvering power of Muslims' *vis-à-vis* Israel.[93] Yet, actually, the main questions that seemed to concern Tehran at the time were strategic interests and the security of the Gulf, as well as economic considerations (mainly oil production and price). The election of Khatami was viewed as a good point for a new start.

Iran welcomed the 'process of rapprochement' with its Arab neighbors. 'Iran has entered a new era of international cooperation and regional integration', wrote the *Tehran Times*. It pointed out that Iran's foreign policy was now based on 'détente', 'mutual respect' and 'dialogue.'[94] *Iran News* added that, with the changing times, regional countries should fulfil their historic responsibility and 'get rid of foreign dominance'. Above all, it continued the conciliatory tone typical of the post-election era: 'Regional countries should remember that we have a thousand reasons to stand united, while there is not a single reason for us to stand apart.' Judged by the positive response of the regional media to Khatami's election, Iran believed that the opportunity for 'a new era of peace in the region is truly ahead'. But it made it clear, that 'before anything else, foreign forces must go home now'.[95]

Consequently, the intensity of mutual contacts became impressive.

The ICO summit hosted by Iran (in December 1997) was crowned by a series of intensive meetings between Saudi Crown Prince 'Abdallah Bin 'Abdul-'Aziz (deputy prime minister and commander of the Saudi National Guard), and senior Iranian officials, including Khamene'i. The visit to Saudi Arabia by Rafsanjani in February 1998 was viewed as a 'qualitative shift' in this 'historic reconciliation'. His meetings resulted in an agreement to establish permanent cooperation to prevent a further decline in oil prices and define a joint action plan aimed at improving the oil market within the OPEC framework. Rafsanjani declared that the visit was the opening of a 'new phase' in Iran-Saudi ties.[96] During a visit to Tehran by the Saudi foreign minister, Prince Sa'ud al-Faysal in May 1998, the two sides also agreed to further expand bilateral ties. Finally, Khatami's visit to Saudi Arabia in May 1999, the first by an Iranian President since the Islamic Revolution, best symbolized this process of rapprochement. It was also an indication of Khatami's determination to improve Iran's relations with its Arab neighbors, including Iraq. Hailing the recent 'atmosphere of understanding' that had emerged in the region, Khatami stressed his country's aim 'to reduce tensions and to reinforce common aims and values'. The principal aim of his visit, he said, was 'to get closer to more sensitive and more fruitful' understanding in the region.[97] Several economic and trade agreements were signed and discussions held on the future of regional security and cooperation, the Middle East peace process and the three disputed islands in the straits of Hormuz.[98]

In line with the new spirit under Khatami, Mohammad Sadr (Iranian assistant foreign minister for Arab and African affairs) stressed the need to move away from slogans and rhetoric to direct action that would reaffirm the fraternal ties between Iran and its Arab neighbors. Such relations, he suggested, should be free from any superiority complex, and based on real friendship and long-term interests. Iran, he reiterated, was 'determined to normalize fully' its relations with its brothers 'in the Arab homeland', to 'open up fully and widely toward its neighbors' among the member-states of the Gulf Cooperation Council (GCC).[99] Defense Minister 'Ali Shamkhani also tried to mitigate Arab concerns over Iran's military arsenal and maneuvers in the Gulf. These were, he said, only the means to enhance his country's defense capabilities, assuring 'all our brothers in the region' that Iranian forces 'will never be used against them'. Iran, he said, was even ready 'to defend the interests of the Gulf states if exposed to any danger'. After all, its military power 'is part of the Islamic World's power', and aimed at 'repelling aggression and confronting challenges'.[100]

Even more profound differences divided Iran and Iraq – with which Iran had recently fought a long and bitter war. In the general mood of realism, Iran improved its ties with Baghdad, yet a looming suspicion hindered bilateral relations and clouded efforts for rapprochement. The long war, the still open question of prisoners of war, Iraqi support for the *Mojahedin-e Khalq,* and general Iranian hostility to the ideology of Saddam Husayn's Iraqi Ba'th regime, are among the problems souring mutual relations. The lack of respect and trust between the two countries is clearly evident if one examines the verbatim attacks (such as in summer 1999, while commemorating 11 years to the end of the war).

The general trend towards improving ties with the Gulf states began under Rafsanjani, but gathered momentum under Khatami. None of the basic problems (ideological disparities, Gulf security, the three islands, oil production, the Arab countries' support for Iraq in the war with Iran, the close ties of most Arab states with the United States and their support for the Arab–Israeli peace process) has been resolved. Nor have recent statements by Iranian officials mitigated the concerns of Arab states in the Gulf and beyond. The new relationships were essentially based on recognition of Iran's needs and the limits of its power on the one hand, and the recognition by its Arab neighbors of Iran's importance and the political change in Iran, and the advisability of attempting to resolve their differences in friendly ways. But, for the time being, Iran has managed to maintain calm and cordial relations, better than at any other time since 1979. Nevertheless, Iran's closest relations are with Syria on the one hand and Islamist movements on the other.

Iran's relations with the member-states of the Steadfastness Front (mainly Syria) had been comparatively good since 1979 and improved further during the Iran–Iraq war and the war in Lebanon. After the change of regime in Sudan in 1989, the Islamic regime in Khartum became one of Iran's major allies in the region. Although there were some signs of incipient differences between Iran, Syria and Libya, the identity of their views on most regional and global issues kept their alliance alive during the first years of the Islamic regime. Since the mid-1980s, Libya's active role in the region has significantly diminished, but Iran's relations with Damascus remained close and extensive.

Tehran's ties with Syria have been the closest it has had with any foreign state since the revolution. This has been so despite some basic disagreements and conflicting opinions on major questions. In addition to the Ba'thist Arab-national ideology, Tehran was displeased with Syria for its support for the GCC, Syria being one of the 'six-plus-two' states that issued the 'Damascus declaration' and its participation in the US-led coalition in the 1991 War. Iran also resented the suppression of Islamism in Syria and did not fully share Syrian policy in Lebanon which was often in conflict with Iranian interests and politics. Syria's peace talks with Israel in 1994–96 were clearly not in line with Iran's policy. Yet Tehran proved fairly tolerant of such disagreements with its major ally.

Syria's peace negotiations with Israel in 1994–96 were not in line with Iran's interest and policy. Iran was also displeased over the more conciliatory approach taken by Damascus towards the resumption of peace talks with Israel under Ehud Barak in 1999. In 1991 *Abrar* warned that Syria, which had already lost its credibility as an anti-imperialist power by participating in the Gulf war, was committing another mistake by taking part in the Madrid Conference.[101] Having failed to dissuade Damascus, Tehran moved on to advise Syria of the appropriate stance to adopt. It pressured Damascus not to be content with liberating the Golan Heights alone, but to liberate Jerusalem as well, promising that – if this were achieved – one billion Muslims would be behind it and its name 'will be imprinted indelibly in the annals of history'.[102] *Ettela'at* pointed to the objective (mainly economic) difficulties facing Syria and the change in the global order that had forced Syria to participate in the Madrid Conference.[103] Nateq-Nuri said explicitly that Iran was unwilling to destroy its close ties with Syria without sufficient reason.[104] This was another sign of realpolitik.

In this context, too, some new voices were heard recently, reflecting the more diversified views expressed in Iran, mainly in the reformist press. *Neshat* took a fresh attitude on this issue following the election of Barak, stressing that Lebanon was occupied (*eshghal shodeh*) not only by Israel, but by Syria too. While Israel occupied the south of Lebanon, Syria occupied large portions of the country, including Beirut, leading to 'negative reactions' by the people living there. For the people of Lebanon, it declared, 'there is no difference whatsoever' between Syrian and Israeli occupation. Lebanon would not achieve freedom and independence merely with the withdrawal of Israel and the South Lebanese Army. As long as the Syrian troops remained, the situation would continue to be 'unfavorable' (*namosa'ed*) for the Lebanese people.[105] There have been a number of such articles, mainly since 1999, representing a new approach, although it is confined to narrow circles, with very few daring to give it full expression.

Islamist movements were the most natural allies for revolutionary

Iran. Consequently, Iran endeavored to cultivate close ties with them, although many Muslim countries, including Egypt, Turkey, Saudi Arabia and Iraq, have hindered such efforts, limiting Tehran's access and direct contacts.

The growth of Islamism in different Muslim countries became noticeable in the 1970s. When seen from a distance, Islamism appears as a monolithic and uniform movement, with some goals, leadership profile and motivation in common. Upon closer scrutiny, however, the movement is not monolithic: despite many shared features, the various Islamist movements have distinctive roots, character and politics. Nevertheless, such movements drew inspiration and encouragement from the Iranian revolution; and Tehran, because of its self-image as 'the mother of all Islamic revolutions', was committed to guide, encourage and support them – at least so far that this did not conflict with its basic interests.

Although Iran's attitude towards such movements and its (moral and material) support for them is not identical, there seem to be several similarities in their inter-relationships. Tehran considers their success a tribute to its own revolution, a manifestation of the spread of its doctrine and influence, and a token of its dominance in the Muslim world. It is encouraged by their growing power and is confident that they will soon emerge triumphant in their respective regions. Therefore, Tehran believes, such movements (like the Hizballah) deserve ideological and moral encouragement, as well as financial and logistical support, from Iran.

The main impact of the Iranian Revolution was manifested not in the major Muslim states, but in tightly knit, numerically small movements, mostly within Shi'i populations. Yet even here the real measure of the Iranian role in their emergence is far from clear. Even in the case of movements for which Tehran has claimed credit (such as Hizballah and Amal in Lebanon, or *al-Da'wa* and *al-'Amal* in Iraq, or Islamic Jihad and Hamas in the West Bank and Gaza), the exact connections between these movements and the Iranian revolution is not sufficiently clear. And the support that Iran was ready to extend to them (even to such groups as the Iraqi Shi'is) is questionable (see above).

Although Iran has limited leverage over the Arab states, it has been more successful in forging ties with Islamist movements, mainly Hizballah, Islamic Jihad and Hamas. Iran took pride and claimed credit for its support. (See Chapter 8.)

The Hizballah has long been the flagship of the Iranian revolution abroad. It maintains a similar philosophy to that of the Islamic regime, it upholds the struggle for the *mostaz'afin* and suppressed people, it presents a successful example of the influence of the Iranian revolutionary creed, it fights Israel, and generally maintains loyalty to Tehran. Ideologically speaking, the Hizballah seem even more loyal to Khomeini's dogma than the Iranians themselves, at least in the 1990s. Their leaders have often been invited to Tehran, and Iranian officials have visited them occasionally. Iran has also maintained a militant militia in Lebanon and provided significant support for the movement.

After initial hesitation, Iran also developed close ties with Hamas. Historically, rather than supporting the Palestinian Sunni Muslim Brotherhood, which constituted Hamas' hard core, Tehran cultivated the Palestinian Islamic Jihad, a staunchly pro-Iranian militant organization. Iran takes pride in having 'a major role' (*naqsh-e beseza'i*) in the formation and the philosophy of Islamic Jihad.[106] Hamas for its part initially rejected the Iranian model. Since the 1991 Gulf war, however, a significant change may be discerned. Following the Oslo Accords in 1993, Tehran's interest, motivation and actual patronage for the Palestinian Islamist movements became still more manifest. (See the following chapter.)

Viewed from Tehran, Hamas had the same advantages as Hizbollah had, with a certain added value. Thus Hamas offered another front for Iran to demonstrate its Islamic leadership, an arena for involvement in the Arab–Israeli conflict, and another ally bordering on the holy lands. Moreover, Hamas seemed determined to struggle against Israel; was better able to strike inside Israel (than the Hizballah); and attracted a greater international interest. Ideologically, too, it is an ideal partner: although Sunni, it bases its ideology on similar Islamic foundations; it rejects Israel's right to exist, and it is determined to combat Israel, imperialism and 'their puppets'. Iran was proud to serve, to use Ahmad Khomeini's phrase, as the repository (*poshtvaneh*) of the Palestinians' uprising.[107] Yet Iranian success in Lebanon, as among the Palestinians, had probably less to do with its 'skilful diplomacy or the appeal of its Islamic message', than with 'internal characteristics and regional developments'.[108]

The rejectionist Palestinians, for their part, expected more meaningful, practical support from Tehran – above and beyond what Iran seemed willing or able to provide – not mere slogans. Iran, in fact, 'did keep [up] its drum beat of opposition and seemed intent on assuming the mantle of chief opponent of Israel'.[109] But to what extent it was ready to jeopardize its interests for the sake of the Palestinian cause has yet to be seen. For Iran, as some Iranian intellectuals maintained, support for

Hamas was relatively low cost, but offered significant dividends. This may explain the continued support of such movements by Tehran. (See the following chapter.)

Judged by the initial expectations of the Iranian revolutionaries the influence of their doctrine in the world of Islam, although not negligible, was still limited. Yet this does not necessarily mean that Islamism has lost its appeal or ceased to inspire other people and movements. Clearly, although, as Keddie suggests, the impact or influence of individuals and movements is 'inherently unmeasureable',[110] given the harsh realities experienced by people in different parts of the Muslim world, the Iranian example undoubtedly attracts many Islamists. Regardless of the apparent difficulty of Islamist rule – in Iran as in Sudan and Afghanistan – in solving problems facing the people, they may prefer to concentrate on the full half of the glass: the success of the Iranian Revolution in toppling the regime of the Shah, which enjoyed the support of a forceful army and the backing of the greatest world power (the United States). Yet, while the Iranian Revolution encouraged Islamists, it also created significant barriers to their ultimate success. Governments are aware of the challenge, have developed the necessary countermeasures, and are fighting back. Although this does not ensure their success, it is an indication of their awareness and effort. The outside world also seems much more tolerant towards suppressive measures applied against the Islamists by their own governments. In fact, the Iranian example has proved that its ideology can be an efficient means of inciting people *against* policies and rulers, although it has so far proved a less potent tool *for* constructive solutions and effective governance. In the final account, this was another significant cause for the limited appeal of its revolutionary creed in the region.

IRAN AND ITS NON-ARAB NEIGHBORS

The Islamic Revolution also opened a new chapter in Iran's relations with its non-Arab neighbors. While most of its neighbors viewed with concern the dramatic change in Iran, the changes in the region, in turn, influenced Iran. The disintegration of the Soviet Union – and the subsequent independence of six Muslim republics to the north of Iran – opened new opportunities for Iran and also presented it with policy dilemmas and challenges. In Afghanistan, it was the Soviet invasion of 1979, the ensuing civil war and the emergence of Islamist rule under the Taliban that influenced Iran. Ideological and strategic differences with

Turkey formed another major focus of contest in Iran's close neighborhood.

Although both Iran and Turkey are Muslim and neighboring states, there has always been a significant ideological disparity between revolutionary Tehran and Ankara. In many ways, these two non-Arab countries represent diametrically different visions of religion and state, and two distinctive prototypes of Islamic government in the contemporary Muslim Middle East.

Turkey is the most secular Muslim country in the Muslim Middle East; an ally of the USA, with NATO bases within its territory, and the only Muslim country, apart from Egypt, which had relations with Israel at the time when the revolutionary regime came to power in Iran. Several new developments since then have further clouded relations between Iran and Turkey: the deepening alliance between Turkey and Israel, the divergent interests of Turkey and Iran in Central Asia and Transcaucasia, and the close ties forged between Iran and Syria (with which Ankara had tense relations). Furthermore, while Turkey accused Iran of supporting Islamist movements (including those operating in Turkey), Iran blamed Turkey for its anti-Islamic and anti-Iranian policy (including Turkey's 'hosting' of Iranian opposition movements). By contrast, economic interests (and Turkey's position as an important transit route to Iran) and mutual concern over the Kurdish challenge presented some common ground for the improvement of ties. The Iranian government, thus, pursued its customary two-tier policy, yet the hard-liners were highly critical both of Turkish policy and of their government's response – indeed lack of appropriate response – to it. Relations between Tehran and Ankara thus shifted between cooperation and competition, between tranquillity and tension.

A major and constant issue of friction throughout the last two decades was the two countries' divergent approaches to Islamism. Ankara viewed Iran as implicitly or explicitly encouraging Islamism in Turkey. Tehran blamed Ankara for an anti-Islamic policy and for stepping up restrictions on its political and cultural cadres in Turkey. Iran also charged Turkey with supporting and training Iranian opposition movements (i.e., the *Mojahedin-e Khalq* and the royalists).[111] Tehran was also concerned by what it viewed as a Turkish scheme, supported by Washington, to play a major role in Central Asia. It maintained that unlike Iran, which was acting there out of pure Islamic faith, Turkey was pursuing its self-interest, or the interests of foreign countries. Ankara was condemned for seeking to penetrate the region to improve its 'ailing economy', bolster its strategic importance, and serve US interests.[112] In fact, Iran claimed that Turkey had been transformed into a satellite of US foreign policy.[113] The independence of the new Muslim republics of Central Asia and Transcaucasia added a new element of contention, as both Ankara and Tehran sought to strengthen their influence in this region.

Several new factors emerged during the late 1990s which added to the tension. The most evident of these was the strengthening alliance between Turkey and Israel. Iran viewed this alliance as a direct military threat, particularly the April 1996 pact that allowed Israeli fighter jets to train in Turkish airspace. Foreign Minister Velayati stated that 'the advance of Israeli aircraft to the Iranian borders' would constitute 'an act of war'.[114] Yet, on this issue too, there were differences among Iranian domestic camps. While hard-liners used rough language to describe Turkish policy, Khatami often used milder language.[115] The coming to power of the Islamic Rafah (Welfare) Party, led by Necmettin Erbakan in June 1996, raised hopes in Iran for a new era in mutual relations, which were stimulated by the Rafah Party's strong pre-election opposition to the Turkish–Israeli alliance.[116] (In August 1996, a week after the USA announced penalizing foreign investment in Iran's energy sector, Iran and Turkey signed a huge gas supply deal worth $23 billion.) Eventually, the Turkish army ensured that the new government did not affect foreign policy. In any case, the brief blooming of ties between Iran and Turkey ended after the Islamic government was dismissed and the Rafah Party outlawed in January 1998. Tehran followed Turkey's politics with concern, but needed relations with its neighbor, regardless of ideological disparities and conflicting interests.

The independence of the Muslim republics of the former Soviet Union has to some degree changed the face of the Middle East, and had significant influence on their neighboring states (Iran and Turkey). Here, too, national interest triumphed over dogma in Iranian politics. Iran was careful not to antagonize Moscow and to maintain good relations with different governments in Central Asia and Transcaucasia. None of them was inclined towards an Islamic order, and most maintained close relations with Turkey and the United States (and even with Israel). For all its desire to expand its ideological influence in this region, regional stability and mutually beneficial bilateral relations proved much more powerful in dictating Iran's actual politics there.

Relations with Russia remained a basic consideration in formulating Iran's attitude toward the northern Muslim republics. Nothing should be done in Central Asia that might jeopardize friendly relations with Moscow, endanger arms supplies, or slow down the growth of economic ties with Russia. Foreign Minister Velayati made it clear that avoiding a 'clash with Moscow' was a major Iranian concern in shaping its policy.[117] Tehran even seemed less obsessed with the Soviet policy towards its own Muslim citizens (see above). Another Iranian aim was to preserve peace on its northern frontier. It wished to avoid instability and disorder, and to bar the spread of negative influences from (ex-Soviet) Azerbaijan to Iranian Azeris while controlling population movements across the borders with both Azerbaijan and Turkmenistan. Iran also wished to establish firm economic ties (including the construction, among other things, of transportation networks and pipelines), cultural cooperation and solid political ties with the different Muslim republics. Ultimately, Iran hoped, Islamic doctrine would also expand in the new republics.

Both foreign policy calculations and domestic reasons made it important for Iran to expand its presence in Central Asia. As a result, Iran operated simultaneously on three levels: enhancing relations with local governments; cooperating with other regional powers (including Moscow); and cultivating ties with local Islamic movements.

Oddly enough, while the propagation of Islalmic doctrine worldwide was an important aim for the Islamic regime, Iranian public statements attached little importance to neighboring Soviet Muslims during the first decade following the revolution. Tehran was careful not to target the Muslim republics in its ideological crusade. Yet it could not altogether ignore its neighboring coreligionists. In a rare and direct reference just before the 1979 revolution, Khomeini told a journalist that Soviet Muslims 'are our brothers. We are brothers of all Muslims; it is a basic Islamic principle that each Muslim supports other Muslims.'[118] But he would usually not go beyond such generalities. Clearly, prudence and a regard for vital interests have continued to prevail in the official Iranian approach.

A similar stance was evident on the eve of the disintegration of the Soviet Union. As Iran began contacts with Soviet Muslims, officials were careful to make clear that this was being done with Moscow's consent. The *Tehran Times* remarked typically that although Iran recognized the Soviet Muslims' 'rightful demands', it also had 'very good relations with the central Soviet Government', and wished to maintain them.[119] Tehran made clear that peace and stability were its primary concern in this strategic and sensitive region and that Iran was doing its fair share in this regard.[120] National considerations also led Tehran to seek good relations with local governments in the Muslims republics of the former Soviet Union, although none could be considered an ideal Islamic

regime. Iran took pains to allay Russian concern, disclaiming any intention of spreading its dogma in the territories of the former Soviet Union.
Velayati added that Iran would not interfere in the domestic affairs of
the Muslim republics nor impose friendship on them; rather it would
strive for good neighborly relations.[121]

Regionally, Iran sought to form new associations for reciprocal cooperation (mainly economic and cultural). These were meant both to
promote its regional and national ambitions and to block attempts by
others to claim pride of place. Therefore, Iran initiated multilateral cooperation schemes based on religious solidarity, economic and regional
interests and linguistic and cultural affinity, hoping to establish itself as
a pivotal element in any future regional alignment. In 1992, Iran hosted
the summit conference of the Economic Cooperation Organization
(ECO). In addition to using the ECO as a vehicle for economic cooperation, Tehran hoped also to make itself the 'center for regional developments' and to play 'a principal role in any political and economic
groupings'. Rafsanjani asserted: 'Co-operation should certainly be
carried out via Iran. For links between the north and the south, the east
and the west, these countries and Europe, Europe and Asia everything
should cross Iran – oil and gas pipelines, railways, communication
routes and international airports.'[122] Clearly, a major interest of Iran
was the gas and oil pipelines from the Caspian Sea region. Iran opted for
a pipeline passing through its territory, while the USA (backed by
Turkey) was opposed.

Differing considerations influenced the scope and nature of Iran's
relations with each of the Muslim republics: one is Shi'i (Azerbaijan),
two are on territory adjacent to Iran (Azerbaijan and Turkmenistan),
and one has cultural affinity with Iran (Tajikistan). Iran has made
vigorous efforts to strengthen bilateral ties with each of them.

Over time, the general trend in Iranian policy was one of greater
realism, less euphoria and enthusiasm, with the emphasis on Islam being
usually toned down in formal contacts. More dogmatic factions within
the Iranian establishment continued to press for a more doctrinaire and
activist policy, but government policy remained more restrained. True,
Islamic revolutionary goals continued to be pursued (such as the distribution of copies of the Qur'an, the teaching of Persian, the distribution of
textbooks, and the training of young clerics), but they received less
publicity, and expressions of enthusiasm about them were muted. What
'Abbas Maleki termed the 'initial euphoria',[123] characteristic of the early
Iranian response to their independence, had considerably subsided some
two years later. While earlier Velayati had said that Iran did not view its

relations with the Muslim republics 'like a businessman' (*manand-e yek tajer*),[124] Rafsanjani maintained that 'the major part' of his visit to five of the republics in 1993, 'concerned business'. Moreover, during this important tour, 'Rafsanjani seemed determined to show himself as statesmanlike rather than ideological'.[125] (For his visit see also above.)

Clearly, Iran has real and significant interests in Central Asia and Transcaucasia. Yet mindful of Central Asia's needs and sensitivities as well as its own national interest, Iran has focused for the most part on politically and ideologically neutral topics in its inter-governmental dealings. At the same time, Tehran strove to foster firm economic ties. That Tehran seeks a 'return to Islam' in Central Asia, and is willing to support it is beyond argument. But precisely what it is doing, and how much it is willing to sacrifice for this cause, are matters of dispute. Finally, at least in the short term, Tehran needs good relations with Moscow no less than with the new Islamic governments. If ideology laid down the priorities, Tehran would have preferred ties with Central Asian peoples first, relations with their governments second, and ties with Moscow third. In actual fact, the scale of Iranian priorities seems rather different, reflecting its interests and realpolitik rather than an ideological drive.

To conclude this brief overview of Iran's relations with its non-Arab neighbors, tensions with both Pakistan and Afghanistan should be mentioned. Tehran condemned Islamabad for scheming to organize the Taliban and to establish them in Kabul. The Taliban were depicted by Iran as an 'Afghan *pustin* [fur cloak]' which has been sewn by the United States, paid for by Saudi Arabia and worn by the Pakistani army.[126] Troubled by the growing influence of Pakistan in Afghanistan, Iran repeated this line in the summer of 1998, when tension between Iran and Afghanistan reached a new peak. (After its diplomats were found dead in Mazar-e Sharif, Iran went so far as to build up a military force along the border and to issue well-publicized threats.) Iran accused Pakistan, the United States, Saudi Arabia and even Israel of being the founders and financiers of the Taliban.[127] It expressed displeasure with the Taliban's interpretation of Islam and tried to dispel the common association of the Taliban with Islamic Iran in global public opinion.[128] The Taliban's aim, *Tehran Times* wrote, was to establish only 'a so-called fundamental Islamic regime' in Afghanistan.[129] Iran, therefore, highlighted the ethnic nature of the conflict in Afghanistan,[130] using every opportunity to denounce the Taliban's 'barbaric' behavior.[131]

Twenty years after the revolution, the Middle East is not what Iran wished it to be, and the impact of the Islamic Revolution has remained largely limited. Rather than the ideology of the revolution, it was primarily the interests of the state that dictated Iran's regional policy. Nor is Iran what its neighbors feared in 1979 it would become. It seems more concerned with responding to developments than with initiating major new policies. Iran is usually not on the offensive; it feels as much threatened as it appears threatening to others.

In the late 1990s many Iranians viewed relations with Iraq and Afghanistan as the two major and most immediate strategic concerns. Iran felt 'sandwiched' between these two bordering Muslim states, which were viewed as posing a serious challenge to its national interests.[132]

With such a troubled neighborhood, Israel and the Arab–Israel conflict seemed far away. Yet even here Iran still seemed determined to play an active role.

NOTES

1. Interview with *al-Mustaqbal*, 13 January 1979; *al-Safir*, 18 and 19 January 1979; Radio Tehran, 7 May 1979 – DR, 8 May 1979. See also, Khomeini, Al-Hukuma al-Islamiyya, pp. 34–7.
2. Radio Tehran, 13 February 1979 – SWB, 15 February 1979.
3. *Al-Safir*, 19 January 1979.
4. For the disqualification of presidential candidate, Jalal al-Din Farsi, in the first presidential campaign in 1980, because his father was an Afghan, see Menashri, *A Decade of War and Revolution*, p. 120.
5. Khomeini even rejected Ayatollah Khalkhali's proposal to name it the 'Muslim Gulf'; see *Kayhan* (Tehran), 29 May 1979. In May 1981, Prime Minister Mohammad 'Ali Raja'i issued a statement saying that Persian Gulf was the 'correct historical and original name', and ordered its use in all official documents; Radio Tehran, 7 May 1981 – SWB, 9 May 1981.
6. James Piscatori, *Islam in the World of Nation-States* (Cambridge: Cambridge University Press, 1986), p. 111.
7. Marvin Zonis and Daniel Brumberg, 'Khomeini, the Islamic Republic of Iran, and the Arab World', *Harvard Middle East Papers*, 5 (1987), p. 74.
8. Ramazani, 'Iran's Foreign Policy', p. 395.
9. Shireen Hunter, 'Iran and the Spread of Revolutionary Islam', *Third World Quarterly*, 10/2 (April 1988), pp. 731–2.
10. Mottahedeh, 'The Islamic Movement', p. 108. For a detailed discussion, see David Menashri, 'Iran's Revolutionary Politics: Iranian Nationalism and Islamic Identity', in Leonard Binder (ed.), *Ethnic Conflict and International Politics in the Middle East* (Miami, FL: University Press of Florida, 1999), pp. 131–54.
11. Khomeini, *Kashf al-Asrar*, p. 337.
12. R. K. Ramazani, 'Khomeyni's Islam in Iran's Foreign Policy', in Adeed Dawisha (ed.), *Islam in Foreign Policy* (Cambridge: Cambridge University Press, 1984),

p. 17. Reprinted in Ramazani's, *Revolutionary Iran: Challenge and Response in the Middle East* (Baltimore, MD: Johns Hopkins University Press, 1986), p. 20.

13. Khomeini, *Kashf al-Asrar*, p. 424.
14. Ibid., pp. 285–6.
15. *Al-Safir*, 18 and 19 January 1979.
16. Khomeini, *Al-Hukuma al-Islamiyya*, pp. 34–5; see also Hamid Algar, *Islam and Revolution* (Berkeley, CA: Mizan, 1981), pp. 48–50. Similar views were also expressed by Ayatollah Hosein 'Ali Montazeri in interviews with *Kayhan* (Tehran), 16 and 18 January 1979.
17. *Ettela'at*, 14 August 1979.
18. See, for example, *Khabarnameh-ye Jebheh-ye Melli* (organ of the National Front), no. 7 (30 October 1978); nos 21 and 22 (21 and 22 November 1978).
19. Radio Tehran, 1 May 1979 – DR, 3 May 1979.
20. Radio Tehran, 12 September 1980 – SWB, 15 September 1980.
21. *Kayhan* (Tehran), 19 December 1982.
22. *Danesh-e Ejtema'i* [Social Science], textbook for fourth grade in high schools (Tehran, 1986–87 edition), p. 92.
23. *Kayhan* (Tehran), 24 October 1983.
24. *Kayhan* (Tehran), 30 September 1982.
25. *Ettela'at*, 7 March 1984.
26. Radio Tehran – DR, 30 October 1984.
27. *Kayhan* (Tehran) 21 February 1985.
28. Tehran TV, 24 August 1996 [DR].
29. Majid Khadduri, *Political Trends in the Arab World: The Role of Ideas and Ideals in Politics* (Baltimore, MD: Johns Hopkins University Press, 1970), p. 8.
30. Ann K. S. Lambton, *Qajar Persia* (Austin, TX: University of Texas Press, 1987), pp. 279–80.
31. Roger Savory, 'The Export of Ithna Ashari Shi'ism: Historical and Ideological Background', in David Menashri (ed.), *The Iranian Revolution and the Muslim World* (Boulder, CO: Westview, 1990), p. 14.
32. Savory, 'Export of Ithna Ashari Shi'ism', p. 35.
33. Richard Cottam, *Nationalism in Iran* (Pittsburgh, PA: University of Pittsburgh Press, 1979), pp. 135, 145.
34. Hunter, *Iran and the World*, p.10.
35. Textbook for fourth grade of high school in social science (*Ta'limat-e Ejtema'i*, edition of 1986–87), pp. 132–40.
36. *Ettela'at*, 29 September 1980.
37. Fourth-year textbook in Persian for elementary schools (*Farsi* edn, 1981–82), pp. 194–5.
38. Fifth-year textbook on social science for elementary schools (*Ta'limat-e Ejtema'i*, edn of 1982–83), pp. 34–5.
39. Golpaygani, for example, maintained that Iraq's policy *vis-à-vis* the Shi'is demonstrated that it had no respect for religious principles. He asked Muslims to show their disgust at Iraqi insults aimed at their holy places, the Iraqi massacre of Muslims, and the oppression of the Iraqi people: *Ettela'at*, 19 March; Radio Tehran, 18 March 1991 – DR, 19 March 1991.
40. IRNA, 18 March 1991 – DR, 19 March 1991.

41. See their statements quoted in *Ettela'at*, 10, 16 and 30 March 1991, respectively.
42. On the different Kurdish Iraqi factions see, Ofra Bengio, *The Kurdish Revolution* (in Hebrew; Tel Aviv: Hakibutz Hameuhad, 1989), pp. 33–9.
43. Zalmay Khalilzad, 'Iranian Policy Toward Afghanistan Since the Revolution', in Menashri (ed.), *Iranian Revolution and the Muslim World*, pp. 235–41.
44. *Iran Times*, 29 October 1993.
45. A detailed discussion of Iran's policy can be found in David Menashri (ed.), *Central Asia Meets the Middle East* (London: Frank Cass, 1998), especially chapters on Iran by Shireen Hunter, Brenda Sheffer and David Menashri, and those on Turkish policy by Philip Robins and William Hale.
46. For such Iranian concern, see *al-'Alam*, 18 January 1992; *Ettela'at*, 30 October, 3 November 1993.
47. Shireen Hunter, 'Iran and Transcaucasia in the Post-Soviet Era', in Menashri (ed.), *Central Asia Meets the Middle East*, mainly pp. 115–17; *Abrar*, 28 June 1992 – DR, 29 June 1992; Tadeusz Swietochowski, 'Azerbaijan's Triangular Relationship: The Land Between Russia, Turkey and Iran', in Ali Banuazizi and Myron Weiner (eds), *The New Geopolitics of Central Asia and its Borderlands* (Bloomington, IN: Indiana University Press, 1994), p. 130.
48. Galia Golan, *Russia and Iran*; *Respublika Armrniya* (in Russian), 14 May 1997, as quoted in DR.
49. For the angry remarks traded between Velayati and Hasanov at the press conference see: *Iran News*, 5 March 1996.
50. *Salam*, 9 December 1995.
51. William Samii, 'Iranian Attitudes Toward the Kosovo Crisis', *Policy Watch* no. 386 (The Washington Institute for Near East Policy, 23 April 1999). See also, Samii, 'Iran Sees Western Plot in Kosovo Crisis', RFE/RL, Iran Report, 2/23, 7 June 1999.
52. Iran Calls for UN Resolution on Kosovo Crisis, IRNA, 3 June, 1999 [DR].
53. Tehran Television, 19 May 1999 [DR].
54. Tehran Television, 29 April 1999 [DR].
55. *Salam*, 5 May 1996.
56. *Jahan-e Islam*, 13 September 1992 – DR, 14 October 1992.
57. In an Iranian communiqué of 9 February 1993: IRNA, 9 February 1993 – DR, 10 February 1993.
58. Hunter, *Iran and the World*, pp. 13, 42.
59. Tehran TV, Roundtable with election candidates, 20 May 1997 [DR].
60. S. Lotfian, 'Iran's Middle East Policies Under President Khatami', *Iranian Journal of International Affairs*, 10/4 (Winter 1998–99), pp. 429–30.
61. *Tehran Times*, 15 August 1998 [DR].
62. Saad, *Image of Arabs*, pp. 7–8.
63. Mirza Aqa Khan Kermani, *Maktub-e Shahzadeh Kamal al-Dowleh be Shahzadeh Jalal al-Dowleh, Seh Maktub* [Letter of Prince Kamal al-Dowleh to Prince Jalal al-Dowleh, three letters] (n.p.: Mard-e Emruz, 1991). See also Jaleh Pir-Nazar, 'Chehreh-ye Yahud dar Athar-e Seh Nevisandeh-ye Motejadded-e Irani' [The Portrayal of Jews in the Works of Three Modernist Iranian Writers], *Iran-Nameh*, 13/4 (Spring 1995), pp. 488–90 and Joya Blondel Saad, *Image of Arabs*, pp. 6, 15.

64. Kermani, *Maktub Shahzadeh*, pp. 79, 82, 101–2, 154–5, 158–9. See also Mangol Bayat, *Mysticism and Dissent: Socioreligious Thought in Qajar Iran* (Syracuse, NY: Syracuse University Press, 1982), pp. 157–61.
65. Saad, *Image of Arabs*, p. 15. For a similarly 'dark and harsh image of Iran' in a school textbook in Arab States, see Talal Atristi, 'The Iranian Image in Arab School Books', *Discourse*, 1/1 (1999), pp. 103–56.
66. Sadeq Hedayat, *Karavan-e Islam* [The Caravan of Islam] (n.p.: Sazeman-e Jonbesh-e Nasionalisti-ye Daneshgahiyan, 1983), see mainly pp. 39–41; Hasan Kamshad, *Modern Persian Prose Literature* (Cambridge: Cambridge University Press, 1966), pp. 108–9.
67. Saad, *Image of Arabs*, pp. 33–59.
68. Ibid., p. 14.
69. Ibid., p. 14; Manuchehr Dorraj, p. 111.
70. Saad, *Image of Arabs*, pp. 61, 65.
71. Ibid., pp. 92–7.
72. Ibid., pp. 98–9; Jalal al-e Ahmad, *Gharbzadegi* [Plagued by the West], trans. Paul Sprachman (New York: Caravan Books, 1982), pp. 15, 29.
73. Saad, *Image of Arabs*, p. 101.
74. *Ettela'at*, 3 September 1996 [DR].
75. Tehran TV, 22 August 1996 [DR].
76. Tehran TV, 15 January 1998 [DR].
77. IRNA, 19 November 1988 – SWB, 21 November 1988.
78. Radio Tehran, 29 November 1988 – SWB, 1 December 1988.
79. Radio Tehran, 19 November 1988 – SWB, 21 November 1988.
80. *Ettela'at*, 2 January 1982; Radio Tehran (in Arabic), 7 February – DR, 8 February 1982.
81. Such views of the Fahd Plan were expressed, among others, by Khomeini (Radio Tehran, 16 November 1981 – DR, 17 November 1981), Khamene'i and Montazeri (Radio Tehran, 17 November 1981 – DR, 18 November 1981) and Rafsanjani (Radio Tehran, 20 November 1981 – DR, 23 November 1981).
82. Radio Tehran, 6 July 1989 – SWB, 10 July 1989.
83. Radio Tehran, 7 July 1989 – SWB, 10 and 11 July 1989.
84. Radio Tehran, 10 July 1989 – SWB, 12 July 1989. Mohtashami then called for the 'Al-Sa'ud clan' to be on trial for the 'crimes it has perpetrated . . . against Islam'. Radio Tehran, 14 July 1989 – SWB, 17 July 1989.
85. Bruce Maddy-Weitzman, 'Inter-Arab Relations', *MECS* 1991, pp. 139–44. The declaration was issued by the foreign ministers of Egypt, Syria, Saudi Arabia, Kuwait, Bahrain, Oman, Qatar and UAE.
86. *Der Spiegel*, 25 March 1991 – DR, 26 March 1991.
87. *Ettela'at*, 10 March 1991.
88. *Jomhuri-ye Islami*, 16 March 1991.
89. *Tehran Times*, 26 August 1992 – DR, 9 September 1992; *Financial Times*, 11 September 1992.
90. Radio Tehran, 15 September 1992 – SWB, 17 September 1992; *Jahan-e Islam*, 13 September 1992 – DR, 14 October 1992.
91. *Tehran Times*, 15 August 1998 [DR].
92. IRNA, 26 December 1996 [DR].

93. *Tehran Times*, 8 October 1996 [DR].
94. *Tehran Times*, 15 August 1998 [DR].
95. *Iran News*, 6 August 1997 [DR].
96. Radio Tehran and IRNA, 6 March 1998; *Al-Sharq al-Awsat* (London), 31 May 1998 [DR].
97. Tehran TV, 20 May 1999 [DR]
98. *Al-Jazirah*, 17 May 1999 [DR]; *al-Ahram*, 1 June 1999 [DR]; *al-Sharq al-Awsat*, 18 May 1999 [DR].
99. *Al-Sharq al-Awsat*, 22 November 1997 [DR].
100. *Al-Ittihad* (Abu Dhabi), 12 July 1998 [DR].
101. *Abrar*, 5 August 1991.
102. *Tehran Times*, 5 October 1994 – DR, 14 October 1994.
103. *Ettela'at*, 29 July 1991.
104. *Ettela'at*, 25 May 1994.
105. See article by Hasan Fathi in *Neshat*, 15 June 1999.
106. Seyyed Hadi Khosrowshahi, 'Intifada: Harakatha-ye Islami dar Sarzeminha-ye Eshghali' [Intifada: Islamic Movements in the Occupied Territories], *Siyasat-e Khareji*, 5/1 (Spring 1991), p. 44.
107. Tehran TV, 21 October 1992 – DR, 22 October 1992.
108. Hunter, *Iran and the World,* pp. 125–6.
109. *Iran Times*, 17 September 1993.
110. Keddie, *Iran and the Muslim World*, p. 118.
111. *Abrar*, 9 May 1992; *Jahan-e Islam*, 22 June 1992 – DR, 2 July 1992; *Tehran Times*, 10 September 1992 – DR, 23 September 1992.
112. *Abrar*, 4 February and 4 May 1992; *Jomhuri-ye Islami*, 3 May 1992; *Jahan-e Islam*, 22 June 1992 – DR, 2 July 1992; and a commentary broadcast over Radio Tehran, 7 May 1992 – DR, 15 May 1992.
113. *Jahan-e Islam*, 22 June 1992 – DR, 2 July 1992.
114. *Neue Zuercher Zeitung* (Zurich), 5–6 October 1996 [DR].
115. See some typically harsh statements by Khamene'i in Radio Tehran, 12 July 1996, by Mohsen Reza'i, in IRNA, 6 January 1998 and by Larijani, in Tehran TV, 14 March 1996 [DR]. For a more moderate approach, see statement by Khatami, in IRNA, 13 September 1998 [DR].
116. *Kayhan* (Tehran), 10 August 1996; Radio Tehran, 12 August 1996 [DR].
117. *Al-Safir*, 27 November 1993.
118. 'Hokumat-e Islami-ye Iran, Vezarat-e Ershad-e Islami', *Sahifeh-ye Nur* (Tehran: Vezarat-e Evshad-e Islami, 1985–86), III, p. 31, as cited in Shirazi, *Melliyatha-ye Asya-ye Miyaneh*, p. 339.
119. *Tehran Times*, 18 August 1991 – DR, 23 August 1991.
120. *Kayhan International*, 23 January 1993 – DR, 28 January 1993.
121. *Hamshahri*, 28 January 1993 – DR, 28 January 1993.
122. *Ettela'at*, 18 February; Radio Tehran, 17 February 1992 – DR, 18 February 1992.
123. *Tehran Times*, 22 February 1993; DR, 5 March 1993.
124. *Ettela'at*, 30 December 1992.
125. *Iran Times*, 29 October 1993.
126. *Jomhuri-ye Islami*, 23 October 1996 – DR, 23 October 1996. Similarly, *Tehran Times* wrote on 2 October 1996 that the takeover in Afghanistan 'was

designed in Washington, financed in Riyadh, and logistically supported by Islamabad'.

127. See *Jomhuri-ye Islami*, 14 July 1998 [DR]; IRNA, 16 August 1998 [DR]; *Iran News*, 31 August 1998 [DR]. Mohsen Aminzadeh (deputy foreign minister for Asia and Oceania) said that Israel and the United States were 'behind such plots in Pakistan and Afghanistan'. See *Discourse*, 1/1 (Summer 1999), p. 38.

128. Tehran TV, 23 April 1998 [DR].

129. *Tehran Times*, 28 September 1996. See also statements by Foreign Minister Velayati (Tehran TV, 30 October 1996 – DR, 30 October 1996) and Ayatollah 'Ali Meshkini (*Tehran Times*, 27 October 1996).

130. See a series of interviews with Dr 'Ala' al-din Borujerdi explaining the Pashtunist nature of the Taliban. Tehran TV, 23 April 1998 [DR]; *Jomhuri-ye Islami*, 12 May 1998 [DR]; *Mobin*, 15 August 1998 [DR].

131. Tehran TV, 14 September 1998 [DR].

132. This was often stressed by Iranian academics. For Iranian security considerations, see Lotfian, 'Iran's Middle East Policies', pp. 420–48; and a Roundtable discussion published in *Discourse*, 1/1, pp. 5–48.

8

Israel: 'The Enemy of Iran and Islam'

One major area in which Iran's revolutionary policy remained excessively uncompromising was in its inherent hostility toward Israel and in its persistent and resonant rejection of Zionism and the legitimacy of the Jewish state of Israel. The revolutionary creed in this regard remained unequivocal and was reflected in such terms for Israel as the 'Lesser Satan', or 'the unlawful child' of the 'Great Satan' (i.e., the United States). Israel was perceived as the enemy of Iran and Islam, and as a threat to the whole of mankind. The revolutionary goal, as one of its major slogans stated, was similarly uncompromising: 'Israel should be eliminated' (*Isra'il bayad mahv shavad*) from the earth. The slogan, 'Death to Israel' became a central theme in Iranian revolutionary politics. The animosity to Israel was by and large the main issue in which revolutionary policy remained highly consistent and uncompromising.

Iran and Israel do not share a common border, have had no wars between them and have no claims on each other's territory. Moreover, under the Pahlavi regime and mainly since the 1960s, the two countries had enjoyed close ties, in fact, a strategic alliance. Although even then the relations between the two countries were not formal, they gradually developed into what an Iranian official at the time described, in an interview with the author, as 'relations of love without a marriage contract'.

Iran is a Shi'i and Persian state – in a predominantly Sunni and Arab region – with a history rich in tension with its Arab (and non-Arab Muslim) neighbors. Thus, under the Shah, while seeking close ties with the West and striving for social and economic reforms, Iran viewed Israel as a natural ally. The Shah also seemed to believe that through his ties with Israel, Iran would benefit in Washington and gain the support, among others, of the US media and business communities.

Israel, which was then struggling to consolidate its new state and in search of recognition and legitimacy in the Muslim world, viewed Iran as an ideal ally. In the 1950s Israel's first prime minister, David Ben-Gurion, developed the concept of 'peripheral states'. In a nutshell, this prescribed that, having no relations with its immediate neighbors, Israel should seek the friendship of 'the neighbors of the neighbor'. Israel was surrounded by hostile Arab countries – some of which (like Egypt) and their ideological creed (i.e., Arab nationalism) – presented serious challenges to Iran as well. This seemed to appeal to the Shah. Consequently, then, close ties were developed between Israel and the states of Iran, Turkey and Ethiopia – the countries of the periphery from the Israeli viewpoint. Iran was an especially important country in the region because of its strategic location, its size and economic potential, it was a Muslim (though not an Arab) state, and seemed to have no reason for conflict with Israel. Additionally, in historical memory of many Israelis, King Cyrus the Great was remembered as the benevolent leader who granted the Jews freedom.

This period of close ties came to an end with the ascendancy of the Islamic regime which regarded – and continues to regard – Israel as its arch-foe. In fact, among all the countries found blameworthy by the revolutionary movement upon taking power, Israel was indicted on more accounts than any other state by the Islamic regime. While Iran gradually renewed ties with most countries, the attitude to Israel has not yet changed in any official or meaningful way. Moreover, Iran's Islamic arguments have put the Arab–Israeli conflict on a totally different footing – a religious crusade as against a political–national conflict. Iran's involvement in Lebanon and its moral, political and material support for the Islamist and Palestinian movements (such as Hamas, Hizballah and Islamic Jihad) have involved Iran more directly in the conflict, presenting a serious challenge to Israel. Indeed by viewing the Palestine question as 'an Islamic one' Iran intensified its involvement.[1] Its attempts (actual or alleged) to purchase and develop weapons of mass destruction and the missile technology to deliver them were viewed as a serious challenge to Jerusalem. Finally, Iran's opposition to the Middle East peace process and its support for the anti-peace camp added to the challenges facing the fragile process of peace-making, presenting yet another difficulty for Israel.

The hostile attitude to Israel had its roots in Khomeini's dogma, and in the view of the Iranian ruling elite there have so far been no sufficient pragmatic considerations to convince Tehran to retreat from this entrenched enmity. In fact, this was one of the rare issues on which the revolutionary ideology and the national interests, as defined by the Islamic regime, seem to coincide. Not only conservatives, but pragmatists too, support such a view in their public statements. Thus, Iran's position was a mixture of ideological conviction (the denial of the right of the Jewish State to exist, rejection of the Shah's policy and hostility to Western capitalism and imperialism) and the state interests as perceived by the ruling elite.

Tehran's customary charges against Israel included the injuries done to Islam by Jews throughout Islamic history, the usurpation of Islamic lands by Israel and its control over Jerusalem. It was also blamed for serving as the 'foster-child' of Western imperialism and as the prime executor of 'plots' in the Muslim world and the instigator of anti-Iranian policy in Washington and, in fact, throughout the world. Revolutionary Iran also held Israel's good relations with the Shah against it. Moreover, the new regime was motivated by an aspiration for Islamic leadership and for greater centrality in the Middle East, and determined to demonstrate the success of the revolution – to its own people, to public opinion in the Muslim world and to the entire world. Therefore, it viewed it as its duty to hoist the anti-Israeli flag higher, to denounce the Arab leaders who negotiated with Israel for peace, and to provide support for those actively confronting it. Since the revolution, Tehran has become an active player in the conflict and the most hostile anti-Israeli state.

The profound dogmatic deviations since 1979 and the significant policy changes since Khatami's election notwithstanding, Tehran's policy in this regard has remained generally consistent. Although more moderate attitudes may have influenced many Iranians, who do not necessarily view Israel as the major concern of Iran, the official line so far has been one of total rejection and animosity towards Israel.

Yet, even in this realm, as will be shown, some initial signs of change can be discerned. These have so far been restricted mainly to non-official statements, and have been made (often indirectly and generally in vague language only), by individuals lacking meaningful political power. Moreover, such expressions – limited as they were – have always been guarded by numerous pre-conditions and were accompanied by continued official – and non-official – rejection of Israel and its policies in the harshest possible ways. Yet, gradually, more pragmatic views have been expressed, some even in public.

This chapter studies in some detail the Iranian attitudes towards Israel, concentrating on the ideological and declarative stances of the Islamic Republic towards Israel, the Arab–Israeli peace process and the Israeli regional policies. Of all the attitudes and policies of Iran, the question of Israel seems to be one that has not undergone substantial change in the course of the two last decades. Furthermore, the formulation of the Iranian position toward Israel encapsulates an array of values, beliefs and emotions, which have dominated the attitudes toward regional politics – chief among these, their attitudes towards Western imperialism, world capitalism and Islamic solidarity. These charges and pronounced statements against Israel may further explain the difficulties involved in retreating from such entrenched positions. In line with the general approach adopted in this study, the discussion below deals primarily with the ideological positions and statements expressed by Iranian officials, polemicists and intellectuals.

THE IDEOLOGICAL BASIS FOR ANIMOSITY

Ideologically, Iran's rejection of Israel's right to exist was utterly unequivocal and totally uncompromising. It became one of the most fundamental tenets of its revolutionary creed and was repeatedly stressed in Khomeini's writings and statements prior to the revolution. This was not a tactical position, filling a vacuum left by the failure of Arab leaders to confront Israel but an expression of the Islamic regime's identification with the tragedy of the Palestinians and its opposition to Israeli control over Palestine. It was the duty of the Muslim world to correct this historical injustice. Khomeini's repeated references to the issue, at least since the early 1960s, gave further meaning to the Iranian attitude.[2] Many of the leading revolutionaries have repeatedly stressed the issue and some (such as Rafsanjani and Velayati) have even written essays on the question.[3]

The initial 'sin' was Israel's very existence. Iran, therefore, categorically denied its right to exist, regardless of boundaries and actual politics. This constituted an important pillar of Khomeini's creed, and turned into one of the most dogmatic elements characterizing the revolutionary regime's first two decades in power. It reflected a deep sense of religious mission, sincere identification with the Palestinian problem and resolute opposition to Israel's existence, policies and its control over Jerusalem. It was, as one Iranian source has put it, even 'deeper than our opposition to the United States'. While the animosity to the latter is 'due to its 'anti-human politics', Israel 'is illegitimate by its very basis, foundation and structure', wrote an Iranian newspaper in 1999. Moreover, if the United States did, one day, change its policy, it would 'cease to be a major enemy'. But Israel would always remain an enemy, 'under all circumstances'. As long as 'a Zionist regime exists [even] in part of Palestine' it vowed, Iran's struggle against it will continue.[4]

Due to its self-image as the proponent of the Islamic cause, Tehran took the lead in rejecting Israel's right to exist. Although some of its main arguments were similar to those that had been raised earlier in Arab political discourse, significant religious elements were injected into them, marking them off from the previous Arab–national claims and from the attitude held in wide segments of the Arab world in the 1990s. Most profoundly, in this regard, was the tendency 'to Islamize' the Arab–Israeli conflict, 'to sanctify' Palestine and to stress the religious obligation to struggle for its liberation. In this regard, the Iranian position had much more in common with the claims of the Islamist movements (such as Hamas, Islamic Jihad and Hizballah) than with the claims of Arab nationalists in the 1960s and the 1970s.

According to this premise, Judaism constituted a faith, not a nation. Therefore, Jews were not entitled to a state of their own, and certainly not by depriving the Palestinians of their legitimate rights, let alone one in the heart of the lands of Islam with Jerusalem as its capital. Making this their focal point, Islamists often went on 'to sanctify' Islamic Palestine in a hitherto unprecedented manner. In the past, even such prominent figures as Hasan al-Banna had spoken of Palestine as the 'heart of the Arab world and the knot of the Muslim peoples' but had not used this kind of sanctifying terminology. In fact, the patriotism of Islamist movements, such as Hamas, encompassed 'divine factors which endow it with a spirit of vitality'.[5] Its leaflets speak of Palestine as the 'Promised Land' (*al-watan al-maw'ud*) of Islam, 'a term' which Sivan argues 'has no basis in Muslim tradition and is evidently copied from the Zionist religio-political vocabulary'.[6] Islamization of the conflict, in the sense of 'injecting massive doses of Islamic symbols, ideas, and values into an already difficult situation',[7] characterized the Iranian Islamic approach. Moreover, in their view, Israel was not only the enemy of Islam, but also of the whole of humanity. Thus, in 1971, Khomeini appealed to pilgrims heading for Mecca to liberate Palestine from the grasp of Zionism, presenting it as 'the enemy of Islam and humanity'.[8] This, too, was common to other Islamists. The Charter of the Lebanese Amal Movement states that Zionism poses 'the real and continuing danger' to 'the values in which we believe, to the entire region, and to the whole of humanity'.[9] Having undertaken this worldwide mission, Iran saw it as its duty to enlighten Muslim peoples about their sacred duty.

Iran thus viewed the Arab–Israeli conflict as involving two diametrically opposed powers: the absolute good embodied in Islam and blasphemy personified by its rivals; the struggle between righteousness (*haq*) and falsehood (*batel*), between light and darkness.[10] In the eyes of many Islamists, the conflict was between 'Jews and gentiles',[11] an attitude inherent in Iranian writings and statements. Israel, they argued, was the

'absolute evil'. Therefore, as the Lebanese leader Nabih Berri maintained, 'whoever stands against it' becomes 'an absolute good'.[12] The
'dispossession of the Palestinians', Imam Musa al-Sadr added, initiated
'a struggle between right and wrong, occupied and occupiers, oppressed
and oppressor'. While Israel is 'an absolute evil' and an 'historical
aberration', the Palestinian revolution is 'the ideal and most sacred of all
revolutions', a cause that every believer should uphold.[13] It was the duty
of the Islamic Revolution to lead, guide and support the camp of the
believers.

In line with this philosophy, Iranians typically maintained that Israel
was 'by its very nature (*zata*) against Islam and the Qur'an', as shown
even in the time of the Prophet (*surat al-ma'idah*).[14] It was, therefore, the
religious duty (*taklif-e shar'i*) of every Muslim to confront it.[15] This was
imperative given the fact that Israel was established in the first *qiblah*
('direction of prayer', i.e., Jerusalem). The liberation of Palestine is not
only the sacred duty (*vajeb*) of the Palestinians, but of all Muslims,
everywhere. Again, Iran as a leading Muslim state should be in the front
line of such a crusade. This sense of duty should not disappear with the
passing of time, since time cannot turn any falsehood (*batel*) into righteousness (*haq*) and is unlikely to change the usurping nature of Israel.

For Iran, the main aim was not 'to establish peace' (*ijad-e solh*), but
to regain rights (*ehqaq-e haq*) and to establish justice (*ejra'-ye 'edalat*).
Even if Palestinian refugees refrained from returning to their homeland
– because they had no choice or had become accustomed to living away
from Palestine – and even if the Palestinians who currently live in Israel
were forced to acknowledge its existence, the Zionist regime would
always remain a 'usurper and illegitimate'. Neither the betrayal by Arab
leaders and the leaders of Palestinian organizations themselves, nor
international recognition could provide Israel with any legitimacy. This
was not only a Palestinian issue, but a Muslim religious crusade. As one
Iranian newspaper put it, 'even if we are more Palestinian than the
Palestinians, we are only fulfilling our [sacred] duty'.[16]

In line with their Arab counterparts, revolutionary Iranians also
rejected the Zionists' claim that Palestine was the historical home of
Jews. Today's Jews, they claimed, were not the offspring of Patriarch
Abraham; by contrast, the Arabs have lived in Palestine throughout
history. Arabs are the descendants of the Canaanites and Phoenicians,
who controlled Palestine for 1,500 years, wrote Rafsanjani.[17] Similarly,
'Ali Akbar Behbudikhwah maintained that while the Jews had lived in
Palestine only for a short while, Palestinians 'are the children of the same
Palestinians and the Canaanites and the other original tribes'. Jewish

claims of a historical right to Palestine were, therefore, totally baseless, from the legal and historical point of view. 'Palestine is not the historic homeland of the Jews', Behbudikhwah thus concluded.[18] Palestine had never been a Jewish 'national homeland' (*vatan-e melli*). A Jewish 'presence' (*hozur*) was evident only during the reigns of Kings David and Solomon, as compared with 2,500 years of Arab residence.[19] Such historical facts, Khamene'i asserted, 'cannot be ignored' with the passage of 50 years.[20]

Another typical and related charge was that Israel is a fabricated state. This, too, was a repetition of similar charges made previously in the Arab world. Rafsanjani enumerated the damage done by this flimsy (*pushali*) state of Israel to the Muslim world.[21] Khamene'i asked whether Palestine could 'be wiped from the world's map and replaced with a fabricated and false state by the name of Israel?'[22]

Velayati devoted a whole chapter in his book *Iran va Mas'aleh-ye Felestin* to the Shi'i clerics' rejection of 'the separation of Palestine', and to their attempt to save it from foreign invaders. The clerics had viewed the sale of lands to Jews before Israel's independence as tantamount to waging a 'war against Islam' (*jang ba Islam*) and trampling (*paymal*) on the faith of Islam. Those who acted in this manner were like infidels (*kuffar*). Iranian–Shi'i '*ulama*' in Iraq, Velayati added, were also among the first to oppose Palestine's separation, calling for a *jihad* to save the world of Islam from such an affliction.[23] Iran was thus duty-bound to follow their directives and to fulfil Khomeini's own creed to eliminate the anti-human state of Israel. On this point hostility to Israel was linked with basic revolutionary-Shi'i tenets stressed by Khomeini in the 1970s, especially the duty of the believer to confront injustice and oppression actively. There was no better way to demonstrate religious devotion or practice martyrdom (*shehadat*) than to engage in the battle for the liberation of Jerusalem.

In his 1979 message to *hajj* pilgrims, the first since taking over as head of the Islamic regime, Khomeini made his stance on this issue loud and clear. Since 'the first *qibla* of the Muslims', i.e., Jerusalem, has 'fallen into the grasp' of Israel, he said, it was the duty of every Muslim 'to prepare himself for battle against Israel'.[24] Rafsanjani's book *Isra'il va Qods-e 'Aziz*, similarly maintained that this struggle was the sacred duty (*vazifeh*) of 'every Muslim and of anyone who believes in justice'.[25] Velayati in his book, *Iran va Mas'aleh-ye Felestin*, also stressed that Palestine – the 'heart of the Muslim world' – has become 'one of the first priorities of Iran's foreign policy'.[26] *Iran News* spelled out the Iranian attitude by declaring that Israel is now Iran's 'enemy number one'.[27]

Israel was accused of not only occupying Palestine, but also of destroying Muslim holy places. Having long castigated Israel for 'burning the al-Aqsa Mosque' in 1969, Iranian revolutionaries now alleged that the Israelis were encouraged by their rabbis to believe that by the year 1999 Solomon's Temple would be rebuilt on the ruins of the mosque.[28] As a typical commentary on Radio Tehran maintained, the Zionist policy of insulting, and whenever possible destroying the Islamic sacred places, has been most evident in the occupied territories. To achieve 'their illegitimate gains they have taken every measure to annihilate other divine religions'.[29] The opening of the archaeological tunnel in Jerusalem in September 1996 provided another opportunity to express such views more forcefully. The foreign ministry spokesman, Mahmud Mohammadi, warned that such 'desecration of the Muslim holy places' was 'a prelude to the erasure of Islamic sites in Jerusalem'.[30] Majlis deputy, Ebrahim Baysalami, made similar charges, claiming that this new 'conspiracy', aimed at the 'destruction of the Al-Aqsa Mosque', was an insult to Muslim beliefs and an attempt to eliminate 'Islamic values'.[31] *Jomhuri-ye Islami* also viewed the 'digging [of] criss-cross tunnels' around the al-Aqsa Mosque as aimed 'at its gradual destruction'. This it claimed, making a connection with the peace process, was not only disastrous in itself, but an insult to all Muslims and 'a further mockery' of 'disgraced Arab governments, who humble themselves by stretching begging hands toward the Zionists', in search of compromise (i.e., peace).[32]

For hard-liners like Velayati, such developments only revealed the 'savage nature' of Israel. They also demonstrated that the Arab leaders only 'harbored idle dreams' that Israel would 'show compassion, mercy, and goodwill'. In fact, Israel 'has been founded on and has its basis' in the killing of Palestinians and violating their basic rights.[33] Addressing the UN Security Council in 1996, Velayati pointed to 'the desecration of Islamic holy places and the indiscriminate massacre' of innocent Muslims.[34] In this context, Israel's 'endeavor to Judaize Jerusalem' has only 'highlighted the religious factor underlying Israel's rejection of the Palestinian people'. This and the 1969 al-Aqsa fire provided Islamists everywhere with a similar pretext to reiterate 'not only the religious significance of Jerusalem, now more directly threatened, but also the need to Islamize the conflict in order to harness the greater potential of Muslims worldwide'.[35]

Although the duty to support the camp of the true believers is common to all Islamists, it is unusual for it to be incorporated as a part of government policy, as in Iran, where it is also echoed by various domestic camps and the established clergy. Indeed, the Iranian government's emphasis on the Palestine question is even more marked than in other Islamist regimes, such as those in Sudan or Afghanistan with their more limited capabilities. But the charges against Israel are not based only on purely religious arguments.

When the Islamic regime took over, one yardstick used to measure its allies and foes was the degree of their closeness to the former regime. Animosity towards Islam and hostility towards Iran were thus inter-related, as was the rejection of Israel for its own demerits and mal-practice, for its serving the goals of imperialism, and for its anti-Iranian policy since the revolution. According to this view, Israel's hostility to Islam is not limited to Palestine, but extends to all Muslim lands, includ-ing Iran. In a speech on 3 June 1963, Khomeini declared that 'Israel does not wish' the Qur'an, the *'ulama'*, or any single learned man 'to exist in this country'. It was Israel that assaulted the Fowziyeh Madrasa in Qom by means of 'its sinister agents'. Israel wishes 'to seize your economy, to destroy your trade and agriculture, to appropriate your wealth' and to remove from its way 'anything it regards as blocking its path', most notably the Qur'an.[36] Iranian preachers, Khomeini alleged, were even warned not to speak up against the Shah or against Israel. Khomeini therefore wondered: 'What is this tie ... between the Shah and Israel that makes SAVAK consider the Shah an Israeli? Does SAVAK consider the Shah a Jew?'[37] In an open letter to Prime Minister Amir 'Abbas Hoveyda on 16 April 1967 Khomeini warned him against concluding 'a treaty of brotherhood' with Israel, 'the enemy of Islam and the Muslims'.[38] Following the 2,500th anniversary of the monarchy in 1971, Khomeini further accused the government of asking for Israeli help to prepare the celebrations. Israel was portrayed as 'that stubborn enemy of Islam and the Qur'an, which a few years ago attempted to corrupt the text of the Qur'an, and now imputes to the Qur'an unworthy statements'. Israel, Khomeini added, planned 'to occupy all the lands of Islam up to Iraq and (God forbid) to destroy the noble shrines of Islam!'[39] In a message to *hajj* pilgrims in 1971 Khomeini portrayed Israel as 'the universally recognized enemy of Islam and the Muslims', that, with the help of the Shah's government, has 'penetrated all the economic, mili-tary, and political affairs' of Iran. This, he said, had turned Iran into 'a military base for Israel' and 'by extension, for America'.[40] Thus, in the minds of many revolutionary Iranians, Israel was behind every sinister scheme. In making such points they often exaggerated wildly. A school textbook blamed Israel even for supporting Iraq in its war with Iran. Even the Israeli attack on Iraq's nuclear reactor in 1981 was 'another example of the conspiracy' between Israel and the Arab states against Iran.[41]

On this point, Khomeini's charges were also linked with his deep anti-imperialist sentiments, something that was shared by some lay intellectuals who resented imperialism and whatever resembled it. In Khomeini's words, Israel was created by imperialism 'in order to suppress and exploit the Muslim peoples', and has been supported ever since 'by all the imperialists'.[42] The West, Al-e Ahmad added, has 'planted Israel as a cover for its own misdeeds'. It has 'planted Israel in the heart of the Arab lands so that the Arabs should forget the real troublemakers in the midst of Israel's trouble-making . . . the French and the American capitalists'.[43] In an article headed 'Israel an Imperialist Phenomenon', a school textbook attributes the creation of Israel to an imperialist plot to divide the Arab world in order to perpetuate imperialist influence in the region. This, it claims, was done in cooperation with Jewish capitalists who were after profits. Thus, 'the political and economic motives were combined' in collaboration with wealth (*zar*) and power (*zur*), to give birth to Zionism, which resembled its father – imperialism.[44] (For Khomeini's anti-imperialist statements, see Chapter 6.)

Kamal Kharrazi maintained in 1998 that Israel is 'the only remaining racist regime in the world'. Israel was created on the basis of political and racist motives, and was supported by foreign powers. Such powers wished 'to establish for themselves a base in the heart of Muslim countries' in order to prevent the growth and progress of Islamic countries and the emergence of a 'united Muslim collectivity'. With the formation of Israel, he added, 'they made the Muslim countries turn all their efforts to confronting such a regime', so that instead of focusing on the development of their region and solving their own problems, 'they had this problem to deal with'. The great powers 'have created such a nest here and have caused disunity and the exhaustion of the resources of Islamic countries'. They had 'political and racist motives' and 'succeeded in placing a number of Jews, a number of Zionists, and to lay the basis for such a usurper regime'.[45]

This was not of course the first 'encounter' of Islam and the Christian world in the Holy Land. Much as in Arab writing, the case of the Crusaders has repeatedly been mentioned in Iranian references to the problem of Palestine. These also made a link between Zionism and imperialism, politics and faith. Like the Crusaders, the new imperialists of the West sensed that they were unlikely to achieve their goal unless they took over the 'heart' of the Muslim world, i.e., Palestine. Yet, while in the past the West sought to achieve its goal through the Church, now it has moved on to use politics and 'indirect strategy' – the foundation of Israel – and to gain doubly: to free itself of the Jews and to divide the Muslim world. The Zionists, Velayati maintained, are thus the 'new crusaders' (*salibiyun-e jadid*). To draw the link, he quoted General Edmund Allenby who upon entering Jerusalem said: 'Now, the Crusades are over', and French General Henri-Joseph-Étienne Gouraud who declared at the tomb of Saladin: 'We have returned, O Saladin!'[46] Imperialists created Israel as their tool, and Israel acted at their bidding. The allusion to the Crusaders gave some comfort, however. While stressing Israel's military strength and the use of force, Iranians often made the point that its presence in the region – just as that of the Crusaders – was only temporary. Reiterating a much-quoted example in Arab writing, President Rafsanjani predicted in 1997 that Israel's fate would be similar to that of the Crusaders, who were even more bloodthirsty and barbaric than the Zionists,[47] but ultimately failed.

Nevertheless, as long as it exists, Israel would continue to endanger Iran and the entire region. Israel was also accused of seeking to realize its historical vision – 'the Nile-to-Euphrates dream'.[48] This diabolical scheme was unquestionable. Rafsanjani maintained that Zionists were striving to achieve their historic goals 'from Lebanon to the Nile and from the Mediterranean to the Euphrates'.[49] Reiterating this point, Behbudikhwah added that Israel viewed the whole region as its 'sphere of living' (*faza'-ye zist*), threatening the sovereignty and territorial integrity of all the Arab states.[50] Similarly, *Jumhuri-ye Islami* maintained that Israel's goal was to establish its rule (*salateh*) 'from the Nile to the Euphrates', claiming that this could be demonstrated by the design of the Israeli flag: the two blue strips on the flag and the star in its middle.[51]

Over time, some Arabs attributed Western support of Israel as part of a Judeo-Christian (or Zionist–Crusader) conspiracy against Islam. Western imperialism, which until then had generally been perceived as a drive for resources and markets, came to be depicted increasingly as 'the hidden image of the crusades undertaken by Western Christians against Muslims of the East'.[52] Thus the creation of Israel, according to Velayati, was a 'diabolical action' intended to 'create a Zionist and anti-Islamic fracture in the heart of the political geography of Islam'. Its aim was to transfer 'the historical crisis between Christians and Jews of Europe to the Islamic World' and convert it into a crisis between Jews and the Muslims of Palestine. It was 'a historic deal' which 'absolved Jews of the death of Jesus Christ' and materialized the 'aspiration of extremist and racist Jews in setting up a Jewish state'. It was not Christianity that offered 'such a recipe', but the 'Crusader mentality of the West influenced by Roman gladiator thinking'.[53]

The Vatican's recognition of Israel in 1993 was seen as another 'Inauspicious Trinity' (*tathlith shum*) of capitalism, Catholicism and Zionism against Islam. *Salam* addressed 'an open petition' to Jesus Christ, blaming the Vatican for pardoning the Jews for having crucified Him. The Vatican's reward to Zionism for their betrayal of Christ, the newspaper suggested, was now intended to help the crooked, the Zionist–Jews, to massacre the Palestinians. The Pope, it wrote, thus preferred 'money and power', over 'morality and humanity'.[54] The Vatican became the bearer of the flag of 'the adulterated (*napakiha*), the unclean (*pelidha*) and the crooked (*nahonjariha*)'. *Ettela'at* suggested that by preferring interest over ideals and divine goals, and by approving such a 'dirty deal', the Vatican's conscience went into 'eternal deep freeze'.[55] This was the reward that the Church has given Israel for the Jews' betrayal of Jesus Christ.[56]

If there was a recognition of Jewish suffering, their distress was attributed to Christendom. In the world of Islam, it was usually maintained, Jews had always lived in peaceful coexistence with their Muslim brethren.[57] It would, therefore, be inappropriate and unjust to ask the Palestinians 'to compensate the Jews' for the sufferings inflicted on them by Christians. Again, this was not a charge put forward by Iranians only. Many others acknowledged that 'the Jew is a sufferer of injustice', but claimed that this had been inflicted on them 'at the hands of the Christian West'. In fact, according to this argument, Jews had more rights under Islam than under Zionism. While Zionism wanted Jews to settle only in Palestine, Islam gave them the right to settle anywhere in the Middle East.[58] Reiterating a similar point, Velayati added that the Europeans, willing to 'resolve the Jewish problem', decided to settle them in Palestine, forcing the Jews on the region and causing problems for themselves as well as for the Arabs.[59] Sirus Naseri, Iran's delegate to the United Nations in Geneva argued that, because 'Europe did not want the Jews' and was anxious to get rid of them, it had tried to establish a state for them. Thus the Palestinians were being called to 'pay the price of Europeans' crimes in Auschwitz and Treblinka'.[60]

As in the rest of the Muslim Middle East, the 1967 war was a turning point in formulating anti-Zionist – and pro-Palestinian and pro-Arab – sentiments. Many Islamists argued that the war was a 'punishment for misplaced trust in the promise of alien ideologies'. For Hasan Ma'mun of al-Azhar, for example, the defeat was a *mihna* (religious test): 'God has punished us that we may go back to Him.'[61] Although Iran continued to maintain close relations with Israel, some Iranians changed their attitude toward Israel at that time.

Such a change of attitude is evident in the writings of Al-e Ahmad, before and after the 1967 war. In the account of his trip to Israel in 1962, Al-e Ahmad expressed sympathy for the Jews and for Israel's achievements, particularly its efforts to assimilate new emigrants through education and the accomplishments of the kibbutz system. A clear anti-Arab sentiment can be found in his writings at the time. As he has put it, 'I, the non-Arab Eastern man . . . having been beaten so many times by this ignoble Arab, am happy at the presence of Israel in the East . . . that can cut the oil pipelines of these [Arab] sheikhs.'[62] In his *Aghaz-e Yek Nefrat* (The Beginning of an Hatred), written immediately after the 1967 war, however, he no longer viewed Israel as a progressive and democratic country, but primarily as an agent of Western imperialism. The Arab then became the brother: 'The conscience of the Iranian intellectual should be bothered', he wrote, 'by the fact that Iranian oil burns in the tanks and airplanes that are killing his Arab and Muslim brothers'.[63]

Iranians often made the point that inter-communal rifts within Israel (mainly the ethnic divide between Ashkenazi and Sephardi) would ultimately lead to Israel's destruction. Ethnic rifts have also been cited as evidence of racist tendencies inherent in Zionism. Alongside similar Arab claims, Iranians argued that the attitude of the Ashkenazi (Jews from Western countries) towards the Sephardi (oriental Jews) represents a sort of racism. A study on Iranian Jews, published in Iran in 1990–91, claimed that oriental Jews in Israel were separated from the Ashkenazim in matters of religion (*nezamat-e shar'i*) and social status (*mowqe'iyyat-e ejtema'i*), and that oriental Jews were second-rate citizens in Israel.[64] This point was repeated in an official collection of documents entitled, 'Documents on the Immigration of Iranian Jews to Palestine'.[65] The existence of a 'sort of animosity' (*guneh-ye doshmani*) between Sephardim and Ashkenazim is also stressed in Velayati's book on Palestine.[66]

Beyond and above all this, Iranians attacked Zionism as a racist ideology, as shown in its attitude to the Palestinians. In the early days of the Iranian Revolution Montazeri said that Zionism was a continuation of the same Jewish racism that had existed in ancient times: Zionists today were equivalent to the Jews of the past and vice versa.[67] This, too, was in line with similar charges among other Islamists. Therefore, because of its 'racist and anti-human' qualities, it was the duty of all human beings to confront Zionism.[68] Israeli attitudes to the Palestinian *intifada* (uprising) were viewed as yet another sign of its fundamental racism. Again, a direct line was drawn between Judaism, Zionism and Israel although officially all three are declared to be separate issues.[69] (See below.) An article entitled, 'Plague in the Name of Zionism', published in *Ettela'at*, viewed Zionism as one of the main calamities of the century. It betrayed 'the credulous' Jews and debauched them. More than that, 'Zionism seduced mankind'. Zionism, the article claimed, was even more harmful than the two world wars.[70]

More often than not, these numerous charges combined to produce a multi-dimensional and categorical rejection. One example of this was an article published by *Jomhuri-ye Islami* on the occasion of 'International Jerusalem Day' in January 1999. Under the title, 'Israel: The Big Fitna [sedition] of the Twentieth Century', it enumerated the main Iranian claims, with a typically harsh tone. Israel, it argued, was not an indigenous (*bumi*) entity, but had been forced on the region by foreign conspiracies. Incompatible with the surrounding environment, it was imposed, through the force of arms and the political tricks of its founders, to serve as the forward battlefront post of the forces of arrogance in the heart of the Muslim world. The Zionist regime was 'a microbe that has inflicted disease on the region'; the Middle East can be cured only by totally removing this tumor from its body. Israel was not, and cannot be, a 'natural phenomenon'. Zionists and Muslims are a 'union of paradoxes'. The goal in the creation of Israel was not the 'founding of a homeland' for the Jews, but the forging of a tool to undermine and fragment the world of Islam. There was, therefore, no option but to 'dismantle' this pariah state and the 'return [of] the terrorists' that had established it to the places from where they 'had been provoked to conquer Palestine'. In another article the newspaper called on all Muslims and their governments to mobilize all their potential to resolve (*hal va fasl*) this great problem (*ma'zal-e bozorg*) in line with the 'will of the Muslim world' and to 'cleanse this shameful stain (*lakeh-ye nang*) off the world of Islam'.[71]

The religious aspects in the Islamists' approach to the question of Palestine, and their allegations of Western support for Israel and its involvement in Iran prior to the revolution were bound to involve arguments against Jews and Judaism as well. Such attitudes were not uncommon in Iranian history, and were reinforced by the political realities in the region, borrowing both from local traditions and from the canon of Western anti-Semitism.[72]

Iranian history has known periods of hostility to Jews. Biases concerning Jews and Arabs (Semites) can be discerned in the writings of such modern Persian authors as Kermani and Hedayat.[73] Khomeini's ideology, as developed prior to his taking power, also contained anti-Jewish elements. On the very first page of his *Al-Hukuma al-Islamiyya*, Khomeini pointed out:

> Since its inception, the Islamic movement has been afflicted with the Jews, for it was they who first established anti-Islamic propaganda and joined in various stratagems, and as you can see, this activity continues down to our present day.[74]

Khomeini accused Jews of distorting Islam, mistranslating the Qur'an, and taking over Iran's economy. Jews were depicted as imperialist spies, agents, and fifth columnists and seen as the real power behind the imperialist plot to take over the whole world.[75] The Prophet of Islam 'eliminated' the Jews of the Bani Qurayza, he said, because they were a troublesome group, causing corruption in Muslim society and 'damaging Islam and the Islamic state'.[76] He added:

> We see today that the Jews have meddled with the text of the Qur'an and have made certain changes in the Qur'an they have printed in the occupied territories and elsewhere . . . We must protest and make the people aware that the Jews and their foreign masters are opposed to the very foundations of Islam and wish to establish Jewish domination throughout the world.[77]

In his book *Towzih al-Masa'el* (Elucidating the Problems), his guide to Muslims for daily life written in the early 1960s, Khomeini emphasized the Shi'i doctrine of the ritual impurity of unbelievers (*nejasah*), listing 'eleven things which made one unclean', including sperm, dogs, pigs, carrion and unbelievers.[78] A school textbook on Islamic culture and religion, discussing 'impure things' (*chizha-ye napak*), refers to causes of disease (microbes and viruses) and then lists impure things, including dogs, pigs, alcohol, excrement and infidels.[79]

Once the revolution had succeeded, however, venomous attacks made by Iranian Islamists gave way to more balanced and tolerant statements about the Jews. Immediately after Khomeini's return to Iran, some prominent figures of the Jewish community met the Ayatollah to affirm their community's allegiance and to make a plea for protection. They made the point that Judaism and Zionism were two totally distinct issues. Khomeini adopted the formula: 'We distinguish between Jews and Zionists. Zionism has nothing to do with religion.' This official distinction – vague as it often appears – is still generally endorsed in official statements.

In reality, manifestations of anti-Jewish sentiment continue to abound, even in the pronouncements of senior government officials. To begin with, as in the Arab world, the distinction between Jews, Israel and Zionism has often remained blurred.[80] There are many references to Israel as a 'bunch of Jews' or to its government as 'a government of unbelievers, of Jews'. In the same vein, American Jews often are termed 'Zionists' and there are occasional references to seventh-century Jews as 'the Zionists of [the Prophet] Muhammad's time'. Khomeini himself made some revealing slips. In a 1982 speech, he began by saying that those who follow in the path of Jesus were worse than the Jews, even if it was 'impossible to say that there is something worse than the Jews'. He then pulled himself up, adding quickly: 'I mean the Jews of Israel.'[81]

As the following passage from a recent article in *Resalat* shows, the terms 'Jews' and 'Zionists' are often used interchangeably. The author wrote about 'the Zionists' who arrived in the United States 'empty-handed' from Europe and became 'influential in the American economy'. In fact, it would be hard to describe Jews who left Europe for the United States as Zionists. Nevertheless, the article maintained that these 'Zionists' have 'plundered the assets of the poor strata of America and set up cartels, trusts, great factories, and banks with huge financial resources'. It continued, providing an explanation for the harassment of Jews: 'They took control of the economic jugular of America' and 'played an important role in determining the fate of . . . the American nation and took control of the reins of [its] government'. The Zionists' control has penetrated so deep, it added, that they 'can paralyze' the American economy. It is therefore 'probable that one day, like Hitler, they will order the annihilation and uprooting of Zionists in America to protect themselves from the influence of these saboteurs'.[82]

Jews were occasionally blamed for their inherent animosity to Islam, and extremely harsh language was used to denounce them. Thus, Hojjat ul-Islam Mohammad 'Ali Allahi stated in 1984 that ever since the birth of Islam 'the corrupt [Jewish] culture . . . a culture of covetousness, a life of usury and interest, treachery, aggression, murder, and sowing divisiveness . . . developed a front against the culture of Islam'.[83] In 1995 Khamene'i referred to Jews as 'those who are subjected to wrath and are wicked'. He then made a link between old Judaism, modern Zionism and the harm done to Muslims, including Iranians. He alleged that those Zionists who lack 'identity and essence', today because of the ugly behavior of some Arab leaders, dictate to other countries how to behave against Iran. The very existence of Israel in the region is therefore superfluous (*ziyadi ast*), he concluded.[84]

Moreover, Iranians – like other Islamists today and Arab nationalists earlier – often convey the message that Jews control the governments of the countries in which they reside (mainly the United States), and even worse, that they betray these governments (preferring the interests of Israel). The case of Jonathan Pollard (convicted in the United States for spying for Israel) provided the context for even harsher accusations in this regard. In a different vein, a public meeting organized by the regime claimed that Marxism was a Jewish plot and that Salman Rushdie's *Satanic Verses* was part of the Israeli conspiracy to destroy Islam.[85] *The Protocols of the Elders of Zion* and venomous anti-Semite caricatures are also routinely published under the auspices of the Islamic regime.

The stress on Jewish control over the world economy became more forceful in the mid-1990s in conjunction with three other major developments: the growing economic difficulties in Iran, US sanctions and the Arab–Israeli peace process, and a series of economic summits (especially in the 1994 Casablanca summit). In this way, world Zionism was linked directly with the anti-Iranian policy of the United States. Thus the *Tehran Times* wrote that the United States' anti-Iranian policy manifested 'the extent of Jewish influence in the decision-making in the United States'.[86] President Clinton's pro-Israeli and anti-Iranian stance, another newspaper argued, was aimed 'to please the rich and influential Jewish lobby in Washington' in order to secure his re-election.[87]

The appointment in late 1996 of Madeleine Albright as US secretary of state was perceived as a further substantiation of Iranian charges. Albright, born a Jew and 'supported by the affluent Jews' in the United States, it was alleged, had clear pro-Israeli leanings. The US National Security Council adviser, Anthony Lake, and US ambassador to Israel, Martin Indyk, who had 'compiled and propounded' the US dual containment doctrine were among 'the staunchest supporters of Israel'.[88] This illustrated US bias in the Middle East and, no less importantly, its anti-Iranian leanings. *Jomhuri-ye Islami* wrote, that the fact that some of the key positions in US Middle East policy formulation were held by Jews and 'about 80 percent of America's mass media network' are 'in the hands of the Zionists', shows the 'octopus-like network of Jews and Zionists' in the US administration.[89] More importantly, Iranians seemed convinced that Israel was orchestrating all imperialist acts against Iran. In this case, they believed it was 'the tail that wagged the dog'.[90] In fact, it was often claimed, 'the political capital' of the United States 'is Tel Aviv'.[91]

The 1994 Casablanca economic conference was seen as the starting point for Israeli economic control over Arab markets that would 'entail further economic misery' for them.[92] The conference was viewed as 'one of the most dangerous gatherings aimed at selling the dignity, honor, independence and assets of Arab countries to the Zionist regime'.[93]

Accusations of Jewish control of the media have long been basic tenets of anti-Semitic literature in the Arab world and in Iran too. Zionism, this 'despised octopus', having used its control over the media to brainwash readers, wrote *Resalat*,[94] had now moved to the film industry 'to attract sympathy in favor of Jews and political Zionism'.[95] According to this logic, movies from *The Ten Commandments* to *Shoah* represented the new 'school of Zionist Cinema'. Under the pretext of revealing the atrocities that Jews had suffered, they used the Holocaust cynically to advance their political – anti-Palestinian – goals. One example cited recently was *Schindler's List*.[96]

Curiously, Iranian sources have often stressed the harm done to Jews in a fairly objective way although this is often claimed to stress that such atrocities occurred in the West, and to link them to 'the Holocaust of our days' – that of the Palestinians.[97] It is argued that just as the Europeans had the right to fight Hitler, so the Palestinians have the right to confront 'the Zionist invaders'.[98] To quote Rafsanjani, the state of Israel 'is illegal, just as the Nazis' presence in France was'.[99] *Kayhan* also castigated Jews for viewing Muslims as 'inferior peoples', who were only born to slavery (*bardegi*) and doomed to remain forever in bondage. This began from the day Jews expressed a preference for Isaac over Isma'il, both sons of Abraham. Given this 'megalomania', it concluded, it was odd that 'the Jews' now stressed that peace was being made between the Children of the Patriarch Abraham.[100] Iranian sources argued further that the 'Talmudic mentality' approves 'the logic of force'[101] and 'advocates the annihilation of the Muslims and legitimizes the shedding of their blood'.[102] While Islam forbids terrorism, *Kayhan* wrote, their 'misleading Torah' explicitly commanded them: 'Kill their [enemy's] men, women, and children; kill even their cattle and sheep; burn their farmlands and destroy their abode.' The 'thought process' of the Zionists and of Hitler 'is the same'.[103] Iranian sources reiterated such comparison between Zionism and Nazism following Israeli attacks on Palestinians or Lebanese, such as Operation Grapes of Wrath, in 1996.[104] The following commentary in *Tehran Times* reflects these multi-dimensional charges as well as the harsh language used in this regard. It denounces what it terms the 'Kosher brotherhood', as a group 'too long intent on Goebbels-style propaganda, acting helpless and crying wolf as the occasion required, picking random targets for destruction and annihilation throughout the Middle East'. It acts as an 'American envoy at one time, at other times acting plenipotentiaries for some European states', and at others as 'trained henchmen and paid killers, becoming pimps and tarts as the occasion requires'.[105]

The trial in France of Roger Garaudy, who was convicted by a Paris court in February 1998 for contesting the view that the Holocaust amounted to a crime against humanity, was used to confirm Iranian claims against Israel, Zionism, world Jewry and the West. Garaudy's invitation to Tehran in April 1998 was used by certain groups to familiarize Iranians with his views and buttress their own ideological message. Many Iranians then condemned Israel for bringing about a 'Palestinian holocaust' and blamed the West for bringing Garaudy to trial while simultaneously protecting Rushdie. Meeting Garaudy on 20 April, Khamene'i pointed to the similarities between Zionism and Nazism, and castigated the West, which on the one hand 'deplores the racist behavior of the Nazis toward the Jews' but supports the Zionists, 'who have the same behavior as that of the Nazis'. He stated that supporting the Zionists is as bad as supporting Nazi Germany and Hitler.[106] Khatami regretted that 'a thinker' and 'a believer' like Garaudy was brought to trial just for publishing research 'about the Jews and the Zionists', which is 'displeasing to the West'.[107] The hard-line press went much further. The 'false slogan of the murder of millions of Jews', one newspaper wrote, was a 'ridiculous pretext' which Zionists had taken to 'fabricating and propagating' in order to convince world opinion of the need to establish a Jewish state.[108] Garaudy was tried even though his claim 'is not far from the truth' and even though many scholars considered the events of Auschwitz to be a 'big lie'. It is quite possible, another paper suggested, that instead of 'writing the history' of the Nazi gas chambers, Western thinkers have 'invented history'.[109] Another Iranian newspaper defended the right of scholars to doubt the 'so-called Holocaust' which is the 'brainchild of the Zionists' to 'seek sympathies' and 'grab billions of dollars annually from the West'. To keep their 'weapon of blackmail vibrant' they make innocent people like Garaudy the 'targets of their irrational attacks'. While scholars doubted the authenticity of the Holocaust, no one could deny 'the 1996 Holocaust' committed by Israel in Lebanon.[110] Unlike the crime committed by Rushdie, Garaudy's statements were 'just historical facts'.[111] Elaborating further on Garaudy's trial, *Kayhan International* claimed that the West had turned into 'an obvious hostage to the theory of "original sin"', to the extent that countries like France did not mind violating their own founding principles to appease the Zionists. Garaudy's trial was a 'judicial holocaust' and the 'trial of freedom of speech', it wrote. Perhaps, it suggested, 'Europe wants to atone for its [own] periodic persecution of Jews', ignoring the fact that Jews 'enjoyed every basic right' in the Muslim world.[112]

The circumstances that led to Khatami's election, his relatively pragmatic policy and the more moderate statements following his election were bound to lead to some relaxation in the statements regarding Jews. Some Iranians had advocated dialogue between Islam and other faiths, including Judaism, long before Khatami's election. Such voices have grown louder and more frequent since then.

The deputy minister of Islamic guidance, Mohammad 'Ali Taskhiri, supported dialogue 'among the divine religions'. This dialogue could also include Jewish scholars, he said, provided they 'dissociate themselves from Zionist mentality'.[113] Khatami's associates, who joined him on his visit to Lebanon shortly before his election, stressed his openness to dialogue with other faiths and his call to renounce religious fanaticism.[114] Mohsen Kadivar reminded his coreligionists that even the Prophet Muhammad and Imam 'Ali 'conducted talks with Jews' and signed treaties with them.[115] Moreover, the 'truth of Islam does not mean the absolute falsehood of Judaism and Christianity'. Kadivar concluded that although 'complete salvation and reward' belonged to Muslims, nevertheless, 'we can both believe in one supreme truth and also not consider other religions and followers of other religions as completely false'.[116] (For Shabestari's views on this subject, see Chapter 6.) Khatami rejected anti-Semitism as 'a Western phenomenon' with 'no precedent' in the world of Islam, where Jews and Muslims 'have lived harmoniously together' for centuries. 'In the east we have had despotism and dictatorship, but never fascism or Nazism', he said.[117] Meeting the leader of Hamas, Shaykh Ahmad Yasin, on 2 May 1998, Khatami said: 'We have no differences with the Jews, but we are against Zionism'.[118] Usually, however, mild references to Jews were combined with harsh language against Zionism, which was often blurred with Jews. Thus, Kharrazi said in an interview that the creation of Israel was not a religious issue, but 'a politically motivated act, a racist act'. It was based on the Zionist philosophy which believes that the Jews 'should be forced, tempted, and taken to this part of the world' to create 'a Zionist base at the heart of Islamic countries'. It was 'the political aim of the great powers' to create Israel, and they succeeded 'in laying the basis for such a usurper regime'.[119]

Generally speaking, the charges against Israel, Zionism and world Jewry remained harsh and often inter-related. That said, there was undoubtedly a conscious effort on behalf of Iranian officials to at least follow Khomeini's dictum and distinguish between Israel and Zionism, on the one hand, and Jews on the other. Even though the above distinction remained largely blurred, their main goal clearly was to denounce Israel and oppose the peace process. With regard to these issues, the Iranian ideological approach and actual policy have remained basically unchanged. Furthermore, these sets of beliefs and attitudes have been shared by most domestic groups and political camps, which otherwise are often opposed to each other. All in all, the harsh rhetoric has persisted and dominated the Iranian approach in this regard more than other areas of political debate. And yet, although no dramatic change has been discerned in Iran's attitude towards Israel since the election of Khatami, there have recently been some differences in nuances and a more diverse language even with regard to the delicate questions related to Israel (see below).

PRAGMATIC CONSIDERATIONS AND OPPOSITION TO THE PEACE PROCESS

As has been pointed out, with very few exceptions, whenever ideological revolutionary convictions clashed with the interest of the state, Iran's state interests ultimately triumphed, forcing a change in its actual policy. Yet such a retreat did not result from new preferences, but was usually imposed by harsh realities. (In a few cases, Iran pursued its revolutionary goals even to the point of impairing its national interests, such as jeopardizing its relations with European countries while in pursuit of Iranian opposition leaders in Europe and reiterating the *fatwa* against the author, Salman Rushdie.) Iran's attitude to Israel was one of the rare examples of adherence to dogma. In this case, so far, ideological hostility does not appear to have clashed with the pragmatic interests of the state, to a degree of forcing a change in such focal dogmatic conviction.

To begin with, Iran's anti-Israeli stance has enhanced its credentials as a major regional power and a leading Islamic state, dovetailing with its ambitions. With other rejectionist states having withdrawn from the scene, as a result of strategic choice (as in the case of Syria), military defeat (Iraq), or marginality (Libya), Iran saw its leadership of the anti-Israel campaign as a means of enhancing its credentials as a major regional power. Moreover, while most Arab states had abandoned their sacred duty to confront Israel, Iran continued to hoist the flag of Palestine, thereby bolstering its pretensions to Islamic leadership. Because of its self image as the major center of anti-US politics Tehran also regarded it as its duty to oppose any US-led initiative aimed at strengthening its hold over the region. It viewed itself as the major foe of 'America's unlawful son' (i.e., Israel) and believed it as its responsibility to oppose any initiative aimed at legitimizing its existence. Tehran also viewed the success of the Palestinian Islamist movements – as well as the Hizballah – as a tribute to its own revolution, a manifestation of the spread of its influence in the region, and evidence of its Islamic leadership. It therefore felt committed to guiding and supporting them – and viewed its support as serving Iranian interests.

Focusing on international issues could also help to divert public attention from pressing domestic problems, to demonstrate success, to highlight Iran's regional importance and to display the regime's adherence to dogma. The uncompromising stance also helped the pragmatists in the regime to display adherence to the ideals of the revolution and thus to satisfy the more dogmatic circles. Iran had consistently supported the Islamist struggle and identified with its cause. Abandoning it could harm its regional plans and alienate hard-liners at home. Even more important was the fact that the political costs involved in gaining these benefits were considered low, compared to the benefits. In a way, some scholars observed, Tehran 'could afford to talk tough while actually doing very little to prevent the Arab slide towards compromise'.[120] Finally, Tehran did not believe that the peace process could resolve the conflict, nor did it trust the Israelis to fulfil their own undertakings. As a Tehran Radio commentary maintained, their 'performance during the last half century clearly shows' that signing agreements 'will never stop the Zionists from showing their extreme hatred towards Muslims and Islam'.[121]

Thus, the basic Iranian attitude remained extremely hostile from the time the new regime came to power. Even before the seizure of power Khomeini had declared Israel a major enemy. Upon coming to power he called on Muslims everywhere to proclaim 17 August 1979 – the last Friday of the month of Ramadan in that year – 'Jerusalem Day', so as to demonstrate solidarity with the 'rights of the Muslim people of Palestine'.[122] This date is still commemorated in Iran annually, marking a major event. On the occasion of the first 'Jerusalem Day' Khomeini called for a campaign to liberate Jerusalem saying: 'If every Muslim was to pour a single bucketful of water on Israel, it would be drowned by an uncontrollable flood.'[123] Yet the animosity went far beyond rhetoric. Iran's support for Islamist movements (see Chapter 7), its presence in Lebanon and its support for Hizballah were some of the main areas of actual encounter between the two states.

Khomeini's unwavering anti-Israeli stand 'has set a legacy' from which the regime is finding it 'difficult to extract itself'. This legacy has been compounded by Khamene'i who, succeeding Khomeini in 1989, 'became increasingly ideological' and continued to uphold the initial dogma. Even 'the moderate leadership' in Iran 'feels compelled to rhetorically reject Israel and the peace process'.[124] For some revolutionaries, the struggle against Israel constitutes one of the essential goals of the revolution. Many, however, eventually ceased to view this aim as practical, or an immediate revolutionary goal. Given the harsh realities at home and new developments in the region, they were not unwilling to reshape their priorities. Yet the decision continues to rest with the conservatives who guard against retreat from dogma, especially if such a major change seemed imminent. At this stage, it is not even clear how much the pragmatists want to retreat from this principle.

Iran's firm position becomes all the more manifest when contrasted with the gradual move toward peacemaking in the Middle East in the 1990s. Tehran viewed the peace process as a treachery (*khiyanat*) against Islam[125] and a contradiction of Islamic aims,[126] and censured the Arab leaders for abandoning their duty to confront Israel. Tehran used every possible opportunity to criticize the United States, to denounce Israel and to condemn the Arab states as well as the Palestinian leadership who were parties to the peace process. It wished to lead the anti-peace camp, calling for a *jihad* (holy war) to save Palestine. It took pride in the fact that Iran alone continued to hoist the flag of Palestine.

When the Madrid conference was convened in October 1991, Tehran organized an international conference, which aimed to unite the movements opposing the peace process. Tehran viewed it as its Islamic responsibility to lead the anti-peace camp – an issue on which the different domestic camps were generally in agreement at the time. Yet there have certainly been differences and contradictory pressures have been at work. According to Shireen Hunter, such an Iranian policy, which stood in contradiction to the otherwise 'general conciliatory, pragmatic trend' in Iran's diplomacy at the time, was prompted largely by pressure from the hard-liners. It was also 'a reaction' to Iran's isolation and marginalization in the region and 'an effort to show that Iran was a country to be reckoned with' and that its pragmatism 'should not be taken for granted'.[127] In initiating the meeting in Tehran, Baktiari maintains, the hard-liners may have also wished to 'compensate' for their own stance in the 1991 Gulf war, and to place Rafsanjani in an 'ideological dilemma'. He was thus left 'to take a tough position on the issue' when 'he was involved in improving relations with Western countries'.[128]

Nevertheless, the opposition to the Madrid initiative united most domestic power groups, at least in their public statements. Tehran wished not only to fill the vacuum left by Arab leaders who were seen to be compromising with Israel, but also to promote the role of Iran and the Muslim world in the emerging new world order following the fall of the Soviet Union. Ayatollah Ardabili viewed the process as a US scheme to make Israel the 'absolute lord of the region so that we [Muslims] become the servant of the servant of America'.[129] The Middle East sector of the new world order, others feared, only meant 'domination and, ultimately, the exploitation of the Middle East'.[130] The Madrid conference was thus viewed as a tool to strengthen Israel with the Arabs receiving in return nothing but 'disgrace and contempt'.[131] For Ahmad Khomeini this represented a US plot to draw the Arabs into a humiliating compromise, in order to ultimately undermine Islam.[132] Tehran therefore castigated the 'reactionary' Arab states participating in the conference, who had bowed down before the United States, which now wanted them to grovel before Israel as well.[133]

However, an examination of the arguments raised by different strands of Iranian domestic political opinion reveals significant variants. While radicals and conservatives alike called for concrete action against US interests and the Arab states, Rafsanjani and his more pragmatic associates stopped short of advocating such measures. Mohtashami led the hard-line approach suggesting that as part of its 'doctrine and duty' Iran should lead the struggle against the United States and Israel. In his view, Muslims 'must use various means to obstruct this conference'.[134] He viewed the very participation in the conference as a 'declaration of war against Islam' and threatened that the revolutionary and martyr-nurturing offspring of Ayatollah Khomeini would turn the world into a graveyard and an inferno for the United States, the Zionists and their mercenaries. 'Based on the *shari'a*', Mohtashami argued, all participants in the conference should be considered *mohareb* (waging war against Islam) and must face a death sentence. 'It is the duty of Muslims in the world to carry that out.'[135] Proceeding from the same premise, he said that it was necessary to 'target all the US objectives throughout the world'.[136] Ardabili called for the formation of resistance cells to fight US interests worldwide, promising that anyone killed in this struggle would 'definitely be a martyr'.[137] He urged devout believers to 'kill Americans'.[138] *Jahan-e Islam* similarly called for a worldwide Islamic mobilization to inflict blows on US interests all over the world.[139] Rafsanjani did not go that far, however. He only vowed that the Arabs would never give up Palestine, and that, one day the 'Muslims will rise up against the Israeli mischief, and America will be left with

[Muslims'] spite and hatred forever'.[140] Khamene'i was more radical than Rafsanjani, but less so than Mohtashami. He threatened that Arab leaders negotiating with Israel would find their rule shaking,[141] and that those participating in the conference would be 'hated by their nations',[142] promising that the 'faithful Palestinian combatants will continue to stay on the scene'.[143]

When the Oslo Accords were signed in September 1993, Tehran convened another conference on Palestine, pledging to spare no effort to defeat them and promising 'limitless support' for their opponents.[144] The official voice from Tehran, radicals and pragmatists alike, was very harsh. They found it crucial to defend Palestine and focused their attacks on Yasser 'Arafat. Rafsanjani vowed that Muslims would not let 'this treason pass lightly', and urged the Islamic states to use their oil wealth and weaponry to revoke the agreement.[145] Khamene'i, calling for an Islamic counterattack to foil the agreement, castigated 'Arafat as a 'notorious, disgraced person' and wondered who had allowed him at all to negotiate in the name of Palestine.[146] 'Arafat's 'treachery' was even more painful than that of Egyptian President Anwar Sadat's peace initiative, since the latter, at least, had retrieved his territory from Israel, while the Palestinians had gained nothing in return.[147] Rallies protesting against the agreement were held in various cities, proclaiming 'readiness to destroy' Israel and to raise the flag of Islam throughout the world.[148] *Majma'-e Ruhaniyyun-e Mobarez* called on the Iranian people to provide 'unconditional support to the glorious intifada' and advised the Iranian government 'to place all its resources' at the service of 'this sacred movement'.[149] *Jomhuri-ye Islami* added that, Palestine being an inseparable part of Islam, no one could make concessions over it and termed the Oslo Accords a sign of enslavement to 'the enemies of Islam' and an act of 'treason and abjectness',[150] the punishment for which was death.[151] Iran continued in its rhetoric against the peace process and, at least at the declaratory level, no significant change could be traced at that time.

Iranians remained generally skeptical of Israel's intentions, even when their main ally, former Syrian President Hafiz al-Asad, was negotiating for peace with Israel, and continued to censure Israel even more vigorously when Israeli–Syrian talks came to an halt in 1996. Velayati represented the general view of the government at that time. 'The Arab people are resentful', he said, 'they do not wish to be humiliated' by compromising with Israel. Iran does not wish to 'create tension with any country', but will also not hesitate 'to defend Islam, Iran, Islamic values . . . and will continue to stand steadfast'. An Israeli military reaction against Iran, he said, 'cannot be completely ruled out', but in such a case Iran 'would not remain silent spectators in the face of aggression'. If Israel resorts 'to such irrational behavior', it would 'suffer from the fall out more than anyone else. Iran has brilliant experience in the field of defense and would certainly give the aggressor an unforgettable lesson.'[152]

Given the already charged situation in the region and the fragile process of peacemaking, Iran's policy placed further obstacles on the path to peace. The Islamic components of Iran's revolutionary creed and its uncompromising stance represented some additional difficulties for Israel as did Iran's actual support and encouragement for the Islamist movements. Although the exact level of Iran's support for Islamist movements is unclear, its actual involvement was meaningful. Velayati stated in 1999, that 'all our friends and enemies know perfectly well', that 'Iran is the [main] supporter of the Hamas and the Hizballah in their struggle against Israel'.[153] In addition, Israel focused on two main allegations: first, Iran's attempts to acquire weapons of mass destruction and the missile technology to deliver them (see Chapter 5) and, second, accusations of Iranian support for terrorism.

Although the concepts of *shehadat* (martyrdom) and *jihad* (holy war) are common to Islamic thought, suicide-type operations were introduced into the Arab–Israeli arena mainly after the Islamic Revolution. Iran viewed martyrdom as *tabrik* (blessing) and the armed struggle as the only way to achieve the Palestinian goals. Iran offered moral support to the Palestinian militant resistance, justified the 'sweet actions' of martyrdom-seeking (*shehadat-talabaneh*),[154] and praised the Palestinian movement as a sign of the growth of 'revolutionary Islam'.[155] For many Iranian leaders, this was the only language 'Jews understand' and the only path to secure the legitimate rights of the Palestinians.[156] Accusations that Iran was behind acts of terrorism (in Argentina, London, New York) were dismissed as Jewish or Zionist propaganda. In fact, Iranian sources often claimed, Muslims were themselves the victims of terrorism, as in Bosnia, Azerbaijan, Chechnya and Palestine. Velayati complained that when Muslims struggled for liberation, 'Western propagandists put the label of terrorism on them.' But those responsible for the massacres of Deir Yasin and Kafr Qasem [i.e., Israel] 'are hailed as advocates of democracy and Western human rights'.[157]

Although Iran did not publicly support the acts of terrorism that led to many casualties in 1994–96 within Israel, it came close to justifying them. Typically, Radio Tehran claimed, following one such blast, that under the circumstances the Palestinians were left with no choice 'but to fight the enemy'.[158] *Jomhuri-ye Islami* termed it a 'just struggle', which has been carried out by 'heroes' and taught Israel 'a serious and effective' lesson, demonstrating that Islamic activists will 'not show any indulgence in avenging Israel's crimes'.[159] Other Iranians called the perpetrators of a suicide attack in 1996 'heroic youth of Islam' and termed their acts 'divine retribution'.[160] Since Muslims believe in 'an eye for an eye and in violence for violence', one newspaper wrote, the Palestinians were justified in resorting to the only path open to them – 'revolutionary rage' – in order 'to answer violence with violence'. It expressed the hope that their revolutionary rage will continue until the 'complete annihilation of Israel'.[161] While insisting that 'we do not approve of terrorist acts', President Rafsanjani argued that the Palestinians 'do not have any other means of defending themselves'.[162]

There were, however, some relatively moderate statements even at that time, with Iranian officials disclaiming support for the opponents of the peace process and some – mainly the intellectuals and the press – voicing more forthright opinions. Typical of such a pragmatic tone was the statement by Rafsanjani, who said that, when we see that 'this whole process is unjust, we state our opposition as a matter of principle. But if the content of the peace plan is just, the substance is just, we shall go along with it.'[163] The generally hard-line secretary of the SNSC, Hojjat ul-Islam Hasan Ruhani, stated that although his country was not optimistic about the Oslo Accords, Iran neither intends to take action against it nor to interfere in the process. In a subsequent interview in *Ettela'at*, he added that, although Iran will not hesitate to adopt any measure to vindicate the right of the Palestinians, it was not seeking to pursue any military actions against this 'shameful accord'.[164] *Salam* lamented that when officials move away from domestic forums (underlining the fact that Ruhani's statement was made while on tour in Europe), they distanced themselves from the firm stances expected of them.[165] Such views, *Jomhuri-ye Islami* noted, reflected an 'overtly different' position from Iran's otherwise 'very clear stance'.[166] Though some pragmatic observations could be found throughout the 1990s, they became much more open, frequent and daring after Khatami's election.

SIGNS OF A MORE NUANCED ATTITUDE

Although all domestic groups seemed confident of the justice of the revolutionary stance, there were signs over time of a more diversified tone in the approach of few. Moderate expressions were infrequent, they were usually voiced by people with no official standing and were usually coupled with reservations and significant preconditions. Yet they revealed some cracks in the otherwise united front against Israel and the peace process. The gap may have been even wider than was reflected in public statements.

Hard-liners continued to view any compromise as a betrayal of the sacred revolutionary mission. Yet, given Iran's own domestic difficulties, its limited power to reverse the trend, and the fact that the Palestinians were making the move of their own choice, some Iranians began to doubt the advisability of being 'more Palestinian than the Palestinians'. Iranian academics who visit the West report a more moderate reaction to Israel among intellectuals and the common people in Iran. Foreign scholars who visit the country usually come back with similar observations.[167] Evidently, a growing number of Iranian intellectuals came to recognize that, under the circumstances, it was impractical and unwise for Iran to take the lead in opposing a process that the Arab leaders themselves endorse. Such observers often maintain that Israel is certainly not the prime concern of the Iranians. Clearly, there were more moderate statements since the early 1990s. They gained force after Khatami's election, and further intensified in the aftermath of the elections in Israel and the formation of the government of Ehud Barak. It is not clear how much support such emerging voices have in Iran. Such views have not yet produced any major policy change, nor have they led any of the main rival camps in Tehran to publicly doubt the need for Iran's firm stance on the issue. However, there have been more moderate voices and public statements in this regard. Interestingly, even such a basic doctrinaire concept is no longer beyond debate.

Certainly Khatami himself did not spare harsh words when referring to Israel. He often used terms like racism and fascism to denounce Israel and its politics. Yet one element was noticeable in his statements all along – that Iran would not disrupt any just agreement reached between the two sides. However, even this was often coupled with doubts about the possibility of achieving a just peace settlement and the reiteration of the right of return for all Palestinian refugees.

Reiterating Iran's opposition to the peace process in his first news conference after victory, Khatami pledged not to take action to disrupt it. Iran was 'interested in peace and tranquility', he said, on condition that 'the rights of all sides' were observed. No peace could be established, he said, 'except with the restoration of the legal rights of all Palestinian people'. However, Iran was 'not going to [undertake] any intervention in this matter' and would only 'keep the right' to express its views. Still, we 'think that the current process will not come to any conclusion'.[168] At his oath-taking ceremony in the Majlis, he reiterated that Iran welcomed a genuine peace in the Middle East 'based on justice', and was ready to play a fair and impartial role to advance it based on United Nations resolutions.[169]

In an interview with CNN television in January 1998 Khatami continued to express disbelief in the possibility of achieving a real and just peace, but denied any intention to disrupt the attempt to reach such a peace. He made it clear that Iran opposed the peace process 'because we believe it will not succeed'. Yet 'we do not intend to impose our views on others or to stand in their way'. In his view, all Palestinians, including those in the Diaspora, should have 'the right to express their views about their land'. Regrettably, the unbridled American support for the 'racist and terrorist regime' of Israel does not serve US interests nor the Jewish people. As for the peace process, Khatami believed that it would fail, because 'it is not just'. Iran, however, was ready 'to contribute to an international effort to bring about a just and lasting peace', he added.[170] Addressing the United Nations General Assembly on 21 September 1998, Khatami reiterated that peace and security in the Middle East would be established only through the recognition of the right of all Palestinians to exercise sovereignty over their ancestral homeland, but that Israeli rule had made coexistence impossible. Palestine is the home of all Palestinians – Muslims, Christians and Jews – and not the laboratory for the violent whims of Zionists, Khatami noted.[171]

Adopting a more belligerent tone at the Tehran ICO summit in December 1997, Khatami reiterated that genuine peace could be established 'only through the realization of all the legitimate rights of the Palestinian people, including the inalienable right to self-determination, return of refugees, [and] liberation of [all] the occupied territories'. Yet 'the hegemonic, racist, aggressive and violent nature' of Israel manifested in 'the systematic and gross violation of international law, pursuit of state terrorism and development of weapons of mass destruction, seriously threatens peace and security in the region'.[172] The Arabs, he said, have already realized that they were dealing 'with a racist, terrorist, and expansionist regime'.[173] Addressing the children of Lebanese martyrs, he went further in describing Israel as 'the most prominent manifestation of international terrorism'.[174] On Jerusalem Day in 1998, reiterating Iran's commitment to support the deprived, he again attacked 'the racist' Zionist regime as the 'root of tension' and blamed the United States for supporting that 'racist, bullying regime, that focal point of state terrorism'.[175] Meeting Shaykh Yasin in Tehran, Khatami again termed Zionism a 'continuation of fascism', adding: 'I am sure that the future will be in favor of the righteous and to the benefit of the Palestinian people resisting [Israel].'[176] For him, too, Israel has been, and continues to be the plague (*ta'un*) of the region and of the world.[177] In their public statements at least there was not much difference between some of Khatami's statements and those of Khamene'i on this issue.

Still, Khamene'i's tone was usually harsher and more uncompromising, reflecting the view of the more doctrinaire elements and thus balancing pragmatic statements by other observers. Addressing the Revolutionary Guards on 17 September 1997, he thus vowed that, ultimately Israel would be wiped off the pages of history itself.[178] At the Tehran ICO summit, he described the peace process as 'unjust, arrogant, contemptuous' and altogether 'illogical'.[179] For Khamene'i, Palestine was the frontline of Islam's war against infidelity. At a meeting with Shaykh Yasin, he promised Iran's support and said that Iran would not recognize Israel 'even for one hour' and would 'continue to struggle against this cancerous growth'.[180] This set the tone for many hard-line statements. *Kayhan International*, reiterating the customary revolutionary credo that 'Israel should be erased from the map of the Middle East', maintained that Israel was the only country 'which is not recognized' by Iran.[181] It claimed that the 'peace' negotiations were not 'genuine, honest and objective', and that the United States was biased towards Israel, while Arab governments which supported the peace talks ignored the violations of Palestinian rights. Peace could only be achieved with the restoration of the complete rights of the Palestinians.[182] Even 'at the cost of its own national interests', *Iran News* declared, Iran 'can never compromise' on the question of Palestine. The liberation of Palestine, it added, continued to be 'at the core' of Iran's policy.[183] Aware of some milder statements, the hard-line *Jomhuri-ye Islami* urged officials to avoid vague statements and to adhere fully to the explicit and accepted policy – that the Zionist regime was illegitimate and that this 'cancerous growth' must be uprooted completely.[184]

As with its stance on earlier agreements between Israel and the Palestinians, Iran also criticized the Wye agreement of 1998. *Kar va Kargar* reiterated that Iran's 'pivotal policy' of defending Palestinian rights has over time 'become firmer and stronger'. For more than 50 years Palestine had been under the occupation of 'a malicious, racist, and rebellious group' and currently, the al-Aqsa Mosque is under the claws of the Zionists. 'The era of compromise agreements' has ended. A 'rootless movement' (i.e., the Palestinian Authority) cannot accept any 'shameful agreements and submit to any humiliation'. The newspaper declared: 'We will bury the boot-wearers of Zionism.'[185]

More importantly, no substantial change could be discerned in Iran's support for Hizballah or other Islamist movements opposing the peace process, although criticism of such an alleged tendency was voiced by some hard-liners. In fact, with the possibility of renewed Israeli–Syrian peace talks late in 1999, Israeli sources pointed to more concentrated efforts by Iran to supply arms to the Hizballah directly.[186] Generally, animosity to Israel remained the main issue over which there has been much agreement among the main rival camps, or at least in their public statements.

Yet, from time to time, relatively moderate views were also expressed, sometimes even pointing to some positive elements within the Israeli state, or questioning the advisability of Iran's continued hostility. With all their reservations and pre-conditions, such expressions signaled a measure of change, at least in some segments of Iranian society.

Mainly after Oslo, some observers acknowledged Israel's existence as a fact that had to be reckoned with and some even pointed to its achievements. Farhang Raja'i, then professor at Tehran's Beheshti University, maintained that, although engaged in war since its independence, Israel had managed to develop and avoid becoming a tool in the hands of others,[187] contrary to expectations. Ahmad Naqibzadeh, another professor at Tehran University, pointed to Israel's 'numerous achievements', in the realm of economic development, and its effort to provide equal opportunities to all its people.[188]

From time to time, Islamists surmised that 'Israel's existence as a Jewish' state, explained its success in its wars. They often remarked that 'Israel wins because it is faithful to its religion, and the Arabs are defeated because they are insufficiently devoted to Islam'.[189] Although the 'Jewish State' was not a religious state like Iran or Sudan, and its leaders are not religious, Naser Hadiyan maintained in 1995, that its attempt to incorporate religion and the principles of Zionism was instrumental in attaining its goals. He argued that Israel had tried to fit old concepts into new realities and the emerging needs of the new state, and used religion as a tool to indoctrinate young soldiers.[190]

In due course, some Iranians also acknowledged that international realities – mainly as they were established following the collapse of the Soviet Union – worked to the advantage of Israel.[191] Ahmad Naqibzadeh said that the Arab–Israeli conflict began with interference by international elements and that the recent Arab tendency to compromise was in part the result of the new international circumstances.[192] Seyyed Kazem Sajjadpur, an Iranian observer, claimed that 'entirely new circumstances' had developed in the early 1990s.[193] Although the author did not suggest a change in this regard, for many in Iran such new realities meant a need to readjust Iranian policies in one way or another.

Some went as far as to claim openly that, regardless of the revolutionary slogans, Israel could not be annihilated. Farhang Raja'i reminded his fellow Iranians that even after 2,000 years Jews had not ceased to exist. One cannot terminate a nation, he pointed out, stressing that even the Prophet Muhammad had not tried to annihilate the Jews, but only to incorporate them.[194] Ahmad Naqibzadeh seconded him. We raise the slogan 'Israel should be eliminated', but is this at all practical? Most states in the world now spoke about achieving a just peace in the Middle East, rather than the destruction of Israel, he noted. Moreover, if the Palestinians themselves decided to make peace with Israel, no other state had the right to be more Palestinian than the Palestinians (literally, to be a bowl that is warmer than the soup; *kaseh daghtar az ash*), or to condemn them for making peace. Yet, he too did not believe it would be easy to resolve the problem.[195] Such statements became more outspoken after Khatami's election.

The weekly *Arzeshha*, edited by the former minister of intelligence, Mohammad Reyshahri, set out to answer questions being raised regarding Iranian policy on this question. That the newspaper felt the need to answer such questions attested to their prevalence, at least in certain segments of the society.

Under the title 'Why the Islamic Republic has turned more Palestinian than the Palestinians' it first enumerated the questions and then refuted them in turn. Every year, such people argued, numerous demonstrations were held in Iran 'in support of the oppressed people of Palestine', where it was stressed that Israel should be erased and eliminated (*mahv va nabud shavad*). 'Disregarding whether this desire is possible or logical, the following question is also raised: have not we become a bowl warmer than the soup (*kaseh daghtar az ash*)?' Palestine has its own representative organizations, which after years of struggle can now achieve their goals better 'by turning to the path of peace' and thus regaining lands to establish a Palestinian state. They may also have concluded that by 'pursuing the past practices' they would not be able 'to free even one iota (*vajab*) of the lands of this country'. In the midst of all this, Iran 'has turned even more Palestinian than the Palestinians and it accuses the leaders of the Arab states and the heads of the Palestinian organizations of betrayal and compromising. Is this [Iranian] policy, which is not acceptable even to the Palestinians themselves, at all logical and wise?'[196] The newspaper answered such questions, of course, but their presentation and the need to answer them was, nevertheless, a sign of the prevalence of such queries in Iran.

The change of government in Israel and the election of Barak in May 1999 has not been followed by any marked softening in Iran's approach. For the Islamic regime, the problem emanates not from the policy of any specific party in Israel, but is inherent in the very nature of the Zionist regime. Many Iranians, therefore, saw no basic differences in the approach of the two main parties in Israel (in their attitude to the question of Jerusalem, Jewish settlements, Jewish immigration, and Israel's racist policy towards the Arabs of Israel). The Likud Party, wrote *Jomhuri-ye Islami*, was in many ways even preferable to the Labor Party. After all, Labor governments engaged in four wars against the Arabs, perpetrated the worst crimes and have a more malicious and negative record. Moreover, the difference between the two parties was not in their goals, but only in the ways prescribed to achieve them. The personal record of Barak (and his own crimes in Lebanon) did not bode well either. Therefore, any expectation of change under Barak was merely a hollow hope and a childish and naive dream. Other articles in the same newspaper stressed the Zionist expansionist vision (from the Nile to the Euphrates), and alluded to Ben-Gurion's alleged belief that the Zionist vision could be achieved by either military or political means.[197] This, it suggested, was the main difference between Likud and Labor and the essence of the change brought about by the elections.

Others pointed to some innovation, although not sufficient change, with Barak's election. *Tehran Times* viewed the election of Barak as a 'White Revolution' (i.e., one achieved by ballots), aimed at creating fundamental changes devoid of clashes and bloodshed. Binyamin Netanyahu, whose 'illogical policies' had inflicted great losses, was crushed by the white revolution 'because of his heedlessness to the people's demands and ideas'. Yet, in spite of his promises during his election campaign, Barak 'took a harsh stance' upon entering office. Like Netanyahu, 'the high number of votes for Barak has taken away his wisdom and made him ignore the people who voted for him'. Barak 'should know that the people voted for the restoration of peace. Therefore, if he followed the unwise and self-serving policies of the past, he would be the next victim of the 'sharp blade of the ballot-papers'.[198] Nevertheless, there was a recognition that the people of Israel, at least, had opted for peace – a point not readily acknowledged in Iran. Another article in the *Tehran Times* even suggested that the Arabs should help

Barak, if Yitzhak Rabin's pledges were, in fact, to be honored. Many people in the West and some in the Middle East 'breathed a sigh of relief', the newspaper wrote, hoping that Barak would 'inject new life into the dead peace process'. In fact, many saw little prospect of Barak taking substantive steps toward 'respecting the rights of the Palestinians and establishing peace in the region'. The paper suggested that the Arab states and 'Arafat 'should first see' whether Barak was willing to fulfil Rabin's commitments. 'If so, they should give him the help he needs.'[199]

At this stage more moderate views were also expresed. *Neshat*, for example, pointed to divergent views in Israel regarding the Arab world, and recognized the will of some domestic trends, including Ehud Barak, to achieve peace. It pointed to fundamental differences between Netanyahu and Barak, and believed that the latter would strive to lead Israel on to the path of peace.[200] This moderate approach gained significant support from 'Abdollah Nuri. Answering charges raised against him on his trial (November 1999), he made clear at the outset that he did not support Israel. Yet he questioned the logic of the Iranian approach. 'Arafat', he said, 'fought Israel all his adult life, with a sense of mission, courage and determination. Would it be wrong to maintain that he knows what is good for the Palestinian people?'

'What kind of logic is it,' he asked, 'that everyone has the right to speak and decide on Palestine and on the [fate of the] Palestinians, but the Palestinians themselves do not have such a right?' Why should we claim the right to impose our own views on them? Is it logical that we maintain good relations with countries that negotiate with Israel, but whoever voices such views in Iran is brought to trial? True, we cannot fight the Palestinian Authority in the territories, but why should we not fight them in Tehran. If Iran considers the leaders of the Palestinian Authority to be traitors, why does it not hand over the Palestinian embassy in Tehran to its 'cherished friends', Hamas and the Islamic jihad? Or, maybe, Nuri continued to mock the Iranian policy, we actually pursue the right policy, but only continue to raise the old customary slogans. In fact, as the Arab countries do not opt for war, with what political, economic or military power do we want to fight Israel? What do Iranians gain from such an attitude, except being blamed for supporting terrorism? Today, the Palestinians have a government, that we recognize, and they are in charge of deciding on behalf of their own people. The current situation is not ideal, but we must come to terms with realities and avoid being 'a bowl warmer that the soup'. Therefore, Nuri went as far as to suggest, that even over the question of Israel, Khomeini's views should be re-examined in light of the changing circumstances.[201] Limited and restricted as they may appear, such expressions represent a more nuanced attitude and signs of 'alternative thought' even on the delicate issue of Israel and the peace process.

The Islamic Revolution introduced a turning point in the relations between Israel and Iran. The close and friendly ties between the two governments under the monarchy turned into a strategic alliance, to which the revolution put a dramatic end. Subsequently, the Islamic regime viewed Israel as the most evil of all its enemies. Israel for its part missed no opportunity to stress the 'Iranian threat' to Israel and Iran's 'evil character', using the harshest possible terms to denounce the Islamic regime and its politics. In fact, Israel volunteered to lead the anti-Iranian camp, just as much as Iran undertook to lead the anti-Israeli camp.

The hostile attitude to the politics of revolutionary Iran was one of the rare issues on which there seemed to be no major difference between different political camps in Israel. Former prime minister Rabin missed no opportunity to stress the 'Iranian danger', censuring Iran's 'dark regime' and the 'turbid Islamic wave' that it produced, blaming Iran for acts of terrorism and presenting it as a major threat to the free world. His favorite phrase in referring to post-Khomeini Iran was 'Khomeinism without Khomeini'. The former prime ministers Shimon Peres and Binyamin Netanyahu generally continued the same line. The policy of 'dual containment' and subsequent US sanctions against Iran were in line with Israeli interests and Israel launched a vigorous campaign against Iran.

Israel did not rest content with stressing the threat. It publicized its effort to combat the potential challenge, and even made open threats directed at Tehran. On 20 January 1993, the Labor deputy in the Knesset, Ephraim Sneh, now deputy defense minister, stressed three elements that combined to make Iran 'a threat to Israel and the region': its ideology, its expansionism and its military arsenal. He asked the Knesset to put the issue of 'the Iranian danger, mainly that of nuclear power [high] on its agenda'.[202] In a public lecture in December 1994 General Uzi Dayan, head of the planning branch of the Israel Defense Forces, said that, 'serious escalation in the nuclear capabilities of Iran and Iraq may lead Israel to a decision [to take action against Iran] already in 1995'.[203] When Israel received F-15-I attack fighter jets in January 1998, the Israeli media stressed repeatedly that their range would encompass Iran.[204] Ephraim Sneh even called for the building up of a capability to carry out a pre-emptive strike against Iran, so as to foil its ability to hit Israel with nuclear weapons.[205]

These are only a few examples of a long list of Israeli statements stressing the 'Iranian threat' or the 'Iranian danger' and designed to threaten Iran. Tehran responded by mocking the Israeli threats, but apparently could not altogether disregard them as part of Israel's campaign to hinder Iran's military programs as well as its efforts to expand its foreign ties. Responding to General Dayan's statement, *Tehran Times* deplored Israel's 'expansionist, annexationist policy' as the real threats to the region and rejected such remarks as 'closer to rumbling than sensible statements of a wise statesman'. It added: 'Although any attack by the Zionist regime on Iran's nuclear power plants is far from expectations, history bears witness that such an attack would be repelled by any means with irreparable repercussions'.[206] *Kayhan* wrote that Israel, which currently possessed 200 nuclear bombs, was striving to maintain its strategic edge even in conditions of peace and, unlike Iran, was unwilling to sign international agreements to control the spread of such weapons. It accused both the Unites States and Israel of adopting a common strategy to prevent the acquisition of nuclear capability by the Muslim states. Although Israel threatened Iran, it should keep in mind that the realities in the region were different from those that prevailed in 1981, when Israel attacked Iraqi nuclear installations, and that Iran had proved how determined it was to defend itself and to confront Israel.[207] The Iranian defense minister 'Ali Shamkhani had no qualms about the Israeli threat. In a discussion in 1999, he said that, 'on the whole', Israel was still 'the major source of threat' for Iran.[208]

However, with the passage of time some signs of change can be seen in the Israeli approach too. For one thing, Rabin's government (and other Israeli governments since) have made it clear that Israel does not have any conflict with the Iranian people or with Islam. Already under prime minister Netanyahu, Israel's defense ministry adopted a more moderate policy towards Iran. Consequently, Israeli terminology chose to refer to Iran as a 'threat' not as an 'enemy' or 'danger'. It was similarly recommended to avoid public anti-Iranian statements. Moreover, there are more diverse attitudes among top Israeli policy-makers, with some even suggesting to reconsider Israeli policy towards Iran.[209] Clearly, under Barak, the anti-Iranian rhetoric has significantly decreased. This may be viewed as a minor modification, yet, given the sensitivity of the issue, it still represents an important step forward.

During the two decades of the Islamic regime, there has been significant dogmatic deviation and the adoption of pragmatic policy choices by Tehran. The revolution has matured, recognized the limits of its power and allowed greater room for national considerations in shaping foreign policy. Ideological, political and personal struggles for power also pervaded political life. All this did not lead yet to any significant official change in Iran's attitude towards Israel. However, judged by its national interests, Israel does not seem to pose a greater threat to Iran than Iran's immediate neighbors. Indeed, in spite of intense anti-Israeli indoctrination, for most Iranians Israel remains a distant foe, while their main concern is Iran's 'near abroad' and its internal situation. Since in almost all cases revolutionary policy has been dictated by interests rather than ideology, it seems that the main obstacle to change in Iran's policy in this regard should be sought in the political, not just in the ideological, realm. This does not necessarily portend an immediate change in Iran's attitude towards Israel. In fact, the significant dogmatic changes in numerous other policy realms may even make a softening of Iran's policy on this issue more arduous in the short term. That the animosity to Israel has become the main, if not the last 'card' in Iran's revolutionary creed makes it even more difficult to reverse. In many ways, retreating from this policy may amount to an open admission that the revolution has eventually failed. Furthermore, even in the realm of state interest and pragmatic considerations, which often prevail over Iranian revolutionary dogma, the threshold of a major policy change towards Israel has not yet emerged. Moreover, in the final account, the Iranian attitude toward Israel is also likely to be influenced by the developments on the Arab–Israeli (and Israeli–Palestinian) fronts. Nevertheless, over 20 years after the revolution, some initial signs of change can be discerned.

NOTES

1. Rafsanjani on Tehran TV, 1 February 1993 – DR, 3 February 1993.
2. For Khomeini's views on Israel and Zionism see his collected statements in Ruhollah Khomeini, *Dar Jostoju-ye Rah az Kalam-e Imam: Az Bayanat va E'lamiyeha-ye Imam Khomeini* [In Search of the Path through the Words and Statements of Imam Khomeini], especially vol. 19, *Felestin va Sahionism* (Tehran: Sepher, 1984–85). For Khomeini's statements regarding Jews see in the same series, volume on *Azadi-ye Aqaliyatha-ye Mazhabi* [The Freedom of Religious Minorities] (Tehran: Amir Kabir 1984–85). See also, Algar, *Islam and Revolution*, pp. 117, 120, 176, 210, 214, 276. For excerpts from Khomeini's statements in Arabic, see *Al-Imam Khomeini wal-Qadiya al-Filastiniyya* (n.p.: Al-'Uruwa al-wuthqa, 1979).
3. ['Ali Akbar] Hashemi Rafsanjani, *Isra'il va Qods-e 'Aziz* [Israel and the Beloved Palestine] (Qom: Azadi, n.d.), pp. 5–6. Rafsanjani devoted much attention to the Palestinian issue, before the revolution. When he was exiled in 1963 to Rafsanjan, and in order to do something to help the struggle, he took with him a copy of the book *al-Qadiya al-Filastiniyya* [The Palestinian Question] (by

Akram Zu'aytar) and prepared an article on the issue. He says that the book influenced him. While reading it, he often cried. He thought his time in exile could be a good opportunity to translate the book into Persian, since under the Shah's anti-Islamic and anti-Arab policy, people had no knowledge of '*Isra'il-e ghaseb*' [The Usurper Israel]. Among the charges levelled against him later was the translation of Zu'aytar's book. See Mas'ud Razavi, *Hashemi va Enqelab* [Hashemi and the Revolution] (Tehran: Hamshahri, 1997), pp. 454–6. See also Velayati, *Iran va Mas'aleh-ye Felestin*. A long list of books have been published by Iran's former ambassador to the Vatican, Seyyed Hadi Khosrowshahi. See Seyyed Hadi Khosrowshahi, *Harakat-e Islami-ye Felestin: az Aghaz ta Intifada* [The Islamic Movement of Palestine: From the Beginning through the Intifada] (Tehran: Ettela'at, 1996), which includes a chapter on 'Izz al-Din al-Qassam.

4. *Arzeshha*, 18 January 1999.
5. Meir Litvak, *The Islamization of Palestinian Identity: The Case of Hamas* (Tel Aviv: Moshe Dayan Center, 1996), pp. 10–3.
6. Emmanuel Sivan, 'The Mythologies of Religious Radicalism: Judaism and Islam', *Terrorism and Political Violence*, 3/3 (Autumn 1991), p. 73.
7. Raphael Israeli, *Fundamentalist Islam and Israel: Essays in Interpretation* (Lanham, MD: University Press of America, 1993), p. 63.
8. Algar, *Islam and Revolution*, p. 195; from *Khomeini va Jonbesh*, pp. 56–7.
9. Augustus Richard Norton, *Amal and the Shi'a: Struggle for the Soul of Lebanon* (Austin, TX: University of Texas Press, 1987), p. 146.
10. For this Islamist view, see Reuven Paz, 'Emdat ha-Tenu'ot ha-Islamiyot ha-Radikaliot kelapi ha-Yehudim ve ha-Zionut beyaminu' [The Position of the Islamic Radical Movements towards the Jews and Zionism in our Days], in Ilan Pape (ed.), *Islam ve Shalom* [Islam and Peace] (Giv'at Haviva: ha-Makhon le-Kheker ha-Shalom, 1992), pp. 46–65.
11. Yvonne Haddad, 'Islamists and the "Problem of Israel": The 1967 Awakening', *Middle East Journal*, 46/2 (Spring 1992), pp. 268–9.
12. See statement by Nabih Berri in Norton, *Amal and the Shi'a*, p. 77, and *Monday Morning*, 1–7 February 1982.
13. *Al-Nahar*, 11 January 1975; *Sawt al-Mahrumin*, 1/2 (28 July 1978), as cited in Majed Halawi, *A Lebanon Defied: Musa al-Sadr and the Shi'a Community* (Boulder, CO: Westview, 1992), p. 147.
14. It says: 'It was because they reneged on the covenant that We cursed them and turned their hearts to stone. . . . there are but a few of them who will not stoop to treachery and deceit.' Yet, it continues: 'However, you must forgive them; and if you see them doing wrong, pass by in silence and do not upbraid them.' *The Quran*, trans. Colin Turner (London: Curzon Press, 1997).
15. 'Ali Akbar Behbudikhwah, 'Naqd-e Towjihat-e Ta'rikhi-ye Sahionism dar mowred-e Mashru'iyyat-e Rezhim-e Qods', *Siyasat-e Khareji*, 3/2 (June–August 1368/1989), pp. 314–17. See also statement by Nateq-Nuri in IRNA, 7 February 1997 – SWB, 8 February 1997.
16. *Arzeshha*, 18 January 1999.
17. Rafsanjani, *Isra'il va Qods-e 'Aziz*, p. 5.
18. Behbudikhwah, 'Naqd-e Towjihat-e Tarikhi', pp. 317–41.
19. *Jomhuri-ye Islami*, 24 August 1995.
20. Radio Tehran, 9 October 1996 – DR, 11 October 1996.

21. Rafsanjani, *Isra'il va Qods-e 'Aziz*, p. 43.
22. Radio Tehran, 9 October 1996 – DR, 11 October 1996.
23. Velayati, *Iran va Mas'aleh-ye Felestin*, pp. 163–8.
24. Algar, *Islam and Revolution*, p. 276 and *Jomhuri-ye Islami*, 25 September 1979. See also Khomeini's message to pilgrims in 1980 in Algar, *Islam and Revolution*, p. 301 and *Jomhuri-ye Islami*, 13 September 1980.
25. Rafsanjani, *Isra'il va Qods-e 'Aziz*, p. 45.
26. Velayati, *Iran va Mas'aleh-ye Felestin*. p. 13.
27. *Iran News*, 9 April 1996.
28. IRNA, 7 February 1997 – SWB, 10 February 1997.
29. Radio Tehran, 1 July 1997 [DR]
30. Radio Tehran, 26 September 1996 – DR, 27 September 1996.
31. Another member of the Majlis added that the fight against world imperialism and Zionism could not be confined to the political, economic and military struggle, as the cultural dimension was no less important. *Resalat*, 2 October 1996 – DR, 17 October 1996.
32. *Jomhuri-ye Islami*, 28 September 1996 – DR, 4 October 1996. See, similarly, *Iran News*, 28 September and 14 October [DR].
33. Tehran TV, 28 September 1996 – DR, 1 October 1996.
34. IRNA, 28 September 1996 – DR, 1 October 1996. Addressing the ministerial coordinating meeting of the ICO (2 October), Velayati added: 'Today our sanctuaries . . . are being shamelessly targeted. Our brothers and sisters . . . are murdered in cold blood.' IRNA, 2 October 1996 – DR, 4 October 1996.
35. Yvonne Haddad, 'Islamists and the "Problem of Israel"', pp. 268–9.
36. Algar, *Islam and Revolution*, pp. 177–8.
37. Ibid., pp. 178–80.
38. Ibid., pp. 192–3.
39. *Khomeini va Jonbesh*, pp. 36–53; cited in Algar, *Islam and Revolution*, p. 201.
40. *Khomeini va Jonbesh*, pp. 56–7; in Algar, *Islam and Revolution*, p. 197.
41. Textbook in history, Tarikh, III grade, Rahnema'i (Intermediary Education), edition of 1360 [1981–82], p. 109
42. See Khomeini's letter to Iranian students in the West (10 July 1972) in *Khomeini va Jonbesh*, pp. 98–9; Algar, *Islam and Revolution*, p. 210.
43. Saad, *Image of Arabs*, p. 113; from Al-e Ahmad, *Lost in the Crowd*, p. 73.
44. Textbook in History: Tarikh, III grade, Rahnema'i, 1981/2, p. 90.
45. Tehran TV, 22 January 1998 [DR].
46. Velayati, *Iran va Mas'aleh-ye Felestin*, p. IV in English introduction and pp. 89–90, 181–2. (Interestingly, both statements are also mentioned in the Charter of Hamas.) Rafsanjani also mentioned the episode of the Crusaders and their defeat by Saladin in his book, *Isra'il va Qods-e 'Aziz*, pp. 12–13.
47. IRNA, 7 February 1997 – SWB, 10 February 1997.
48. See statements by Nateq-Nuri (IRNA, 7 February 1997 – SWB, 8 February 1997).
49. Rafsanjani, *Isra'il va Qods-e 'Aziz*, p. 43.
50. Behbudikhwah, 'Naqd Towjihat-e Tarikhi', pp. 314–17.
51. *Jomhuri-ye Islami*, 24 August 1995.
52. Haddad, 'Islamists and the "Problem of Israel"', pp. 281–2.
53. Velayati, *Iran va Mas'aleh-ye Felestin*, pp. IV–VI in English introduction.

54. *Salam*, 25 December 1993. See also *Ettela'at*, 26 January 1994.
55. *Ettela'at*, 27 November 1993.
56. *Kayhan* (Tehran), 9 January 1994.
57. See article in *Jomhuri-ye Islami*, 24 August 1995.
58. Ismail R. al-Faruqi, 'Islam and Zionism', in J. Esposito (ed.), *Voices of Resurgent Islam* (Oxford: Oxford University Press, 1983), pp. 263–7.
59. Velayati, *Iran va Mas'aleh-ye Felestin*, pp. 53, 183–4, *passim*.
60. *Kayhan* (Tehran), 1 March 1994.
61. Haddad, 'Islamists and the "Problem of Israel"', pp. 267, 274.
62. Jalal Al-e Ahmad, *Safar be Velayat-e 'Ezra'il* [Journey to the Province of the Angel of Death] (Tehran: Ravaq, 1984), pp. 59–62; Saad, *Image of Arabs*, p. 121.
63. Al-e Ahmad, *Safar be Velayat-e 'Ezra'il*, pp. 91–2; Saad, *Image of Arabs*, p. 121.
64. 'Ali Asghar Mostafavi, *Iranian-e Yahudi* [The Jews of Iran] (Tehran: Bamdad, 1990–91), pp. 159–60.
65. Marzie Yazdani (ed.), *Asnad-e Mohajerat-e Yahudiyan-e Iran be Felestin* [Documents on the Immigration of Iranian Jews to Palestine] (Tehran: Sazeman-e Asnad-e Melli, 1996), pp. 38–9, in editor's introduction.
66. Velayati, *Iran va Mas'aleh-ye Felestin*, p. 17.
67. *Ettela'at*, 29 December 1979.
68. Behbudikhwah, 'Naqd-e Towjihat-e Tarikhi', pp. 314–17.
69. For such Iranian attitudes, see articles on Iran by David Menashri, in annual account, *Anti-Semitism Worldwide* (Tel Aviv: Tel Aviv University, Project for the Study of Anti-Semitism, 1994), pp. 165–72; 1995/96, pp. 195–8; and 1996/97, pp. 205–8.
70. *Ettela'at*, 23 February 1995.
71. *Jomhuri-ye Islami*, 14 January 1999.
72. 'Islamic antisemintism', Kramer has observed, tends 'to see Israel as a symptom of some larger conspiracy against them – either Western, or Jewish, or a sinister combination of the two'. Yet, for Muslims to portray the Jew as 'the eternal Jew' and as 'the arch conspirator', there must be more at work than Islamic tradition and Israeli policy. They also borrowed, he wrote, 'from the canon of Western religious and radical antisemitism'. Martin Kramer, *The Salience of Islamic Fundamentalism*, Institute of Jewish Affairs, Report No. 2 (October 1995), pp. 4–8.
73. Jaleh Pir-Nazar, 'Chehreh-ye Yahud', pp. 483–502.
74. Khomeini, *Al-Hukuma al-Islamiyya*, p. 7.
75. Abrahamian, *Khomeinism*, pp. 123–4.
76. Khomeini, *Al-Hukuma al-Islamiyya*, p. 83.
77. Khomeini, *Al-Hukuma al-Islamiyya*, p. 121. See also Algar, *Islam at Revolution*, p. 127.
78. Khomeini, *Towzih al-Masa'el*, pp. 15, 18.
79. *Farhang-e Islami va Ta'limat-e Dini* [Islamic Culture and Religious Studies], fifth year, elementary school, edition of 1360 [1981/82], pp. 121–2.
80. As Peretz argues, for Islamists 'all these terms are odious, and what distinction, if any, exists among them is irrelevant'. Don Peretz, *The Intifada: The Palestinian Uprising* (Boulder, CO: Westview, 1990), p. 102.
81. *Jumhuri-ye Islami*, 20 September 1982.

82. *Resalat*, 7 February 1998 [DR].
83. *Ettela'at*, 28 February 1984.
84. *Ettela'at*, 8 January 1995.
85. *Iran Times*, 7 December 1990; Abrahamian, *Khomeinism*, p. 124.
86. *Tehran Times*, 16 March 1995.
87. *Iran News*, 28 September 1996 – DR, 4 October 1996.
88. *Jomhuri-ye Islami*, 8 December 1996 [DR].
89. *Jomhuri-ye Islami*, 26 October 1997 [DR].
90. *Tehran Times*, 25 September 1994 – DR, 30 September 1994.
91. *Kayhan* (Tehran), 29 June 1998.
92. *Tehran Times*, 31 October 1994 – DR, 1 November 1994.
93. *Jomhuri-ye Islami*, 2 November 1994 – DR, 4 November 1994.
94. *Resalat*, 3 January 1994.
95. *Kayhan* (Tehran), 16 February 1994.
96. *Kayhan* (Tehran), 16 February 1994. See also, *Resalat*, 3 January 1994.
97. *Kayhan* (Tehran), 1 March 1994.
98. Radio Tehran, 20 October 1994 – DR, 21 October 1994. See also *Kayhan* (Tehran), 1 March 1994.
99. *Le Figaro*, 12 September 1994 – DR, 13 September 1994.
100. *Kayhan* (Tehran), 31 October 1994.
101. Radio Tehran, 26 February 1994 – DR, 28 February 1994.
102. *Kayhan al-'Arabi*, 27 February 1994 – DR, 7 March 1994.
103. *Kayhan* (Tehran), 11 March – DR, 18 March 1996.
104. *Kayhan* (Tehran), 21 April 1996.
105. *Tehran Times*, 28 December 1997.
106. IRNA, 20 April 1998 [DR].
107. Tehran TV, 19 January 1998 [DR].
108. *Jomhuri-ye Islami*, 14 January 1999.
109. *Resalat*, 13 January 1998 [DR].
110. *Tehran Times*, 4 April 1998. This is a reference to the tragic Israeli attack in Lebanon which claimed the lives of over 100 Lebanese civilians.
111. *Kayhan International*, 17 February 1998 [DR].
112. *Kayhan International*, 20 April 1998 [DR].
113. *Al-Safir*, 4 June 1997 [DR].
114. *Al-Riyad*, 8 June 1997 [DR].
115. *Hamshahri*, 15 November 1998 [DR].
116. *Salam*, 1 January 1998.
117. IRNA and Tehran TV, 8 January 1998 [DR].
118. IRNA, 2 May 1998 [DR].
119. Tehran TV, 22 January 1998 [DR].
120. Ehteshami, *After Khomeini*, p. 157.
121. Radio Tehran, 6 July 1997 [DR].
122. Radio Tehran, 7 August 1979 – SWB, 8 August 1979.
123. *Daily Telegraph*, 17 August 1979.
124. Hooshang Amirahmadi, 'The Islamic Republic and the Question of Palestine', *Middle East Insight*, 10/4–5 (May-August 1994), pp. 50–4. Amirahmadi maintained, that 'One major problem with Iran's Palestine policy is its largely ad hoc nature and confused direction. A coherent policy has never been spelled

out and changing phases of Iran's policy have made a bad situation look worse. The only constant theme in Iran's approach to the Palestine question has been the rejection of Israel as a legitimate entity.' He added that even after the Oslo accord (see below), Iran's policy continued to be 'the same old ad hoc approach'.

125. See Yazdi's statement in *Ettela'at*, 11 September 1993; *Iran Times*, 17 September 1993.
126. *Ettela'at*, 14 September 1993. See also *Kayhan* (Tehran), 15 September 1993 – DR, 13 October 1993; *Ettela'at*, 18 and 19 September 1993; *Jahan-e Islam*, 18 September 1993 – DR, 30 September 1993.
127. Shireen Hunter, *Iran After Khomeini* (New York: Praeger, 1992), pp. 134–5.
128. Baktiari, *Parliamentary Politics*, pp. 214–15.
129. Radio Tehran, 2 August – DR, 5 August 1991. Similarly, *Ettela'at*, 3 August 1991.
130. *Jomhuri-ye Islami*, 20 July 1991.
131. *Jomhuri-ye Islami*, 23 July 1991.
132. Radio Tehran, 6 August 1991 – DR, 6 August 1991; *Ettela'at*, 6 August 1991.
133. *Jomhuri-ye Islami*, 23 July 1991.
134. *Al-Diyar*, 28 October 1991.
135. Radio Tehran, 30 October 1991 – DR, 30 October 1991; *Abrar*, *Financial Times* and *Jerusalem Post*, 31 October 1991.
136. *Abrar*, 22 October 1991; IRNA, 22 October 1991 – DR, 23 October 1991.
137. Radio Tehran, 4 October 1991 – DR, 7 October 1991; *Ettela'at* and *Financial Times*, 5 October 1991.
138. Radio Tehran, 22 November 1991 – DR, 25 November 1991; *Ettela'at*, 23 November 1991.
139. *Jahan-e Islam*, 2 November 1991.
140. *Ettela'at*, 10 August 1991; Radio Tehran, 9 August 1991 – DR, 9 August 1991.
141. Radio Tehran, 31 July 1991 – DR, 2 August 1991; *Ettela'at*, 1 August 1991.
142. *Ettela'at*, 31 October 1991; IRNA and Radio Tehran, 30 October 1991 – DR, 31 October 1991; *Financial Times*, 31 October 1991.
143. *Ettela'at*, 26 August 1991; IRNA, 25 August 1991 – DR, 27 August 1991.
144. *Ettela'at*, 11 September 1993; *Iran Times*, 17 September 1993.
145. *Iran Times*, 17 September 1993.
146. *Iran Times*, 24 September 1993. See similarly *Ettela'at*, 9 October; Tehran TV, 16 September – DR, 17 September; *Ettela'at*, 18 September 1993. It should be recalled, however, that 'Arafat was the first prominent figure who visited Tehran after the revolution in February 1979. Yet, shortly afterwards relations between Tehran and the PLO turned tense.
147. *Resalat*, 14 September 1993 – DR, 27 September 1993.
148. *Iran Times*, 24 September 1993.
149. *Resalat*, 19 September 1993 – DR, 30 September 1993.
150. *Jomhuri-ye Islami*, 13 and 14 September 1993.
151. *Jomhuri-ye Islami*, 15 September 1993 – DR, 15 September 1993.
152. See interview with Velayati in *Ettela'at*, 3 September 1996 – DR, 23 September 1996.
153. *Jomhuri-ye Islami*, 4 April 1999.

154. *Resalat*, 23 January 1994; *Kayhan* (Tehran), 24 January 1994; Radio Tehran, 26 February 1994 – DR, 28 February 1994; *Salam*, 17 February 1996.
155. *Jomhuri-ye Islami*, 28 February 1996, 6 March 1996; *Salam*, 5 March 1996; *Kayhan* (Tehran), 11 March 1996.
156. *Resalat*, 23 January 1994; *Kayhan* (Tehran), 24 January 1994; *Ettela'at*, 26 February and 1 March 1994; Radio Tehran, 26 February 1994 – DR, 28 February 1994. *Jomhuri-ye Islami*, 6 March 1996.
157. Velayati, *Iran va Mas'aleh-ye Felestin*, p. 7 in the Introduction.
158. Radio Tehran, 23 January 1995 – DR, 23 January 1995.
159. *Jomhuri-ye Islami*, 24 January 1995 – DR, 30 January 1995.
160. IRNA, 4 March 1996 – DR, 6 March 1996.
161. *Khorasan* (Meshhed), 10 March 1996 – DR, 29 May 1996.
162. Rafsanjani's interview with *Der Spiegel*, 14 October 1996 – DR, 17 October 1996. See also his statement quoted by IRNA, 11 March 1996 – DR, 12 March 1996.
163. *Middle East Insight*, 11/5 (July–August 1995), p. 11.
164. IRNA, 22 September 1993 – DR, 23 September 1993; *Ettela'at*, 7 October 1993 – DR, 18 October 1993.
165. *Salam*, 26 September 1993 and 3 October 1993 – DR, 7 October 1993; See also *Jomhuri-ye Islami*, 27 September 1993 – DR, 6 October 1993.
166. *Jomhuri-ye Islami*, 27 September – DR, 6 October 1993.
167. Amirahmadi, 'Question of Palestine', pp. 50–4; Eric Hooglund, 'Iranian Views of the Arab–Israeli Conflict', *Journal of Palestine Studies*, 25/1 (Autumn 1995), pp. 86–95.
168. Reuters and IRNA, 27 May 1997.
169. *Iran News*, 5 August 1997 [DR].
170. Khatami's interview with CNN, Tehran TV, 8 January 1998 [DR].
171. IRNA, 21 September 1998 [DR].
172. IRNA, 9 December 1997.
173. IRNA, 14 December 1997.
174. *Kayhan* (Tehran), 2 September 1997 [DR].
175. Tehran TV, 19 January 1998 [DR].
176. *Tehran Times*, 3 May 1998. See also IRNA, 2 May 1998 [DR].
177. *Jomhuri-ye Islami*, 10 August 1998.
178. *Jomhuri-ye Islami*, 18 September 1997.
179. IRNA, 9 December 1997.
180. Tehran TV, 2 May 1998 [DR].
181. *Kayhan International*, 17 December 1997 [DR].
182. *Kayhan International*, 7 August 1997 [DR].
183. *Iran News*, 3 August 1997.
184. *Jomhuri-ye Islami*, 4 October 1997.
185. *Kar va Kargar*, 14 January 1999 [DR].
186. *Yedi'ot Aharonot*, 7 October 1999.
187. *Faslnameh-ye Khavarmiyaneh*, 1/1 (Summer 1994), Roundtable, p. 26.
188. 'Shenakht Siyasatha-ye Dakheli va Khareji-ye Isra'il', Roundable, *Faslnameh-ye Khavarmiyaneh*, 1/3 (Winter 1994), pp. 468–73.
189. Ghassam Salame, 'Islam and the West', *Foreign Affairs*, No. 90 (Spring 1993), p. 29.

190. Naser Hadiyan, 'Mahiyyat-e Gheyr-e-Madani-ye Dowlat-e Isra'il', *Faslnameh-ye Khavarmiyaneh*, 2/1 (Spring 1995), pp. 104–5.

191. Farhang Raja'i in *Faslnameh-ye Khavarmiyaneh*, 1/1 (Summer 1994), p. 11.

192. *Faslnameh-ye Khavarmiyaneh*, 1/1 (Summer 1994), pp. 7–9.

193. Seyyed Kazem Sajjadpur, 'Siyasat-e Mahar-e do-janebeh dar theory va 'amal', *Siyasat-e Khareji*, 8/1–2 (Spring–Summer, 1994), pp. 25–42.

194. *Faslnameh-ye Khavarmiyaneh*, 1/1 (Summer 1994), p. 24.

195. *Faslnameh-ye Khavarmiyaneh*, 1/1 (Summer 1994), pp. 31–5.

196. *Arzeshha*, 18 January 1999.

197. *Jomhuri-ye Islami*, 25 May 1999.

198. *Tehran Times*, 31 May 1999, 1 and 2 June 1999 [DR].

199. *Tehran Times*, 20 May 1999 [DR].

200. See article by Hasan Fathi, *Neshat*, 29 June 1999.

201. Nuri, *Showkaran-e Eslah*, pp. 144–51.

202. See proceedings of the Knesset, 20 January 1993 (Internet database).

203. *Yedi'ot Aharonot* and *Ha'aretz*, 30 Decemebr 1994.

204. See a critique by Ze'ev Schiff, in *Ha'aretz*, 20 January 1998.

205. *Ma'ariv* and *Yedi'ot Aharonot*, 27 September 1998.

206. *Tehran Times*, 3 January 1995.

207. *Kayhan* (Tehran), 15 January 1995.

208. *Discourse*, 1/1 (Summer 1999), p. 25.

209. Author's interview with prominent Israeli officials. See also *Ha'aretz*, 8 July, and 8 and 10 August 1999. In April 2000, minister of justice, Yossi Beilin, suggested the need for Israel to reconsider its Iran policy.

Epilogue

The evolution of the main processes discussed in this book peaked in 2000. The Majlis election (held in two rounds on 18 February and 5 May) was a microcosm of recent momentous changes in Iranian society, evident in grave internal strife, and added to existing tensions. The main political trends then crystallized into two major camps, representing different philosophies and policies: advocates of reform and champions of continued conservatism. This rivalry revolved primarily around basic domestic issues that had evolved in recent years: questions of religion and state, Islam and democracy, the status of the *vali-ye faqih*, and the still unfulfilled expectations – mainly in the realms of political freedom and social and economic difficulties. Foreign-policy issues remained marginal, accentuating unfolding domestic disputes, for example, a rapprochement with the United States set against adherence to the revolutionary creed. This also articulated the inherent dichotomy between the popular voice and the institutions of power and clerical rule (see Chapter 5).

With such major issues at stake, the two competing camps viewed the elections as means not only to secure their sway in politics, but also to determine the course of the revolution, the regime and even the destiny of Islamic movements worldwide. Tension intensified as the balance of power was put to the test after the new Majlis began its work in late May.

To supplement this book's discussion and update it to three years after Khatami's election to the presidency – less than a year before the end of his first term – this Epilogue seeks to provide a preliminary analysis of the major domestic trends that evolved up to summer 2000. It begins with a study of the pro-reform camp's remarkable ascendancy and their electoral victory in February; it moves on to discuss the conservatives' countermeasures between the two rounds of the elections; and it ends with some tentative observations on the balance of power as the new Majlis began its term.

PRELUDE: THE OFFENSIVE OF THE REFORMISTS

The spring of 2000 marked the pinnacle of the pro-reform drive, signaling a period of unprecedented openness and liberalism. True, Iran had experienced occasional brief intervals of liberalism in its modern history, such as in the early 1940s (following the abdication of Reza Shah), in the early 1950s (the movement led by Mosaddeq), or prior to the fall of the Shah and before the consolidation of the Islamic regime. But on these occasions the central government had been weak, and thus forced to tolerate such tendencies. In the late 1990s, by contrast, the regime seemed stable, but significant segments within the revolutionary system endorsed a policy of reform and change.

The magnitude of change was best reflected in the press, which has in turn accelerated the process of openness. Having played a principal role in the domestic debate throughout the 1990s, the press turned into a major symbol of change and the struggle for freedom at the end of the decade. The multiplicity of newspapers, the diversity of views they presented and the level of free expression came abundantly into focus after Khatami's election, reaching a peak after the summer of 1999. The press played a crucial role in expanding the boundaries and defining the scope of public debate, and proved a vital tool for propagating new ideas and enlisting support for them. At no other time had there been so many new papers and journals, enjoying such a degree of freedom, and expressing such a diversity of viewpoints with such a fervor and sense of mission. Here, too, there had previously been occasional intervals of openness. But then, again, the regime had been weaker, the circle of readers limited and the press less vibrant. By late 1999 almost all the taboos were broken and most crucial issues were being critically debated – the system of government, relations with the United States and even the value of leading the opposition to the Arab–Israeli peace process. Newspapers mushroomed, circulations rocketed and people welcomed their appearance with enthusiasm. A new generation of investigative columnists emerged – brave, penetrating and determined – questioning basic revolutionary axioms and harshly criticizing leading revolutionary figures (mainly Rafsanjani). The press thus turned into a major arena of public debate.

Enterprising journalists used the freedom of expression both to popularize the concept of civil society and to give wider currency to the view that religion itself is subject to different interpretations – as leading intellectuals have also maintained (see Chapter 1). They created a forum for a 'much-needed and long-absent debate', maintaining a watchdog role, exposing violations of rights and leading the discussion on extremely sensitive issues.¹ As can be seen throughout this book, some newspapers adopted a daring line before 1997 (for example, *Salam*, *Payam-e Daneshju-ye Basiji*) but have since gradually adopted a more critical attitude; others began more recently, often to replace banned newspapers, but continued to propagate the critical line even more assertively. Among them were *Jame'eh* (replaced subsequently by *Tous*, *Neshat*, *Akhbar-e Eqtesad* and *'Asr-e Azadegan*), *Aftab-e Emruz*, *Fath*, *Hoviyyat-e Khish*, *Sobh-e Emruz*, to cite but a few. Concurrently, other papers continued to support the conservative line and to uphold genuine revolutionary values, using equally harsh language to denounce their rivals, with a similar degree of passion and fervor – among them *Kayhan*, *Ya le-Tharat al-Hosein*, *Jebheh*, *Sobh*, *Resalat*, *Qods*, *Jomhuri-ye Islami*. Radio and television generally followed the official conservative line. Khamene'i, too, has generally aligned himself with the conservatives. For him, the reformist papers were 'the crawling cultural advance of the enemy'.² The reformist newspapers, although operating in a minefield, led the struggle with impressive determination and a sense of mission (for a list of newspapers see the Appendix).

Hand in hand with the blossoming of newspapers and journals, a refreshing wave of book publication has been noticeable, often containing unprecedented criticism of basic ideological tenets and realities in the country. Among the most important of these publishing marvels were those written by the 'jailbirds': Nuri's *Showkaran Eslah* (Hemlock for Advocate of Reform); Ganji's *Talaqqi-ye Fashisti az Din va Hokumat* (The Fascist Interpretation of Religion and Government); and the dialogue between Nuri and Ganji, *Naqdi Bara-ye Tamam-e Fosul* (Critique for All Seasons) (excerpts from these works are quoted in Chapters 1, 6 and 7). Other such titles are: 'Abbas 'Abdi, *Dar Masir-e Azadi* (On the Road to Freedom), Mohsen Kadivar, *Daghdagheha-ye Hokumat-e Dini* (Apprehensions of Religious Government), 'Emad al-Din Baqi, *Goftogu ba Sa'id Hajariyan* (Dialogue with Sa'id Hajariyan). These books set off a flurry of debate and a redefinition of the public agenda.

After late 1999, political activities evolved around movements that come close to representing formal parties. The pro-reform camp proved extremely active, determined to use the momentum of its electoral victories in 1997 and 1999 to win a majority in the Majlis. This, it was believed, would remove a major obstacle in the path of reform, giving the president greater freedom to advance his programs. That leading reformists like Nuri, Shams al-Va'ezin and Kadivar were in jail and newspapers occasionally banned did not seem to weaken their camp.

Each newspaper that was closed was replaced by another, often more critical; and the leading jailed figures continued to incite their supporters from prison, while their replacements were determined to pursue their predecessors' course. The conservatives were then resolved to maintain their hold over the institutions of power and to block the emerging power of their rivals; yet they hesitated to take bold steps to reverse the course of events.

Neither the pro-reform nor the conservative camp was unified. They both lacked a popular membership base and their platforms were usually bland. Some movements, like *Jebheh-ye Mosharekat-e Iran-e Islami* (Islamic Iran Participation Front; officially launched on 5 December 1998 and led by the president's brother, Mohammad Reza Khatami), seemed well organized; others were formed around a leading figure, or a general concept. On 13 November 1999, 18 groups came together to form a loose coalition of the supporters of the movement of the Second of Khordad (23 May 1997) with the aim of forming a unified election strategy. The conservative camp encompassed the old ideological revolutionary groups such as *Jame'eh-ye Ruhaniyyat-e Mobarez* (Society of Combatant Clergy) and *E'telaf-e Peyrovan-e Khatt-e Imam va Rahbari* (Coalition of the Followers of the Imam's Line and the Leadership). A third group comprised the opposition within the Islamic system, such as *Nehzat-e Azadi* (Freedom Movement) and *E'telaf-e Niruha-ye Melli-Mazhabi* (Coalition of National-Religious Forces).

While the two main political trends emanated from and were interrelated to the ruling system, their differences were nevertheless deep, reflecting the basic divisions in society. The reformists identified with the spirit of the Second of Khordad; the conservatives with 22 Bahman (11 February; revolutionary victory in 1979 and the ideas of Ayatollah Khomeini).

The *Mosharekat* pledged to turn the Majlis elections into a new Second Khordad and adopted the slogan that served Khatami in 1997, 'Iran for all Iranians'. The movement linked 'justice' and 'freedom', calling for 'reform, freedom and economic welfare' and 'justice, freedom and spiritual values', and stressing that reform stems from, rather than clashes with, the revolution. The youth had created the Second of Khordad, Mohammad Reza Khatami stated, and they would now 'create another Second of Khordad'.[3]

The Second of Khordad movement was extremely active, but there were significant disagreements among its various components over issues such as the lists of candidates, the appropriate economic policy, and the correct attitude to the United States. Most groups wished to limit the number of clerics in the list, but *Ruhaniyyun-e Mobarez* advocated larger clerical representation and formed a separate list. Also in contention was whether to include Rafsanjani. Some groups favored his inclusion (such as the *Kargozaran*, or House of the Workers), while others, who viewed him as the symbol of the government's misconduct, made his exclusion a matter of principle. Akbar Ganji led the campaign against 'Ali Akbar Rafsanjani, which became known as the 'Akbar versus Akbar' battle. He charged Rafsanjani with responsibility for the assassination of dissidents during his presidency (see Chapter 5), and of prolonging the war with Iraq (and thus of being responsible for the casualties and destruction). He termed him 'the Red Eminence', because of his 'responsibility' for bloodshed.[4] Others followed suit, criticizing Rafsanjani mercilessly. The reformists generally held a milder attitude towards the United States. In a letter from jail dated 17 December 1999, Nuri asked: 'How did Iran benefit from the slogan "Death to America?"' Has such rhetoric 'developed our economy' or promoted any of our national goals?[5] His brother 'Ali Reza Nuri, too, favored a realistic stance towards foreign countries.[6] Montazeri, often viewed as the 'living conscience' of the clergy, lent his support to them (in January 2000), upholding the popular right to make decisions. No stable government can be established, he said, 'unless it is popular', and the Supreme Leader is 'not infallible', and cannot claim 'absolute power'. People can 'elect' and even 'depose him'. Iranians, he said, are not against the Islamic system, but they resent the dictatorship practiced by a certain faction that 'has monopolized Islam' under 'the pretext' of defending it. They are the greatest 'enemy of Islam', he said.[7]

The conservatives denounced the reformists and their philosophy as dangerous to the regime and to the faith. They warned people not to be deluded by their slogans, tellingly suggesting that the enemies of the revolution wanted the reformists to win. Ayatollah Mesbah Yazdi again set the tone, supporting harsh measures and urging true believers to use violence, if necessary, to answer those who deviate from the correct path: 'If someone tells you he has a new interpretation of Islam, hit him in the mouth.' Rafsanjani added that reformers were 'unjust' to question Iran's performance in the war. 'Killing people's confidence is more dangerous than AIDS', he said.[8] *Kayhan* and other conservatives then compared Montazeri with those who had opposed Imam 'Ali.[9]

The deep and broad gap between the camps was evident in their campaign. Pro-reform candidates were often shown sporting a broad smile – emulating Khatami, who has been nicknamed *Seyyed Khandan* (Smiling Seyyed) – and wearing suits; conservatives appeared grim-faced and mostly shabbily dressed in their campaign posters. While pro-reform male candidates normally wore designer stubble, conservatives usually sported bushy beards. Reformers used Persian words, studiously avoiding words of Arabic origin; conservatives peppered their speeches with Arabic quotations. The average pro-reform candidates had relatively high levels of education, were usually natives of large cities, and many of them were businessmen, journalists, professors and writers; their rivals usually hailed from smaller towns or rural areas, and were more representative of the *bazaar*, the clerical elite, the farming community and lower-level civil servants. Pro-reform candidates upheld political freedom, economic development and social change, while their rivals put the emphasis on defending the revolution and Islam, putting economic development (*towse'eh eqtesadi*) before political development (*towse'eh eqtesadi*).[10]

The conservatives appealed for mass disqualification of 'unfit' candidates. The student Basij of Tehran University urged the Council of Guardians to bar not only the 'third stream' (anti-revolutionary, *monafeqin*), but also the 'second stream' (liberals of all sorts) – the 'new *monafeqin*', who, taking advantage of official negligence, had penetrated the system to occupy major positions, in order to act against it. They were no better than the Iraqi troops who had invaded Iran and worse even than the 'third stream', as they were operating in disguise.[11]

The Council of Guardians appeared more hesitant to disqualify candidates than they had been in the previous elections (see Chapter 2). Nevertheless, it disqualified some 10 per cent of the 6,851 aspirants, including resolute advocates of reform like 'Abdi, Hamid Reza Jala'ipur, 'Ali Rashidi, Ahmad Zeyd Abadi, Tabarzadi, 'Ezzatollah Sahabi and Ebrahim Yazdi. Several key figures, including 'Abdollah Nuri and Mohsen Kadivar, had previously been jailed. Many more did not even register, understanding they would not be approved anyway. The reformists viewed their disqualification as negating the principle of republicanism and people's rights.[12] The contention that the Council could judge better what was good for the people, said 'Ali Reza Nuri, was another sign of their striving for guardianship and mastership.[13]

The election results confirmed resolute popular support for reform. The reformist trend maintained its margin of victory from the presidential and the municipal elections (70 per cent of the seats decided in the first round). According to the initial results announced for Tehran province, the leading reform candidates gained impressive support in the capital: Mohammad Reza Khatami (61.2 per cent), Jamileh Kadivar (47 per cent), 'Ali Reza Nuri (45.6 per cent), Mohsen Armin (41.8 per cent),

Hadi Khamene'i (41.8 per cent). The conservatives barely managed to secure the election of Rafsanjani (25.6 per cent), the last of the province's 30 seats, just passing the 25 per cent threshold for victory in the first round. Even after the final results were announced, following numerous recounts (see below), the victory of the pro-reform camp remained solid throughout the country. Voters had supported a policy of change, and opted to replace the old guard with a new breed of largely untested politicians dedicated to reform.

THE CONSERVATIVES STRIKE BACK

Following the first round, the conservatives seemed determined to check the growing power of their rivals. The reformists aimed to cement their victory by securing approval of the results of the first round by the Council of Guardians and winning more seats in the second round of the elections.

Moving onto the offensive, the conservatives operated on several parallel lines: directing warnings at their rivals; alerting people to the 'danger' they represented to Islam and the revolution; and taking actual steps against them (such as nullifying the results in several constituencies, banning newspapers and arresting more pro-reform figures).

Stern warnings against the reformists were issued by clerics, basing their argument on religious grounds, and by the security forces, using the logic of power. They portrayed their opponents as emissaries of the anti-revolutionaries, acting against the revolution and Islam. To intimidate their rivals, before the elections, the conservatives had portrayed the reformists as American agents; such accusations were intensified afterwards. Mesbah Yazdi went so far as to state that a former head of the CIA had traveled to Iran with a suitcase full of dollars to distribute among reformist journalists and other 'cultural agents' of the USA.[14] In his view, the crimes of those who speak of a new interpretation of Islam, who conceal, distort or turn its principles upside down, was greater than the killers of Imam 'Ali: 'they are no better than the devil'.[15] Rafsanjani drew parallels between the situation in 2000 and the civil strife that had followed the revolutionary takeover – then and now, those who contest the clerical leadership were agents of foreign powers, he said. They put 'freedom against Islam' and questioned the accomplishments of the revolution, thus paving the way for those who want to take over the country.[16] Rafsanjani's comparison between the situation then and now, and between President Khatami and the deposed President Bani Sadr, was very revealing. On 14 April Khamene'i himself endorsed 'lawful' violence (*khoshunat*) – to punish those who commit transgressions – but denounced 'unlawful' violence, aimed at usurping people's rights. He supported 'Islamic reforms', arguing that the revolution itself was the greatest reform movement, but warned against reforms championed by the Unites States and the other enemies that threatened to destroy Islamic values. However, he advised people not to act 'against the law' even 'for the sake of your sentiments' or in support of 'a person'.[17] He even praised Khatami as a 'defender of the system and the revolution'.[18]

Although violence was mostly prevented, some acts of violence did take place between the two rounds of the elections. Most conspicuous was the near-fatal attempt on Sa'id Hajariyan's life (12 March 2000). Once a prominent official in the ministry of intelligence, Hajariyan had become a leading reformist. Using harsh language, he and like-minded reformists called for the extremist philosophies to be thrown into the dustbin of history. For people like Soroush, Hajariyan was a victim of a fascist interpretation of Islam. The attempt on his life, he suggested, was not an isolated case but the culmination of a long process, which had been supported by official agencies and had not been denounced by the 'silent clerics'.[19] Ganji accused Mesbah Yazdi of having influenced the ministry of intelligence and of having approached elements in that ministry to discuss an alleged scheme against President Khatami, Kadivar, Nuri, Shabestari and Soroush.[20] Violence also erupted in constituencies in which the election results were annulled (see below). Yet, evidently, both sides – each for its own purposes – wished at this stage to check violence.

The crackdown on the pro-reform press best signaled the conservatives' determination to block the reform movement. Escalation in rhetoric preceded the actual banning of the pro-reform organs. In two speeches (14 and 20 April 2000) Khamene'i said that although there were many good people among them, and while the 'sound transfer of information' is acceptable, some of them 'try to sow discord, create tension' and 'spread pessimism'. He complained that 'ten to 15 papers', apparently guided 'by one center', were inciting the public. The 'constitution and main policies are insulted, small events are magnified, the atmosphere is filled with libel'. This is not freedom of the press, he said, this is press 'charlatanism'.[21]

Given the popularity of the pro-reform press and their sharp criticisms, the authorities had earlier banned several such newspapers (*Jame'eh, Neshat, Salam*), some of which were replaced by others, even more critical. The conservatives decided to put an end to this game of cat and mouse. The press law, passed in the waning days of the Majlis, gave the courts power to close newspapers summarily and to control who owned or worked for them (see below). On 23 April 2000, 12 newspapers and journals were banned. By early August another 12 had been banned, and many of their editors, owners or leading journalists had been arrested (including Ganji, Shams al-Va'ezin, Jala'ipur, 'Isa Sahar-Khiz, Baqi, Zeyd Abadi). Other intellectuals and student leaders (such as 'Ezzatollah Sahabi, Tabarzadi, Mehrangiz Kar, Shahla Lahiji, Shirin 'Ebadi) were also put behind bars. The Second of Khordad front, viewing the ban on these newspapers as 'illegitimate', blamed a 'power mafia', which 'is set to trample' upon the interests of 'Islam, the revolution, the system, and the state'.[22]

The Council of Guardians also overturned the victories of about a dozen reformists, alleging voter intimidation, vote-buying and biased electoral officials. This decision sparked protests and riots in some of the affected districts, in which several people were killed and many arrested. The Council also delayed for two months the decision regarding the second-round elections for the 66 seats in which no candidate passed the 25 per cent threshold to gain a seat in the first round, before finally setting a date (5 May 2000). The results for Tehran remained undecided for three months, and eventually the reformers won there by a landslide (see below).

Foreign media also reported an alleged plot between security and media officials. Mutual suspicion prevailed. The conservatives feared that their rivals would use the Majlis to derail the revolutionary regime, and the reformists feared a plot to annul the results or even to remove the president. While pledging to 'try to be tolerant with duped elements and criminals', a Revolutionary Guards' statement pledged that if necessary, 'the enemies will feel [the pain of] its blows in their skull' so that 'they will forever be stopped from hatching plots'. They denounced 'the champions of American-style reforms' and raged against 'certain members of the press' who promote 'unbridled and ill-defined reforms'. They warned: 'Traitors and reactionaries have reemerged like a malignant tumor and speak of an end to the revolution and [the] elimination of Islam.'[23]

The second round of the elections was thus held in an atmosphere of growing suspicion and distrust. The reform camp again proved strong nationwide, securing two-thirds of the 66 seats contested. Facing the conservatives' offensive and fearful that a misguided counter-step would provide a pretext for annulling the elections, the pro-reform people demonstrated impressive restraint, or as Jala'ipur put it, an 'active silence'. This was their response, Mohammed Reza Khatami said, to the 'illegal means' used to suppress its progress. He hoped that 'everyone would now bow' to the popular vote, so that 'the pure ideals' of the revolution and the programs of the president 'will be materialized'.[24]

Finally, following Khamene'i's urgings, the Council of Guardians approved the Tehran results on 20 May 2000. Claiming that the elections had been riddled with widespread fraud, vote-rigging and irregularities, it nullified 726,000 votes (out of 2,290,000) in 534 (out of 3,000) polling stations. Reformers nevertheless won 26 of the 30 seats. The most important change was the upgrading of Rafsanjani from slot 30 to slot 20, and the victory of the conservative Gholam'ali Hadad 'Adl (replacing the only candidate of the national-religious front who had made it into the Majlis according to the initial count). Two other pro-reform candidates – 'Ali Akbar Mohtashami and Eliyas Hazrati – won the runoffs. Altogether, the pro-reform camp seemed to have secured almost 200 of the Majlis 290 seats. Given the election system and past experience, the exact breakdown of the factional affiliations could not be determined with any certainty. Yet one point was clear: for the first time since 1979 the Majlis was not dominated by the conservative clerics.

Rafsanjani's position was a major issue in the reformist–conservative contest. Having initially cautioned him not to run, the reformists subsequently targeted him mercilessly. He lost further credit after being associated with the crackdown on pro-reform investigative journalists who had linked him to the murders of dissidents and the series of killings in Iran (see Chapter 5). The endless reports about 'the fortunes' amassed by his family further tarnished his reputation. The support of his daughter, Fa'ezeh Hashemi, turned her into another target. Having gained the second place in Tehran in 1996, now she lost her seat. Rafsanjani withdrew on 25 May, stating that poisonous propaganda 'by enemies' had created an ambiguous atmosphere, which 'could be used by internal and foreign enemies'. He had entered the race 'to protect national unity', he said, and withdrew 'for the same reason'.[25] Rafsanjani, who had been the first speaker of the Islamic Majlis and had served two terms as president, coming to be regarded as one of the strongest and most powerful personalities in Iran after Khomeini himself, had suffered a devastating humiliation. The 'slap voters delivered to Rafsanjani' was matched by the defeat of conservative stalwarts across the country.[26] However, Rafsanjani maintains his post as head of the Expediency Council, empowered to approve legislation; and the conservative clergy still control significant power bases. The reformists, for their part, have established firm influence over another bastion of power, but their ability to advance reform legislation is not clear – as debate on the press bill is already showing at the time of writing.

The contest between the rival camps was internal and the main topics in dispute were domestic. Yet issues of foreign policy, particularly policy towards the United States, were unceasingly controversial and came to the fore most forcefully during the elections. Conservatives, faithful to the spirit of 1979, cut off all debate on the issue with the revolutionary slogan 'Death to America'. Reformists pledged to review the matter, often suggesting that normal relations with the United States, and détente in foreign relations at large, could serve Iran's national interests better. Following the first round of the elections, Mohammed Reza Khatami said (on 22 February 2000) that the new Majlis would support the government policy of détente and even accelerate it, typically requiring of Washington that it take the first step of a milder approach.[27] More generally, however, they maintained that propagating an absence of relations with the United States as a value or maintaining that relations with the United States are against the interests of Islam – as conservatives often claimed – was an insult to logic and far from rational. Forming ties has nothing to do with values, they insisted, and should reflect nothing but national interests. Moreover, while the *faqih* may outline basic guidelines, it is up to the foreign ministry to formulate actual policy.

Washington for its part viewed the election as an 'event of historic proportions', signaling Iranians' preference for 'openness and engagement'.[28] President Clinton expressed the hope that the new Majlis would usher in a period of 'openness and freedom', praising Iran as 'one of the most wonderful places in all human history'.[29] The US administration has also moved gradually to soften trade sanctions. In December 1999 it allowed Boeing to sell parts to Iran's national airline, so as to ensure the safety of its passenger aircraft. Secretary of State Madeleine Albright then threw a big rock into the already troubled waters of Iranian politics. In a most conciliatory speech (on 17 March 2000), she acknowledged that the 'democratic winds' in Iran are 'refreshing'. As a step towards bringing down the wall of mistrust, she declared an easing of the economic sanctions, a step that enables Americans to import carpets and such food products as dried fruits, nuts and caviar from Iran, and enables Iranians to purchase such products as corn and wheat from the United States. 'The United States is willing either to proceed patiently, on a step-by-step basis' or 'to move very rapidly if Iran indicates a desire and commitment to do so', she concluded.[30]

Iranian reactions to Albright's announcement typified the internal dichotomy in the country. President Khatami said later (11 July 2000) that a 'new turn' had taken place in Iran's relations with the United States, but urged the Clinton administration to be more ambitious in pursuit of reconciliation. He regretted that, except for minor changes, 'no concrete steps' had been taken.[31] Foreign ministry spokesman Asefi observed 'positive and negative points' in Albright's speech. Although 'past accusations were repeated', she had 'tried to admit America's past mistakes and present a new and different attitude'. By contrast, Hasan Ruhani, secretary of the Supreme National Security Council, viewed the lifting of sanctions as an improper American attempt to reward certain forces in Iran. The Americans, he said, 'are offering a piece of chocolate to what they see as [positive] developments inside Iran', which is 'a very ugly and unacceptable move'. American policy remained 'the same hostile policy', he said, and Albright's speech only indicates 'interference in Iran's internal affairs'.[32] *Kayhan* then called for the bringing to trial of American politicians of the past 50 years, just as Hitler and his associates had been brought to trial after World War II. It also accused mercenary journalists and the local lackeys of the United States of being ignorant of its blood-sucking nature.[33] Khamene'i, too, rejected Washington's offer and accused its leaders of the past 50 years of having supported Iranian dictators who are now in hell, and of currently supporting their emissaries – their dirty waste and refuse (*tofaleh* and *zabaleh*).[34] Hence, the attitude to the United States, though marginal in the campaign, was another major divide and at the heart of the stormy debate between reformists and conservatives.

A Stormy Climate: In the Aftermath of the Majlis Elections

The February elections were conducted in an atmosphere of unprecedented freedom. Symbols that had hitherto been held holy lost their sacred status and fundamental taboos were broken. Clearly, people voted against past politics and opted, instead, for reform and new ideas.

The reformist trend gained further strength and reformism encompassed larger segments of society and wider spheres of policy. The process of change that had been boosted with President Khatami's election gained greater steam and reached a new peak. The reformists' victory was decisive and they seemed determined to pursue their course of action and fulfill their campaign pledges. Yet, faced with the conservatives' countermeasures, the reformists had to change pace, even if this did not necessarily mean changing direction. The clerics in power appear to be widely unpopular, among certain segments of Iranian society. The elections also showed how anguished people in Iran are after two decades of Islamic rule. The decline of clerical representation in the Majlis seemed, thus, a blow to the ruling conservative elite, not only to individual contenders.[35]

Carried forward on the wave of their electoral victory, the reformists initially seemed over-optimistic about the prospects of reform. The Majlis vote was an earthquake, of the magnitude of the Second of Khordad, said Jala'ipur.[36] Others viewed the election as a milestone in Iran's contemporary history, signaling a rejection of custodianship or mastership over the people, and a denial of those who behaved as 'the father' (*pedarsalari*), with the people opting instead for freedom and democracy. People have rejected those whose use-by-date has expired, added 'Isa Sahar-Khiz, in order to vote for people who speak and look like themselves, and who care about the people rather than about advancing their personal goals. As the new Majlis is considerably younger than the previous one, it also signaled a generation change – moving responsibility on to the younger generation.[37] The elections proved once more that Iranians are active in the political scene, said Zeyd Abadi, counseling the conservatives – and the reformists too – always to heed the popular voice.[38] The old traditions were 'forever' consigned 'to the archives of history' exulted *Fath*. Those officials who had enjoyed the 'sweet taste' of power, believing that they could continue to benefit from the system, had now learned that they can be removed by the people.[39]

Moreover, the elections proved that it was the people who had led the reform movement not vice-versa; more than shaping the movement, President Khatami was its product. This is seen in the impressive support for hitherto unknown candidates, like Mohammad Reza Khatami, 'Ali Reza Nuri and Jamileh Kadivar (whose brothers turned into symbols of the movement), for Hadi Khamene'i (brother but adversary of the Supreme Leader), and in the failure of Fa'ezeh Hashemi to gain election. Demography also favors the reform movement, at least for the long run, as the young had supported reform *en masse*. Moreover, the support for the reformist trend was impressive countrywide, even among the rank and file of the armed forces. Although it was not a 'second revolution', it was an important signal of popular support for reform.

Yet the road to meaningful transformation seemed filled with significant impediments. To begin with, the president himself views his reforms as being part of the essence of the revolutionary system. Although the conservatives have suffered a 'crushing defeat', they have not been booted out of public life. They continue to control major power centers – such as the Council of Guardians, the judiciary, the Revolutionary Guards – and can usually rely on the support of the Supreme Leader. It is also not clear whether the new (and mostly unknown) Majlis members possess the leadership qualities to lead the reformist movement to actual success. In fact, because of the rapid change in the composition of the Majlis, there are not many 'heavy-weight' parliamentarians. Many of the prominent reformists, including the three who won the highest vote in Tehran, have little or no experience in government. The reform camp is far from unified, and it is not clear how long its components will be able to stick together or to agree on a common agenda. That personalities such as Karubi, Khalkhali and Mohtashami (leading radicals less than a decade ago) are now part of the reform list is a telling indicator of the extent of change, but also poses questions about the cohesion of the reform camp and their future policy. Some of the reformists did not spare their criticism of President Khatami – for his failure to implement reform as swiftly and comprehensively as they had deemed necessary. Clearly, the people do not seem to be satisfied any longer with pledges of a better future, but demand practical solutions to their pressing problems. The vote signaled disillusionment and made clear the popular choice, but what the actual policy will be, or whether the president will be able to meet the growing expectations, remains unclear. The fact that he has already been in office three years, and that within a year another presidential election will take place, add to the challenges facing him. All in all, the reformists' euphoria after the sweeping victory in February 2000 is being balanced by a growing realism and their ambitions are being trimmed by sobering realities. The reformists have proven determination, but also an impressive measure of caution.

The short time that has elapsed since the elections is insufficient to determine the direction in which the country is now heading, or the meaning of the reformists' parliamentary victory for actual politics. The domestic struggle continues, even more forcefully, with the same major issues coloring the internal debate: the system of *velayat-e faqih* and the role of the Supreme Leader; the quest for freedom and social and economic betterment; and Iran's relations with the outside world, particularly with the United States.

Evidently, the reformists wished to use their victory to advance their electoral pledges, mainly in the realm of 'political development' – more specifically, to strip the press law of restrictive amendments added in the last days of the outgoing Majlis and to unshackle the banned newspapers; to depoliticize the court system and to define crimes such as 'insulting religion' that courts used in order to jail people for political ends. It soon became clear, however, that the conservatives were determined to prevent major changes. As against the reformists' stress on popular support for their line, the conservatives emphasized the centrality of the clerical voice in the Islamic system; while the pro-reform camp appealed for 'political development', the conservatives cautioned them first to cure the economic wounds and put 'economic development' highest on the agenda.

For the reformists, 'political development' was the highest priority, and the amendment of the press law was their first major test-case. On 18 June 2000, 151 Majlis members wrote to Ayatollah Hashemi Shahrudi, the head of the judiciary, criticizing the judiciary's harsh attitude towards the press and intellectuals, and urging him to stop the closure of newspapers at once.[40] The Majlis voted to give top priority to a new press law to protect newspapers from suspension before trial and to shield journalists from criminal prosecution. The conservatives were determined to block the law, and continued to ban the remaining pro-reform newspapers (*Bahar*, the last major pro-reform organ, was banned on 8 August 2000). Quashing the reformists' goal, Khamene'i, in an extraordinary move, ordered the Majlis to scrap the bill. In his letter read out at the Majlis on 6 August 2000, he termed the new bill a threat to the fundamental pillars of the system. It would endanger national security, unity and faith, he wrote, if the enemies of the revolution infiltrate the press. The present press law 'has prevented such a calamity so far' and amending it 'is not in the interests of the country'. The decision aroused loud arguments and caused scuffles in the Majlis. Speaker Karubi was forced to comply, stating that it is 'our duty to obey the leader's order' and that the system is based on submission to the 'absolute rule of the Supreme Leader'.[41]

Khamene'i's interference was crucial in countering the reformists' plans to amend the press law, but it contained an even graver message for the pro-reform camp. Until then, Khamene'i had usually succeeded in appearing to give some support to each side of the political divide. He had praised the president occasionally as a true heir to the values of the revolution, and proclaimed support for reform, maintaining that the Islamic revolution itself was an exemplary reform movement. Iran has both to preserve values and to pursue reform, he had said, the two camps being like 'two wings' of 'one bird' (*yek parandeh*), which ought to work in harmony to drive the revolution on to new horizons.[42] Yet as the Supreme Leader, Khamene'i has been closer to the conservatives all along and his main concern has been staunch adherence to the revolutionary creed. He stepped in to check the critical trend the press was following (including harsh criticism of the *velayat-e faqih* doctrine); a move also meant to make it clear that, no matter how loud the popular voice, the final decision rests with the supreme religious authority. In accordance with their strategy, the reformists again demonstrated restraint, although some Majlis representatives protested loudly. Mohammad Reza Khatami hinted at 'special schemes' aimed against the Majlis had it not complied with the will of the Supreme Leader.[43] Although it is not yet clear whether such a harsh intervention was an isolated case or signaled a more active endorsement of the conservative line, Khamene'i's move served as a reminder to the reformists of the current real limits of their power.

Khamene'i's move was directly related to one of the most basic questions in contention: the authority of the *vali-ye faqih* and the weight of the clerical voice as against the popular will (see Chapter 1). Ayatollah Mohammad Yazdi, the former head of the judiciary, continued to uphold (on 30 June 2000) the exclusive legislative right of the clergy. People have endorsed democracy in the framework of Islam, he said, and they cannot ignore the views of the clerics.[44] His successor, Ayatollah Hashemi Shahrudi – who had been viewed as relatively moderate when he assumed office in 1999 but firmly supported the conservative line thereafter – seconded him, maintaining (on 31 July 2000) that deep understanding of religious law is a prerequisite for legislation. By contrast, the chairman of the legal committee of the Majlis, Naser Qavami, maintained that the Majlis is entitled to approve laws – which is its main task. Ayatollah 'Aba'i Khorasani (another member of the committee) added that many laws have no religious connotations and that generally legislation should not be an exclusive domain of the clergy.[45] Carrying the argument further, Mohammad Reza Khatami said that, while clerics are entitled to guide the people, they should not present their own ideas as representing the views of the people – people are entitled to define the reform they desire.[46] Montazeri once again added his weight in support of the reformists. In a letter on 7 August 2000, he again rejected the concept of 'the absolute rule of the *faqih*', and defended the people's right to determine policy. The Supreme Leader is not infallible, he reiterated, warning that overruling parliament could lead to despotism. The Supreme Leader's intervention in issues such as the press law is illogical and leads to instability; one is not supposed to ban newspapers out of fear of the enemy's influence, just as it would be against logic to destroy the water pipes just because the water is polluted.[47]

While the reformists stress 'political development', the conservatives emphasize 'economic development'. In truth, the economy continues to pose a serious challenge (see Chapter 4). The basic difficulties have not been mitigated, even after the dramatic rise of oil prices in the last year. There seems to be little economic planning, and the government acts mostly to resolve immediate problems as they emerge rather than engaging in long-range planning. There is a growing sense of alienation, as gaps between the rich and poor are not bridged. Moreover, many Iranians resent the situation in which those who were part of the system (*khodi*) benefited, while those outside the system (*gheir-e khodi*) did not. In early July, there were disturbances – related to social and economic grievances – in different cities. In Abadan, where riots began after electricity and water had been cut during extremely hot days, anti-government slogans were also voiced (several people were reportedly killed).

Either out of deep and sincere conviction or as a tool to censure the government, the conservatives have continued to focus on its economic failures. Meeting Majlis members on 18 June 2000, Khamene'i urged them to abandon petty issues and trivial intellectual argumentation, and to devote themselves more seriously to resolving the complex economic difficulties of the country. Portraying a gloomy picture of people's daily life, he urged the government to focus on securing people's livelihood (*ma'ishat*) – otherwise there would be no religion, no morale and no hope.[48] Ayatollah Hashemi Shahrudi, Mohammad Yazdi and Rafsanjani, among others, seconded him.[49] Mohammad Reza Faker of *Ansar-e Hezbollah* went still further in censuring Khatami's incompetence. Since his election, Faker said, Khatami had proven his strength only in delivering eloquent speeches. While the country is confronted with enemies, his government (and now the Majlis too) were wasting their time defending the rights of Iran's adversaries.[50] While in the past criticism of the government was rejected as anti-revolutionary, grieved Ahmad Pur-Nejati (head of the Majlis cultural committee), now the president is seen as responsible even for the drought, and his opponents portray a worn-out and miserable picture of the country.[51]

While castigating the president and the entire reform camp for their misguided policies, the conservatives continue to label some of the reformists as emissaries of foreign powers. Leading reformists have been blamed for maintaining contacts with the United States and accused of having received money from foreign agencies.[52] Khamene'i stated (on 9 July 2000) that Western imperialism led by Washington has conspired to undermine the Islamic regime, just as it did with the USSR.[53] The danger, such charges implied, was not in a 'Gorbachev' (that is, with Khatami), but the 'Yeltsins' that might follow.

More than two decades after the revolution, the struggle over the future path of Iran is not yet over. Recently, domestic controversies have further deepened and turned increasingly harsher and more open. In sum, as was demonstrated in the 2000 Majlis election campaign, this is a struggle between the initial ideals of the 1979 revolution (22 Bahman) and the new spirit of President Khatami's movement (the Second of Khordad). It is a struggle between conservatism and reformism, idealism and pragmatism, religion and state, isolationism and globalization. It is equally a contest between the institutions of power and the emerging civil society; between the old guards and the new generation. While growing demand – and support – for reform has been noticed, the conservative establishment is struggling to preserve loyalty to the revolutionary dogma. With time, almost all taboos have been removed, and Iranians – more than others in the region – are now debating among themselves the fundamental questions facing their nation. It is a profound and comprehensive debate, on questions of religion and state, Islam and democracy, idealism versus national interests, and on attitudes towards the outside world. Khatami, who was elevated on a wave of public support, is now being criticized by the conservatives for moving too fast; simultaneously he is being castigated by many reformists for being too slow and hesitant and for having failed to fulfill the people's expectations for real change.

While the conservatives have been struggling to block reformism and the reformists seem resolved to advance their goals, the climate of 'tropical storm', some observers have suggested, was threatening to turn into 'a hurricane'.[54] Even as both camps appear to be determined to advance their particular cause, they have so far seemed to be avoiding a head-on collision. The fierce domestic debate, nevertheless, continues. The Majlis elections have exposed the depth of domestic divides, adding new dimensions to an already profound national argument. The new discourse, in the aftermath of the Majlis elections, seems the precursor of the next presidential elections, scheduled for the summer of 2001. Moreover, it represents a much deeper struggle to define the future course of Iran's Islamic revolution.

Notes

1. Op-Ed by Shaul Bakhash, *Washington Post*, 27 February 2000.
2. *New York Times*, 10 October 1999.

3. *Washington Post*, 17 February 2000.

4. *Sobh-e Emruz*, 19 January 2000.

5. *New York Times*, 21 December 1999.

6. *Hamshahri*, 13 January 2000.

7. *New York Times*, 24 January and 13 February 2000; *Al-Sharq al-Awsat*, 25 May 2000, in *Mideast Mirror*, 25 May 2000. Montazeri's tract was sent by fax to Reuters and the *Guardian* and was published in some Iranian papers on 15 January 2000 (*Fath*, *'Asr-e Azadegan*, *Sobh-e Emruz*, *Azad*). See also *Frankfurter Allgemeine Zeitung*, 20 May 2000.

8. *New York Times*, 24 January 2000.

9. *Kayhan* (Tehran), 16, 23 January 2000.

10. *Al-Sharq al-Awsat*, 15 February 2000 (article by Amir Taheri).

11. *Kayhan* (Tehran), 13 January 2000.

12. Hadi Khamene'i in *Fath*, 12 January 2000.

13. *Hamshahri*, 13 January 2000.

14. *Mideast Mirror*, 11 February 2000.

15. *Resalat* and *Entekhab*, 2 May 2000.

16. *Jomhuri-ye Islami*, 29 April 2000. See also *New York Times*, 29 April 2000.

17. *Jomhuri-ye Islami*, 15 April 2000; *Al-Sharq al-Awsat*, 17 and 18 April 2000, in *Mideast Mirror*, 17 and 18 April 2000.

18. *New York Times*, 27 April 2000.

19. *'Asr-e Azadegan* and *Fath*, 3 April 2000.

20. *'Asr-e Azadegan*, 29 March 2000.

21. *Jomhuri-ye Islami*, 15 and 22 April; IRNA, 20 April 2000.

22. IRNA, 29 April 2000.

23. *Al-Sharq al-Awsat*, in *Mideast Mirror*, 4 May 2000. See also *Al-Sharq al-Awsat*, 12 and 17 April 2000; RFE/RL Iran Report, Vol. 3, No. 15, 17 April 2000.

24. *Washington Post*, 7 May 2000.

25. Radio Tehran, 25 May – SWB, 25 May 2000.

26. *Akhbar al-Khalij*, 21 February, in *Mideast Mirror*, 21 February 2000.

27. IRNA and *Mosharekat*, 22 February 2000.

28. *New York Times*, 21 February; *Mideast Mirror*, 21 February 2000.

29. *The Times* (London), 15 March 2000.

30. Albright's remarks before the American–Iranian Council (17 March 2000), as released by the Office of the Spokesman, US Department of State.

31. *Washington Post*, 12 July 2000.

32. *Mideast Mirror*, 20 March 2000; *Washington Post*, 18 March 2000.

33. *Kayhan* (Tehran), 27 and 28 March 2000.

34. *Kayhan* (Tehran), 26 March 2000.

35. *Jomhuri-ye Islami*, 22 and 24 February 2000.

36. *'Asr-e Azadegan*, 20 February 2000.

37. *Akhbar-e Eqtesad*, 20 February 2000.

38. *'Asr-e Azadegan*, 22 February 2000.

39. *Fath*, 24 February 2000.

40. *Jomhuri-ye Islami* and *Bayan*, 19 June 2000.

41. *Bahar*, 7 and 8 August 2000; *Hamshahri*, 7 August 2000; *New York Times*, 7 and 9 August; *al-Khalij*, 9 August 2000.

42. *Jomhuri-ye Islami*, 13 May 2000.

43. *Bahar*, 8 August 2000.
44. *Jomhuri-ye Islami*, 1 July 2000.
45. *Bahar*, 2 August 2000.
46. *Bahar*, 19 July 2000.
47. Letter by Montazeri answering questions put by the BBC, on 7 August 2000. See also his interview with *Mehregan* (from 28 June 2000).
48. *Jomhuri-ye Islami*, 19 June 2000.
49. IRNA, 1 August (statement by Shahrudi); *Jomhuri-ye Islami*, 1 July (Yazdi) and 5 August 2000 (Rafsanjani).
50. Iranian Students New Agency, 1 August 2000. See similarly an article in *Kayhan International*, 2 August 2000.
51. *Bahar*, 2 August 2000; IRNA, 3 August 2000.
52. See charges against Ganji for maintaining contacts with an American officer and anti-revolutionaries in Turkey: *Kayhan* (Tehran) and *Jomhuri-ye Islami*, 21 May 2000; charges against Soroush, Kadivar and other intellectuals for receiving financial support from foreign agencies, see *Kayhan* (Tehran), 15 July 2000. Soroush and Kadivar's wife denied such accusations: *Jomhuri-ye Islami*, 16 July 2000 (Mohsen Kadivar was still in jail then).
53. *Jomhuri-ye Islami*, 10 July 2000.
54. Thomas Friedman, in *New York Times*, 15 August 2000.

Appendix: List of Iranian Newspapers

Iranian newspapers played a major role in the domestic debate throughout the 1990s. The multiplicity of newspapers, the diversity of views they presented and the level of free expression and criticism have become most visible following Khatami's election, reaching a new peak in 1999 and early 2000. The numerous pro-reform newspapers have played a focal role in the heated political atmosphere, and proved a useful tool for enlisting support on the eve of the Majlis elections. At no other time before in Iran (nor elsewhere in the Middle East) had there been so many new papers and journals, enjoying such a degree of freedom and expressing such a diversity of viewpoints with such fervor and sense of mission. True, in the past there had been occasional brief intervals of openness, such as in the early 1940s (following the abdication of Reza Shah), the early 1950s (under the opposition movement led by Mosaddeq), or just prior to the fall of the Shah (and until the consolidation of the new regime). But on all these previous occasions the regime was weaker, the circle of readers more limited, and the press less developed.

By 1999, it seemed as though almost all the taboos had been removed, and the most critical issues, domestic and foreign, were openly debated, including the basic principles of the system of government and relations with the United States. Pro-reform newspapers took the lead in voicing dissent, as the many references in this book show. They were extremely popular, particularly among the youth and the more educated class. At the same time, other organs continued to preach the more conservative line and genuine revolutionary values, using equally harsh language to denounce their foes, with similar degrees of passion and fervor. The press thus turned into a major arena of public debate. The crackdown on the pro-reform newspapers, mainly after April 2000, and the banning of over 20 newspapers and journals since then, has somewhat checked this wave of colorful press, at least for the time being. Yet, their impact would be difficult to ignore.

The story of the press in this sensitive juncture of Iranian history deserves a comprehensive study, which will undoubtedly follow. As this book draws heavily on the Iranian press, the list below briefly delineates the main papers used, or referred to in this study, as a guide for the readers.

The characterization of newspapers here, however, should be treated with caution. During the past decade, some newspapers have wavered in their tendencies, even on key issues, as have certain politicians. A few of them expressed diversified views, in an attempt to reflect the different prevailing viewpoints. Others where published for a period too short to allow judgment. Also, certain leading journalists served on the editorial boards of or contributed to several newspapers simultaneously; in some cases, the same people ran more than one paper. Moreover, with the banning of newspapers they were replaced by others, often with the same line and editorial staff. Newspapers were discontinued and then reappeared, sometimes under the same title, at other times with a new name. With these caveats in mind, the list below portrays the general line of the papers at the time of their use in this book. For certain items (mainly newer papers), the names of key people (editor, managing director, publisher, or leading journalists) are given in brackets.

Name of Publication	Place and Frequency	General Attributes (journalists affiliated with the newspaper, or main contributors)
Aban	Tehran, weekly	pro-reform; issued after Khatami's election; one of the most adamant in its criticism; banned on 23 April 2000 (Mohammad Hasan 'Alipur)
Abrar	Tehran, daily	generally supports a conservative line (Seyyed Mohammad Safizadeh)
Aftab-e Emruz	Tehran, daily	pro-reform; published since 1999; banned on 23 April 2000 (Fereydun 'Amuzadeh Khalili)
Akhbar	Tehran, daily	generally expresses middle-of-the-road views (Ahmad Safa'ifar)
Akhbar-e Eqtesad	Tehran, daily	pro-reform; published after *Neshat*'s ban in September 1999 and followed its line; usually carried identical articles as in *'Asr-e Azadegan*, with greater stress on economic issues; banned on 24 April 2000 ('Isa Sahar-khiz, former official in the ministry of Islamic guidance)

Arya	Tehran, daily	pro-reform; banned on 23 April 2000 (Mohammad Reza Zohdi)
Arzeshha	Tehran, weekly	hard-line (Mohammad Mohammadi Reyshahri, former minister of intelligence and founder of the Association for the Defense of Revolutionary Values)
'Asr-e Azadegan	Tehran, daily	pro-reform; continued *Neshat* after its closure in September 1999 and followed its line; banned on 23 April 2000 (Mashallah Shams al-Va'ezin, Hamid Reza Jala'ipur, Mahmud Shams)
'Asr-e Ma	Tehran, bi-weekly	pro-reform; organ of *Mojahedin-e Enqelab-e Islami*, in the coalition of 'Second of Khordad' (Mohsen Armin)
Ava	Najafabad, bi-weekly	close to Ayatollah Montazeri; banned on 27 April 2000 (Mustafa Izadi, Mohammad Hasan Hamedi)
Azad	Tehran, daily	pro-reform; banned on 23 April 2000 (Mohammad Reza Yazdanpanah)
Bahar	Tehran, daily	pro-reform, very close to President Khatami; issued following the massive ban of newspapers in April 2000; banned on 8 August 2000 (Sa'id Pur-'Azizi)
Bahman	Tehran, weekly	published before the 1996 Majlis elections to support pragmatic line and reconstruction; supported Rafsanjani; discontinued after the 1996 elections ('Ata'ollah Mohajerani, vice-president under Rafsanjani and minister of Islamic guidance under Khatami)
Bamdad	Stockholm, weekly	cultural, political and social journal; gives expression to dissident views (Bahram Rahmani)
Bamdad-e Now	Tehran, daily	pro-reform; banned on 23 April 2000 (Abul-Qasem Golbaf)
Bayan	Tehran, daily (formerly monthly)	first published in the early 1990s (monthly) and was extremely critical of Rafsanjani and his government's policy; re-appeared in late 1999 (daily) to continue the banned *Salam* (and was published by its press); unofficial organ of *Majma'-e Ruhaniyyun-e Mobarez*; banned on 25 June 2000 ('Ali Akbar Mohtashami, former minister of interior)

Discourse	Tehran, quarterly	published since 1999 by the Center for Scientific Research and Middle East Strategic Studies, in English (Seyyed Hosein Musavi, Executive Director; Mahmud Sari' al-Qalam, editor)
Echo of Iran	Tehran, monthly	an English-language survey; contains analysis, reports and profiles; published in Tehran since the early 1950s
Entekhab	Tehran, daily	generally middle-of-the-road (Taha Hashemi, member of the Fifth Majlis, 1996–2000)
Ettela'at	Tehran, daily	one the main newspapers since the mid-1920s; now generally conservative, but much less hard-line than *Kayhan* – the other major paper from pre-revolution days (see below)
Farda	Tehran, daily	pro-reform; discontinued due to lack of financing (Ahmad Tavakkoli, minister of labor and social welfare in the early 1980s)
Faslnameh-ye Khavar-e Miyaneh	Tehran, quarterly	published since summer 1994 by the Center for Scientific Research and Middle East Strategic Studies (Mohammad 'Ali Mohtadi)
Fath	Tehran, daily	pro-reform; continued *Khordad* (after its closure in November 1999); banned on 23 April 2000 ('Ali Hekmat, 'Emad al-Din Baqi)
Goftogu	Tehran, quarterly	journal focusing on social and cultural issues (Reza Saqafi)
Gozaresh-e Ruz	Tehran, daily	pro-reform; banned on 23 April 2000 ('Ali Mohammad Mahdavi Khorrami)
Hamshahri	Tehran, daily	founded and edited since the early 1990s by the then Mayor of Tehran, Gholamhosein Karbaschi; supported pragmatism and economic rehabilitation; was an important organ of the Executives of Construction in the 1996 Majlis elections (Karbaschi, Mohammad 'Atrianfar)
Ham-mihan	Tehran, daily	founded by Karbaschi prior to the Majlis elections of 2000 (who was then released from jail), supporting the Executives of Construction. Initially was believed to support Rafsanjani, though often adopted a more pro-reform and critical line towards him. Banned on 16 May 2000

Hoviyyat-e Khish	Tehran, bi-weekly	organ of the Islamic Union of University Students and Graduates; strong pro-reform line; critical of the concept of *velayat-e faqih*; often also critical of Khatami for being, in its view, too hesitant; banned in early 1999 (Heshmatollah Tabarzadi)
Iran	Tehran, daily	organ of the Islamic Republic News Agency; relatively mild tone (Hosein Zia'i)
Iran Daily	Tehran, daily	organ of the Islamic Republic News Agency; relatively mild tone; in English (Mohammad Khoddadi)
Iran-e Farda	Tehran, monthly	pro-reform; banned on 23 April 2000 ('Ezzatollah Sahabi, Reza 'Alijani)
Iranian Journal of International Studies	Tehran, quarterly	published since1994 by The Institute for Political and International Studies (founded in 1983); in English (Seyyed Sadeq Kharrazi; Bahram Mas'ud)
Iran News	Tehran, daily	in English; middle-of-the-road (Mohammad Soltanifar)
Iran Times	Washington DC, weekly	publishes the main features of the week, for Iranians living abroad; Persian with an English section (Javad Khakbaz)
Iran Weekly Press Digest	Tehran, weekly	issued since 1987; summary of weekly news and reports (Faramarz Ghazi)
Jahan-e Islam	Tehran, daily	published by Hadi Khamene'i (the brother, but adversary, of 'Ali Khamene'i) and was very critical of Rafsanjani's government in his second term as president, and therefore was then banned; resumed in 1999 and subsequently discontinued
Jame'eh	Tehran, daily	published since mid-1998; pro-reform; one of the most critical papers prior to its banning, after five months (Hamid Reza Jala'ipur, Mashallah Shams al-Va'ezin)
Jebheh	Tehran, daily	extremely hard-line; reflecting views of *Ansar-e Hezbollah*; banned in May 2000 – the only hard-line organ which was then banned (Mas'ud Dehnamaki)

Jomhuri-ye Islami	Tehran, daily	organ of the Islamic Republican Party; represents the conservative line
Kar va Kargar	Tehran, daily	middle-of-the-road; recently supporting greater reform ('Ali Rabi'i, Morteza Lotfi)
Kayhan	London, weekly	an opposition organ, contains news and critical articles (not to be confounded with *Kayhan* daily published in Tehran, see below)
Kayhan	Tehran, daily	founded in the early 1940s; now supports an extremely hard-line position (Hosein Shari'atmadari)
Kayhan al-'Arabi	Tehran, daily	in Arabic; generally follows the line of *Kayhan* daily
Kayhan-e Hava'i	Tehran, weekly	in both English and Persian; includes the main weekly news published by *Kayhan* daily ('Ali Akbar Darini)
Kayhan International	Tehran, daily	in English; follows *Kayhan* daily's line, though in a somewhat more moderate fashion (Hamid Najafi)
Khordad	Tehran, daily	pro-reform; very critical of government policy; banned in November 1999 ('Abdollah Nuri)
Kiyan	Tehran, monthly	a literary and cultural journal containing analytical articles
Khorasan	Meshhed, daily	hard-line position (Hosein Ghazali)
Mellat	Tehran, daily	issued on 22 May 2000, pledging to support the reform movement; banned the following day (Sa'id Haqqi, 'Ali Mothbat)
Me'yar	Tehran, monthly	pro-reform, very critical of the hard-line policy (published by Ebrahim Zalzadeh who was murdered in Tehran in 1997)
Mobin	Tehran, weekly	pro-Khatami ('Ali Mohammad Ghariba'i, Kamal Moradi)
Mosharekat	Tehran, daily	organ of the *Mosharekat* movement; published since 1999 in a bid to continue the banned *Salam*; banned on 27 April 2000 (Mohammad Reza Khatami, the president's brother)

Neshat	Tehran, daily	continued the banned *Tous* and followed its critical and pro-reform line; banned in September 1999 (Shams al-Va'ezin, Latif Safari)
Panjshanbeha	Tehran, weekly	issued by the group publishing *Hamshahri* (Jaleh Osku'i)
Payam-e Azadi	Tehran, daily	pro-reform; banned on 23 April 2000
Payam-e Daneshju-ye Basiji	Tehran, weekly	students organ; very critical of Rafsanjani's government; supports reform; formerly *Payam-e Daneshju*
Payam-e Hajar	Tehran, weekly	pro-reform; banned on 23 April 2000 (A'zam Taleqani, the daughter of Ayatollah Seyyed Mahmud Taleqani)
Qods	Meshhed, daily	conservative; highly critical of President Khatami (Seyyed Jalal Fayyazi)
Rah-e Now	Tehran, weekly	pro-reform; very critical of Rafsanjani; banned in September 1998 (Akbar Ganji, one of the journalists most critical of the hard-line policy and of Rafsanjani; in jail since April 2000)
Resalat	Tehran, daily	published since the 1980s; one of the main organs of the conservatives (Amir Mohebbiyan)
Ruzegar-e Now	Paris, monthly	contains critical articles against the regime's policy (Isma'il Pur-Vali)
Salam	Tehran, daily	one of the most critical newspapers of the early 1990s; representing the views of *Majma'-e Ruhaniyyun-e Mobarez*; banned temporarily several times (such as prior to the 1996 Majlis elections) and its editors brought to trial, but it continued to voice harsh criticism (mainly against Rafsanjani's policies); since the mid-1990s *Salam* advocated a greater measure of openness and reform and expressed more moderate views; banned in July 1999 (Mohammad Musavi Kho'iniha; 'Abbas 'Abdi)
Siyasat-e Khareji	Tehran, quarterly	contains articles on Iran's foreign policy and international affairs in general

Sobh	Tehran, bi-weekly	major organ of the conservatives (Mehdi Nasiri)
Sobh-e Emruz	Tehran, daily	pro-reform, highly critical of the conservatives; banned on 27 April 2000 (Sa'id Hajariyan, adviser to President Khatami, was wounded in an attempt on his life on 12 March 2000; Akbar Ganji)
Tehran Times	Tehran, daily	now generally close to the Supreme Leader; supported a measure of pragmatism under Rafsanjani ('Abbas Salimi Namin)
Tous	Tehran, daily	replaced *Jame'eh* (with the same line and editorial staff); extremely moderate, banned about two months later
Ya le-Tharat al-Hosein	Tehran, weekly	a hard-line organ; published by *Ansar-e Hezbollah* ('Abdul-Hamid Mohtasham)
Zan	Tehran, daily	generally pragmatic; focusing on women's issues; banned in April 1999 after having published parts of a new year's message on behalf of Farah Diba (Fa'ezeh Hashemi, Rafsanjani's daughter)

Glossary

akhund	in the past usually a general title for high-ranking clerics; more recently used as synonymous with *molla* (Ar. *mulla*; see below), usually referring to low-ranking clerics, often slightly pejoratively
Al	the people of, clan, family of
'alem	(Ar. *'alim*) a person who is learned in religious law and its sources (pl. *'ulama'*)
ansar	lit. the helpers or champions of; the Medinian followers of Prophet Muhammad; now used to denote certain groups supporting the revolution (such as *Ansar-e Hezbollah*)
ayatollah	lit. 'sign of God'; a distinguished *mojtahed*
ayatollah 'uzma	grand *ayatollah* (pl. *ayatollah 'uzam*)
basij	mobilization; paramilitary militia (subordinated to the Revolutionary Guards) in support for the regime against foreign enemies (such as in the war with Iraq), or domestic opposition
Bonyad-e Mostaz'afin va Janbazan	Foundation of the Dispossessed and Self-Sacrificers; a charitable foundation that had become a sizeable business conglomerate
Bonyad-e Shahid	Foundation of the Martyrs
fatva	(Ar. *fatwa*); a religious judgment or ruling by a leading *'alem*
faqih	a jurist specializing in the field of *fiqh*; jurisprudent; jurisconsult
fiqh	religious law, jurisprudence
fitna	sedition; a revolt with religious aspirations
ghayba	occultation of the Imam, in expectation for his return as the *Mahdi* (for Twelver Shi'is, the Twelfth Imam)

hadith	the traditions concerning the sayings and deeds of the Prophet Muhammad (and in Shi'i Islam also of the Imams)
hajj	the pilgrimage to Mecca; *Hajji* – one who has performed the *Hajj*
haram	things that are prohibited by religious law
harim	the interior of a household, occupied by women and children (*andarun* in Persian)
hijra	emigration; the flight of the Prophet from Mecca to Median, in AD 622
hojjat ul-Islam	lit. the proof of Islam; refers to relatively high-ranking cleric, lesser though than an *ayatollah*
hokumat	government or governance
ijtihad	lit. exertion, endeavor; the process of reaching an independent legal judgment in deciding matters relating to religious law by employing reason and principles of jurisprudence (*usul al-fiqh*)
'ilm	knowledge (mainly regarding that of religious law and the sources of religious law)
imam	in Twelver Shi'ism, one of the 12 hereditary successors of the Prophet, beginning with Imam 'Ali; used also to designate a religious leader of the community; leader of congregational prayer
imam jum'ah	leader of Friday congregational prayer
ithna 'ashariyya	lit. the Twelvers; the branch in Shi'ism (dominant in Iran) that believes in 12 imams (the first being 'Ali and ending with the Hidden Imam, Muhammad b. Hasan)
jihad	lit. striving for the cause of religion; holy war undertaken to expand the boundaries of Islam or to defend Islam
Kargozaran-e Sazandegi-ye Iran	The Executive of Iran's Construction; a political movement formed before the 1996 Majlis elections in support of greater pragmatism
khan	tribal chief; a general title of respect
madhhab	a school of law
madrasa	a religious seminary
majles-e khobregan	Council of Experts (officially, *shura-ye khobregan-e rahbari* – Council of Experts [for deciding on questions] of the Leadership); elected by the people; empowered to select a new Supreme Leader

Majlis	*Majles-e Shura-ye Islami*; the Iranian parliament
manteq	logic; one of the traditional subjects in the theo-ogical seminaries
marja'-e taqlid	source of imitation; a prominent scholar whose rulings and practices are a binding example for his followers
maslahat	state or public interest
mofsed fil-arz	corrupt of the earth; one who is charged with spreading corruption
mojtahed	one who is legally eligible by diploma to exercise *ijtihad*
molla	a cleric (Ar. *mulla*); the term does not denote a hierarchical gradation; usually refers now to a low-ranking cleric, typically a preacher; see also *akhund*
morshed	a spiritual guide
mostakbarin	the arrogant, affluent classes (also used to denote the superpowers, mainly the USA)
mostaz'afin	disadvantaged classes, underprivileged
Pasdaran-e Enqelab-e Islami	Revolutionary Guards (lit. the Guardians of the Islamic Revolution); a paramilitary organization with a strong ideological affinity to the conservative leadership
SAVAK	State Intelligence and Security Organization; so called after the initial of its Persian name: *Sazeman-e Ettela'at va Amniyyat-e Keshvar*
seyyed	a descendent of the Prophet
shar'	religious jurisdiction
shari'a	the canonical law of Islam, as defined by orthodox authorities
shura	council
shura-ye negahban	Council of Guardians (comprised of six clerics appointed by the Supreme Leader and six jurists chosen by the Majlis and approved by him), charged with reviewing laws passed by the Majlis to determine whether they are in conformity with Islamic law and compatible with the constitution
shura-ye tashkhis-e maslahat	roughly, the Expediency Council; a body formed in 1988 to resolve disagreements between the Majlis and the Council of Guardians; expanded in 1997 and is headed by Rafsanjani since the end of his presidential terms

taqlid	emulation; the process of following and emulating the practice and pronouncement of a *mojtahed* in matters relating to religious law
tollab	(Ar. *tullab*), students of *madrasa*
'ulama'	(sing. *'alim*; lit. learned persons), the religious class
vaqf	(Ar. *waqf*) endowment, established for religious or charitable purposes
velayat-e faqih	(Ar. *wilayat al-faqih*); guardianship or vicegerency of the jurisconsult; the concept that the right to rule belongs to those who are learned in jurisprudence
zolm	injustice, oppression (Ar. *zulm*)

Bibliography

In Persian

Al-e Ahmad, J. *Safar be Velayat-e 'Ezra'il* [Journey to the Province of Angel of Death]. Tehran: Ravaq, 1984.

Bani Sadr, A. *Eqtesad-e Towhidi* [Economy of Divine Unity]. N.p.: Ettehadiyeh-ye Anjomanha-ye Islami dar Orupa, 1978.

Behbudikhwah, 'A. A. 'Naqd Towjihat-e Tarikhi-ye Sahionism dar mowred-e Mashru'iyyat-e Rezhim-e Qods' [Historical Justifications Concerning the Legitimacy of the Occupying Regime of Jerusalem], *Siyasat-e Khareji*, 3/2 (June-August 1989), pp. 314–44.

Behnam, J. *Iranian va Andisheh-ye Tajaddod* [The Iranians and the Thought of Modernity]. Tehran: Farzan, 1996/97.

Ganji, A. *Naqdi Bara-ye Tamam-e Fosul: Goftogu-ye Akbar Ganji ba 'Abdollah Nuri* [Critique for All Seasons: Akbar Ganji's Conversation with 'Abdollah Nuri]. Tehran: Tarh-e Now, 1999–2000.

Ganji, A. *Talaqqi-ye Fashisti az Din va Hokumat* [The Fascist Interpretation of Religion and Government]. Tehran: Tarh-e Now, 2000.

Ganji, A. *Tarik-Khaneh-ye Ashbah: Asib-shenasi Gozar be Dowlat-e Demokratik-e Towse'eh-gara* [Ghosts' Darkhouse: Pathology of Transition to the Developmental Democratic State]. Tehran: Tarh-e Now, 1999.

Hadiyan, N. 'Mahiyyat-e Gheir-e Madani-ye Dowlat-e Isra'il', *Faslnameh-ye Khavarmiyaneh*, 2/1 (Spring 1995), pp. 99–111.

Hedayat, M. Q. *Khaterat va Khatarat* [Memories and Dangers]. Tehran: Rangin, 1950–51.

Hedayat, S. *Karavan-e Islam* [The Caravan of Islam] N.p.: Sazeman-e Jonbesh-e Nasionalisti-ye Daneshgahiyan, 1983.

Hokumat-e Islami-ye Iran, *Sahifeh-ye Nur* [A Collection of Imam Khomeini's Statements]. Tehran: Vezarat-e Ershad-e Islami, 1985–86.

Kadivar, M. *Nazariyeha-ye Dowlat dar Feqh-e Shi'eh* [Views on Government in Shi'i Jurisprudence]. Tehran: Nashr-e Ney, 1376 [1997–98].

Kadivar, M. and M. M. Shabestari. 'Din, Modara va Khoshunat' [Religion, Tolerance and Violence], *Kiyan*, 45 (January–March 1999), pp. 6–19.

Kermani, M. A. K. *Maktub-e Shahzadeh Kamal al-Dowleh be Shahzadeh Jalal al-Dowleh, Se Maktub* [Letter of Prince Kamal al-Dowleh to Prince Jalal al-Dowleh, Three Letters]. N.p.: Mard-e Emruz, 1991.

Khatami, M. *Zamineha-ye Khizesh-e Mashruteh* [The Circumstances Behind the Emergence of Constitutionalism]. Tehran: Paya, n.d.

Khatami, M. *Bim-e Mowj* [Fear of the Wave]. Tehran: Sima-ye Javan, 1995.

Khatami, M. *Az Donya-ye 'Shahr' ta Shahr-e 'Donya'* [From the World of the City to the City of the World]. Tehran: Nashr-e Ney, 1997.

Khomeini, R. *Dar Jostoju-ye Rah az Kalam-e Imam: Az Bayanat va E'lamiyeha-ye Imam Khomeini* [In Search of the Path through the Words and Statements of Imam Khomeini]. Vol. 19, *Felestin va Sahionism* [Palestine and Zionism]. Tehran: Sepher, 1984–85.

Khomeini, R. *Dar Jostoju-ye Rah az Kalam-e Imam: Azadi-ye Aqaliyatha-ye Mazhabi* [In Search of the Path through the Words and Statements of Imam Khomeini: The Freedom of Religious Minorities]. Tehran: Amir Kabir, 1984–85.

Khomeini, R. *Kashf al-Asrar* [Unveiling the Secrets]. Tehran: 1979 [1944].

Khomeini, R. *Towzih al-Masa'el* [Elucidating the Problems]. Tehran: 1962.

Khosrowshahi, S. H. *Harakat-e Islami-ye Felestin: az Aghaz ta Intifada* [The Islamic Movement of Palestine: From its Inception to the Intifada]. Tehran: Ettela'at, 1996.

Khosrowshahi, S. H. 'Intifada: Harakatha-ye Islami dar Sarzeminha-ye Eshghali' [Intifada: Islamic Movements in the Occupied Territories], *Siyasat-e Khareji*, 5/1 (Spring 1991), pp. 32–50.

Mostafavi, 'A. A. *Iranian-e Yahudi* [Iranian Jews]. Tehran: Bamdad, 1990–91.

Nuri, 'A. *Showkaran-e Eslah* [Hemlock For Advocate of Reform: The complete Text of Nuri's Defense at the Special Clerical Tribunal]. Tehran: Tarh-e Now, 1999.

Pir-Nazar, J. 'Chehreh-ye Yahud dar Athar-e Seh Nevisandeh-ye Motejadded-e Irani' [The Portrayal of Jews in the Works of Three Modernist Iranian Writers], *Iran-Nameh*, 13/4 (Spring 1995), pp. 483–502.

Rafsanjani, 'A. A. Hashemi. *Israel va Qods-e 'Aziz* [Israel and the Beloved Holy Land]. Qom: Azadi, n.d.

Razavi, M. *Hashemi va Enqelab* [Hashemi and the Revolution]. Tehran: Hamshahri, 1997.

Sajjadpur, S. K. 'Siyasat-e Mahar-e do-janebeh dar Theory va 'Amal', *Siyasat-e Khareji*, 8/1–2 (Spring–Summer 1994), pp. 25–42.

Salehpur, J. 'Naqdi bar Nazariyeh-ye "Farbehtar az Ideolozhi"' [Critique on the View of 'More Substantial than an Ideology'], *Jahan-e Islam*, 5 (June–July 1994), pp. 23–7.

Shabestari, M. M. 'Islam va Masihiyat-e Orupa'i' [Islam and European Christianity], *Siyasat-e Khareji*, 4/3 (September–November 1989), pp. 409–15.

Soroush, 'A. K. 'Dark-e 'Azizaneh-ye Din' [Precious Understanding of Religion], *Kiyan*, 4/19 (May–June 1994), pp. 2–9.

Soroush, 'A. K. *Farbehtar az Ideolozhi* [More Substantial than Ideology]. Tehran: Sarat, 1993.

Tabarzadi, H. 'Nagofteha-ye Enqelab: Rah-e Halli Bara-ye Sakhtar-e Siyasi-ye Ayandeh-ye Iran' [The Unspoken Words of the Revolution: A Solution for the Future Political Structure of Iran], *Mehregan*, Spring 1999 (Internet edition).

Taleqani, M. *Islam va Malekiyyat* [Islam and Ownership]. Tehran: Entesharat-e Masjed-e Hedayat, 1954.

Velayati, 'A. A. *Iran va Mas'aleh-ye Felestin* [Iran and the Question of Palestine]. Tehran: Daftar-e Nashr-e Farhang-e Islami, 1997.

Yazdani, M. (ed.) *Asnad-e Mohajerat-e Yahudiyan-e Iran be Felestin* [Documents of the Immigration of Iranian Jews to Palestine]. Tehran: Sazeman-e Asnad-e Melli, 1996.

IN OTHER LANGUAGES

Abrahamian, E. *Khomeinism: Essays on the Islamic Republic*. Berkeley: University of California Press, 1993.

Aghajanian, A. 'Ethnic Inequality in Iran: An Overview', *International Journal of Middle East Studies*, 15 (1983), 211–24.

Akhavi, S. *Religion and Politics in Contemporary Iran: Clergy–State Relations in the Pahlavi Period*. Albany, NY: SUNY Press, 1980.

Al-e Ahmad, J. *Gharbzadegi* [Plagued by the West], trans. Paul Sprachman. Delmar, NY: Caravan Books, 1982.

Algar, H. *Islam and Revolution: Writings and Declarations of Imam Khomeini*. Berkeley, CA: Mizan, 1981.

Amirahmadi, H. 'The Islamic Republic and the Question of Palestine', *Middle East Insight*, 10/4–5 (May–August 1994), pp. 50–4.

Amuzegar, J. *Iran's Economy under the Islamic Republic*. London: I.B. Tauris, 1993.

Amuzegar, J. 'Islamic Fundamentalism in Action: The Case of Iran', *Middle East Policy*, 4/1–2 (1995), pp. 22–33.

Atrissi, T. 'The Iranian Image in Arab School Books', *Discourse*, 1/1 (Summer 1999), pp. 103–56.

Ashraf, A. and A. Banuazizi. 'The State, Classes and Modes of Mobilization in the Iranian Revolution', *State, Culture and Society*, 1/3 (Spring 1985), pp. 3–40.

Bakhash, S. 'Iran: The Crisis of Legitimacy', in *Middle Eastern Lectures*. Tel Aviv: Moshe Dayan Center, 1995, pp. 99–118.

Bakhash, S. 'Iranian Politics Since the Gulf War', in R. Satloff (ed.), *The Politics of Change in the Middle East*. Boulder, CO: Westview, 1993, pp. 63–84.

Bakhash, S. *The Reign of the Ayatollahs: Iran and the Islamic Revolution*. New York: Basic Books, 1984.

Baktiari, B. 'Iran's New President', *Middle East Insight*, 13/1 (November–December 1997), pp. 16–23.

Baktiari, B. *Parliamentary Politics in Revolutionary Iran: The Institutionlization of Factional Politics*. Gainesville: University Press of Florida, 1996.

Banuazizi, A. 'Faltering Legitimacy: The Ruling Clerics and Civil Society in Contemporary Iran', *International Journal of Politics, Culture and Society*, 4/4 (1995), pp. 563–78.

Banuazizi, A. 'Iran's Revolutionary Impasse: Political Factionalism and Societal Resistance', *Middle East Report*, 24/191 (November–December 1994), pp. 2–8.

Banuazizi A. and M. Weiner (eds). *The New Geopolitics of Central Asia and its Borderlands*. Bloomington: Indiana University Press, 1994.

Bayat, A. 'Squatters and the State: Back Street Politics in the Islamic Republic', *Middle East Report*, 24/191 (November–December 1994), p. 10–14.

Bayat-Philipp, M. *Mysticism and Dissent: Socioreligious Thought in Qajar Iran*. Syracuse, NY: Syracuse University Press, 1982.

Bill, J. 'The United States and Iran: Mutual Mythologies', *Middle East Policy*, 2/3 (1993), pp. 98–106.

Boroujerdi, M. *Iranian Intellectuals And The West: The Tormented Triumph of Nativism*. Syracuse, NY: Syracuse University Press, 1996.

Bulatao, A. R. and G. Richardson. *Fertility and Family Planning in Iran.* Washington, DC: The World Bank, 1994.

Chubin, S. *Iran's National Security Policy: Capabilities, Intentions and Impact.* Washington, DC: Carnegie Endowment, 1994.

Clawson, P. *Business as Usual? Western Policy Options Toward Iran.* Washington, DC: American Jewish Congress, 1995.

Clawson, P. *et al.* (eds). *Iran Under Khatami: A Political, Economic and Military Assessment.* Washington, DC: Washington Institute for Near East Policy, 1998.

Clawson, P. (ed.) *Iran's Strategic Intentions and Capabilities.* Washington, DC: National Defense University, 1994.

Cottam, R. W. *Iran and the United States: A Cold War Case Study.* Pittsburgh, PA: University of Pittsburgh Press, 1988.

Cottam, R. W. *Nationalism in Iran.* Pittsburgh, PA: University of Pittsburgh Press, 1979.

Dabashi, H. *Theology of Discontent: The Ideological Foundations of the Islamic Revolution.* New York: New York University Press, 1993.

Dawisha A. (ed.) *Islam in Foreign Policy.* Cambridge, MA: Cambridge University Press, 1984.

Dorraj, M. *From Zarathustra to Khomeini: Populism and Dissent in Iran.* Boulder, CO: Lynne Rienner, 1990.

Ehsani, K. '"Tilt But Not Spill": Iran's Development and Reconstruction Dilemma', *Middle East Report*, 24/191 (November–December 1994), pp. 16–24.

Ehteshami, A. 'After Khomeini: The Structure of Power in the Iranian Second Republic', *Political Studies*, 39/1 (March 1991), pp. 148–57.

Ehteshami, A. *After Khomeini: The Iranian Second Republic.* London: Routledge, 1995.

Eisenstadt, M. *Iranian Military Power: Capabilities and Intentions.* Washington, DC: Washington Institute for Near East Policy, 1996.

Esposito, J. (ed.) *The Iranian Revolution – Its Global Impact.* Miami, FL: Florida International University Press, 1990.

Esposito, J. *The Islamic Threat: Myth or Reality?* Oxford: Oxford University Press, 1992.

Esposito J. (ed.) *Voices of Resurgent Islam.* Oxford: Oxford University Press, 1983.

Fairbanks, S. C. 'Theocracy versus Democracy: Iran Considers Political Parties', *Middle East Journal*, 52/1 (Winter 1998), pp. 17–31.

Golan, G. *Russia and Iran: A Strategic Partnership.* Discussion Paper no. 75. London: Royal Institute of International Affairs, 1998.

Haddad, Y. 'Islamists and the "Problem of Israel": The 1967 Awakening', *Middle East Journal*, 46/2 (Spring 1992), pp. 266–85.

Halliday, F. 'An Elusive Normalization: Western Europe and the Iranian Revolution', *Middle East Journal*, 48/2 (Spring 1994), pp. 309–26

Hashim, A. *The Crisis of the Iranian State.* London: Oxford University Press, 1995.

Helfgot, L. M. 'The Structural Foundations of the National Minority Problem in Revolutionary Iran', *Iranian Studies*, 13/1–4 (1980), pp. 195–214.

Hooglund, E. 'Iranian Views of the Arab–Israeli Conflict', *Journal of Palestine Studies*, 25/1 (Autumn 1995), pp. 86–95.

Hooglund, E. 'The Pulse of Iran Today', *Middle East Insight*, 11/5 (July–August 1995), pp. 40–7.

Human Rights Watch. *Guardians of Thought: Limits of Freedom of Expression in Iran*. New York: Human Rights Watch, 1993.

Human Rights Watch. *Human Rights Watch World Report – 1996*. New York: Human Rights Watch, 1996.

Hunter, S. *Iran After Khomeini*. New York: Praeger, 1992.

Hunter, S. 'Iran and the Spread of Revolutionary Islam', *Third World Quarterly*, 10/2 (April 1988), pp. 730–49.

Hunter, S. *Iran and the World: Continuity in a Revolutionary Decade*. Bloomington, IN: Indiana University Press, 1990.

Kamshad, H. *Modern Persian Prose Literature*. Cambridge: Cambridge University Press, 1966.

Kanovsky, E. *Iran's Economic Morass: Mismanagement and Decline Under the Islamic Republic*. Washington, DC: Washington Institute for Near East Policy, 1997.

Katzman, K. *US–Iranian Relations: An Analytic Compedium of US Policies, Laws and Regulations*. Washington, DC: The Atlantic Council of the United States, 1999.

Kazemi, F. 'Civil Society and Iranian Politics', in A. R. Norton (ed.), *Civil Society in the Middle East*. Leiden: Brill, 1996, pp. 119–52.

Keddie, N. R. *Iran and the Muslim World: Resistance and Revolution*. New York: New York University Press, 1995.

Keddie, N. 'Iran: Change in Islam, Islam and Change', *International Journal of Middle East Studies*, 11/4 (1980), pp. 527–42.

Khadduri, M. *Political Trends in the Arab World: The Role of Ideas and Ideals in Politics*. Baltimore, MD: Johns Hopkins University Press, 1970.

Khatami, M. *Hope and Challenge: The Iranian President Speaks*. Binghamton, NY: SUNY, 1997.

Khatami, M. *Mutala'at fi al-Din wal-Islam wal-'Asr* [Studies on Religion, Islam and the Era]. Beirut: Dar al-Jadid, 1998.

Khomeini, R. *Al-Hukuma al-Islamiyya* [The Islamic Government] (in Arabic). N.p.: 1970.

Lambton, A. K. S. *Qajar Persia*. Austin: University of Texas Press, 1987.

Lazarus-Yaffe, H. 'Ha-Shi'a be-torato ha-politit shel Khomeini' [Shi'ism in Khomeini's Political Thought], *Ha-Mizrah Ha-Hadash*, 30 (1982), pp. 99–106.

Lewis, B. *The Middle East and the West*. New York: Harper & Row, 1964.

Litvak, M. *The Islamization of Palestinian Identity: The Case of Hamas*. Tel Aviv: Moshe Dayan Center, 1996.

Lotfian, S. 'Iran's Middle East Policies under President Khatami', *The Iranian Journal of International Affairs*, 10/4 (Winter 1998–99), pp. 420–48.

Matin-asgari, A. 'Abdolkarim Sorush and the Secularization of Islamic Thought in Iran', *Iranian Studies*, 30/1–2 (Winter–Spring 1997), pp. 95–115.

Menashri, D. *Iran: A Decade of War and Revolution*. New York: Holmes & Meier, 1990.

Menashri, D. (ed.) *The Iranian Revolution and the Muslim World*. Boulder, CO: Westview, 1990.

Menashri, D. 'The Islamic Revolution in Iran: The Consolidation Phase', *Orient*, 25/4 (April 1984), pp. 499–515;

Menashri, D. 'Shi'ite Leadership: In the Shadow of Conflicting Ideologies', *Iranian Studies*, 3/1–4 (1980), pp. 119–45.

Miller, J. *God Has Ninety-Nine Names: Reporting from a Militant Middle East.* New York: Simon & Schuster, 1996.

Mottahedeh, R. P. 'The Islamic Movement: The Case of Democratic Inclusion', *Contention*, 4/3 (Spring 1995), pp. 107–27.

Nafisi, A. 'The Veiled Threat', *New Republic*, 22 February 1999, pp. 24–9.

Najmabadi, N. 'Iran's Turn to Islam: From Modernism to a Moral Order', *Middle East Journal*, 41/2 (Spring 1987), pp. 202–17.

Norton, A. R. *Amal and the Shi'a: Struggle for the Soul of Lebanon.* Austin: University of Texas Press, 1987.

Paz, R. "Emdat ha-Tenu'ot ha-Islamiyot ha-Radikaliot kelapi ha-Yehudim ve ha-Zionut beyaminu' [The Position of the Radical Islamic Movements towards the Jews and Zionism in Our Days], in Ilan Pappé (ed.), *Islam ve Shalom* [Islam and Peace]. Giv'at Haviva: ha-Makhon le-Kheker ha-Shalom, 1992, pp. 46–65.

Pipes, D. 'Ambitious Iran, Troubled Neighbours', *Foreign Affairs*, 72/1 (1993), pp. 124–41.

Pipes, D. 'There are no Moderates: Dealing with Fundamentalist Islam', *The National Interest*, 41 (Fall 1995), pp. 48–57.

Piscatori, J. *Islam in the World of Nation-States.* Cambridge: Cambridge University Press, 1986.

Rajaee, F. *Islamic Values and World View: Khomeyni on Man, the State, and International Relations.* Lanham, MD: University Press of America, 1983.

Rajaee, F. 'A Thermidore of "Islamic Yuppies"?: Conflict and Compromise in Iran's Politics', *Middle East Journal*, 53/2 (Spring 1999), pp. 217–31.

Ramazani, R. K. *Revolutionary Iran: Challenge and Response in the Middle East.* Baltimore, MD: Johns Hopkins University Press, 1986.

Ramazani, R. K. 'Iran's Foreign Policy: Both North and South', *Middle East Journal*, 46/3 (Summer 1992), pp. 393–412.

Roshandel, J. 'Iran, Nuclear Technology and International Security', *Iranian Journal of International Affairs*, 8/1 (Spring 1996), pp. 151–70.

Rouleau, E. 'The Islamic Republic of Iran: Paradoxes and Contradictions in a Changing Society', *Middle East Insight*, 11/5 (July–August 1995), pp. 55–6.

Roy, O. 'The Crisis of Religious Legitimacy in Iran', *Middle East Journal*, 53/2 (Spring 1999), pp. 201–16.

Roy, O. *The Failure of Political Islam.* Cambridge, MA: Harvard University Press, 1994.

Saad, J. B. *The Image of Arabs in Modern Persian Literature.* Lanham, MD: University of America Press, 1996.

Sachedina, A. 'Who Will Lead the Shi'a? Is the Crisis of Religious Leadership in Shi'ism Imagined or Real?', *Middle East Insight*, 11/3 (March–April 1995), pp. 24–8.

Al-Sadr, M. B. *Iqtisaduna* [Our Economy]. 4th edn. Beirut: Dar al-Fikr, 1973.

Salame, Gh. 'Islam and the West', *Foreign Policy*, 90 (Spring 1993), pp. 22–37.

Sher, N. *Comprehensive US Sanctions Against Iran: A Plan for Action.* Washington, DC: AIPAC, 1995.

Shirley, E. G. [pseud.]. 'The Iran Policy Trap', *Foreign Policy*, 96 (Fall 1994), pp. 75–93.

Shirley, E. G. [pseud.]. 'Fundamentalism in Power: Is Iran's Present Algeria's Future?', *Foreign Affairs*, 74/3 (May–June 1995), pp. 28–44.

Sick, G. 'A Sensitive Policy Toward Iran', *Middle East Insight,* 11/5 (July–August 1995), pp. 21–2.

Sivan, E. 'Radical Islam and the Arab–Israeli Conflict', in M. Curtis (ed.), *Antisemitism in the Contemporary World*. Boulder, CO: Westview, 1986, pp. 61–9.

Sivan, E. 'The Mythologies of Religious Radicalism: Judaism and Islam', *Terrorism and Political Violence*, 3/3 (Autumn 1991), pp. 71–81.

Snyder, R. 'Explaining the Iranian Revolution's Hostility Toward the United States', *Journal of South Asian and Middle Eastern Studies*, 17/3 (Spring 1994), pp. 19–31.

Steinbach, U. 'The "Second Islamic Republic": A Theocracy on the Road to Normality', *Aussenpolitik*, 1 (1990), pp. 73–90.

Tonchev, Plamen. 'China and Iran: A New Tandem in World Energy Security', *Iranian Journal of International Affairs*, 10/4 (Winter 1998–99), pp. 485–94.

Vakili, V. *Debating Religion and Politics in Iran: The Political Thought of Abdolkarim Soroush*. New York: Council for Foreign Relations, 1996.

Zonis M. and D. Brumberg. *Khomeini, the Islamic Republic of Iran, and the Arab World*. Harvard Middle East papers, 5 (1987).

Index